DEVELOPMENT IN JUDGING MORAL ISSUES

The Bureau of Education Research Fund,

designed to support books originating within the

College of Education of the University of Minnesota,

supported publication of this volume.

Development in Judging Moral Issues

James R. Rest

Department of Social, Psychological,
and Philosophical Foundations of Education
University of Minnesota

UNIVERSITY OF MINNESOTA PRESS □ MINNEAPOLIS

Copyright © 1979 by the University of Minnesota.
All rights reserved.
Published by the University of Minnesota Press,
2037 University Avenue Southeast,
Minneapolis, Minnesota 55455
Printed in the United States of America

Library of Congress Cataloging in Publication Data

Rest, James R
     Development in judging moral issues.

     Bibliography: p.
     Includes index.
     1. Moral development. 2. Moral development —
Testing. I. Title.
BF723.M54R47   155.4'18   79-22755
ISBN 0-8166-0891-1

To Ann and Susan

Foreword

by Lawrence Kohlberg

I am pleased to have been asked to write a foreword to Jim Rest's important book. Jim has asked me to discuss his book from my perspective on the last twenty years of research in moral development.

My own involvement in this research history dates from 1955, when I commenced my dissertation (Kohlberg 1958), with the intent of carrying forward into adolescence Piaget's (1932) pioneering investigation of the development of moral judgment in children. In studying moral development in adolescence, I decided to use Piaget's general assumptions and method. This meant first a focus on moral judgment, and a definition of moral judgment in terms of judgments of justice. Like Piaget, I assumed that the child's active moral constructions, as distinct from his passively learned assertions of adult moral clichés, would center on the child's sense of justice. Like Piaget, in focusing upon reasoning about justice, I assumed that the developing child was a philosopher, constructing meanings around universal categories or questions, such as the question of fairness. So as a means of eliciting such reasoning, I chose to present hypothetical dilemmas of ancient vintage that had been discussed by philosophers. The assumption that the cognitive-developmental approach makes, of the child as philosopher, is the assumption of structuralism. I was drawn to the assumption of structure before discovering Piaget and had spent some years doing diagnostic and research work examining unconscious and affective structures from a psychoanalytic framework. I eventually found frustrating the research into unconscious mental structures beneath culturally conforming responses, in trying to interpret "signs," since I was seldom entirely convinced by my own interpretations. In contrast, the Piagetian study of moral reasoning seemed to reveal mental structures directly. The response of children and adolescents to my hypothetical dilemmas were clearly structurally patterned and clearly their own. Though often attempting to conform and give "the right answer," students gave reasons far from what I or the adult culture expected, reasons with their own clear inner logic. These constructions convinced me of the second major assumption of Piaget's cognitive-developmental approach, the stage assumption, that these cognitive constructions were qualitatively unique and proceeded through an invariant sequence or order.

My dissertation, an elaboration and reassertion of Piaget's stage approach, added tentatively described fourth, fifth, and sixth stages to the three stages of moral judgment described by Piaget (1932). For theoretical guidance in interpreting my material on these later stages, I turned to McDougall (1908), Dewey (1895), Mead (1934), and especially to J. M. Baldwin (1906). My data also led me to question many of the details of Piaget's first three stages and to provide a slightly different account of these early stages (Kohlberg 1958, 1964).

Rest's (1969) University of Chicago dissertation represented a second major step in the research history. At the time Rest launched his dissertation only two basic efforts had been made to validate the stages described in my dissertation. The first was the work of Turiel and myself replicating my dissertation studies in other cultures: Turkey, Taiwan, and Yucatan. These studies showed that group age trends showed the same types of thought developing in the same order in the cultures studied. The second was Turiel's (1966) experimental documentation that the amount of assimilation of material at other stages was predicted by the stage-order hypothesis; that is, groups of adolescents exposed to the next stage up would assimilate judgments to which they were exposed more than would groups exposed to stages two above or one below their own.

These studies, like my dissertation were deficient as validating stages because they relied on group data or group averages. The stage hierarchy hypothesis could predict these group averages better than chance, but the stage hypothesis demanded far more in the way of internal order in the individual. Rest's thesis provided the first clear evidence of internal order supporting the stage hierarchy hypothesis. It indicated an almost errorless hierarchical Guttman scale in comprehension of each stage and clear evidence that comprehension never went more than one stage beyond spontaneous production or usage of the stage. Rest's study, and the cross-cultural data, were the data featured for an optimistic 1969 statement of expectations for "Stage and Sequence: the Cognitive Developmental Approach to Moralization" (Kohlberg, 1969). The statement advised caution until individual longitudinal data were shown to have the order shown in group data, but its spirit was one of confident steady advance in an established paradigm.

Implementations in practice followed. Blatt (1969) had demonstrated that classroom dilemma discussion led to moral judgment advanced in line with the stage sequence model. Accordingly, immediately after the programmatic statement on developmental research (Kohlberg 1969), I wrote an equally programmatic statement on stages of moral development as a basis for moral education (Kohlberg 1971). This vision brought Rest, Blatt, and myself from Chicago and Turiel from Columbia to Harvard in what eventually became the School of Education's Center for Moral Education.

The first order of business for the group at Harvard was not programmatic advance, however, but attending to some major cracks in the paradigm, faults that could be viewed as cracks in the theory, the methodology, or both. These cracks were anomalies of sequence in the results of the longitudinal data on my dissertation subjects reinterviewed every three years for 12 years (Kramer 1968). These data had not been available for assimilation at the time the programmatic statements were written. When faced, it meant a halt in use of my dissertation stage-definitions and rating system. I had been able to ignore the defects in my dissertation method as long as research consisted in relating group data to prior theoretical expectation. My first interpretation of the longitudinal anomalies was not to critique the method but to report failure of the sequence hypothesis itself, to report existence of "retrogression" in the college years (Kohlberg and Kramer 1969). Further reflection by Turiel (1974) and myself (Kohlberg 1973b) led to reassertion of the sequence hypothesis but acknowledged failure in the details of both stage definition and of measurement method. Retrogression to Stage 2 was reinterpreted as a transitional "Stage 4½," the breakup of conventional morality without the consolidation of a more principled morality. Theoretical dispute about these two interpretations forced us to face the fact that we did not have an adequate assessment methodology in the methodology of my 1958 dissertation. I had, in fact, never thought the method was adequate. My thesis described stages not as true stages but as ideal-type moral orientations. Longitudinal study was necessary not only to validate but to define an invariant sequence of stages. I did not consider that my dissertation provided a "test" or "scale" of moral judgment development, but rather that it was an exploratory assessment method. In terms of reliability, the thesis data indicated that the method led to consensus between raters or between dilemmas sufficient for research on groups and comparing age (or other group) averages in terms of theoretical hypotheses. The data did not justify the method as an individual test in terms of test-retest and other criteria of test reliability locating individual subjects.

Some years after Rest and I had concluded that the dissertation method was inadequate, Kurtines and Greif (1974) concluded the same. They were, however, led to recommend throwing out the theoretical stage baby with the assessment method bathwater. Anomalies in the data, they concluded, invalidated both the theory and the assessment method at the same time. Logically one cannot, as they did, question both the theory and the method at the same time. Rest and I questioned the method, prior to fundamentally questioning the theory.

Accordingly in 1970, Rest and I concluded that there was no point in going on with the kind of research covered in my 1969 article, studies characteristic of a first phase of moral development research. The first phase, we concluded, had delineated the broad outlines of culturally universal qualitative patterns of development of moral judgment and demonstrated the fruitfulness of the cognitive-developmental theoretical assumptions for research. The second phase, we thought would have to be methodological, the construction of a valid and reliable test or assessment of moral judgment development. Jim left Harvard to take a position at Minnesota with a determination to further this second basic phase of research. This book is the story of this phase of research and its results, as it developed at Minnesota.

More slowly and uncertainly, we at Harvard also started in a divergent but complementary direction of second-phase research. The test construction phase at Harvard was very slow, only arriving at a standardized interview and scoring manual with acceptable reliability and validity this year (Kohlberg, 1979; Colby, 1979; Colby, Gibbs, and Kohlberg, in preparation). These test-construction steps were taken in line with the assumptions which Rest in this volume calls "the simple stage model." These assumptions include the following:

1. A majority of an individual's spontaneous reasoning can be classified at a single stage (or at most two adjacent stages).
2. Movement in time is always from the individual's major stage to

the next stage in the sequence. Each new stage is a reconstruction or transformation of the prior stage.

3. Each stage is described in terms of formal structures of reasoning, not in terms of the content of judgments and values such structures generate.

In line with these conceptions, the first Harvard efforts involved revising stage-definitions around "construction cases" in our longitudinal sample, and rating these cases by a clinical method requiring a rater who could theoretically distinguish the stage structure from content. This effort led to dropping the sixth stage as a reliably rateable stage in our longitudinal data but confirming sequence in clinical ratings for the other five stages (Kohlberg and Elfenbein, 1975).

Encouraged by these clinical results, the Harvard group went on to develop a more objective and reliable interview and scoring method. This method led to results consistent with the simple stage model after blind scoring of a longitudinal "sealed sample." Though reliable, the method is lengthy and complex, since the manual makes fine distinctions between content and structure on specific items. This method concludes the Harvard program of second phase research and, with the complementary completion of the Minnesota second phase program, opens up the prospect of a third phase of research that returns to the many theoretical problems unsolved in the first phase.

This book reports the Minnesota program of second phase research, which got off the ground with a test almost 10 years earlier than the Harvard program. Rest concludes, and I agree, that he has relatively successfully completed this phase of research. His data indicate first, that he has developed a test that is reliable and valid according to the usual research standards of reliability and construct-validity of psychological assessment. His data indicate, secondly, solid support for the cognitive-developmental assumptions given preliminary support by first phase research. Rest's successful conclusion of a second phase of research means that he has greatly contributed to the establishment of a paradigm of research in moral development.

Paradigms in Kuhn's (1962) sense are still relatively few and rare in contemporary psychology. A paradigm represents a sufficient agreement in a field on (a) problems requiring explanation, (b) theoretical assumptions for such explanations, (c) methods of measurement, and (d) types of study design so that different researchers can do studies leading to similar conclusions or at least conclusions meaningful to all concerned. The findings reported here support Rest's belief that his linking a cognitive-developmental moral judgment theory with an elaboration of a method defines a paradigm in the study of morality (whether taken together with, or independent of, the Harvard work in the field). Rest summarizes the findings of one hundred studies with his measure as demonstrating:

1. Moral judgment is developmental. One very major source of variation in Rest's measure of moral judgment is age, and other major sources of variation due to social experience are developmental, that is, they are related to amount and complexity of experience.

2. The processes involved in moral judgment development are cognitive. Rest's measure of moral judgment preference and recognition is related to conceptual comprehension of moral judgment, to intelligence and other cognitive variables.

3. While related to cognition, moral judgment is moral; it is not merely the application of cognitive skills or intelligence to moral questions or situations. Measures of moral judgment correlate with measures of moral attitudes, choices, and behavior to an extent not accounted for by IQ or other "pure cognitive" variables.

These findings by Rest and his colleagues, using his DIT measure, are consistent with findings using our method of qualitative stage categorizations of spontaneous responses to dilemmas (Kohlberg 1969; Colby 1979). Rest's work, then, supports and clarifies the fundamental assumptions of the cognitive-developmental approach to moralization. It provides a broader, more solid data base for moral judgment in a variety of American natural groups and populations than does the Harvard work. An alternate to the complex Harvard method of scoring spontaneous interview material, Rest's method of assessing moral judgment is demonstrated here as having good reliability and good construct validity for many research purposes involving high school or adult populations.

So far I have discussed the work reported in this book from the point of view of similarities to the Harvard work. There are of course, divergences from the Harvard method and research program. These may be best understood in terms of the findings of Jim Rest's own dissertation and the conclusions and directions it suggested to him at the end of the 1960s. As mentioned earlier, Turiel had constructed a classic study (1966) supporting the hypothesis that the moral stages formed a hierarchy, assimilating reasoning at the next stage up. Turiel, Rest, and I (Rest, Turiel, and Kohlberg 1969) became interested in determining whether this hierarchy could be defined purely by the cognitive characteristics of the stages, that is, whether the stages could be shown to be a hierarchy of comprehension. If such were the case, sequence in spontaneous production could be understood as a function of the intersecting two dimensions of the stages, their increasing difficulty of comprehension and their increasing attractiveness or preferability if (partially) comprehended or understood. Rest's (1969) dissertation tested these hypothesized hierarchies of comprehension and preference and related them to spontaneous production and assimilation of new reasoning. At the time it represented the most convincing evidence that the stages formulated in my dissertation formed a qualitative hierarchy.

As also mentioned earlier, just after Rest (1969) had obtained such orderly data on a stage hierarchy of comprehension and preference, discrepant data on spontaneous production appeared, the longitudinal data indicating cracks in the sequence (Kohlberg and Kramer, 1969). The disorder in the Kramer longitudinal data could not lead Rest to question the idea of moral stages or the cognitive developmental interpretation of moral judgment, since it was just these assumptions that generated the empirical hierarchy found in his dissertation. But it could, and did, lead him first to question the simple stage assumptions behind the longitudinal study. A hierarchy of qualitative stages was upheld by his dissertation, but one not requiring simple stage assumptions. Furthermore, at the time of Rest's dissertation, the data on spontaneous production did not fit the simple stage model. In both Rest's data and in the longitudinal data (Kohlberg and Kramer 1969) subjects had fewer than 50% of the responses at their major stage. Subjects often used significant amounts of three or even four stages. Longitudinally, an excessive number of subjects skipped stages, or regressed. It was entirely reasonable, then, for Rest to question the simple stage model.

Rest's dissertation led him, secondly, to question the methodology that awarded a privileged position to spontaneous production in defining or assessing stage. Rest's own data on comprehension and preference yielded data more orderly than spontaneous production data in terms of stage theory. The only lack of fit of the comprehension or preference data to the stage model was its fit to the simple stage model. By definition, comprehension and even preference data should indicate comprehension and preference of many stages, not one. In such data the hypothesis of stage hierarchy, not the hypothesis of use of a single stage, was critical for cognitive-developmental theory. Development in such preference and comprehension data could be reflected by a profile or by amount of highest stage usage; it could be, or need not be, reflected in a single stage location. If one abandoned the simple-stage assumption, there was no particular reason to award spontaneous production a privileged position in assessing moral judgment development. For some purposes, recognition might be better than production. If one wished to predict such decisions as voting, comprehension and preference of stage might be a better predictor than spontaneous usage. Rest felt a methodological preference for spontaneous production could only come from empirical findings, not theoretical assumption.

Third, Rest's dissertation led him to question a rigid distinction between content and structure in defining and assessing moral judgment development. This distinction can only be maintained in assessment if assessment is limited to staging spontaneous production. In recognition (comprehension and preference) tasks the subject's reactions are focused on content related to structure, not structure itself. From the point of view of structural theory, a subject need not be self-consciously aware of his own stage structure, or that of others, and hence not react consistently to structure in recognition tests. Structural consistency, then, should be found only by a psychologist abstracting structural features from spontaneous responses, not from the subject's own abstractions of structure in recognizing and preferring the judgments of others.

Rest's questioning of the simple stage model and related assumptions was entirely in line with empirical findings at that time. It led him to begin development of the DIT, a recognition test of moral development. Clearly, a multiple choice test of moral development has marked advantages in diminishing psychologists' efforts in scoring. It was less the increased efficiency, however, than the increased scoring reliability that led Rest to favor this format. In fact, as this book reports, the DIT can claim not only reliability, but construct validity as well, since results with it conform to expectations derived from the cognitive developmental theory and cannot be accounted for by interpreting the test responses as other than cognitive developmental or other than moral.

The DIT does not pretend to be a test predicting to spontaneous production or assigning an individual to a single stage. It is not an indictment of the DIT's construct-validity, that it correlates only moderately with stages of spontaneous production. Such correlations are sufficient for the construct validity of his test, since they indicate that two different tests of cognitive moral development tap the same general domain. From the point of view of the Harvard group, the moderate correlations between the DIT and our measure support the construct validity of the Harvard measure as well as the Minnesota measure.

The researcher is likely to ask, however, which test is better or has more (construct) validity, the Harvard or the Minnesota test? In one sense, Rest and I would agree that the Harvard test is better: it is better if one wishes to test implications of simple stage theory, since the test was constructed and validated according to the criterion of the simple stage construct. Insofar as one wishes to research the implications of the general cognitive-developmental theory underlying both tests, there is no reason to claim the Harvard test is better. Indeed, a number of research purposes or considerations might warrant considering the Minnesota test the test of choice, apart from the consideration of economy and the more extensive data base. The first is that very consideration that makes the Harvard test better for studying implications of simple stage theory, the consideration that the Minnesota test makes fewer theoretical assumptions than the Harvard test. The second consideration is that, in a sense, the Minnesota test is more "broad spectrum" or at least taps a different band of the spectrum than the Harvard test. The Harvard test assesses only spontaneous production: the DIT assesses recognition, comprehension and preference (and hence at least indirectly spontaneous production). Many responses influenced by moral judgment development may represent more the recognition than the spontaneous production dimension of moral development. An example Rest studied is candidate choices in an election, which would seem to depend on a voter's comprehension and preference for a candidate's political position and reasoning, not upon his capacity to spontaneously produce political reasoning like the candidate. The Minnesota test is more broad spectrum, secondly, in that it does assess content related to structure rather than endeavoring to assess "pure structure." Many of the response correlates of moral judgment development presumably require the mediation of content associated with structure. As in the example used, if moral development is to predict voter choice, it is through content mediation, for example, preference for a candidate's "liberalism."

A loose partial analogy may clarify the problems in comparing the Minnesota and Harvard tests, the analogy of comparing tests of general intelligence or mental development. Binet and Simon envisaged constructing a broad-spectrum test of intelligence or of general cognitive development. The test was not to be based on a specific theory of cognitive development but on (a) a conception of a general function of cognition or cognition elaborated in Spearman's theory of "g" and (b) the idea of regular cumulative cognitive age-development reflected in, but distinct from, specific school and home learn-ing. The Binet test achieved construct validity partly because results fitted these assumptions, partly because empirical research findings using it fit the general conceptions of common-sense or ordinary-lan-guage usage of the concept "intelligence." Piaget initiated a second phase of research into the development of intelligence by stage-theo-retical analyses, originally to the Binet, later to assessments of his own. These analyses eventually led to the construction of a standard-ized test of Piagetian mental development, the Pinard and Laurendeau (1969) tests. Presumably the Pinard and Laurendeau is a better test to use in elaborating specific Piagetian hypotheses, but not a better broad spectrum test of intelligence.

Unlike the intelligence tests, not enough empirical research results are in on either moral test to recommend which one should be used. In the meantime, however, I believe this volume helps lay the foun-dation for a third phase of research that will address these and many other questions.

Preface

When confronted with a complex moral problem, people do not necessarily agree on what is at stake, and not surprisingly they diverge in their judgments about solutions, advocating different courses of action. The central thesis of this book is that the differences among people in the ways they construe and evaluate moral problems are determined largely by their concepts of fairness, that it is possible to identify and describe these basic concepts, and that more adequate and complex concepts of fairness develop from less adequate simple ones. This book describes the course of development in people's moral thinking, the research strategies and instruments used in studying the phenomena, and the conclusions and findings from over a hundred studies; in the light of these empirical findings, it reexamines many theoretical issues and suggests next steps in research.

In 1969, Lawrence Kohlberg's Center for Moral Development at Harvard was just the place to entertain audacious grand schemes. The Center was filled with energetic activity; there was a sense of being in the vanguard of a new psychological and educational movement. It seemed clear that Behaviorism was losing its hold on the field of personality and social development, and that soon much interest and energy would be directed towards the processes and organization of thinking. For years, Kohlberg had disregarded Behaviorism's edicts and had a wealth of ideas for extending Piaget's general approach. Moreover, the apathy of psychologists toward the study of morality was changing. The Civil Rights movement, the student protests, and the debate over the Vietnam War dramatized how differently people think about the issues of social justice. Psychological studies of moral thinking seemed more and more important and relevant. Kohlberg's theories were directly applicable to politicians' pronouncements, SDS pamphlets, Supreme Court decisions, and newspaper editorials.

Along with the exhilarating sense of being in a vanguard, however, some of us had an uneasy feeling that the theorizing had gone beyond a solid data base. Difficulties were apparent in the most fundamental research operation—the method of assessing moral judgment. Without a set of definite, validated procedures for assessment, theories were difficult to relate to concrete cases. Completed studies provoked much interest and generally supported the theory, but in 1970, there were few studies, and these involved a limited number of subjects and contained many loose ends. Aside from the volumes of theoretical speculation, a reader could go through all the hard data in a weekend.

Kohlberg had begun to revise his system for scoring moral judgments in 1968. His primary interest, however, was not to put together a handy instrument, but to devise a theoretical system to represent the logic of moral thinking, analogous to Chomsky's work on syntactic structures. The complexities of this task are bewildering, and the progress slow.

Alternative schemes for assessing moral judgment became a compelling interest for me. Instead of attempting to devise structural models of different moral philosophies, couldn't I use some of the characteristic features of different stages as markers of development? Instead of individual interviews, couldn't multiple-choice techniques be tried? Kohlberg supported the general idea of developing an alternative method of assessment, seeing that this method could assist the research effort. But at times the enterprise seemed foolhardy. The clinical interview seemed to be *the* way to study thinking; any other method seemed inconsistent with what was unique and valuable in the cognitive development approach. Some saw a multiple choice test akin to the alchemists' folly of attempting to change lead into gold, doomed to failure on basic principles.

After moving to Minnesota, I devised a multiple-choice questionnaire (the Defining Issues Test), and by 1971 I had some pilot data that were most promising. A number of graduate students became interested in the project, and we collected the data that were the basis for the first publication of this work in 1974.

Positive reactions to the research and to the instrument gained momentum, and requests to use the test came in—to date, about 800 researchers from the United States and from a dozen other countries. Mark Davison joined the faculty at the University of Minnesota, bringing with him a background in psychometrics and measurement theory, and he immediately became involved in the projects. The findings of other researchers using the Defining Issues Test substantiated and extended our Minnesota findings. In 1974 I put together a manual on the test, and when choosing a cover for it, I asked the printers, "Do you have anything in gold?"

It would be gratifying to think that all of the interest in the Defining Issues Test has been due to the scientific community's impression of our insights into assessment problems, cunning in crafting an instrument, clear vision about construct validation, dazzling empirical findings, and reconceptualization of basic ideas. Instead, I admit to receiving some letters like the following:

Dear Sir,

My dissertation committee says I have to include a measure of moral development in my study. I tried to use Kohlberg's test, but since I'm not that interested in moral judgment, I'd like to use yours, which I heard is quick and easy. Please send me a copy of the text right away because I'm supposed to collect data next week.

The journal articles, dissertations, and manuscripts that report findings on the Defining Issues Test now form a stack over ten feet high. This book condenses and interprets these findings and ideas. Unlike the situation in 1970, there is now a substantial data base. Because of the theoretical richness of the moral judgment construct, its body of replicated and interlocking findings, and its potential social usefulness, moral judgment research is in an enviable position in psychology.

I wish to acknowledge the contributions of the dozens of researchers who shared their findings with me, and who sent in their raw data for use in our data bank. Specific names and references are cited throughout the book. Most notably, my colleague, Mark Davison, has contributed to so many aspects of this work that it would be impossible to list them all, but his special interests are described in Chapter Eight, which he wrote. More than twenty students at the University of Minnesota have aided in this research, and I wish to acknowledge especially the continuing efforts of James Carroll, Jeanette Lawrence, Douglas Marston, Edgar McColgan, and Steve

Robbins. Generous financial support has come from the University of Minnesota Graduate School, especially in crucial times. The research has been funded also by the Spencer Foundation, National Institute of Mental Health, and the University of Minnesota College of Education. I wish to thank Anne Colby, John Gibbs and Tom Lickona for reading early drafts of the book and making many detailed suggestions and helpful comments; Carol Masters for editing the manuscript and making ten thousand corrections and clarifications; and the College of Education for providing funds to offset some of the publication costs of this book.

Contents

DEVELOPMENT IN JUDGING MORAL ISSUES

1

Introduction

Jean Piaget and Lawrence Kohlberg have been most influential in shaping research on moral judgment. In the 1930s, Piaget's major work in moral judgment, as well as his other work during that period, received little attention from the academic community. Kohlberg's work in the 1950s and early 1960s was similarly ignored. Into the 1960s, most psychologists were wary of studying inner mental processes. In addition, many scientists in the Eisenhower era were uneasy about studying a topic like morality, since it was associated with stodgy moralists, muddleheaded do-gooders, and Communist-hunters.

In contrast, since the mid-1960s the study of cognition has become a major interest in psychology. Major social events have focused attention on moral issues. The Civil Rights movement, the student protests, the Vietnam War, Watergate, the women's movement all have emphasized issues of social justice, thus making it difficult for thoughtful people not to be concerned about morality. These two developments—psychology's turn to cognition and society's concern with moral issues—have provided a favorable context for moral judgment research. The specific impetus for this research, however, is the theoretical direction given by Piaget and Kohlberg, whose ideas have brought many people into the field. Currently, hundreds of studies are done per year on moral judgment, and the topic now is well represented in college textbooks, handbooks, and journals, and at conventions.

3

Piaget

In the 1930s, Piaget's book *The Moral Judgment of the Child (1932)* was in stark contrast to other investigators' work on moral thinking at the time. Pittel and Mendelsohn (1966) reviewed the various earlier approaches. The main interest of the other researchers was to use verbalizations to predict behavior—such as juvenile delinquency or classroom cheating. A common research strategy was to devise questionnaire items that it was hoped would have high correlations with behavioral measures. The verbal material or paper-and-pencil responses were not seen as reflecting an underlying *organization* of thinking, as Piaget theorized, but rather, the verbalizations were conceptualized as representing ignorance of rules and moral teachings, or as self-reported revelations of inner tendencies to do wrong. Pittel and Mendelsohn remark on the success of this approach:

> Attempts to assess moral values have frequently focused on observable behavior from which values are inferred, or have attempted to predict overt behavior from subjective values. Rarely have subjective values been studied in their own right.
>
> While the delineation of the links between values and behavior is clearly a desirable objective, many investigators, in their eagerness to focus on behavior, have paid insufficient attention to the conceptualization of moral values and the appropriate methods for their measurement. Both experience and the research literature point to the complexity of the relationship between moral values and moral behavior. Simplistic models of this relationship have led to a failure of prediction, a consequent rejection of assessment techniques and thus to a proliferation of test devices, apparently in the hope that something might predict moral behavior (p. 22).

Piaget's cognitive developmental approach provided a way to study subjective values in their own right. Other researchers' aim was to explain the occurrence or nonoccurrence of some behavior that had significance from the researcher's (or society's) point of view; a subject's verbalizations were interesting only insofar as they predicted behavior. In contrast, Piaget aimed to explain why a subject values certain things from the person's own point of view. Verbalizations were regarded as interesting for what they revealed about the inner world of the subject. Piaget interviewed children about many kinds of moral situations, finding that they had definite intuitions about moral right and wrong; however, their point of view seemed to be drastically different from that of an adult. Piaget characterized the difference between child and adult points of view by postulating different underlying cognitive organizations, each with its particular logic and way of interpreting experience. Piaget did not assume that the world looks the same to all people — as if the world were simply there for anyone to apprehend directly with their senses. Piaget was impressed with the complexity of mental operations involved in making sense out of experience. His genius has been in analyzing the kinds of cognitive constructions that are necessary to achieve the most basic understandings of the world. People may not be aware of the cognitive structuring that is going on "behind the scenes" (and rarely are their thoughts as explicit as codified philosophies); nevertheless, individuals do have definite intuitions about how the world works and about what is fair. The psychologist's job is to capture the logic and pattern of these intuitions by postulating underlying cognitive structures that, in effect, account for what is intuitively obvious to the person. Piaget characterized the young child's moral point of view as "moral realism" or "heteronomous morality," in which the child is aware of moral rules and duties, but does not see them as social arrangements and human devices for regulating cooperative interaction. Rather, the child assumes moral rules are fixed in the nature of things, like natural, physical laws, and are the same for everyone. Only gradually does the young child realize that moral rules are cooperative arrangements among equals, agreed upon for mutual benefits. This latter point of view is called "autonomous morality."

One fundamental tenet of the cognitive developmental approach, then, is that a person's perception of reality is cognitively constructed, and one aim of the psychologist is to identify and describe these basic cognitive structures. A second fundamental tenet is that cognitive structures *evolve* — that there is a developmental progression by which the earlier cognitions are elaborated to accommodate greater complexity in experience. In support of the claim of a developmental progression, Piaget's book is filled with examples of young children's moral thinking contrasted with older children's thinking. These examples are presented both as empirical evidence for the theory of the developing structure of moral judgment, and as illustrations of the logical primitiveness of the younger child's thought and the greater conceptual adequacy of the older child's thought.

In summary, Piaget accomplished many things in his 1932 book:

1. He defined the problem area and the theoretical construct of moral judgment. Before Piaget, a psychological construct called "moral judgment" did not exist, nor were psychologists involved in identifying the basic logical structures underlying people's judgments, or describing how these structures successively develop.

2. Piaget introduced methods for studying a subject's moral judg-

ment. Most characteristic is the presentation of an episode or story to the person to evoke discussion and an explanation of the subject's views. An important part of his work also involved the observation of children's game behavior.

3. Piaget identified a dozen specific features in children's moral thinking for making inferences about their underlying thought structure. The features include "immanent justice," "intentionality," "relativism of perspective," etc. (see Kohlberg 1964, for brief review, pp. 396-400; see also Hoffman 1970, pp. 265-271). Also, Piaget gave an extensively argued rationale in each case for the younger child's thinking being more primitive than the older child's.

4. Piaget provided some empirical data in support of his theory, almost exclusively the numbers of subjects at different ages whose responses were scored as different types. By today's journal standards, such cross-sectional age trend data would not count for much without data on scoring reliability, subject consistency, statistical tests of significance, or covariance with I.Q. (or other tests of discriminate validity). However, these refinements are secondary to Piaget's pointing researchers to a key empirical test of cognitive developmental theory—namely, to look for age-related differences in types of responses—and this has been the most extensively used paradigm in cognitive developmental research.

Piaget's approach did not provide a complete research program for the study of morality. Strictly speaking, his study of moral judgment only provides a limited characterization of the cognitive structures underlying people's verbalizations and of how these structures change over time. Many interesting questions about the psychology of morality are not directly addressed by this research. The investigator cannot do everything at once: He or she has to set priorities, placing some questions ahead of others. Other research approaches have played different hunches. Currently, no single theory or research approach adequately treats all aspects of the psychology of morality. The cognitive developmentalist puts priority on trying to understand morality from the inside out—that is, by first attempting to understand how the subject sees the world, what his pressing concerns are, what possibilities for action he sees. In contrast, behavioristic approaches attempt to discover regularities in human behavior from an external point of view, relating the occurrence/non-occurrence of observable behavior to objective events in the environment. While there is a clear incompatibility in research strategy between the two approaches, one day an integration may be achieved. The point is that the study of morality is multifaceted and Piaget's approach prioritizes certain phenomena, certain questions, and certain research strategies.

Kohlberg

Kohlberg's dissertation in 1958 begins a second phase in moral judgment research. His contributions have elaborated the cognitive developmental approach, expanded its research program, and applied the ideas to education. Although American psychology in the 1950s and 1960s was dominated by Behaviorism (both the "hard" and "soft" varieties, Radical Behaviorism and Social Learning Theory), Kohlberg has been an American advocate for a cognitive developmental approach to the study of personality and social development. His 1969 chapter in *The Handbook of Socialization Theory and Research* is his most extensive statement, and he is regularly called on to provide counterpoint to the behaviorist theme. Contrasting the cognitive developmental approach with that of the behaviorist, he calls attention to fundamental assumptions in research approaches. He argues that "morality" cannot be defined in terms of conformity with the prevailing group norms, for it remains a philosophical rather than a behavioral concept; a person's morality cannot be assessed without knowing that person's point of view and intentions. Furthermore, Kohlberg maintains that behavior has an underlying structure; it is not an aggregation of disconnected responses triggered by external stimuli. Human beings must be viewed as active organisms, who construct interpretations of their activity in making plans. While the environment provides the context in which humans learn, plan, and act, the organization of human behavior is not a simple reflection of environmental configurations. These statements may seem bland and obvious today, but it must be remembered that in the 1950s and 1960s, the possibility of studying cognition was hotly debated, as was the notion that there were developmental trends in human behavior. These were the days before Social Learning Theory became *Cognitive* Social Learning Theory (e.g., Mischel and Mischel 1976; Bandura 1977; see Aronfreed's discussion of changes in theory, 1976).

Kohlberg provided a new method of assessing moral judgment that provided new information about it, which in turn has prompted new characterizations of its structure. His dissertation began as a replication study of Piaget's work, with a different data gathering procedure. Instead of using Piaget's story pairs designed for younger children (see Chapter 4 for further discussion), Kohlberg presented older subjects (10 to 16 years instead of 4 to 13 years) with complex moral dilemmas and interviewed them about what they thought should be done and why. Two of Kohlberg's dilemmas are as follows:

Heinz and the Drug Dilemma

In Europe, a woman was near death from a special kind of cancer. There was one drug that the doctors thought might save her. It was a form of radium that a druggist in the same town had recently discovered. The drug was expensive to make, but the druggist was charging ten times what the drug cost him to make. He paid .$200 for radium and charged $2,000 for a small dose of the drug. The sick woman's husband, Heinz, went to everyone he knew to borrow the money, but he could only get together about $1,000, which is half of what it cost. He told the druggist that his wife was dying, and asked him to sell it cheaper or let him pay later. But the druggist said, "No, I discovered the drug and I'm going to make money from it." So Heinz got desperate and broke into the man's store to steal the drug for his wife. Should Heinz have done that? Was it wrong or right? Why?

The Captain's Dilemma

In Korea, a company of Marines was way outnumbered and was retreating before the enemy. The company had crossed a bridge over a river, but the enemy were mostly still on the other side. If someone went back to the bridge and blew it up as the enemy were coming over it, it would weaken the enemy. With the head start the rest of the men in the company would have, they could probably not be able to escape alive; there would be about a 4 to 1 chance he would be killed. The captain of the company has to decide who should go back and do the job. The captain himself is the man who knows best how to lead the retreat. He asks for volunteers, but no one will volunteer. If he goes himself, the men will probably not get back safely and he is the only one who knows how to lead the retreat. Should the captain order a man to go on this very dangerous mission or should he go himself? The captain finally decided to order one of the men to stay behind. One of the men he thought of was one who had a lot of strength and courage but he was a bad trouble maker. He was always stealing things from the other men, beating them up and wouldn't do his work. The second man he thought of had gotten a bad disease in Korea and was likely to die in a short time anyway, though he was strong enough to do the job. Should the captain have sent the trouble maker or the sick man? Why?

Kohlberg found that Piaget's two stages with a dozen features did not adequately describe the kinds of reasoning produced by these subjects. Kohlberg identified dozens of features in the recurrent responses of subjects; furthermore, the thinking seemed to cluster into six stages instead of Piaget's two. The brief characterizations of the six stages are well known (Kohlberg 1964, p. 400):

Stage 1. Punishment and obedience orientation.

Stage 2. Naive instrumental hedonism.

Stage 3. Good-boy or good-girl morality of maintaining good relations, approval of others.

Stage 4. Authority maintaining morality.

Stage 5. Morality of contract, of individual rights, and of democratically accepted law.

Stage 6. Morality of individual principles of conscience.

Any stage scheme needs to be described in terms of the specific features that judges are to use in scoring a given interview, how each feature of a stage is part of a unified system of ideas, and how each stage is conceptually more adequate than the previous stage. From 1958 to about 1968, the features for scoring were listed but were not systematically related to the core unifying idea of each stage. The grounds for claiming that one stage was more advanced than another were essentially that the earlier stages fail to make crucial distinctions that the later stages make (e.g., distinguishing the moral value of human life from physical objects or the person's social status). Around 1968-1969 Kohlberg began to revise the description of scoring features, attempting to devise a scoring system keyed to the fundamental categories and distinctions of moral philosophers. For instance, philosophers distinguish different kinds of moral questions (e.g., Who has a responsibility to act in a given situation? Assuming responsibility to do something, exactly what should a person do? If a person fails to perform his duty, how should he be treated?), different principles of justification (justice, utility, prudence, perfection, etc.), and different social systems or institutional contexts (law, affectional relations, property, punitive justice, etc.). Kohlberg attempted to devise a taxonomy in which a subject's thinking could be classified in terms of these features, in effect providing a way of analyzing all possible moral philosophies. As might be imagined, the complications in devising such a scheme are bewildering, and this philosophical work is still unfinished. In 1971, Kohlberg published his most extensive discussion of how his six stages form an order of increasing cognitive adequacy (pp. 195-213). In the 1971 presentation, one stage is better than its predecessor not only in terms of being more differentiated (as in the earlier discussions), but also in terms of taking account of increasingly complex problems (e.g. how to organize a society). The highest stage is also characterized as being more often "reversible," one of the properties by which Piaget contrasts the relative adequacy of cognitive structures. By 1976, however, Kohlberg was describing moral stages in terms of different kinds of "social perspective": the perspective of an individual considering his own interests (at Stages 1 and 2), or the perspective of an individual who sees himself as a participant in a group whose members share expectations (at Stages 3 and 4), or the perspective of a rational moral individual "who has made the moral commitments or holds the standards on which a good or just society must be based" (1976, p. 36: Stages 5 and 6). These ideas will be further discussed in the next chapter. Over the years Kohlberg revised definitions of the stages, changed the basis for claiming that higher stages are conceptually more adequate than lower stages, and changed the scoring of interviews.

The work on the scoring system has gone slowly and has been undergoing many revisions, but recently (July, 1978) the Harvard group has finished a version that they intend to keep in its present form. The development of the scoring system is notable (if not unique) in using longitudinal data from the same subjects, some tested six times at three-year intervals over eighteen years. Virtually all other developmental schemes have used cross-sectional data (groups of different subjects at different ages). Using longitudinal data places greater constraints on devising a scoring system (because the same subject scored at later points in time cannot have scores out of sequence) but also has greater potential for capturing true ontogenetic change than cross-sectional data (in which no track of *individual* development is possible, and so the developmental sequence represents *group* differences). Over the years, a scoring system was developed so that a single subject at a particular testing would have scores mostly at one stage and over many testings would have scores that showed step-by-step invariant sequence. In meeting these two criteria, stages were redefined and scoring criteria were modified so as to produce the desired pattern. Recently (Colby 1979; Kohlberg 1978) data were reported on over thirty longitudinal subjects who show almost perfect invariant sequence. However, whether the system can be generalized to other data is still unknown. Also, since the latest scoring system has so recently been put into final form, little is known about its other empirical properties—such as its divergent validity (discussed in Chapter 4 and 6), its basic psychometric properties, its usefulness in explaining "real-life" phenomena. Nevertheless, the new scoring system is an impressive accomplishment in that it effectively manages the inherent problems of all interview data: defining a unit of analysis, devising a taxonomy that scorers can use with astonishingly high agreement, and relating the discriminations used for scoring to theoretically meaningful categories. One is particularly impressed in comparing the clarity, organization, and specificity of the recent scoring system to the 1958 scoring system.

Despite the revisions in the scoring system, a great amount and variety of research has been done over the years. These studies have gone beyond Piaget's in using the more elaborated six-stage model, in testing many more hypotheses than did Piaget's research, and in devising new research paradigms. Much of this work has concentrated on examining the stage properties of moral judgment. Kohlberg adopted Piaget's later notion of the stage concept rather than the looser, earlier notion of stages that Piaget had used in his moral judgment work (see Chapter 3 for a detailed discussion of the stage concept). The variety of studies and their major aims can be outlined as follows:

1. Cross-sectional comparisons of older subjects with younger subjects, with the aim of showing that older subjects tend to use higher stages of moral judgment (see Kohlberg 1969 for general discussion).

2. Longitudinal studies following the same subjects over several years and consecutively testing them to see if changes are "upward," according to the theoretical order of the stages (e.g., Kramer 1968; Kohlberg and Kramer 1969; Kuhn 1976; Holstein 1976; White, Bushnell, Regnemer 1978; Kohlberg 1978).

3. Cross-cultural studies to see if age trends in moral judgments of non-American subjects follow the same sequence as American subjects (e.g., Edwards 1978; Grosuch and Barnes 1973; Kohlberg 1969).

4. Intervention studies aiming to show that a subject's development can be advanced by special experimental or educational interventions (e.g., Blatt 1969; Blatt and Kohlberg 1975; Keasey 1972; Selman and Lieberman 1975; Tracey and Cross 1973; Turiel 1966, 1969, 1972).

5. Comprehension studies, aiming to show that comprehension of the stages is cumulative (i.e., if a subject understands Stage 4, he understands the lower stages but not necessarily the higher stages), and to show that above a subject's own predominant spontaneous stage of production, comprehension is increasingly difficult for the subject (e.g., Rest, Turiel, and Kohlberg 1969; Rest 1973).

6. Correlational studies relating moral judgment to delinquency (e.g., Kohlberg and Freundlich 1973), to political activism, and to political ideology (Candee 1976; Fishkin, Keniston, and MacKinnon 1973; Fontana and Noel 1973; Haan 1975; Haan, Smith, and Block 1968), to a life-situation guilt measure (Ruma and Mosher 1967), to ego factors (Sullivan, McCullough, and Stager 1960; Grim, Kohlberg, and White 1968; Krebs 1967), to cheating behavior (Krebs 1967; Schwartz, Feldman, Brown, and Heingartner 1969), to ratings of conduct (Kohlberg 1969), and to helping behavior (McNamee 1973; Rothman 1976; Turiel and Rothman 1972).

7. Studies of prerequisite components of moral judgment, namely

Piagetian Formal Operations and social role-taking (e.g., Colby 1973; Moir 1974; Keasey 1975; Kuhn, Langer, Kohlberg, and Haan 1977; Selman 1971, 1973; Tomlinson-Keasey and Keasey 1974). Much of this research will be further discussed in later portions of this book.

In addition to this involvement in basic research, Kohlberg has been the leading advocate of moral education programs based on cognitive developmental ideas. Teacher training, curriculum development, and evaluation programs have been organized largely through his efforts in moral education. Starting with a small pilot project in a single classroom, moral education programs are now part of the curriculum in many schools, in prisons, and in the governance of a school organized as a "just community" (e.g., Kohlberg 1971, 1973a; Kohlberg and Mayer 1972). (See Purpel and Ryan [1976], for a recent introduction to Kohlbergian moral education programs; see Lawrence [1977], Lockwood [1977], Rest [1974], for reviews.) The educational programs aim to develop the students' capacity to make well-reasoned, adequate judgments. Current evidence suggests that many adults do not reach the highest levels of moral judgment, and so presumably make decisions with less adequate conceptual tools. Yet, the moral decisions that modern people must make are becoming more complicated in our personal lives (e.g., euthanasia, the pill, abortion, wide possibilities in life styles) and in our corporate life (government leaders who corrupt the very institutions they head, difficult tradeoffs between ecology and economic development, the prospects of overpopulation, mass famine, and economic collapse). Some futurists (e.g., Ehrlich and Ehrlich 1974) are pessimistic about the ability of people to face the difficult moral decisions ahead and to reach the unprecedented levels of cooperation required if we are to avert catastrophe. Cognitive developmental moral education programs propose to foster such development in moral decision-making and in social cooperation.

New Directions in Moral Judgment Research

Many studies continue to replicate or directly extend Piaget's and Kohlberg's work. However, beginning in the early 1970s, new lines of moral judgment research appeared that were not completely consistent with earlier lines of research or anticipated in the earlier formulations. Three major centers of activity deserve mention that have differing interests but that see their activities as outgrowths of Piaget's and Kohlberg's work.

1. A considerable number of studies have been devoted to reexamining how children process the stimulus materials that Piaget introduced.

Whereas Piaget's purpose was to demonstrate that older children tend to use more complex ideas than younger children in response to hypothetical moral stories, the recent interest has been to identify features and cues in the hypothetical stories that affect how children perform the task. For instance, comparisons are being made between material presented verbally versus material presented by videotape, between familiar versus unfamiliar materials, between different orders in which elements are presented, between degrees of salience or intensities of situational cues, and so on. Therefore, Piaget-type materials are used and modified not to draw conclusions about developmental differences, but to describe how differing situational features affect information processing. Some of this research is reviewed by Shantz (1975) and is cited in Chapter 3. Clearly in moral judgment research, and in cognitive developmental research in general, a simple stage model of development does not take into account the diversity of factors affecting the performance of subjects in making moral judgments; a complete psychological model of moral judgment needs to give attention to more fine-grained aspects of information processing and decision-making. So far, researchers in this group have not been too concerned with integrating the information-processing perspective with the Piagetian developmental stage perspective.

   2. Another major outgrowth of Piaget's and Kohlberg's work has been the research by William Damon, Robert Selman, and Elliot Turiel. As Damon elaborates in his recent book (1977), these researchers wish to identify and describe the basic organizational principles of social knowledge of children in early and middle childhood. Their approach is similar to Piaget's and Kohlberg's in that social problems are presented to children in one-to-one interviews; each interview is interpreted in terms of one or another general system of ideas; development is portrayed as progress through successive organizations of thinking. For all three researchers, the focus is on their descriptions of developmental stages or levels—in complete contrast to the previous group, who emphasize information processing variables. Although their general research strategy is similar to Kohlberg's, they have defined new domains of social development different from Kohlberg's stages of moral judgment and have developed different interview materials. Selman (1976, 1977) concentrates on how children understand interpersonal relationships like friendship, leadership, and authority. Turiel's (1974) focus is upon nonmoral social regulations and conventions, such as sex roles and etiquette. Damon's emphasis is still within the moral judgment domain but is specifically concerned with issues of distributive justice and authority. The theoretical-descriptive work of

the group is fascinating, and the first round of empirical results have been impressive; however, the psychological model of developmental stages presupposed in this research is still very much that of Piaget and Kohlberg.

3. Research on the Defining Issues Test (hereafter, DIT) is another outgrowth of Kohlberg's and Piaget's work, and is the special focus of this book. This research arose primarily in response to the need for a practical, validated method for assessing moral judgment and the need to establish a data base for the major claims of the cognitive developmental theory. As evidence has accumulated, some of the key ideas of cognitive developmental theory have been reinterpreted — such as the stage concept and the relation of moral judgment to behavior. The ease of administration and scoring, and the comparability of results have attracted hundreds of new researchers into the moral judgment field, and we now have the most substantial integrated body of findings yet assembled on moral judgment.

In contrast to the Damon, Selman, and Turiel research, DIT research is concerned with an older group of subjects (adolescence through adulthood); furthermore, DIT research differs in adopting some different research strategies and in attempting to accommodate the stage-model to aspects of human performance not anticipated in Piagetian-type models of development. On the other hand, DIT research is still most interested in developmental differences, not in information processing analyses; hence, the research differs from that of investigators reexamining Piaget-type materials with an information processing approach.

Preview of the Book and DIT Research

A brief preview of the chapters of this book gives some indication of the scope of DIT research and provides a guide to the reader. Chapters 2, 3, and 4 lay down the theoretical rationale of DIT research. More specifically, Chapter 2 discusses how the word "moral" is being used, to what domain of human functioning "moral judgment" pertains, what features of people's thinking are relevant to a developmental analysis, how these features represent underlying organizations or systems, and in what sense one organization of thinking can be said to be a developmental advance over another.

Chapter 3 discusses the meaning of the word "stage." A simplistic model of development is criticized, and in its place a more complicated model is proposed, truer to the evidence at hand. A proposed model of development has many major and direct implications for constructing a measure of moral judgment and designing studies. Chapter 3 contains a discussion of issues such as "quantitative versus qualitative" analysis, indexing development as a continuous variable versus locating what stage a subject is "in," and the usefulness of the concept of "stage."

Chapter 4 explains the construction of the DIT and its special features. The construction of any moral judgment instrument involves four sets of ideas and decisions; one set has to do with hypotheses about the features of thinking to be studied (for the DIT, this is discussed in Chapter 2). Another set of hypotheses and decisions pertains to devising a data collection procedure that will create material relevant to the construct and that is not too confounded by other determinants. A third set concerns a method or algorithm for integrating the bits of information from various items so as to yield a general score of moral judgment development. A fourth set has to do with the strategy for validating an instrument. An instrument can be no better than the weakest set of ideas and decisions in any one of these four areas. The many decisions regarding the construction of the DIT are discussed in this framework.

Chapters 5, 6, 7, and 9 summarize the empirical findings of DIT research, discuss the designs and rationales of major lines of research, highlight some of the outstanding and exemplary studies, and discuss needs and future directions for research. The first part of Chapter 5 deals with a study of over 5,000 subjects from over 100 different samples collected by over 50 different researchers in all regions of the United States. DIT scores are related to the subjects' age and education, region of the country, sex, socioeconomic class and other demographic variables. In accord with developmental theory, DIT scores are powerfully related to age and education. The second part of Chapter 5 discusses several longitudinal studies in which the same subjects have been followed and retested at two-year intervals. Evidence indicates that generational effects, sampling biases, and testing effects are not serious artifacts that invalidate the age trends. Both the cross-sectional samples and the longitudinal studies are discussed in terms of evidence for the *developmental* nature of moral judgment.

Chapter 6 presents hundreds of correlations of the DIT with other psychological tests and variables. There are four main classes of correlations, and the theoretical questions of interest are different in each of these four:

1. DIT correlations with cognitive developmental variables (such as moral comprehension, Kohlberg's test, Piagetian Formal Operations, etc.) and with IQ and achievement tests are relevant in documenting

the *cognitive* nature of moral judgment. Also of special interest is the relationship between the DIT and Kohlberg's test, since both purport to measure moral judgment as characterized in terms of six stages; Kohlberg's test involves the production of justifications and the DIT involves the evaluation of different ways of stating the important issues of a dilemma.

2. DIT correlations with attitude and (3) behavior measures pertain to the question of whether moral judgment is value neutral and merely an intellectualizing skill, or whether it is related to the value stances that people take and the way they lead their lives. The discussion suggests that at least nine kinds of factors mediate or complicate the relation of moral judgment and behavior.

4. DIT correlations with personality tests reflect on the relation of moral judgment as one aspect of the person's personality to other aspects of personality.

Chapter 7 discusses studies designed to induce change in moral judgment. These are of two kinds: one kind of study considers the effect of changing the subject's test-taking "set," for instance, by asking the subject to fake low or fake high. In this case, increases in scores are an indication of the test's susceptibility to artifacts and construct-alien factors. The second kind of study looks at the effect of experiences designed to facilitate moral judgment advancement faster and further than the normal developmental pace. Most of the studies are of educational programs with quasi-experimental designs.

Chapter 8 by Mark Davison presents a new procedure for scaling DIT responses and a new way of representing subjects' scores on the DIT. Davison demonstrates the superiority of his new index (D) over the previous one (P) by systematically comparing D and P on a variety of reliability and validity criteria, and showing that the D index produces some stronger trends theoretically expected of the moral judgment construct. Since all of the DIT research before 1977 used the P index, Davison's new index begins a new phase in DIT research. Not only does Davison's work provide a more powerful use of the DIT, but it also illustrates a general strategy for test improvement. Furthermore — and most theoretically important — Davison's scaling procedures provide a way of examining the internal structure of DIT items and provide evidence for the developmental stage model.

Chapter 9 summarizes what can be concluded about moral judgment research at present and what I see as the crucial issues in research strategy. For readers with some familiarity with the area, it may be a good idea to read Chapter 9 before the other chapters for the gist of my argument and conclusions, and for selecting chapters of special interest.

2

The Developmental Features of Moral Judgment

The fundamental assumptions of moral judgment research are that a person's moral judgments reflect an underlying organization of thinking and that these organizations develop through a definite succession of transformations. What, then, are these underlying organizations of thinking? How can an underlying organization be identified? How can one cognitive structure be said to be developmentally more advanced than another?

Moral judgment research begins with attempts to answer these questions. One's ideas shape the data collected and how the data are scored and interpreted. Since a person's thought processes or basic cognitive structures cannot be observed directly, the psychologist's description of moral judgment development is speculative, and at best involves a process of guessing, gathering information in accord with these guesses, and then reformulating the guesses in light of the information.

This chapter describes the ideas about moral judgment development that have guided DIT research. As with any developmental scheme, no claim can be made for its detailed accuracy or finality, but the interesting and interpretable research that this approach has generated speaks for its validity. This chapter describes the rationale for various DIT items, explains some differences from Kohlberg's scheme in the characterization of stages, and supports the claim that some types of moral judgments are more advanced than others.

Function of Moral Thinking and
Conditions for Social Equilibrium

I find it helpful to begin this discussion in a way similar to John Rawls' (1971) discussion of a theory of social justice. We begin by observing that every person is born into an association of people. People band together for mutual advantage—for raising the young, for protection, for a division of economic labor, for the pure pleasure of interpersonal stimulation, for sexual stimulation, and so on. Social cooperation makes possible a better life. Therefore participants in a social group have a mutuality of interests for maintaining that group. There is also, however, a source of potential conflict of interests, since each person cannot be assumed to be indifferent to the distribution of the benefits of social collaboration. Thus there are natural tendencies to want to collaborate and cooperate but also tendencies to preserve and protect individual interests.

For simplicity's sake, the present account is written from the point of view of the individual pursuing one's own interests. This is not intended as a view of human nature that asserts that people lack empathy or concern for the welfare of others. Nevertheless, my account makes the weakest assumptions about empathic concerns so as to highlight the problem of balancing interests in social cooperation. If cooperation can be fostered among purely self-interested individuals (the harder case), then there is less of a theoretical problem in establishing cooperation among altruistic individuals (or more likely, individuals with varying degrees of self and altruistic concerns). The account attempts to solve the more difficult problem, for the less difficult are also satisfied with this solution. It should be noted that even among completely altruistic individuals, the means of distribution of the burdens and benefits of cooperative living must still be decided. Even if you were willing to be a slave, there's the question of whose slave you should be. Altruism and empathy don't remove the distribution problem in schemes of cooperation, and to discuss the problem assuming varying degrees of empathy and altruism would make the account more complicated.

A crucial function of moral thinking is to provide a plan for the distribution of the benefits and burdens of social collaboration (see Rawls 1971). Moral rules and principles regulate the basic relationships among people in terms of allocating rights (what kinds of claims a person can make on others in his own interest) and allocating responsibilities (the claims that others can make on their behalf from the person). Moral rules and principles regulate which social arrangements, practices, and institutions are permissible in society, what rights and responsibilities are particular to certain social roles, and what rights and responsibilities are common to all members of society. Hence, moral thinking has to do with the basic terms of cooperation—what I can expect of you, what you can expect of me.

Social collaboration depends on having a stable and reliable enough system of cooperation that people will be willing and able to fulfill their responsibilities. Each member of society needs to be concerned with other people's acceptance of a plan of cooperation. Two conditions for establishing a stable and reliable system of social cooperation are that its participants (1) recognize its norms, and (2) accept and support the system. Regarding the first point, each individual must be aware of the role that he is to play and must have a mutual understanding with others about respective rights and responsibilities. In contrast to the operation of an ant colony or a bee hive, in which coordination of behavior is established by genetic predetermination, complex human activity can be coordinated only by each person knowing what is expected of him. The issue is, then, how can human beings who have direct access only to their own minds come to coordinate their thinking and planning with others? How can mutual expectations about behavior be established? In the discussion of stages that follows, it is claimed that one of the two major factors determining the development of moral thinking is the person's concepts of how people form mutual expectations about the coordination of their behavior. It will be argued that socio-moral development begins with rudimentary concepts of shared expectations (norms established by the demands of a caretaker) and culminates in a concept of mutual expectations founded on a logical analysis of the requirements of an ideal system of cooperation.

The second condition for establishing a stable and reliable system of social cooperation is that there be some way of securing the support of the participants to maintain it. Although each participant may recognize that in the abstract, social cooperation is preferable to isolation, there are many arrangements of social cooperation to choose from. If in a particular system of cooperation some individuals seem to be reaping huge benefits and others, meager benefits, then the less advantaged persons are going to have strong reasons for changing the system. If an imbalance is perceived in the distribution of benefits and burdens, then there are unstablizing forces within that social system. On the other hand, if the rules of a society operate to maximize the welfare of each participant without giving advantages to some people at an undue cost to others, by and large, its participants have a great stake in maintaining the system. In other words, a

balancing of interests creates a stable social equilibrium; each participant is willing to bear his social burdens for the sake of the benefits
of social cooperation, realizing that others reciprocally bear their
respective burdens and receive their proportional benefits. Concepts
of fairness and justice are essentially notions about the balancing of
individual interests and the benefits of cooperation.

In the discussion of stages that follows, the second major factor
determining development will be characterized in terms of how the
interests of participants in a cooperative system are balanced; that is,
each stage has a distinctive concept of justice. The early stages have
only the rudiments of the concept of a stabilized, equilibrated social
system, for they do not view people's relationships within an encom-
passing social system but rather see people as collections of individuals who interact in isolated encounters. Stages 1 and 2 are limited
in the scope of relationships and social interactions that come within
their notice. They are limited in the temporal perspective within
which chains of interactions are noticed. Furthermore, as we move
through the stages we will see that arbitrary factors (e.g., accidents of
birth, historical circumstances) that tend to disequilibrate a social
system are progressively neutralized or otherwise provided for.

In summary, moral judgment is concerned with how the benefits
and burdens of social cooperation are to be distributed (the rules of a
social system that assign people's rights and responsibilities). Moral
development will be analyzed in terms of its successive conceptions
of (a) how mutual expectations among cooperating individuals are
established, and (b) how the interests of individuals are to be equilibrated. Table 2.1 presents the stage characterization on the two major
developmental dimensions and that stage's central concept for determining moral rights and responsibilities.

Note that the word "morality" as used here involves social interaction and does not concern individual values that do not affect other
people. For instance, a person's sense of obligation to improve and
devotion to actualizing his or her fullest potential are not regarded
here as a "moral" value; nor is a preference for "Rock and Roll" over
Beethoven. Not all values are *moral* values. Contrary to some philosophers who use "moral" to include concepts of the good or worthwhile
life, the use of "moral" in this account is restricted to concepts of
justice or fairness. Perhaps it would have been clearer if this research
area had been labeled "fairness judgment" instead of "moral judgment." The label originated with Piaget and has become the traditional term, and should not be confusing if this qualification is kept
in mind.

Stages in Moral Development

In order to describe development, a stage model will be used. More will be said in the next chapter about what is meant by "stage." It will suffice here to say a stage is a logical organization of thinking assumed to underlie the manifestation of certain features of moral judgments.

The present model began with Kohlberg's six-stage scheme, and represents a reformulation of that scheme in the light of my dissertation in 1969. In the process of extensive interviewing (some subjects accumulating as much as 13 hours of interviewing) and working on a scoring system for moral concept comprehension (see Rest 1969, Appendix B), I formed some new ideas about stage characteristics. A first systematic draft of this scheme appeared in 1970 as an unpublished manuscript, and various revisions (1971, 1974, 1976) have been circulated informally since. This scheme provided the basis for the DIT.

To illustrate the present scheme, excerpts from the 1969 study will be used, since the extensive interviews give richer impressions of people's thinking than the short DIT items. (In Chapter 4 DIT items will be given and related to specific concepts of this scheme.) A brief description of the study is necessary to explain the presentation below. The focus was on people's comprehension of moral judgments of the six stages as presented to them in statements. Statements had been prepared beforehand to illustrate the various stages of thinking, advocating one course of action or another for two of Kohlberg's standard dilemmas, the Heinz story and the Captain story (see description in Chapter 1). A statement was presented to a subject, who was asked to restate it in his own words and then to give a criticism or refutation of the statement. The subject's discussion was then scored as comprehending a stage-distinctive idea in the original prototypic statement (scored a "hit") or as not comprehending it (scored a "miss").

The format of the presentation below is (a) to describe theoretically the assumed understanding at each stage of the two factors underlying moral development (namely, concepts of how expectations about each other's actions are coordinated, known, and shared; and concepts about how an equilibrium or balance of interests of people in a cooperating group is achieved). These two factors determine the central concept for assigning moral rights and responsibilities and give logical unity to the various characteristics of people's spoken moral judgments. With each new stage, changes in these two factors account for the changes in how the subject ascribes rights and

Table 2.1. Stages of Moral Judgment

Stage	Coordination of expectations about actions (how rules are known and shared)	Schemes of balancing interests (how equilibrium is achieved)	Central concept for determining moral rights and responsibilities
Stage 1	The caretaker makes known certain demands on the child's behavior.	The child does not share in making rules, but understands that obedience will bring freedom from punishment.	The morality of obedience: "Do what you're told."
Stage 2	Although each person is understood to have his own interests, an exchange of favors might be mutually decided.	If each party sees something to gain in an exchange, then both want to reciprocate.	The morality of instrumental egoism and simple exchange: "Let's make a deal."
Stage 3	Through reciprocal role taking, individuals attain a mutual understanding about each other and the on-going pattern of their interactions.	Friendship relationships establish a stabilized and enduring scheme of cooperation. Each party anticipates the feelings, needs, and wants of the other and acts in the other's welfare.	The morality of interpersonal concordance: "Be considerate, nice, and kind, and you'll get along with people."
Stage 4	All members of society know what is expected of them through public institutionalized law.	Unless a society-wide system of cooperation is established and stabilized, no individual can really make plans. Each person should follow the law and do his particular job, anticipating that other people will also fulfill their responsibilities.	The morality of law and duty to the social order: "Everyone in society is obligated and protected by the law."

| Stage 5 | Formal procedures are institutionalized for making laws, which one anticipates rational people would accept. | Law-making procedures are devised so that they reflect the general will of the people, at the same time insuring certain basic rights to all. With each person having a say in the decision process, each will see that his interests are maximized while at the same time having a basis for making claims on other people. | The morality of societal consensus: "You are obligated by whatever arrangements are agreed to by due process procedures." |
| Stage 6 | The logical requirements of non-arbitrary cooperation among rational, equal, and impartial people are taken as ideal criteria for social organization which one anticipates rational people would accept. | A scheme of cooperation that negates or neutralizes all arbitrary distribution of rights and responsibilities is the most equilibrated, for such system is maximizing the simultaneous benefit to each member so that any deviation from these rules would advantage some members at the expense of others. | The morality of non-arbitrary social cooperation: "How rational and impartial people would organize cooperation is moral." |

responsibilities in a moral dilemma. Conceptual advances in these two factors account for the theoretical claim that each new stage has more adequate conceptual tools for making decisions. The two factors are said to *underlie* moral judgments because it is not assumed that a person is consciously aware of or can articulate these basic notions (just as a three year-old child is not consciously aware of the grammatical structures in his speech patterns, or the Concrete Operational child is not assumed to be aware of Piaget's logico-mathematical groupings supposedly underlying Concrete Operational Thought). The two factors are speculations on my part about what underlies the developmental differences in people's intuitions of fairness at the various stages. (b) After this theoretical discussion of a stage, the specific features in people's observable utterances are described. These are the characteristics that trained judges use to score interview material. The characteristic is summarized in a few words, numbered (e.g., 1a, 1b, 1c), and briefly explained. (c) Then a prototypic statement used in the 1969 study is given to illustrate the stimulus material that was presented to the subject. (d) Then examples are given of the subjects' discussions of the prototypic statement. If the subject was judged to show comprehension of the stage-distinctive idea in the statement, this category is labeled, "Response—scored a 'hit.'" If the subject was judged not to show comprehension, this is labeled, "Response—scored 'miss.'" If the excerpted material comes from a subject's criticism of the statement, it is labeled, "rejection." (e) Finally at the end there is a discussion of what has been accomplished at each stage and what the major inadequacies are.

Stage 1: Obedience: "You do what you're told"

At Stage 1, concepts about mutual expectations and about equilibrated social systems are rudimentary. The child is aware that his caretakers tell him to do certain things and not to do other things. At Stage 1, being moral is being obedient. At this stage the child cannot view the caretaker's rules as mutually shared agreements because (1) the child has no say in determining them, (2) the intent of the caretaker is opaque to the child, and (3) the child sees no coordination of his wishes with those of the caretaker in the formulation of rules. The child does not comprehend any purpose or plan behind the rules, nor any interconnectedness among the rules. They are simply there, like unchangeable, physical laws, and disobedience is uncritically associated with punishment.

Stage 1, as described here, is not necessarily the absolute zero point of moral judgment development, but only the first point of discussion in the present account. In my dissertation and in DIT research, infants and very young children have not been studied, and I leave to other researchers the task of charting the earliest phases of development (c.f. Damon 1977).

Below are listed three representative characteristics of Stage 1, some prototypic statements used in the comprehension study, and the subjects' responses that illustrate the features of this stage:

1a. *Right and wrong are defined simply in terms of obedience to fixed rules.*

The following statement exemplified this characteristic of Stage 1, written in the context of the Heinz story:

Statement—Heinz story: "When you take a drug like that it's stealing. Stealing has always been against the law. That's the way it is; the law is the law." A typical response to this statement, which was scored as comprehending the idea but not agreeing with it, was the following:

Response—scored "hit," rejection: "He shows that he accepts the law, what it says. He doesn't question it. He takes everyone's word for it, it seems like. He doesn't seem to have any of his own ideas about it."

1b. *Punishment inevitably follows disobedience, and anyone who is punished must have been bad.*

Statement—Heinz story: "You shouldn't steal the drug because you'll be caught and sent to jail if you do. Criminals always get caught in the long run. And you'll feel bad thinking how the police will catch up with you."

Response—scored "hit," rejection: "You would have getting caught on your mind. But the idea of saving your wife's life is more important than knowing you are going to have to get punished somehow."

Despite the primitiveness of Stage 1, there is a definite accomplishment here too. At Stage 1 the individual's behavior is coming under the governance of social norms that represent an extra-individual reality. As children extend the caretaker's demands to other children, there are the beginnings of the concept of the generality of rules. At Stage 1 the cooperation of the child with the caretaker is not equal or reciprocal, of course, since the child does not set rules for the caretaker. The child clearly has responsibilities, but his only right is freedom from punishment if he is obedient.

Stage 2: Instrumental Egoism and Simple
Exchange: "Let's make a deal"

Stage 2 represents an advance, in viewing each individual as having his own wishes, motives, and points of view. Other people have self-interests, like oneself, although each person may have a different perspective on situations, and may want to do something different. For Stage 2, an act is right if it does some good for the actor. Hence no longer is morality blind, but serves a purpose. Viewing each person as an independent agent motivated to pursue his own interests, Stage 2 has a concept of social interaction less lopsided than Stage 1's; in Stage 2, each person is an independent operator. Two people may want to cooperate and do each other a favor if it is in each one's interest to do so. We have the beginnings of cooperation, in which each party has rights and responsibilities, as determined in the bargain. Stage 2 bargains are characteristically simple "one-shot" exchanges of favor for favor, a limited form of equilibrated social cooperation. It follows that if two people cannot make a deal, one should not interfere with the other, because each wants to do his or her own thing.

A number of stage characteristics logically follow from these core notions.

2a. *An act is right if it serves an individual's desires and interests.*

Statement—Heinz: "The druggist can do what he wants and Heinz can do what he wants to do. It's up to each individual to do what he wants with what he has. But if Heinz decides to risk jail to save his wife, it's his life he's risking; he can do what he wants with it. And the same goes for the druggist; it's up to him to decide what he wants to do."

Response—scored "hit": "He just says that the individual can do what he wants and his life is in his own hands. This is true—and his thinking, this person's thinking, it is up to him. If he wants to do it, he can do it. No one else can change his mind."

2b. *One should obey the law only if it is prudent to do so.*

Statement—Heinz: "Stay within the law and you can save yourself a lot of trouble. Some laws are pretty stupid, but if you don't obey them, you might get caught and have to pay a fine or spend some time in jail."

Response—scored "hit": "It only deals with the consequences in the individual if he gets caught. . . . (He says) the reason not to break the law is because of the inconvenience to yourself if you get caught . . . the main fault with his statement is that it does not deal with the 'rightness' of breaking the law."

2c. *Cooperative interaction is based on simple exchange.*

Statement—Heinz story: "(Heinz is) running more risk than it's worth unless he's so crazy about her he can't live without her. Neither of them will enjoy life if she's an invalid."

Response—scored "hit," rejection: "He is only worried about what will happen to Heinz, he will be in jail. He doesn't care about his wife . . . or his love for her, or anything, he just says she will just be bedridden and she'll suffer . . . . He's saying that for all the troubles Heinz has to go through, it isn't worth it."

The accomplishment of Stage 2 is to establish a purposiveness to the rules of cooperation, in contrast to Stage 1's blind obedience. Furthermore, at Stage 2 the rudiments of equality and reciprocity are first established in the notion of simple exchange. Cooperative interactions are entered into voluntarily, with each party understood as having something to gain—and that's what makes it fair.

Stage 3: Interpersonal Concordance: "Be considerate, nice and kind, and you'll get along with people"

A crucial advance leading to Stage 3 is what Flavell, Botkin, Fry, et al (1968) have termed "reciprocal role taking." This is the realization that a person is aware that another is thinking about him and also that the other knows that the person knows he is an object of the other's thought, and vice versa. In other words, people can be mutually aware of each other, and of each other's thoughts and expectations regarding one another. Whereas role taking at Stage 2 involves awareness of the other's intentions and desires, role taking at Stage 3 involves awareness that the self and the other are mutually aware that each is thinking about the other (See Selman 1973). Reciprocal role taking therefore provides a new way of coordinating expectations among people ("we have a general understanding," rather than "we've made a deal"). Reciprocal role taking makes possible a new kind of cooperative reciprocity among people: not favor for favor, as at Stage 2, but the reciprocity of enduring friendship. By being able to anticipate what the other's inner goals and general dispositions are, one can form a more stable image of that person than may be apparent in the vicissitudes of the specific outward acts of the person. By having an appreciation of the "inner person," two people may form a more enduring relationship than the single, one-shot exchanges, provided for in Stage 2. Stage 3's concept of relationship entails the establishment of a balance of interests in which each party is thoughtful and considerate of the other's feelings, and each tries to be helpful and supportive. Each favor need not be bargained for, as in Stage 2, and it is not necessary to keep tally of who owes whom because having a stable, positive relationship ("having somebody that cares and that you can count on") is a good in itself. For Stage 3, therefore, morality is a matter of establishing and maintaining enduring positive relationships.

3a. *An act is good if it is based on a prosocial motive.*

Since what is crucial to Stage 3 is that general positive relationships among people are maintained, a person's general inner disposition (his being a good person) is more important than occasional deviant acts undertaken in behalf of sustaining personal relationships.

Statement—Heinz Story: "Stealing is bad, but . . . Heinz isn't doing wrong in trying to save his wife. . . . He is only doing something that is natural for a good husband to do. You can't blame him for doing something out of love for his wife."

Response—scored "hit": "Any good husband that wants to provide for his family and his wife what he should and out of goodness or out of his heart—he will do this, so you can't blame him for doing what he thought was right. . . ."

It may be noted that the Stage 3 statements here are only considering Heinz's good intentions towards his wife and not towards the druggist. One of the deficiencies of Stage 3 is that it can justify (or at least, excuse) action undertaken with good intentions toward one party while disregarding the other parties. This is a "centration" or partial focus on only one of several crucial aspects. An adequate morality must consider all parties involved, must define to whom one has an obligation (to Heinz's wife? to the druggist?) and to what extent one is obligated (should Heinz even go so far as to sacrifice his life to save his wife? sacrifice his life and the druggist's, if necessary?)

3b. *Being moral implies concern for the other's approval.*

One is concerned with conforming one's behavior to what the other expects, because to violate his expectations or to incur his disapproval undermines his being able to count on you, and thus jeopardizes a general positive relationship.

Statement—Heinz story: "If you were so heartless as to let your own wife die, you would feel terrible and everybody would really think you were inhuman. It would be terrible to think of what you allowed to happen to your own wife and what they must have thought when she realized you weren't going to save her."

Response—scored "hit": "Thinking about what she was thinking when she realizes you weren't going to save her might have an effect, but if this person is so heartless and cruel and everything, then it wouldn't bother him."

Response—scored "miss": (Response lacked evidence of awareness of the statement's concern for approval in the eyes of others.) "He's sort of bringing everybody else into it. . . . It sounds like he is trying to cover up for it by bringing everybody else in."

Stage 3's major accomplishment is the concept of a stabilized, continuing cooperative equilibrium based on friendship or personal relationships. Each party in this cooperative system determines his rights and responsibilities by anticipating the feelings, needs, and expectations of the other. The relationship is stabilized (or "conserved" in the Piagetian sense) despite isolated or occasional perturbations, so long as each party discerns that the core, inner person still cares and wants the relationship.

Stage 4: Law and Duty to the Social Order:
"Everyone in society is obligated and protected by the law"

Stage 3 conceptualizes a stabilized system of social interaction based on mutual understanding, but this system is limited to primary group relations based on sentiment. It fails to define guidelines of moral interaction for strangers, for people not of one's liking, or for people outside one's circle of friends or relatives. The ideal of the flower-children notwithstanding, maintaining good interpersonal relationships is not enough to coordinate the interactions of people in a complex society. Stage 4 advances over Stage 3's limitations with a new conception of how shared expectations can be established. In contrast to Stage 2 and 3's role-taking, which depends on face-to-face encounters and learning to interpret social cues and messages from others, at Stage 4 expectations are coordinated through laws by which people can anticipate one another's expectations without knowing one another.

4a. *Right is defined by categorical rules, binding on all, that fix shared expectations, thereby providing a basis for social order.*

Laws establish norms for behavior that are publicly set, knowable by all members of society, categorically and impartially applied, and impersonally enforced as a society-wide concern. A system of shared expectations established by law is particularly threatened by any deviations whatsoever. If people no longer feel a categorical compulsion to comply with law, or if they suspect that others are infringing, the whole system of interlinked expectations is undermined. Without a basis for common understandings, there is chaos in people's minds about what to expect of each other—hence Stage 4's concern that if one deviation to law is allowed, actual social chaos will ensue. Stage 4 is vulnerable to that particular overcompensation popularly referred to as the "law and order" mentality.

Statement—Heinz: "It is a natural thing for Heinz to want to save his wife, but it's still always wrong to steal, You have to follow the rules regardless of how you feel or regardless of the special circumstances. Even if his wife is dying, it's still his duty as a citizen to obey the law. No one else is allowed to steal, why should he be? If everyone starts breaking the law in a jam, there'd be no civilization, just crime and violence."

Response—scored "hit": "If Heinz was allowed to steal, then everyone would have to be allowed to steal, and our society would be one mass of crime and violence. . . . If our streets were filled with crime—I think they would—everyone would live in fear. Heinz surely would not benefit from this. Since everyone is equal, the laws must apply equally to everyone; therefore, Heinz should not receive any special privileges."

Response—scored "miss": "I don't think everyone else should be brought into this—about stealing—it is just about him . . . it should be about him." (This subject apparently saw Heinz's deed as an isolated occurrence rather than as one involving categorical social norms, binding on all, and as an issue of social order.)

4b. *Values are derived from and subordinated to the social order and maintenance of law.*

No personal consideration or circumstance can supersede the law. Safeguarding any value—like life or property—cannot be accomplished by a few people's unilateral actions, but life or property is only safe when *no one* threatens it, when there is a *general* social arrangement whereby others respect it (not just when your friends respect it, as only Stage 3's plan of cooperation provides). Therefore laws have to come before everything else, according to Stage 4, in order to make a society-wide cooperative system work. Stage 4 confuses the maintenance of law as a condition for safeguarding values with the assertion that law is the prime value or the basis of all human values.

Statement—Heinz story: "A human life is important but so is law and order. Stealing is against the law and against the commandments. You can't throw away laws and religion because that's what keeps human life sacred in the first place."

Response—scored "hit": "If you throw them (laws and religion) away, human life would be just sort of chaos. It wouldn't be sacred anymore. . . . If there's no more law and religion it would be like a Communist world. Even that wouldn't be there because there would be no one to regulate them and they'd be looting the stores and killing others and after food and that."

Response—scored "miss": (Subject construes the "value of life" to be a personal predilection rather than a society-wide norm.) "Life should be respected, but a lot of times somebody will die you don't even know. And you don't even care, you know. Or somebody important will die and you won't care. Or sometimes a relative will die and you won't care that much."

4c. *Respect for delegated authority is part of one's obligations to society.*

Individuals are related to each other through their respective roles or "positions" in society. Such "positions" represent the functional divisions of labor deemed useful to accomplish the institution's goals, and are defined without regard to any particular person, but with regard to the particular duties, prerogatives, and rewards appropriate to that function. Each person has a job to do as his part of the division of labor in society, and each person does his job expecting that others will do theirs; this complementarity of roles permits society to function.

Furthermore, one must respect authorities, for an authority does not act on his own but acts on behalf of the whole system. To show disrespect for an authority is to show disloyalty to the whole system of roles, and is a threat to Stage 4's concept of cooperation.

Statement—Captain story: "It's a soldier's duty to obey the captain's commands. It's part of the captain's responsibility to decide about this mission. He doesn't like to be in a position where he has to give such orders but he has to do it. The captain is just doing his job and the soldier must do his."

Response—scored "hit": "The only one that decides right or wrong is society. Society is the one that decides if this captain had the right to make a choice, and either choice he made, behind him is society and the law."

The major accomplishment of Stage 4 is its conception of a stabilized system of cooperation at a society-wide level, extending Stage

3's notion of stabilized relationships by the concept of a formal organization of roles. To each role is attached its particular rights and responsibilities of citizenship. People know what behavior to expect from each other, in that laws and society-wide norms are publicly set for everyone to know and heed.

Stage 5: Societal Consensus: "You are obligated by whatever arrangements are agreed to by due process procedures."

Stage 4 provides a rationale for supporting *established* social arrangements, but not a rationale for choosing between *different* systems of law or different sets of social arrangements. The realization that advances people beyond Stage 4 is that there are many ways of arranging a stable social order; however, some social systems distribute the benefits and burdens of social cooperation very unequally, and do so on arbitrary grounds. What is distinctive about Stages 5 and 6 is that they face the problem of devising a plan for cooperation that minimizes arbitrary inequities and maximizes the stake each individual has in supporting cooperation. Stages 5 and 6 attempt to provide a rationale for choosing among alternative social systems, and to provide guidelines for creating new laws and arrangements.

Previous stages have conceptualized various ways that people can establish shared expectations about their interaction: Stage 2 concepts arrange specific bargains in the interests of each party; Stage 3 conceptualizes friendship relationships based on mutual role-taking; and Stage 4 concepts provide a formal system of social roles that are definable and knowable through laws. But this coordination of perspectives is only possible after laws have been enacted and established. On what basis can new laws be proposed that one can anticipate will be accepted? Stage 5 tries to envision the mind of the hypothetical rational person. Rather than role-taking the minds of specific individuals whom one knows in concrete historical-cultural circumstances, and trying to figure out how to strike a bargain with these actual people, Stage 5 attempts to coordinate perspectives by imagining the terms of agreement that a group of hypothetical rational people would accept. One attempts to justify, therefore, one's plan for social cooperation by imagining what is rational. This procedure of justification is not unlike procedures of justification in logic and science. Piaget's statement is apropos: "Logic is the morality of thought just as morality is the logic of action." (Piaget 1965, p. 398).

The cooperative system that Stage 5 envisions is one based on the law-making process, a process that would draw support from rational people. Stage 5 anticipates that people can reach agreement about their laws if (1) the law-making process reflects the general will of the people, and (2) if certain minimal safeguards of people's welfare are guaranteed for everyone, i.e., certain basic rights like "life, liberty, and the pursuit of happiness."

If the people of a society have fair procedures for choosing their laws, then according to Stage 5 those laws should be viewed by most people as representing the most desired set of social arrangements and providing a basis on which to press claims on others. Although various concrete procedures conceivably could be used to reach societal consensus, historically the procedures of constitutional democracy have been the tools for making laws establishing the equilibrium of interests that Stage 5 sees as fair. Voting is taken as an expression of people's own estimate of their interests. In conditions of free discussion and free elections, ideas and interests come into competition with each other, and compromise and negotiations for votes take place. Hence, the final vote can be assumed to represent the give-and-take of compromise and the molding of interests into balanced public policy that will maximize the welfare of its constituents. Even if an individual feels his interests are contrary to the majority vote in some issues, he is obligated to abide by that vote; laws must be nonoptional and binding on all, and, besides, it is expected that an individual will be on the majority side most of the time and will then want majority policies fulfilled. Note, however, that what is essential to Stage 5 is not that a society adopt the political machinery of Western democracies, but that a social system be regulated by consensus-producing procedures.

The other crucial ingredient in Stage 5's concept of social cooperation is the provision of certain minimal safeguards for everyone. These safeguards are necessary because "the will of the people" almost always will not be unanimous but will be representative of the majority. Even the majority must be prevented from making life intolerable for the minority, for intolerable social arrangements would make it unreasonable for the minority to cooperate. There can be (and have been) laws to which obedience by a minority is self-defeating (for instance, being a completely law-abiding Jew in Nazi Germany). In Stage 5 the term, "basic human rights," refers to the minimum guarantees that any social system must make to the participants in order for them to consider that the general commitment to cooperate is worthwhile.

These characteristics of Stage 5 are exemplified below:

5a. *Moral obligation derives from voluntary commitments of society's members to cooperate.*

Statement—Heinz story: "The law represents the basis of how people have agreed to live with each other. By continuing to live in that society, he has agreed to respect and maintain its laws."

Response—scored "hit": "The people have made the laws up for themselves and they are the ones that have gone together and decided on these laws, so they should follow the laws that they have made."

5b. *Procedures exist for selecting laws that maximize welfare as discerned in the majority will.*

Statement—Heinz story: "Heinz has to respect the general will of his society as it is set down in the law. The law represents the basis of how people have agreed to live with each other."

Response—scored "hit": "I think he meant that the majority of the people have set down laws to live by and because . . . this is how people have agreed to live with each other."

Response—scored "miss": (Subject construed "respecting the general will" as the Stage 3 concern to be personally approved and admired by the others.) "He's saying . . . people are more interested in what your neighbors are going to say about your new car . . . and what people are talking about. In our society today you are more interested in that the Joneses see you in Church. . . ."

5c. *Basic rights are preconditions to social obligations.*

Statement—Captain story: "According to the rules of the army, a soldier can't refuse an order like that, but as a human being, the troublemaker has the right to refuse. When a man enters the army, it is understood that there are going to be risks, but he hasn't agreed to commit suicide."

Response—scored "hit": "He is saying that although you sign a contract when you enter the Service, you have not signed any contract to commit suicide."

Response—scored "miss": "If he's ordered to, he has to. Once he's in, he's got to obey the way everybody has to. Everybody has to go in there and serve his time. If he's drafted, he hasn't got the right to refuse. Even if the whole situation is wrong, that man has to do what he's told."

The major accomplishment of Stage 5 is to provide principles (i.e., consensus government, basic human rights) for setting up a system of social cooperation. It accomplishes the coordination of perspectives by imagining what rational people would accept. The balancing of interests and the appeal of the arrangement are established by instituting procedures for making laws that are viewed as fair. If a person has been allowed to cast his vote, to have his day in court (with all due process), to have his basic rights protected, then there are no grounds for complaint.

Stage 6: Nonarbitrary Social Cooperation: "How rational and impartial people would organize cooperation is moral"

Before going on to Stage 6, it may be helpful to put this discussion in perspective. At every stage there is an intuitive sense of what is right and fair. The developmentalist asserts that this moral sense changes as more complexities of social life are taken into account. The present scheme proposes to analyze the underlying logic of people's moral sense in terms of different social arrangements for distributing the benefits and burdens of cooperation. In order for any set of social arrangements to function, (1) the participants must have some way of knowing what is expected of each of them, and (2) the participants must have some stake in supporting the arrangements by feeling that the balancing of interests is fair. Stage 6 is an advance over Stage 5 with regard to the second condition, i.e., in the establishment of a balance of interests. Recall how this is accomplished in previous stages. Stage 1 provides a normative structure (the caretaker's demands) for the regulation of human interaction; however, in this system of cooperation there is great inequality between parties and hardly any reciprocity. The system comes into being because of the accidents of birth—i.e., who was born first, who is bigger and more powerful, etc. Stage 2 goes a long way toward establishing some equality among participants in a cooperative arrangement through the notion of simple exchange. Stage 2, however, provides only a very temporary and fragmentary system of social cooperation, and is arbitrarily bound by the particular circumstances of parties getting together and having favors that each one wants. Stage 3 provides for a more established, ongoing system of cooperation in friendship relationships, each party being committed to the other's welfare; however, Stage 3 arbitrarily limits cooperation to whatever friendships have been established at a given time. Stage 4 establishes a society-wide system of cooperation in which all participants equally are under the law and in which all are reciprocating, each carrying out his or her own role ("Formal Justice"). Stage 4, however, allows gross inequities and arbitrary distribution of the benefits and burdens of social living, because the social order may be set up legally to give advantage to some at the expense of others (for example, a slave society). Stage 5 attempts to eliminate arbitrary rules by providing procedures for making new rules that reflect the will of the people, giving each person an equal say in determining the arrangements of society and hence each receiving from social cooperation the most that one could hope for while at the same time having a moral basis for pressing claims on others. Stage 5, therefore, has gone a long way in neutralizing inequities and lopsided reciprocity due to accidents of birth, historical accidents, and other arbitrary circumstances. Stage 5, however, attempts to create an equilibrium of social cooperation through the procedures for making laws (through "Procedural Justice"), and therefore has not completely insured that the outcomes of duly enacted laws produce a completely nonarbitrary equilibrium of social cooperation ("Substantive Justice"). Even when laws are enacted that reflect the will of the people, inequities can still exist (particularly for powerless minorities), and the collective judgment of the people at one time may be unfair as viewed by the people at a later time (for instance, the acceptance of slavery in early America). Stage 6 maintains, therefore, that merely because the majority of people want a law (or national policy), that does not make it morally right, for there is a more ultimate test of morality than social consensus.

Stage 6 adopts the same method as Stage 5 for the coordination of perspectives—namely, imagining the mind of the rational person. But Stage 6 pushes this perspective one step further; Stage 6 not only attempts to anticipate what the rational person would accept in terms of procedures for making laws, but, further, to anticipate what principles a rational society would want to end up with for governing its system of cooperation.

The work of John Rawls, 1971, most clearly formulates this starting point for constructing an ethical system, and he elaborates and argues for particular definitions of principles of justice. While the present account borrows heavily from Rawls' work, most other modern moral philosophers can also be understood as formulating moral principles by which an ideal society would be regulated, and invoking these principles as the ultimate criteria for making moral decisions (rather than tradition, friendship ties, or a current consensus). The defining feature of Stage 6, therefore, is its appeal to abstract principles (e.g., Rawls' two principles of justice, Kant's categorical imperative, Brandt's extended rule utilitarianism, etc.) which are so presented that rational, equal, and impartial people could choose them as the governing terms of their cooperative interaction.

The following statements and responses further discuss Stage 6 thinking:

6a. *Moral judgments are ultimately justified by principles of ideal cooperation.*

Statement—Heinz story: "Where the choice must be made between disobeying a law and saving a human life, the higher principle of preserving life makes it morally right—not just understandable—to steal the drug. . . . If Heinz does not do everything he can to save his wife, then he is putting some value higher than the value of life. . . . By not acting in accordance with your sense of the value of human life you would condemn yourself . . . you would know that you have betrayed your own moral integrity."

Response—scored "hit": "He's operating out of a value of human life. It's a higher principle. . . . He's recognized that there are other kinds of values, but he's saying the value of life is higher than these. I think he's making judgments out of principles. . . . (If I didn't act in accord with this value, it isn't that) I'd feel bad because I'm supposed to feel bad, or because of the loss I have had, or because of what other people think of me or a judgment outside of myself. Betrayal by your own moral integrity implies, one, that I organize in my life some system of principles and values, that I live consistently out of these values—or try to live consistently out of these values—and that these values and principles then become organized into really who I am, and how I live, and who man is in this world. And to violate these principles then is to violate my integrity, which is to violate my whole person, and mankind too for that matter."

The above response brings out clearly that the decision to save Heinz's wife is being justified on the basis of a general way of making choices (not just opting for life in this particular situation), that other people would be expected to make the choice this way (not a matter of acting on personal preference or simply choosing what is self-serving in this instance), and that the value appealed to has intrinsic worth for the actor (not being a means to some other goal).

In evaluating subjects' responses to this prototypic statement, it was much more difficult to have assurance of scoring hits than of scoring misses. The system of conceptions that we have just sketched as Stage 6 was often indistinguishable in our data from the less advanced conceptualization (Stage 5B), which takes an individualistic-humanistic stance on this issue (a belief or self-accepted commitment to human dignity *without* a rationale to base it on).

The response below did not seem to see the justification as following from general principles, but rather assimilated the sense of the prototypical statement to be exonerating the motives and good intentions of Heinz, in a Stage 3 way of thinking:

Response—scored "miss"; (assimilation to Stage 3): "He's doing it for his wife, to save a life. He's not stealing for the sake of stealing, it has a purpose and (the statement) thinks it is a good moral purpose."

6b. *Individuals each have an equal claim to benefit from the governing principles of cooperation.*

The Stage 6 concept of cooperation entails that all individuals are viewed as ends-in-themselves and not means for some other good, for cooperation that is not coercive or arbitrary entails respect for the individuals who enter into it and support it.

Statement—Captain story: "It's unfair to single out anyone to go since any human life is the same value. But if someone must go, it should not be based on saying what his life is worth. . . . As a matter of principle you have to look upon every life as sacred. If the troublemaker can do the job best, then he should go, but not because his life is less important."

Response—scored "hit": "The principle behind the decision is the value of human life—that is, to save the most lives possible. . . . The platoon by not volunteering gave the responsibility of decision back to the captain. The sick man or the troublemaker has no right to refuse the order because to do so would be to rate their life as being worth more than the rest of the lives of the platoon. . . ."

There were many subjects whose responses to this prototypic statement clearly show no evidence of anything resembling Stage 6 thinking about "moral equality" and "sacredness of life." In the examples below, note how the Stage 6 notion is assimilated and distorted to other frameworks of thinking, in some cases producing drastically different moral positions.

Response—scored "miss": (Subject confused the fact of individual differences in ability and usefulness with the moral equality of human life.) "He says here that in a way it's unfair to single out anyone to go since any human life is the same value. I couldn't disagree with this more. I think first of all a human life is pretty cheap in our world today. And I think also that there is a very much different scale of value for everyone's life. One man's life is not just as important as another man's life especially when you're working in a society or in a group such as an Army company because there will always be people who are more talented, who are smarter, and who are physically more able. And these people are more important to the group."

Response—scored "miss," assimilation to Stage 4: (Rather than disputing that life was sacred and of equal value, like the above example, most subjects agreed with the Stage 6 statement of life's sacredness and of equal value. But the following example assimilated. equality of life to mean Stage 4's notion of equal protection under the law.) "Well, right in the laws of your country, it says that murder is a felony punishable by the gas chamber or any other way the state or federal government sees fit . . . let's say you only killed a poor alcoholic on skid row—so we only give you five days in jail? No! You'd get the electric chair the same there as if you would have killed Percy's daughter or the Lindburgh baby, or anyone else."

Response—scored "miss," assimilation to Stage 4: (Another subject derived the "sacredness of life" from the Stage 4 notion that people hold useful role positions in society.) "I think every life is sacred but you have to look at every person as part of the whole, like part of civilization or something like the President would have a much better role than the average person, but the average person also has his role to do in the world."

Response—scored "miss," assimilation to Stage 3: (A Stage 3 notion of the sacredness of life was determined on an affectional basis.) "I think every life in itself is sacred, but I think people are biased sometimes, like different lives are more sacred to different people. Like, if my mother died and a stranger on the street dies, I would be much more concerned about my mother."

Response—scored "miss," assimilation to Stage 2: (A Stage 2 notion of "every life is of equal value" simply asserted that values are instrumentally determined.) "I would think that it would just be that you couldn't say anyone like the troublemaker's life was less valuable because less valuable than what? You know, if it was less valuable than another man's life, you just can't tell, because you don't know what the troublemaker may be some day, and you don't know his background, and the other man's background, and even if you did, it would be different to them than it would be to you. And— sometimes maybe you could. Like, just maybe in a few instances, you might be able to where there's somebody really down in the gutter, or a real wino, say—his life just isn't worth anything, even to himself."

Comparisons of Stage Schemes

In this account of the development of moral judgment, the influence of Piagetian theory is conspicuous in many respects. (1) Perhaps the most obvious one is the cognitive-developmental perspective: the various statements that subjects make are assumed to follow from a general underlying orientation, and that these basic ideas are successively modified and transformed with development. (2) Another influence of Piaget's thinking is in making cooperation the central concept of moral judgment development. The present account, like Piaget's (1932), portrays the course of development as starting with the morality of constraint and ending with the morality of cooperation; however, many of the features of Kohlberg's stage characteristics are used to depict stages between these two poles. (3) Morality is seen as part of the evolutionary process of establishing wider and more encompassing systems of equilibrium, in this case, equilibrated social systems. Rather than viewing morality as a transcendental faculty of mankind, as Humanistic Psychology tends to do, morality is portrayed as naturally and gradually evolving as a person's experiences widen and his cognitive development proceeds. On the other hand, morality is not reduced to lower forms of psychological adaptation, such as conditioned avoidance responses (e.g., Eysenck 1976), or operant conditioning (e.g., Goldiamond 1968), or imitation (Bandura and McDonald 1963). (4) Many of Piaget's explanatory devices are used in the present account to describe development: for instance Stage 3's "conservation"; Stage 4's "over-compensation"; the "centration" of Stage 3 on one actor's good motives, neglecting the consequences to other actors; the "neutralization of arbitrary perturbations" so as to create a more "stable and equilibrated system" of cooperation; and the "coordination of perspectives" in role-taking so as to establish a basis for shared expectation.

(5) As in Piaget's (1932), Kohlberg's (1969), and Selman's (1976) accounts of the development of moral judgment, certain acquisitions in role-taking are seen as prerequisite to the development of moral judgment.

Differences with Piaget's stages are quite obvious, given that his dozen or so features are embodied in two stages that studied children from 5 to 13 years of age, whereas the present scheme (and Kohlberg's scheme) attempts to account for development in moral judgment up through professional moral philosophers. One hardly ever has the sense when reading Piaget's characterizations of his older subjects that this is how moral philosophers think.

Comparisons with Kohlberg's stage scheme[1] are more difficult to discuss since there is so much that is borrowed, the differences are subtle, and Kohlberg's stage descriptions have changed over the years. My scheme has six stages whose core characteristics are directly borrowed from Kohlberg's. I use two factors to account for the logical coherence of the features of each stage, and the basis for arguing the greater conceptual adequacy of each stage over its successor. While Kohlberg has discussed somewhat similar notions in one place or another (c.f. 1976, Table 2-1), I have not seen elsewhere the arguments for stage conssitency and logical sequentiality worked out in detail quite the way it is in this chapter. Furthermore, it is not always clear what kind of argument Kohlberg has in mind, and it is amazing how differently some reviewers have construed his stage scheme (e.g., Eisenberg-Berg, in press; 1977; Hogan 1975b, p. 534; Haan, 1978). The present account represents my notion about how a Kohlberg-type stage scheme ought to be understood, namely, in terms of the logic of cooperation, rather than (as other writers have suggested) as "prohibition morality," "romantic individualism," or "imperativist rules handed down by revelation."

While there is a general similarity in overall conceptualization between Kohlberg's scheme and the present one, nevertheless, there is a striking difference in basic architecture. The present scheme has two elements running through the six stages (columns 1 and 2 of Table 2.1); the various subthemes of each stage are the scoring features (or "surface features"), which can be identified in subjects' protocols, and they are simply listed as 2a, 2b, 3a, 3b, 4a, 4b, etc. There is no special relation between 2a, 3a, and 4a, nor between 2b, 3b, and 4b. The various Stage 4 features (e.g., 4a, 4b, 4c) are simply various ways that Stage 4 thinking is manifested in different contexts.

Kohlberg's scheme, in contrast, has a much more elaborate architectural structure. He starts with a philosophical-theoretical analysis (discussed in Chapter 1) of the basic questions that moral thinking addresses, the basic concepts of justification, and the basic social institutions and values found in every society and culture. In principle, every moral judgment can be viewed as an intersection in each of these three sets—e.g., as addressing a particular kind of moral question, as using a particular type of justification, and as arising in reference to some specific social institution. Other kinds of distinctions are also made besides these three sets that we need not go into here. Kohlberg attempts not simply to list a few features of each stage inductively arrived at, but attempts to create a logical grid for analyzing every possible moral judgment—a far more ambitious undertaking than my scheme.

Kohlberg refers to the philosophical sets of distinctions by special names: "element," "norm," "issue," etc. It is not necessary to go into the delineation and rationale for these here (see Kohlberg, et al., 1978), but one of Kohlberg's major architectural decisions has been to consider stages of development as independent of these philosophical distinctions. Kohlberg suggests viewing his scoring system as a tree structure (Kohlberg et al 1978): there are three dilemmas in a form, the interview material in each dilemma is separated into "issues," each issue is separated into "norms" (12 possible), each norm is separated into "elements" (17 possible), and each element is then scored by stage. All four levels of distinctions (issue-norm-element-stage) must be made in order to separate "content" from "structure."

According to Kohlberg's system, the stage score gives no information, for instance, on whether a subject in response to the Heinz dilemma is orienting himself or herself to the maintenance of social order or to the value of life. What is crucial to this developmental analysis is a further differentiation of ways of understanding social order or the value of life. Kohlberg argues that earlier scoring systems did not make a rigorous enough distinction between content and structure—for instance, previously, any reference to social order would have been scored as Stage 4. Kohlberg claims that because of this "confusion of content with structure," there were some cases of longitudinal inversions and much stage mixture in data analyzed by the previous scoring systems (1976). By purging "content" from stage scores, Kohlberg has now obtained a pattern of nearly perfect step-by-step sequence in his longitudinal cases—and these new data show the step-by-step pattern better than any other longitudinal data that I have seen in developmental research. (More will be said about this later.)

Furthermore, Kohlberg's architecture introduces some order into the business of classifying moral judgments, particularly necessary when a scorer is dealing with spontaneously produced judgments from interviews. The scorer's job is a two-phase operation: first, locate the judgment in terms of its "content"; then find its developmental stage. In Kohlberg's earlier scoring system (1958), the scorer's job was to go through all the lists of features until something resembling a subject's moral judgment had been found. If two features on two different lists resembled the subject's response, there were no clear conceptual grounds for deciding under which list to score the response (and in many instances, the lists overlapped). The element-norm-issue scheme attempts to introduce a conceptual structure into lists of features so that a scorer can find his way through the lists and have a conceptual basis for arguing that a particular response belongs here rather than there.

From Kohlberg's point of view, my stage scheme confuses content with structure because the whole apparatus of element-norm-issue is not attended to. Among cognitive developmentalists, charging a researcher with confusing content with structure is more serious than aspersions about one's mother. Since the whole program of DIT research is based on the stage scheme of this chapter, if one cannot find something to say in defense, then the whole enterprise is suspect.

First (a minor point), there is no particular advantage in DIT research for having an apparatus that helps scorers find their way around a complex scoring system because in DIT research, subjects' responses are not being scored—the test is multiple choice. Second (the major point), I question the degree to which "structure" (that which distinguishes the stages from each other) is really distinguished from "content" in the new scoring system, and also I question the value of doing so.

Can stage structure really be dissociated from the content of issues, norms, and elements? Kohlberg seems to indicate this can be done when he talks about "holding content constant" so as to examine structure, and the necessity of not confusing content with structure (1978, Part I, pp. 55 ff). One test of how independent structure is from content is to examine the degree to which each content category is differentiated into six structural stages. If it is really possible to hold content constant while varying structure, then there ought to be 12,240 classifiable moral judgment scores in Form A of the 1978 Scoring Guide (figuring that there are three dilemmas to Form A, two issues in each dilemma, 12 norms for each issue, 17 elements for each norm, and six stages plus four transitional stages). Instead, we find that there are only 184 possible scoring categories listed. Why this shrinkage from 12,240 to 184? Some of the shrinkage can be accounted for in that no Stage 6 responses are defined, owing to the difficulty in finding subjects that far advanced (but this would account for a shrinkage of only 1,224). Some of the shrinkage can be accounted for by the purging of some scoring categories from the scoring manual because they produced stage scores that were discrepant from other stage scores. I do not know how many scoring categories were dropped for the sake of maximizing stage consistency and invariant sequence. However, I believe that the greatest shrinkage derives from the inability to separate "content" from stage distinctions. Stage 1 simply cannot be defined in terms of the "content" of Element #17, "Maintaining social contract or freely agreeing." Similarly, we do not find the higher stage entries on Element #1, "Obeying persons or deity." Each stage cannot be defined in terms of every content category. Note that we are not just missing a few entries here and there, but that the list of actual scoring categories is only about 2% of the logically possible categories if content and structure were completely orthogonal and independent.

What is the advantage of purging issue-norm-element material from stage distinctions? Certainly a developmental analysis should go beyond whether a subject advocates stealing or not stealing in the Heinz story. We want to know why the subject favors one line of action or another, and we want to make some abstract characterization of the way he goes about making moral decisions that would be transferable to other situations. Further, if the subject says, "Don't steal because of the law," we want to know how he is viewing the law — for instance, is it simple fear of legal punishment, is it concern for social order, or what is it? But how fine should we make distinctions? Do we really want to go as far as Kohlberg has gone in purging content from structure?

Consider the following four responses to the Heinz story, which are scored at different stages in the 1978 Manual, but which are all concerned with social order:

1. "If everyone went around breaking the law, things would be wild, stealing, murder. You couldn't live." (Scored Stage 3 — Law, II.9; Part 3, p. 96).

2. "Yes, I mean in general this type of precedent would be established for any kind of a want that somebody wants to satisfy. Just go ahead and rob or something like that, the result would be." (Scored Stage 3/4 — Law, II.9; Part 3, p. 97).

3. "If it's just, if it's necessary to preserve order. [Why do we need laws?] Well, I think without laws there would be chaos, there wouldn't be any order so to speak. I am talking about just laws now." (Scored Stage 4 — Law, II.9; Part 3, p. 107).

4. "Because it is so hard for people to live together unless there are some laws governing their actions. Not everybody is good certainly and we have to go by some code, so to speak, that we have to follow to make sure that everybody has their own individual rights." (Scored Stage 5 — Law, II.17; Part 3, p. 117).

The scoring guide makes these distinctions:

Stage 3: "One should obey the law because if everybody breaks the law there would be chaos, things would be wild, or everything would be topsy-turvy; *OR* because without laws immoral people would cause chaos."

Stage 3/4: "People should obey the law because otherwise laws will no longer be a guide to people; *OR* because otherwise a bad example or precedent will be set; *OR* because otherwise people will steal even if they don't really have to, will steal without thinking, or will think stealing is o.k."

Stage 4: "People should obey the law because the law is essential if society or civilization is to survive; *OR* because the law is necessary for social organization, general social order, or smooth social functioning; *OR* because giving way to individual beliefs or values and decisions will cause disorganization."

Stage 5: "One should obey the law because if individuals are to live together in society, there must be some common agreement; *OR* because laws represent a necessary structure of social agreement."

I think these are pretty fine distinctions. Actually, there are six additional categories which are very close to these four (Criterion Judgments Nos. 14, 17, 18, 20, 22, and 23); and earlier manuals contained a category scored stage 2/3, "One should obey the law because if people start breaking the law and stealing other people's things, everybody will lose out." (Kohlberg et al. 1977, 2/3 — Law, B.9). My point is not that there are no distinctions among these examples, but that the distinctions are very slight in comparison to distinguishing a concern for the affection of a husband for his wife, versus a concern for maintaining law and social order, versus a concern for the basic human rights of anyone. Kohlberg's new system says in effect that these latter distinctions are confusing content with structure, and that the most important set of distinctions to make are like those in the former set. By the new system, a stage score would not reflect the difference between a person oriented to affectional concerns (say, at Stage 3) from a person oriented to social order concerns (which may also be scored at Stage 3); the variance in stage scores reflects the kinds of distinctions illustrated in the examples above. So one must ask: Are these the most psychologically significant discriminations in people's moral thinking?

I have assumed that the most useful unit of analysis is the kind of consideration that a subject brings up (which may have both "content" and "structural" elements in it according to Kohlberg's scheme). If a subject is concerned about law in the sense of maintaining social order, that is Stage 4; if a subject is concerned about law in the sense of worrying about a jail sentence, that is Stage 2. Items on the DIT are written to convey this distinction without distinguishing 10 kinds of concern for maintaining social order. My scheme does not assume that the same kind of considerations are addressed at each stage nor that the logical unity of a stage is best portrayed by a common set of content categories running orthogonally through the stages. Rather, I assume that the type of consideration that a person deems important (e.g., maintaining social order) is indicative of the developmental level in itself.

It is certainly not the case that abstraction for its own sake always leads to more profound and more useful psychological analysis. Kohlberg has introduced four tiers of distinctions (issue-norm-element-stage). It is conceivable that someone else could introduce *five* tiers of distinctions and claim that Kohlberg was confusing structure (newly defined) with content, and so on, ad infinitum. The question is not who can out-abstract whom. Also, the question of defining stages is not settled by appealing to theoretical accounts of stage descriptions, because various theoretical schemes can be proposed that are equally satisfactory on purely logical grounds (c.f., my scheme and Kohlberg's, at different levels of abstraction). Along with Kohlberg, I think the matter must be settled empirically, in terms of the kinds of analysis and distinctions that produce the most useful results. I am not yet decisively swayed by his longitudinal data (impressive as they are) since it is unclear how well those findings will generalize to other samples, it is unknown to what degree stage scores from the new system are confounded with verbal fluency and other performance variables, and it is unknown what characterizations of moral thinking will prove most useful in understanding "real life" behavior. Happily, Kohlberg has provided us with a tool by which these questions can be explored empirically, for with the 1978 Scoring System it is possible both to make the fine discriminations required by that system and also to analyze results by collapsing discriminations.

Finally, in addition to architectural differences, some differences in stage characterizations should be noted. Kohlberg has A and B substages and I do not. Kohlberg has redefined Stage 3 so as to include an "Archie Bunker, law and order" type (Kohlberg, 1976, p. 43), has redefined Stage 2 to include some ideas formerly coded at Stage 3, and has redefined Stage 4 to include some ideas formerly coded as Stage 5. Stage 6 is no longer defined at all in the Scoring Guides, so it is impossible to be coded as a Stage 6. In theoretical discussions, my definition of Stage 6 is less stringent than Kohlberg's (1971). For Kohlberg, to be Stage 6, one must have a deontological philosophy that places justice as the cardinal concept. For me, virtually any philosophy is Stage 6 that construes the ultimate bases of moral obligation as following from a logical analysis of the requirements of cooperation. In my scheme, virtually all major modern moral philosophers are Stage 6; by Kohlberg's, there does not seem to be more than a handful. It should be noted, however, that differences in conceptions of Stage 6 have never made much difference in research findings, because the discriminations necessary to distinguish it from Stage 5 are not well elicited either by Kohlberg's test or the DIT, and the discriminations are not important to most subjects.

Having commented at length on differences in my stage scheme with Kohlberg's, I want to reaffirm the preponderant indebtedness of my scheme to Kohlberg's. In comparison to other characterizations of moral judgment development (e.g., Bull 1969; Eisenberg-Berg, in press; Haan 1978; Hoffman and Saltzstein 1967; Lee 1971), the differences are minor. The reader now has an account of the developmental scheme presupposed in the construction of the DIT. I regard the successes of DIT research as generally confirming Kohlberg's general stage ideas, although the Harvard group have not agreed with some of my minor alterations. I also regard working on developmental schemes as never finished or final, and will want to reexamine the entire matter when item analyses of the DIT are completed and when some more empirical results are available on Kohlberg's new scoring system.

3

The Stage Concept
in Moral Judgment Research

"Most typically, the stage concept is invoked to refer to a mode, pattern, or constellation of behaviors (or dispositions toward behavior) that seem to characterize some definable point in the child's life. . . ." (Flavell and Wohlwill 1969, p. 91). The stage concept as now used in moral judgment research is largely an import from Piaget's post-1940 work on physical and logical concepts. Although Piaget's own major work in moral judgment (1932/1965) used the concept of stage — as have other theorists such as Baldwin (1906), Dewey (1895), and McDougall (1908) — Piaget was very cautious, tentative, and nonspecific about the use of the stage concept in moral judgment research: e.g., "These moralities (heteronomy and autonomy) are due to formative processes which, broadly speaking, follow on one another without, however, constituting definite stages" (Piaget 1932/ 1965, p. 195 — see also Flavell 1963, p. 291). In contrast to Piaget's earlier tentativeness, Kohlberg cites Piaget's later 1960 discussion of the stage concept as defining how "stage" should be construed in the moral judgment area (Kohlberg 1969, p. 352-353; Kohlberg 1971a, p. 4; Kohlberg 1971b, p. 186; Kohlberg 1973, p. 181-182; Kohlberg, Colby, Gibbs, and Speicher-Dubin 1976, p. 31-32). The particular passage from Piaget that Kohlberg so often cites is as follows:

1. Stages imply distinct or qualitative differences in children's modes of thinking or of solving the same problem at different stages.

2. These different modes of thought form an invariant sequence, order, or succession in individual development. While cultural factors may speed up, slow down, or stop development, they do not change its sequence.
3. Each of these different and sequential modes of thought forms a "structured whole." A given stage-response on a task does not just represent a specific response determined by knowledge and familiarity with that task or tasks similar to it; rather it represents an underlying thought-organization. . . .
4. Cognitive stages are hierarchical integrations. Stages form an order of increasingly differentiated and integrated *structures* to fulfill a common function (1960, pp. 13-15).

While Piaget's discussions of the stage concept are invaluable, in recent years an enormous amount of energy has been devoted to explicating the concept and examining its fit with data. It has become evident that the stage concept is used in a variety of ways and that there is no unique model of development that the concept implies. Flavell (1970, 1971; Flavell and Wohlwill 1969) and Wohlwill (1973) have described several variations of the stage model, ranging from simplistic and unqualified models to more complicated and qualified models of development. After reviewing hundreds of developmental studies, these authors along with numerous others conclude that a simple stage model is untenable and urge more complex conceptions as models of cognitive development. It is ironic that moral judgment researchers who have borrowed the stage concept from Piagetian research have been promulgating a less qualified, and more "hard line" concept of stage than is now tenable in the research that brought the concept into being.

What is a "simple stage model" and how does it differ from a more complicated model? What evidence is there that moral judgment researchers have assumed a simple stage model of development? In answering the second question, I will cite quotes from Kohlberg's writings for an academic audience. Other moral judgment researchers (including myself) could be cited as well, but Kohlberg has been so influential in shaping the field that his views on the stage concept have simply been repeated by virtually everyone else doing moral judgment research. In answering the first question, I shall describe the simple stage model in stark terms that may seem to be more caricature than what anyone believes. Presented so explicitly, perhaps no one would agree that these statements fully and accurately represent his views. Yet the quotes that I will produce do seem to suggest this caricatured version of the stage concept, and it seems that many of Kohlberg's followers have understood him in this way.

What difference does it make whether one adopts a simple stage model or not? In the course of this chapter I will show how one's model of development affects major decisions in assessment strategy and research design.

The Simple Stage Model

Kohlberg has articulately contrasted a cognitive-developmental approach with other approaches. He points out that the emphasis of behaviorism on quantitative descriptors of behavior (frequency, amplitude, intensity, latency of responses) contrasts with the cognitive-developmental emphasis on the patterning in behavior and its logical interconnectedness (Kohlberg 1969, p. 348-9). Whereas trait or psychometric approaches view people as aggregates of quantitative dimensions or traits, where each person has more or less of the various traits, a cognitive developmental approach makes use of ideal-typological constructs, again emphasizing the qualitatively different patternings and organizational forms of behavior rather than carving it up into polar dimensions (e.g., Kohlberg 1969, p. 371-2).

Qualitative Descriptors. The special emphasis of cognitive-development on qualitative aspects of behavior is exaggerated in the simple stage model in asserting that *only qualitative* differences are appropriate in developmental analysis and that *quantitative* considerations are antithetical to an interest in cognitive structures. According to the simple model, one person can be said to be different from another in being in a qualitatively different stage, but it is inappropriate to talk about amounts of this stage or that stage. Kohlberg states, "Structural theory does not treat any change as a change in structural competence unless the change is evident in a qualitatively new pattern of response" (1973b, p. 181). Kohlberg criticizes the Defining Issues Test for "assessing a continuous variable of moral maturity rather than discrete qualitative stages" (1976, p. 47).

Stage Unity. The cognitive-developmental idea of "structured wholes" is interpreted by Kohlberg (and many others) to imply that the various aspects of a cognitive structure such as Piagetian "conservation and other aspects of logical operations should appear as a logical and empirically related cluster of responses in development" (Kohlberg 1969, p. 353). Since the various components of a stage function as a unit — they comprise an integrated system — all the components of a structure become operational at the same time, that is, one aspect appears if other aspects appear. Although minor discrepancies exist, the unity of moral development is more striking than the discrepancies. "The stages form a clustered whole. There is a general factor of moral stage cross-cutting all dilemmas, verbal or behavioral" (Kohlberg 1973b, p. 186). "Individuals should be consistently at a stage unless they are in transition to the next stage. . . ." (Kohlberg 1976, p. 47).

Step-by-step Invariant Sequence. Piaget, like Kant, postulates that people mentally operate on what is given in direct experience, to form structures of meaning and the basic categories of knowledge. Such concepts as number, space, time, mass, density, and so forth are not directly read off from our sensations and perceptions, but are the result of a continual organizing activity. Unlike Kant, Piaget maintains that these basic structures of knowing are developed, not established *a priori*; that they derive from the person's general coordinations of actions and abstractions from these coordinations, and are elaborated and extended through accommodation and assimilation. The point here is that cognitive structures are developed progressively, one mediating the next.

Proponents of a simple stage model interpret this position to imply the following: "Stage theory holds that every single individual, studied longitudinally, should only move one step at a time through the stage sequence and always in the same order" (Kohlberg et al. 1976, p. 39). The step-by-step metaphor suggests a staircase rather than a ramp to depict upward movement. A person is on one step one day, then moves to the next step with no backward steps and no skipping to higher steps. Kohlberg repeatedly invokes the step-by-step model, and he claims that studies have confirmed this view: "Fifteen-year longitudinal data on 50 American males in the age period 10-15 to 25-30 demonstrate movement is always forward and always step-by-step" (Kohlberg, 1973b, p. 186; see also 1971a, p. 36 and 42; 1971b, p. 187; Kohlberg and Kramer 1969, p. 103).

Furthermore, Kohlberg claims *invariant* sequence. He allows only two conditions under which a reversal in sequence might occur: "obvious errors in observation or . . . dramatic regression-inducing stress or damage" (Kohlberg et al. 1976, p. 39). Otherwise, "a single case of longitudinal inversion of sequence disproves the stage theory if it is not a manifest case of measurement error . . . . A stage sequence disregarded by a single child is no sequence" (1973b, p. 182).

Error-free, Context-independent Assessment. In a simple stage model, developmental assessment involves determining what stage a subject is in by obtaining a sample of a person's functioning, interviewing the person to find out how he or she thinks, then characterizing the organization of the person's thinking by classifying it in terms of the stages. Assessment or diagnosis is fairly straightforward because (a) the characterizations of the different stages are obvious once one has talked to a variety of people ("The claim we make is that anyone who interviewed children about moral dilemmas and who followed them longitudinally in time would come to our six stages and no others," Kohlberg 1976, p. 47); (b) the specific context or content of an interview does not make much difference in the assessment of a person's stage (*"Intuitive issue scoring* . . . is theoretically the most valid method of scoring, since it is instrument free, that is, applicable to any moral dilemma," Kohlberg 1976, p. 45); and (c) stage assessment is very accurate (Kohlberg refers to the new scoring systems as "relatively error-free tests"—1976, p. 47).

(It should be noted that more recently, Kohlberg has modified his views regarding the error component in all measurement; however, his 1976 views have received greater dissemination and are cited here to exemplify the simple stage model.)

Further features of the simple stage model are not stated explicitly but are sometimes tacitly assumed in various data analyses and in discussions of development. Reference to Figure 3.1 can help make these points more clear. The image of development that is sometimes presupposed includes the following characteristics:

1. A period of development occurs in which each stage has a turn at predominance in use over other stages, and each stage peaks at 100% usage. There are times at which subjects are "pure" types.

2. Step-by-step development implies that the only kind of stage mixture that occurs is between adjacent stages, and then, only two

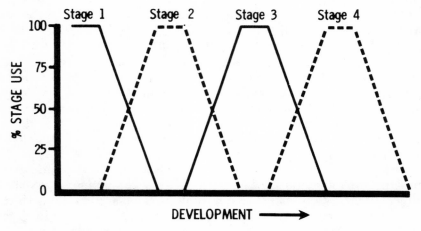

Figure 3.1. Graphic presentation of the simple stage model.

stages mix at a time (e.g., there can be a mix of Stages 2 and 3, 3 and 4, but not a mix of Stages 2, 3, and 4). Step-by-step development implies that a previous stage (the "-1" stage) falls to 0% usage before the higher stage (+1) begins (for example, Stage 2 use falls to 0% before Stage 4 begins).

3. The stages are evenly spaced across development and each stage has a symmetrical and identical rate of onset and decline. This is assumed in averaging stage scores across subjects (that is, moving up from Stage 1 to Stage 2 equals movement from Stage 3 to Stage 4; moving up "one-third a stage" has uniform meaning). (This assumption is made in Kohlberg's use of the Moral Maturity Index — discussed below — and in discussions of stage change.)

4. Periods of transition alternate with periods of consolidation (first there is Stage 1, then transition to 2, then consolidation in 2, then transition to 3).

5. The peak of stage usage is also the peak of stage consolidation. That is, when subjects come to use Stage 3 100%, then they have the best understanding of and facility with Stage 3 that they will ever have. Or, put another way, no further development of a stage's organization of thinking occurs after its usage has peaked. (This is assumed in discussions of subjects being simply "in" one stage and "out" of the previous one, and the next stage being beyond reach.)

Many of the features of the simple stage model stem from the emphasis on analyzing the form or organization of a response instead of a response's frequency, latency, or accuracy. To illustrate this point, the story is often told of Piaget's work with Binet on tests of intelligence — whereas Binet was concerned with the accuracy of an answer, Piaget became interested in the different types of wrong answers that indicated qualitatively different organizations of thinking. It should be noted, however, the simple stage model assumes that inferences about a single response can also be applied generally to the person who has produced that response. For instance, if one analyzes a moral judgment response to fit into a Stage 3 organization of ideas, then the simple stage model goes on to say that the *person* (not only that *response*) is in Stage 3. The simple stage model assumes that people are single-tracked thinkers who cannot operate with more than one organizational program at a time (or two programs, if they are in transition). But notice that this assumption about human thinking does not logically follow from the focus on analyzing the *organization* of thinking rather than the frequency, latency, or accuracy of response. It is an assumption about response systems in the person's head (that there is essentially only one respone system operative at a time). Later it will be argued that an interest in analyzing a *response* in terms of an underlying organization of ideas does not entail that the *person* has only one way of organizing ideas.

Empirical Inconsistencies with the Simple Stage Model

The simple stage model has launched initial research efforts in studying cognitive development. Perhaps in initial research, a more complicated developmental model would have overloaded psychologists already burdened with working out an alternative approach. Whatever the case, as studies have been completed and a substantial body of findings has accumulated, cognitive developmentalists have noted several serious, consistent problems with the simple stage model.

Subject Fluctuation. Flavell and Wohlwill (1969, p. 99) note that when children are in a period of transition in acquiring a structure, for example, conservation of length, they vacillate in the employment of the cognitive structure. Subjects are not clearly "in" one stage or another, but "these structures have a probabilistic character, appearing now in evidence, now absent." Acquisition is not an all-or-none matter, but seems rather to increase in degree of probability that the structure will be in evidence. "The recent Piagetian literature strongly suggests that development is normally gradual rather than abrupt. . . ." (Flavell and Wohlwill 1969, p. 79). Therefore we need to have quantitative as well as qualitative descriptors in an account of cognitive structural development. We need qualitative descriptors to represent the different organizational patterns, and we need quantitative descriptors to represent the degree to which a particular subject is manifesting one or another of these organizational patterns. Moral judgment research gives much evidence of subject fluctuation. Rubin and Trotter (1977) report a correlation of only .44 for stability over 2 weeks, using Kohlberg's 1976 Scoring System. Selman and Lieberman (1975) reported test-retest correlations in the .60s on their measure of moral judgment. Test-retest correlations on the DIT are generally in the .70s and .80s (see Davison, Chapter 8). In a recent longitudinal study, Kuhn (1976) found so much subject inconsistency over a half year interval on a modified version of Kohlberg's scale that she advanced the rather novel proposition that a theory of stage sequence does not even imply "that individuals remain stably categorized as one type or another" (p. 163). On the basis of another longitudinal study, White, et al. (1978) also state, "These preliminary data suggest that there are short-term fluctuations in individual patterns . . . ." Subject fluctuations have also been evident in intervention studies as well (e.g., Blatt and Kohlberg 1975; Turiel 1966). The latest information on the Harvard 1978 Scoring System (Colby 1979) indicates extraordinary test-retest reliability (correlations in the high .90s); however, even with this scheme there is some subject fluctuation over a two-week period. About 30% of the subjects show shifts in their major/minor stage scores—for instance, a subject scored as predominantly Stage 3, with minor Stage 2, shifts to predominantly Stage 2 with minor Stage 3. In short, subjects are not simply "in" one moral stage or another, but fluctuate within a developmental range.

Inconsistencies Due to Test Characteristics. When cognitive structure is assessed, the specific type of testing materials, the instructions and procedures, and scoring procedures can make a big difference to the way subjects organize their responses. For instance, in testing for seriation, a child may be able to order six objects by size, but may not be able to so order 10 objects. A child may give evidence of making transitive inference when making comparisons of height but not when making comparisons of curiosity. In testing for conservation of substance, a child may indicate conservation when asked to point to the level of a glass that the liquid will rise to when poured, but the child may be unable to explain his answer. In short, we get inconsistent indications about a subject's thought structures if we vary the test characteristics.

Flavell and Wohlwill (1969) suggest many kinds of test characteristics that can affect the kind of thought organization a subject exhibits: "the stimulus materials and their familiarity, the manner of presentation of the relevant information and the amount of irrelevant information from which it has to be abstracted, the sheer magnitude of the information load placed on the child in dealing with the problem, the role played by memory and sequential processing of information, and so on" (p. 99). In Flavell's 1970 review of hundreds of cognitive developmental studies, he cites the overwhelming evidence of the effects of test characteristics on structural assessment (pp. 1032-1034).

The moral judgment literature contains much documentation of this same phenomenon. For example, Medinnus (1959) administered two Piaget-type stories to subjects, each story designed to tap the same moral judgment characteristic. He found that children seemed more advanced on one story than on the other, and he suggested that the discrepancy may have been due to differences in the explicitness of relevant story cues and to differences in the familiarity of children with the incidents depicted. Magowan and Lee (1970) systematically investigated the effects of giving children Piaget-type stories describing familiar or unfamiliar settings and found that greater familiarity was strongly associated with more advanced moral judgments. Recently it seems that a major preoccupation of researchers using the Piagetian moral judgment paradigm has been to investigate the effects of varying test characteristics, producing a flood of studies: Armsby (1971); Baldwin and Baldwin (1970); Berg-Cross (1975); Berndt and Berndt (1975); Buchanan and Thompson (1973); Chandler, Greenspan, and Barenboim (1973); Collins, Berndt, and Hess (1974); Costanzo, Coie, Grumet, and Farnill (1973); Crowley (1968); Gutkin (1972); Hebble (1971); Hewitt (1975); Imamoglue (1975); Irwin and Moore (1971); Jenson and Hughston (1971); Johnson (1972); King (1971); Rule, Nesdale, and McAra (1974); Shantz and Voydanoff (1973).

Using the Kohlbergian paradigm, Liebermann (1971) has demonstrated differential "story pull" of the dilemmas in Kohlberg's 1958 test; for example, a Stage 4 response to the Heinz dilemma is rarer than to other dilemmas. Certain stories "pull' out certain stage responses. Leming (1975) found that a set of "practical" moral dilemmas (containing moral conflict situations likely to be found within the life space of the subject) elicited different stage responses than Kohlberg's set (dealing with nonfamiliar dilemmas). A recent study by Crockenberg and Nicolayev (1977) found discrepancies between Kohlberg's Form A and Form B, each set containing dilemmas that raise similar moral issues but vary in details of the story setting. The most recent study of alternate form reliability in the 1978 system reports a correlation of .84 between forms and 85% agreement within half a stage (Colby 1979).

In summary, test characteristics make a significant difference in the manifestation of cognitive structure, and the differences have been much greater than we would have expected from a straight Piagetian view.

Decalage Across Content Domains. It has long been noted in Piagetian research that the various manifestations of concrete operations (conservation of length, mass, weight, transitivity, etc.) are not acquired by subjects concomitantly—in fact there seem to be regular age gaps in the acquisition of many concrete-operational concepts; for example, conservation of mass is regularly attained before conservation of weight. Some of Piaget's writings seem to suggest that all concrete operational concepts should be acquired synchronously—as Toussaint states (1974, p. 992):

> The structuring or *structure d'ensemble* criterion, one of Piaget's defining
> characteristics of the stage construct, postulates that mutual connections
> and reciprocal interdependencies exist between the logical operations, and
> that it is these interrelationships which create the unified system of the
> logical structures that characterize a given period of development. . . .
> Two important consequences that follow from this postulate are: (a) that
> the acquisition or development of a family of related concepts should be
> expected to occur at about the same time, and consequently (b) that solu-
> tions to tasks of related logical structure should be expected to be of equiv-
> alent difficulty. (Quoted from Flavell 1977, 247).

Although some dispute exists over whether the concept of *structure
d'ensemble* (or Piaget's theory) requires synchronous development of
all manifestations of a structure (Flavell 1971; Pinard and Laurendeau 1969), the fact is that synchrony is rare in manifestations of
concrete operations or formal operations. Even when two different
concrete operational concepts, for instance, transitivity of length
and conservation of length, are tested with nearly identical stimulus
materials, there is still no evidence of synchrony (Smedslund 1964).
Flavell states (1971, p. 441), "the available evidence certainly leads
one to believe that tight synchronisms are probably few and far between."

In moral judgment research using Piaget's stage concepts (e.g.,
immanent justice, objective responsibility, retributive justice, expia-
tory punishment) Hoffman's (1970, p. 274) review concludes that
the evidence for synchrony across various concepts is quite ambiguous. One study (Johnson 1972) reported consistency across concepts, but other studies have not.

In moral judgment research based on Kohlbergian stages, it is not
certain what the constituent concepts would be as counterparts, say,
to the conservation of mass, weight, or transitivity in Piaget's concrete
operations. A unit of analysis smaller than the global entity, stage,
has not been clearly established. From time to time various substage
units have been proposed: in 1958, Kohlberg proposed "aspects" as
subunits; in 1970, "modes, elements and categories"; in 1973,
"issues"; in 1975, "criterion concepts"; in 1977, the stage intersects
with an element applied to a norm in response to an issue. Since 1970
I have proposed a different list of "concepts" as discussed in Chapter
2. However, neither the psychological reality nor the theoretical utility of these various substage units has been demonstrated. It is not
clear whether these subdivisions are convenient fictions for scoring
and exposition, or whether there is some reality beyond this. The

"synchrony question," in any case, asks whether all of these substage units reflect the same stage, or different stages. Or how much stage mixture is there in moral judgment scores? (Admittedly stage mixture when computed on responses from several dilemmas will also reflect mixture, owing to story differences.)

In Kohlberg's earlier scoring systems, the evidence quite clearly showed that stage scores for a subject were very mixed. For instance, in 1969 (p. 387) Kohlberg provided a profile of average stage distribution obtained from sentence scoring—this showed that 47% of the responses of the average subject were in his predominant stage, with lesser percentages in adjacent stages. Thus on the average, not even a simple majority (50%) of the responses were at a single stage, and stage mixture of more than two stages were the rule rather than the exception. Likewise, DIT research shows considerable stage mixture: subjects indicate that they think the items of various stages are important.

In the latest system (1978) there is much less stage mixture. A recent paper (Colby 1979) presented 58 longitudinal cases, in which about 61% of the scores were mixes of two adjacent stages, and 39% were single stage scores. In contrast, the 1958 Sentence Scoring System never showed any single stage subjects. Furthermore, in the 1978 system, the predominant stage accounts for about 67% of the total scores assigned; 95% of the scores fall into a subject's two highest stages.

The new Scoring System produces less stage mixture, for several reasons. One of the objectives of the system has been to devise better ways of capturing the underlying structure of subjects' thinking rather than to depend overmuch on fragmentary remarks and concrete word usage. In the previous scoring systems, particularly in the 1958 system, the Harvard group (Colby 1978) believe that too much attention was given to superficial features of subjects' responses, thus generating faulty scoring and exaggerated stage mixtures. By concentrating on larger scoring units (that is, units based on a line of thinking developed in response to *several* interviewer questions rather than scores for every single sentence or word), one assesses more than simple word usage and gets close to the underlying structure of subjects' thinking. The 1978 system has made a significant achievement in defining a unit of analysis in free response interview material, and in doing so, has eliminated a lot of stage mixture.

At first it might seem that the problem of stage mixture disappears once a "truly structural" scoring system is developed (i.e., the 1978 system). There are other reasons, however, that the new system produces less stage mixture:

1. The new system only uses three stories per form rather than the nine originally used in 1958, and with fewer scores from fewer stories, the chance of stage mixture is lessened. If additional stories were used that raised quite different moral issues from those raised in Form A or Form B (issues of the distribution of wealth or of opportunity) there might be more stage mixture. Thus far, there has not really been an attempt to sample the complete diversity of moral dilemmas that are possible and to test the unity or mix of stage scores under those conditions.

2. In the formulation of the 1978 scoring system, some criterion concepts were later discarded if they produced scores that were discrepant with the subject's predominant stage scores. Therefore, the current system does not attempt to encode everything and represent a protocol in terms of a distribution of scores at various stages. The current system is designed to maximize stage purity by omitting criteria that previously have caused discrepant scores. On the one hand, Kohlberg's new system is remarkable and impressive for being able to devise scoring rules that create scores with such stage unity — it gives the measure good internal consistency. On the other hand, such data are not a rigorous test of stage unity or mixture because the scoring rules are biased towards producing unity.

3. A third feature of the 1978 system that reduces stage mixture is the use of "upper stage inclusion rules." Whenever a subject gives material that matches a criterion concept at a lower stage, but elsewhere in the interview gives more elaborated material that logically extends the simpler idea and is scorable at a higher level, the lower stage score is not recorded. For example, suppose that a subject started out discussing the Heinz dilemma with the words given in Chapter 2, page 44 (Example 1), which was scored Stage 3. If later in the protocol the subject gave the material coded as Stage 4 (Example 3), then the Stage 3 code would not be reported on the scoring sheet. Similarly, if in yet another place, the subject gave the material in Example 4, scored Stage 5, then neither the Stage 3 nor Stage 4 material would be recorded. This system assumes that the subject's most complete elaboration (whatever is scored at the highest stage) represents what the subject had in mind when giving the less elaborated material, that the subject's thinking is consistent, even if the verbalization is not. The "higher stage inclusion rule" in effect wipes out lower stage scores, which are simpler or less elaborated versions of a similar point

scored at a higher stage. Therefore, since no record is kept of lower stage scores that are overridden by the higher stage inclusion rule, data from the 1978 scoring system cannot be a very strong test of stage mixture or stage unity. (On balance, this rule is reasonable to have in the 1978 system, given the emphasis on larger integrative scoring units, given the kinds of distinctions emphasized as stage differentiators, and given the clinical observation that in interviews people are sometimes elliptical in discussing their ideas.)

Even if perfect stage consistency were shown in data produced by the 1978 system, and if no problems existed in interpreting the data as a test for stage mixture, there would be yet another challenge to the stage consistency view. Interview material gives a different impression of a subject's organization of thinking than material from other assessment procedures. It is to this phenomenon that we now turn.

Discrepancies Due to Response Mode. A prevalent criticism of Piagetian research is that the favorite method of structural assessment, the clinical interview, may underestimate the structural competencies of the child. In interviewing, a child is credited with having a structure only if he can express it, explain it, justify it, and sometimes argue against other alternatives. This requirement places a great load on a child's linguistic abilities, and—the argument goes—children deficient in linguistic abilities may have competence that they are not credited with at all (see, for instance, Brainerd 1973, 1977; Braine 1959; Bruner 1964; Gelman 1972; see Flavell 1970, pp. 1032-33 for many references). A person may be able to organize his or her actions and make discriminations using a structure without being able to talk about the structure or give evidence in his verbalizations that he has the structure. Piagetian researchers who use non-verbal (or really, less verbal) means of assessment often report earlier ages of acquisition of cognitive structures than do researchers who use more verbally loaded means of assessment. For instance, Braine's disagreement with Smedslund over whether transitive inference first appears in 5-year-olds or 8-year-olds is largely owing to the difference in response mode. (See Miller, 1976, for a review of non-verbal techniques of assessing Piagetian concepts.) A parallel issue arises in role-taking studies: those assessments that require the child to explain and justify something verbally tend to credit the child with cognitive structures much later than assessments that are not so heavily dependent on verbal explanations (see Shantz's 1975 discussion of the discrepancies between Selman and DeVries). It is not uncommon in cognitive developmental research to find discrepancies in attributing structural competence when different response modes are required of the subject.

At first this seems to be simply a discrepancy over methodology: one group of researchers, wanting to be sure that a subject really has a structure, insists on interview methods that give a subject credit for having a structure only if the subject can verbally explicate, justify, and resist counterargument; other researchers argue that such interview methods associate verbal ability too much with structural competence. Such disagreement seems to be a difference in willingness to commit false-negative over false-positive errors, or vice versa. Although it may be argued that requiring verbal explanation is more in keeping with the Piagetian tradition of "la méthode clinique," Brainerd (1973) has strongly maintained that responses not requiring verbal explanation are data more defensible from Piaget's theoretical views on the relation of language to thought processes, and also (1977) that judgment data without verbal explanations have produced clearer age trend patterns than data using verbal explanations.

Beyond the methodological implications, the fact that different response modes do not always agree has implications for the way we think about the notion, "having a structure." A subject may have a cognitive structure at different levels, that is, a subject may first have a structure in a way that can be manifested non-verbally, and then with further development, may manifest the structure verbally, being able to talk about it, explain it, and justify it. In both instances (the non-verbal and verbal) there is a sense in which the child can be said to "have" the structure, but "have" it at different levels. Again, such a view is contrary to the "all or none" view of a simple stage model. Also, it suggests that a given structure may undergo extended development from level to level. As Flavell states:

> Everything we know about intellectual development continually forces us to distinguish between the potential generality of any cognitive tool and the child's current ability to exploit that potential. Although it is still far from clear just how the developmental lag between early buddings and later blossomings ought to be conceptualized . . . , it is simply a fact that the full evolution of any cognitive item almost invariably looks more like an extended process than a punctate episode. (Flavell, 1970, pp. 1038-1039).

Flavell (1971 p. 432-3) reviews evidence showing that a relatively simple structure like transitivity, first manifested perhaps as early as 4 or 5 years old, continues its development through more advanced levels, long into adulthood. A concrete operational structure continues to develop well after the first appearances of formal operations. Applied to Kohlbergian stages this notion implies that concepts, say, of Stage 3, may continue to develop even after concepts of Stage 4 have made their appearance. This idea challenges the simple stage model, which postulates that development in Stage 3 is complete before Stage 4 begins, and challenges the theory that transition periods must alternate with periods of consolidation. Flavel's argument suggests, for instance, that Stage 3 development to very advanced levels may be occurring while Stage 4 is developing to moderate levels and Stage 5 is developing at the earliest levels (see Flavell 1971, p. 427 ff).

In moral judgment research Breznitz and Kugelmass (1967) conducted a particularly interesting study that illustrates the effect of response mode and documents extended development. The structure under consideration was Piaget's notion of intentionality—that is, a subject's use of the intentions of an actor, rather than simply the material consequences of the action, as a criterion in judging. Breznitz and Kugelmass tested intentionality in a number of response modes, including the following:

1. The subject simply rated the actor in a story on a four-point scale of blame; in a set of 12 stories, a subject was credited with intentionality if his pattern of ratings reflected greater weight given to intentions than consequences.

2. The subject had to verbally produce and articulate the criterion of intentionality as a basis for judging an actor, without any suggestions as to what the criterion might be.

3. The actor had to defend and justify the principle of intentionality in competition with other principles and argue why intentionality was a more appropriate basis for making the judgment than the other principles. Breznitz and Kugelmass found that the response modes comprise a Guttman scale, form a definite order of difficulty, thus giving evidence for viewing them as different levels of advancement. Although the first signs of intentionality in making moral judgments seems to appear at least by age 6 (Shantz 1975), this study showed that intentionality was still undergoing development well into adolescence (age 17).

In moral judgment research using Kohlberg's stages, studies by Rest, Turiel and Kohlberg (1969) and Rest (1973) suggest that subjects *prefer* statements (give higher ratings of importance to statements) at stages higher than the stages they can paraphrase, and spontaneously produce statements at even lower stages. Hence a particular type of thinking (e.g., Stage 4) seems to be evident developmentally first in a preference task, then in a paraphrasing-for-comprehension task, then in a spontaneous production task. In these studies, paraphrasing-comprehension was rarely more than one stage ahead of spontaneous production, although preference was further ahead. In comparisons between the DIT (a recognition-rating task) and Kohlberg's test (a spontaneous production and justification task), the DIT credits subjects with higher forms of thinking than Kohlberg's test (Rest et al. 1974; Alozie 1976—discussed more in detail in Chapter 6). On the average, subjects were almost two stages higher on the DIT than on the Kohlberg test.

In summary, cognitive developmental research indicates that the development of cognitive structures proceeds through different levels and that the development can extend years beyond the first manifestation of the structure, even if new structures have made their first manifestations in the meantime.

A More Complex Developmental Model

We have reviewed four kinds of empirical discrepancies present in the simple stage model that occur both in moral judgment research and in Piagetian research: subject fluctuations, inconsistencies due to test characteristics, decalage across content domains, and discrepancies due to response mode. The prevalent reaction of moral judgment researchers has been to acknowledge these discrepancies, but accept them as "decalage," "measurement error," or the sorry state of social science in general. An alternative response is to reexamine our basic developmental model and accept some complications in the model for the sake of better empirical fit. The following complications and modifications are proposed:

1. The notion that a person either "has" or has not a stage is wrong. The manifestation of a certain thought organization is not an "all-or-nothing" matter. Cognitive developmentalists cannot characterize change either in qualitative terms only or in quantitative terms only. Qualitative descriptors are necessary to depict the different logical organizations of thinking; quantitative descriptors are necessary to show the extent and degree to which different structures are operating psychologically in a particular person. The question of developmental assessment should not be, "What stage is a person in?" but rather, "To what extent and under what conditions does a person manifest the various types of organizations of thinking?"

2. Developmental assessment is probabilistic. As Flavell and Wohlwill point out (1969), in the period of transition, subjects fluctuate in using a certain structure of thinking—at first exhibiting the struc-

ture very seldom, then increasing to the point of using it fairly reliably in appropriate situations. During this period of transition, then, we best think of a subject exhibiting a structure in terms of an estimate of probability (40%, 85%, etc.) rather than saying he definitely "has it" or "doesn't have it."

A probabilistic notion of developmental assessment is also appropriate when we consider that differences in test stimuli and content affect the manifestation of a given cognitive structure. No pure, direct assessment of cognitive structure exists that is unaffected by the specific task, content, and response characteristics of the situation. Research has surprised most of us in the large degree to which structural assessments are affected by these "extraneous" factors. Therefore any developmental assessment must take into account all these performance and situational factors in considering the subject's competence to organize his thinking in a certain structure. Several authors cited by Flavell (1977) make this point:

> It is implicitly assumed that the conservation task tests for one thing—a child's logical capacity to treat quantity as invariant. Thus, if he passes the test, he is judged to lack this capacity. On the basis of the results given here and other studies in the literature, it begins to appear that the conservation test evaluates more than one thing. Put another way, it seems that children who pass the conservation test are demonstrating many extralogical skills as well as their logical capacity; whereas children who fail are doing so for any of a number of reasons. (Gelman 1972, p. 88).

> . . . Performance levels under particular conditions are but fragmentary indicators of capacity." (Bortner and Birch 1970, p. 735).

> The relationship between any set of behavioral indices and a mental process, therefore, is an uncertain one, and a diagnosis will always have the status of a working hypothesis. (Smedslund 1969, p. 247).

Therefore the manifestation of a particular cognitive structure in a particular set of tasks gives us only a probabilistic indication whether that cognitive structure would be manifest in any other set of tasks. To the degree that all of the task, performance, and response characteristics are equivalent in two diagnostic settings, we would expect closer agreement between the two diagnoses. But not enough study has been done to identify all the relevant factors and to what degree they affect the subject's particular cognitive organization; therefore, we must regard our assessments as probabilistic.

3. The notion of *step by step* development through the stages is severely challenged by research in cognitive development. It is difficult to consider a subject at a *single* step at any particular time, when such striking stage mixtures occur, owing to content and performance

factors and to different levels of structure development. Rather than moving "one step," a subject may advance in several organizations of thinking simultaneously, for example, moving to advanced levels of Stage 3, to moderate levels of Stage 4, and to the earliest levels of Stage 5. It is difficult to talk about movement out of one stage and into the next when there is so little evidence of developmental synchrony of the constituent concepts of the stages. Instead of alternating phases of transition and consolidation (Stage 2 consolidation, then transition to Stage 3, then Stage 3 consolidation, then transition to Stage 4, etc.), the structure of thinking may continue to develop much beyond the onset of the next stages of thinking (for example, becoming able to explain and critique Stage 3 at the same time that Stage 5 statements can be intuitively discriminated from Stage 4 statements).

Recall that Figure 3.1 depicts the simple stage model of development. Each stage has a period of 100% usage, and this period is assumed to coincide with the time of fullest development and consolidation of that stage. Transition periods of relatively short duration come between each period of consolidation. Stage mixtures only occur between adjacent stages and only two stages can be mixed at a time. The ascending and descending slopes of all the stages are symmetrical, identical in shape and evenly spaced.

For purposes of discussion, consider Figure 3.2 as depicting a much messier and complicated picture of development. Each curve represents a qualitatively different way of thinking; Type 1 is a different logical organization from Type 2, and so on. I have chosen the word "type" here, instead of "stage," because stage suggests that a subject is exclusively one type at one time whereas the research indicates that subjects are mixes of types.[1] In Figure 3.2, no type has a period of 100% usage, and every type does not have a period when it predominates. Type 3 is prevalent at no time; however, it does come to be important at one period and the ascent and descent of Type 3 thinking is a useful marker for the course of development. Mixtures of more than two types occur. The curves are not symmetrical or evenly spaced, and Stage 3 has decreased before Stage 2 has decreased. The order of first acquisition is *not* the same as the order of elimination. Many of the assumptions of the simple stage model and Figure 3.1 are not met. Still, Figure 3.2 depicts a developmental order in the use of the various types of thinking, and a subject's profile of type usage can place him or her along a developmental continuum. If developmental studies of many subjects confirmed that profiles of type usage do shift something like the manner depicted in Figure 3.2,

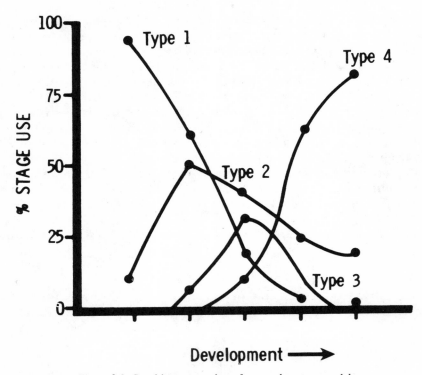

Figure 3.2. Graphic presentation of a complex stage model.

then we would have some very useful information about the course of development even though many assumptions of a simple stage model were not met.

Note also that in this more complex model there is no assumption that the point of highest usage of a type is also the point of its fullest development. It could happen that usage of a type lingers on after the point of prevalence, as Type 2 does at later periods of development. Indeed, we might even entertain the possibility that Type 2 thinking is most completely consolidated and fully understood after new ideas have come to replace it—that a subject might have the clearest vision of a type of thinking in hindsight, looking back at what is rejected but now more completely understood. Recall that in the 1969 study discussed in Chapter 2, subjects were asked to discuss statements written at various moral judgment stages, including stages lower than the subject's own stage of production (that is, if the subject produced judgments at Stage 5, he was asked to discuss statements written at Stages 1, 2, 3 and 4, in addition to Stages 5 and 6).

Quite often it seemed that the thinking of subjects about lower stages was clearer (in seeing the interconnectedness of the ideas, in awareness of the implications, in understanding their logical cohesion as a system) than their thinking about their own stage of current use, which although prevalent, was still confused and lacked closure. It might be useful to refer to some of the examples of "rejection-hits" in Chapter 2. Quite often the rejection material gave the clearest evidence of understanding.[2] Indeed, one of the factors that may prompt change to new and more complex ways of thinking is that a person comes to understand more clearly his or her former ideas and the system they belong to. In summary, increased clarity about and facility with a structure of thinking may continue to develop after that structure declines in use and newer structures have begun to replace it.

According to a more complex model of development, after a theorist has identified qualitatively different types of thinking (and has reason for believing that the earlier types are logically prior to and/or help mediate the formation of the later types), much empirical work remains in charting the ascents and declines of each type and the patterns of overlap. Whereas the simple stage model assumes that all development is of the pattern depicted in Figure 3.1, the more complex model allows the pattern in Figure 3.2 to be a possibility, but one possibility among infinite combinations of intersecting curves. In a more complex model, the logical identification of different types has only begun the work of charting development. Extended empirical work must determine the acquisition slopes, the extent of prevalence, and the rejection slopes for each type—and their overlap with the curves of other types. All of these developmental features cannot simply be assumed to be a series of equally spaced, equally shaped curves with little overlap.

Implications for Developmental Diagnosis

A chief interest in all developmental diagnosis is to locate subjects somewhere in a course of development, whether the course of development is conceptualized in qualitative terms, quantitative terms, or both, as in the present account. A common shortcoming of approaches that emphasize qualitatively different types of structure is that their proponents have assumed that once we have a sample of verbal behavior and once a taxonomy is worked out that gives rules and/or examples for scoring the samples, then we know where a subject "is" developmentally. The problem with such a view is that it fails to take account of the effect that task variables, performance factors, test stimuli, and so on, have on the manifestation of cognitive structures, and it also fails to take account of a more complex stage model, such as that depicted in Figure 3.2.

Method-Specific Assessment

From the foregoing discussion, one of the first implications for developmental diagnosis is that differing methods of gathering data (such as a recognition task asking subjects to rate prototypic statements as against a production task asking subjects to generate solutions to problems and to justify those solutions) are likely to create different impressions of the subject's organizing structures. In other words, all data should be regarded as method-specific unless proven otherwise. So, for example, Kohlberg's statement, "The postconventional level is reached by a minority of adults and is usually reached only after the age of 20" (1976, p. 33) must be understood as referring to only one method of data collection, that of spontaneous production and justification. As has been discussed already, other methods of data collection indicate that recognition of postconventional thinking can occur much earlier, and furthermore, McColgan (discussed in more detail in Chapter 6) suggests that in some circumstances, information about moral judgment recognition may be more significant than information about moral judgment production. McColgan found that the DIT successfully discriminated predelinquent boys from nondelinquent boys whereas the Kohlberg test did not. However, the two main points here are that a full developmental picture of moral judgment must come from a variety of data gathering methods, not just one; and also that particular data gathering methods may be especially useful for special research purposes. For instance, Kohlberg's task might be especially useful in studying the kinds of public statements that political leaders make. The DIT, however, might be more useful in studying how members of the listening audience perceive political speeches.

Not only do different kinds of tasks (e.g., recognition, production, paraphrasing) affect what structures are manifested but so also do the specific test stimuli and materials and contents. For instance, a dilemma about mercy killing may evoke different organizing structures than a dilemma about distribution of wages or a dilemma about civil disobedience. Again, the main implication of the foregoing discussion is to recognize the content-specific and method-specific nature of all developmental assessment. A future goal is to identify the various attributes of test situations that affect the structural organizations of thinking manifested and the extent to which each of these attributes affect them. We shall attempt to develop a classification system that maps out these factors in relation to each other. In the meantime we must regard every assessment of cognitive structure as a compound of the subject's competence in structuring thinking and the performance and situational factors accounting for an unknown proportion of the variance of scores. In the meantime, we can establish certain guidelines:

1. Do not rely on a single test instance (or on responses to one moral dilemma story; collect enough bits of data so that a general picture emerges that is not overly influenced by an idiosyncratic subject-situation interaction or by fluctuations in the subject's thinking. Presumably the more bits of information we have, the greater the chance that extraneous factors will cancel each other out, leaving a truer picture. Contemporary developmental psychology studies often attempt to assess a complicated construct (e.g., cheating, altruism, cooperation, resistance to temptation, etc.) by collecting a single bit of information, or by running a subject through a single experimental simulation. Such reliance on single bits of information is like trying to assess IQ with a single vocabulary item.

2. Build in some diversity of the test stimuli (for example, use a variety of kinds of dilemmas; don't use only dilemmas involving breaking the law to save someone's life) so that a developmental score is based on a representative sampling of possible contexts. We want to be able to claim that our score is the best generalized single indicator of the subject's method of making judgments in a diversity of other contexts. If we use dilemmas involving breaking the law to save someone's life, we might be able to generalize to other dilemmas of this type, but generalization to other kinds of dilemmas would be questionable.

3. Test stimuli, test administration and setting, and scoring procedures should be as standardized as possible. Otherwise we can't know whether differences in developmental levels are due to actual developmental differences or to varying performance factors. Standardization is the best available technique for reducing score variance that is caused by performance factors. Although some psychologists in the Piagetian tradition have claimed that a flexible clinical interview is better for interpreting the true developmental character of a subject's thinking (c.f. Damon 1977), this claim has never been demonstrated, and some writers have demonstrated serious deficiencies with the clinical interview (Brainerd 1973, 1977; Braine 1959; Miller 1976). Clinical interviewing pursues a subject's remarks and therefore is individualized for every subject. This information is valuable in discover-

ing the kinds of thought organizations present, and is indispensable in the first phases of exploratory research, when the scoring categories and the taxonomy of responses are being derived. But once the scoring categories have been defined and the research purpose is to chart a subject's developmental progress, the information gathering procedures must be standardized. Gathering ideas about how to describe the various organizational structures (using an open-ended clinical interview method) is a different business from trying to locate subjects as accurately as possible in a postulated course of development.

Qualitative and Quantitative Assessment

Another implication of the foregoing discussion is that researchers should attempt to measure the extent to which each type of structure is in use. In other words, they should pay attention to quantitative description in addition to qualitative description. If development is as complex as that depicted in Figure 3.2, it is important to know how much of each type of thinking, as well as which types of thinking, are present.

The simple stage model of development has led researchers for a long time to conceptualize the diagnosis question as, "What stage is a person in?" Expecting to find all of a subject's judgments in one stage, researchers have been frustrated in finding that a subject has, say, 15% responses in Stage 2, 47% in Stage 3, 30% in Stage 4, and 8% in Stage 5. One reaction to this situation has been to devise some rules by which information is discarded so that a subject can still be typed into a single stage. For instance, stage typing by *predominant usage* would assign the subject of the example above into Stage 3 — or perhaps 3(4), if subordinate stages were recognized. Or, to stage type in terms of the *highest stage of substantial use*, we might look for the most advanced stage in which a subject has at least 10% usage, and accordingly type the subject as Stage 4. Recently (1976) Kohlberg, et al have adopted new stage typing rules that are more complex, but all these schemes are motivated by a simple stage model of development as is depicted in Figure 3.1. The irony of these schemes of stage typing is that they are sometimes used to support the fiction that only qualitative differences are important in developmental research, yet they depend on quantitative information for their computation.

The problems with indexing development by stage typing are the following: (a) stage typing often throws information away, (b) it may misrepresent idiosyncratic content-specific influences, and (c) it assumes that either initial acquisition or peak acquisition is the most important thing to know about stage usage. The first of these problems, (a) throwing information away, is the most obvious. By using stage typing rules and allocating a subject to, say, Stage 4, we don't know whether the subject had a certain amount of Stage 2 in addition to Stage 4 or a certain amount of Stage 6. These two subjects are likely to be quite different. Furthermore, in earlier studies of stage change, the most striking changes have been upward shifts from low to high stages (for example, at time 1, 15% Stage 2, 47% Stage 3, 30% Stage 4, and 8% Stage 5; at time 2, 5% Stage 2, 37% Stage 3, 50% Stage 4, and 8% at Stage 5). In this case, the loss in Stage 2 is one of the major changes; to represent this situation as a one-step shift from Stage 3 to Stage 4 is to omit information about the change in Stage 2. Furthermore, stage typing is a coarse-grained way of representing development. If we use recent scorings from Kohlberg's 18-year longitudinal study (1978), we see that full stage shifts (2 to 3, 3 to 4, etc.) occur on the average only every 12.3 years (in the 30 subjects presented, only two subjects move more than two full stages, and the average subject moves only 1.3 stages over this whole span).

The second problem of stage typing (b) is related to the fact that certain stories "pull' certain stages more than other stories. For example, on the Heinz and the drug dilemma, it is more difficult than on the euthanasia dilemma to give Stage 4 reasons. Now suppose it were discovered that all the dilemmas currently used made it difficult to give Stage 4 reasons (the dilemmas all biased against Stage 4 reasoning). Stage 4 would be consistently underestimated in subjects, resulting in many fewer Stage 4 subjects than would be obtained from other sets of dilemmas. Whereas other types of indexing (discussed below) might build in some compensation for differences in "story pull," this has not been done with stage typing indices. Chapter 8 shows that Davison's procedure of scaling each individual item in effect creates different scale weights for an "easy" Stage 4 item than a "difficult" Stage 4 item, and therefore has built in a compensating factor in the developmental score for different "story pull" and "item pull."

(c) What is the most important phase of a type's developmental curve: when it starts, when it peaks, or when it decreases? Stage typing a subject as "a Stage 3 subject" because the subject uses more Stage 3 than any other stage is in effect assuming that the most important aspect of stage usage is prevalence or peak use. Alternatively, stage typing a subject as "a Stage 4" subject because the most advanced stage used is Stage 4 is assuming that the most important aspect of stage usage is its beginning use or its acquisition stage. Stage typing rules force us to choose one part of the acquisition curve of stages and to allocate subjects to stages on the basis of when new stages begin, or when they peak, or when they end. If development proceeds according to Figure 3.1, it doesn't make much difference which aspect of the curve we choose, because all these stage typing indices would be perfectly correlated. But if development proceeds more like Figure 3.2, then nonredundant information is present in the acquisition phases, the peak phases, and the end phases and we need to keep all this information for indexing development.

Enough said about stage typing. Another index used by Kohlberg, the Moral Maturity Score, preserves more information about a subject's use of other stages besides his "own" (however defined) and takes into account quantitative as well as qualitative information. The Moral Maturity Score is a weighted average of stage usage ranging from 100 to 600, calculated by multiplying the percent usage of each stage by its number (that is, the Stage 1 percent is multiplied by 1, the Stage 2 by 2, and so on), then adding the products and multiplying by 100. For instance, the MMS for the example cited earlier at time 1 would be calculated as $(2 \times .15) + (3 \times .47) + (4 \times .30) + (5 \times .08) = 3.31; 3.31 \times 100 = 331$. The MMS is a more sensitive index than the various stage typing indices (it is more useful for measuring short term change) and Alozie (1976) found that the MMS had much greater internal consistency than Kohlberg's stage typing indices. However, the MMS in effect makes the assumptions that there is no particular "story pull" in the set of dilemmas that are used; that the stages are equally spaced; that each stage has a period of predominance; that the ascending and descending slopes of each stage curve is symmetrical—in short, the MMS assumes that development is as depicted in Figure 3.1.

So far I have pointed out the problems in the most frequently used methods of indexing. The general charge is that these indices have presumed a simple stage model. In the next chapter I will present our first approach to the indexing problem; most all of the research to date with the DIT has followed this solution, and most all of the research in this book is based on it. In Chapter 8, Mark Davison presents a newer solution based on an ingenious and sophisticated method of scaling developmental data. Future researchers will want to take advantage of Davison's new index. The discussion of devising indices for assessment procedures supposing a more complex model of development will be deferred then to Chapter 4 and taken up again in Chapter 8.

Other Research Problems Due to the Simple Stage Model

In the preceding discussion, I have argued that the simple stage model has misdirected decisions of research strategy in diagnosis. The simple stage model has led to questionable practices on other research issues as well: (1) in the analysis of developmental change; (2) in the analysis of the association of moral judgment with other variables; and (3) in the formation of homogeneous groups of subjects.

1. The simple stage model has led to thinking about developmental change in step by step terms. The "step by step" idea has already been criticized at length, but it remains to suggest an alternative conception of change. I propose thinking of developmental change as an upward shift in the subject's distribution of responses, where "upward" is defined as increases in higher stages or types at the expense of lower types. This notion is illustrated in terms of individual subject profile analysis in my 1975 longitudinal study, and discussed further in Chapter 5. Instead of describing, say, a Stage 3 subject as moving to Stage 4, an example of upward change would be a subject who at time 1 had 5% Type 1, 20% Type 2, 50% Type 3, 20% Type 4, and 5% Type 5; and at time 2 had 0% Type 1, 10% Type 2, 40% Type 3, 45% Type 4, and 5% Type 5 responses. In analyzing change in individual subjects one must be careful about over-interpreting any shift in type usage, given the fact of subject fluctuation and instrument unreliability. A practice employed in the 1975 longitudinal study was to test-retest stability to estimate the range of error in each type's score; then, to count any change in type usage as true developmental change, the shift had to exceed that margin of error (see Rest 1975a, p. 743-4). Davison's new index provides another method for representing upward change, presupposing that change is not a "step by step" matter, but rather a shift in distribution in responses.

2. In studies of the association of moral judgment with other variables, the simple stage model has led researchers to look for stage by stage comparisons—for example, to ask what stage of moral judgment corresponds to what stage of Piagetian stages, or role taking, or comprehension, or ego development, and so forth. In making these comparisons, it is assumed that it makes sense to stage type the subject on both measures. At this point in the discussion it would be redundant to inveigh further on the evils of stage typing. Nevertheless such statements abound in the literature as: "a subject cannot comprehend thinking at more than one stage above his own stage," or "role taking ability at stage 2 is a necessary but not sufficient condition for moral judgment at stage 2," or "Piagetian Formal Operations is a prerequisite

for principled moral thinking"—and in light of the previous discussion we have to question the logic and defensibility of such statements. The problem with such statements is that they represent development as a point rather than as a range within which the subject operates, depending on the test characteristics, response mode, content domain, or level of attainment. Mapping out one developmental variable on another can be done point for point only if it is understood that the points have little generality to other situations, test instruments, response modes, or scoring conventions (which makes point for point comparisons rather trivial). For instance, in some earlier studies (Rest, Turiel, and Kohlberg 1969; Rest 1973), I claimed that subjects cannot comprehend thinking more than one stage above their own stage; but the findings would be different using the DIT as the moral judgment measure instead of Kohlberg's test; or using Kohlberg's 1978 scoring system rather than the 1958 system; or changing the stringency of the comprehension scoring rules; or using a highest substantial usage algorithm rather than a predominant usage algorithm for stage typing. Since developmental assessment is instrument specific, point by point comparisons with other measures have little generality. A correlation between two specific developmental measures (for instance, Kohlberg's 1958 test and the 1969 measure of moral comprehension) is evidence for a general association between the two constructs (moral judgment and moral comprehension), but it is not sufficient to claim stage by stage correspondences.

3. Many studies have grouped subjects by stage typing, assuming subject homogeneity within groups, and also assuming that the stage typing would predict the subjects' moral thinking in new and different situations; that is, stage typing a subject at Stage 3 by Kohlberg's test is presumed to imply that the subject will think in Stage 3 terms when placed in a moral education program in a group discussing new dilemmas. Accordingly, intervention treatments have been designed to be one level above the subject's stage, or two levels above. The discussions of these studies are invariably couched in terms of the simple stage model. Again, the problems with such designs are in the presumption of pinpointing development and the assumption of context-free assessment. Certainly researchers can make probabilistic statements about the relative development of groups of subjects, or about interventions at a high or a low level, but the state of developmental assessment is being strained when a researcher talks about giving a +1 model to a Stage 3 subject.

4

Constructing
the Defining Issues Test

Constructing a way to assess moral judgment is fundamental in moral
judgment research; assessment precedes and is presupposed in every
other research operation. The previous chapter pointed out some of
the difficulties in developmental assessment and presented some of
the desirable features of a developmental measure. The Defining
Issues Test is one approach to the problem. Instead of first presenting
a history of the construction of the DIT I will introduce the DIT in
a more general framework of the major part of constructing any test
of moral judgment. There are four inescapable sets of decisions which
any test constructor faces, and a test can be no better than the weakest set. In this chapter I will discuss the options in each of the four
sets of decisions, and present my reasons for choosing the particular
set of alternatives that resulted in the DIT. I don't view the DIT as a
unique or ultimate solution to the problem of moral judgment assessment, and would hope that other researchers will explore other options. At the same time, I will point out features of the DIT that have
enabled it to overcome some of the difficulties inherent in assessment.

The four major sets of decisions in constructing a test of moral
judgment are as follows: (a) What features of thinking are to be used
in characterizing someone's moral judgment? In Chapter 2, the features used in the DIT have been discussed. Other researchers might
want to use other features, but they must engage in the same kind of

theoretical and descriptive analysis, identifying what features are used and why. (b) What information-collecting procedure (or task) will be used? Kohlberg uses the semi-structured interview about hypothetical moral dilemmas. Rest, 1969, used subjects' discussions of prototypic stimulus statements. Piaget at one point observed children playing marbles and then questioned them about the game. There are many possibilities, and each method has its special difficulties and some methods have special advantages. (c) Once data have been collected from a particular subject, then how does one use this information to index the subject's development? The last chapter discussed difficulties indexing by stage typing according to predominant usage, the highest level of use, and the MMS. What better scoring algorithms are possible and how does one choose among them? (d) How does one validate a test of moral judgment? It is certainly not dust bowl empiricism to ask that any test of moral judgment produce empirical demonstrations of its reliability and validity. But what kinds of studies count in establishing reliability and validity?

Since the first question, identifying features of moral judgment, has already been discussed in Chapter 2, let us move to the second part, data collecting procedures.

Data Collecting Procedures

If moral judgment is an important construct and refers to something pervasive and influential in human functioning, it should be manifested in many ways. If it could be assessed only by interviewing subjects about particular hypothetical dilemmas, then we should question whether the whole field studies a circumscribed, relatively trivial phenomenon of interviewing behavior. On the other hand, if moral judgment is really "the fundamental structure by which people perceive and make decisions about their rights and responsibilities," it should be manifest in many kinds of responses. A great variety of tasks could be used to generate moral judgment material. The following lists a number of them, mentioning some difficulties and advantages, and previous uses in research:

a) *Abstract direct questioning.* One could simply go up to someone and say, "Describe the way you make moral judgments. How do you decide questions of right or wrong? What reasons are important to you in making moral decisions?" As a slight variation in format, one might not ask these questions in a face-to-face interview, but ask subjects to write a 1,000 word essay. This approach has the advantage of being direct. This method has been used by Tapp in her legal development scale (see Tapp and Kohlberg 1971), asking questions such as "What is a law?" "Why should people follow rules?" "What makes a rule fair?" A disadvantage of this method is that it requires subjects to have a reflective awareness of their cognitions and be able to express them in response to an abstract question. In a strict sense, what one assesses is a person's reflective theory rather than the thought operations that guide his or her decision-making. Imagine, for instance, that we asked a three-year-old child, "What makes a sentence grammatical?" Although children at age three are fairly accomplished in decoding and encoding grammatical features, no three-year-old could delineate the grammatical rules operating in his language. A similar case might be true of moral judgment: for most people who are not moral philosophers, their abstract account of their own moral judgments might lead us to underestimate the complexity of their thinking. Another problem in the direct approach is that subjects may not have been schooled in the technical uses of certain words (like "grammatical," "moral," "law") and may answer the question in accord with their own idiosyncratic use of the word, and again give a false impression. For instance, to some people the word "moral" has a special connotation regarding sexual behavior, and their discussion of "what morals mean to me" would not be representative of their concepts of fairness. Abstract questioning is probably most useful in moral judgment research in studying the most advanced forms of moral judgment by people familiar with formal moral philosophical discourse (e.g., moral philosophers, lawyers, politicians, judges, ministers, etc.)

   b) *Justifying solutions to moral dilemmas.* In collecting samples of a person's moral judging, this method presents a moral problem, then asks for a solution and a justification for that solution. This of course is Kohlberg's chief method, and Piaget's to some extent. It has the advantage of being open-ended, so that a subject's own structuring tendencies can be exhibited without constraint. It also is concrete enough that subjects do not need to have worked out a reflective philosophy (as in "a" above). The hypothetical dilemma can be simplified enough that the moral issue is highlighted, thus helping to prevent the subject from getting sidetracked on questions of fact, personality, and other issues that are not specifically *moral* judgments. This method is particularly valuable for discovering the many features of people's thinking that may be used for a developmental analysis, and Kohlberg has identified hundreds of new features (e.g., the "criterion judgments") beyond those identified by Piaget (e.g., intentionality, objective responsibility, immanent justice, etc.).

The usual format of posing a dilemma through a written paragraph can be varied in many ways: by posing the dilemma with a slide-tape presentation (Kohlberg and Selman 1973); by posing the dilemma through dramatic role playing and asking the subject to portray one of the actors and state moral reasoning while in the actor's role (Blasi 1971); by using historical documents and records to pose the dilemma (Lockwood 1972); by asking children how to divide rewards among themselves (Damon 1977); by asking prisoners to talk about actual conflicts in prison life (Hickey 1972); by asking student protesters how they perceive and justify their acts of civil disobedience (Haan 1975); asking women who are contemplating an abortion to disclose their thinking (Gilligan, 1977). A further variation is to examine existing writings, speeches, autobiographical statements, letters, and interviews for discussion of why a person did what he did. Kohlberg has in this manner stage-scored written material from Adolph Eichmann, from a soldier in the My Lai Massacre, from Richard Nixon, and from Martin Luther King. Candee analyzed statements of various Watergate principals (1976).

Interviewing subjects about hypothetical or real moral dilemmas is usually enjoyable for subjects. Major problems arise, however, in trying to interpret what the subjects say. For all data of this sort some kind of scoring system must be devised that can be used independently by other trained judges. Difficulties arise in what to define as the scoring unit, and in how to allocate material to each scoring unit. There is the problem that in open-ended responses, subjects can wander from point to point and not give a systematic inventory of their views, leading to incomplete information and information that is not comparable from subject to subject. Often a subject does not give decisive or complete enough information to make a clear match with one or another scoring category. When an articulate subject spontaneously goes into an extended explanation of his thinking, we understand his thinking; often we quote these subjects in our reports and scoring guides. Most subjects, however, are not so articulate or explicit, and the scorer has to infer what the subject has in mind. Scoring requires considerable skill, training, and time. Even with this investment of time and effort, ambiguities exist as to what the scores represent. Individual differences in verbal expressiveness may result in a scoring difference of several stages; for instance, in the four scoring features cited from Kohlberg's guides in Chapter 2 (page 44), how do we know that a subject who gives the response coded Stage 3 really didn't have the response coded Stage 4 in mind, but was less articulate than the person scored Stage 4? In some studies, subjects have been tested and then re-tested after a short interval, and the subjects have been scored at a lower level at the second testing (c.f. discussion in Chapter 3, page 54). Presumably at the second testing, the subjects have not lost basic cognitive structure, but have just not worked as hard the second time in elaborating what is on their minds. Hence open-ended interviewing is not an uncomplicated source of information about a subject's thought structure, but a mixed result of many processes, skills, and factors.

c) *Comparing acts and actors in stories.* One of Piaget's methods for gathering moral judgment information was to present two stories and ask the subject to judge which story presented a naughtier character. For instance, Piaget (1965, p. 122) used one story depicting a boy who breaks fifteen cups accidentally while entering the dining room, and in the contrasting story, a boy breaks one cup while sneaking some jam out of the cupboard. The subject is asked which boy is naughtier, and if you were the daddy, which one would you punish more? After deciding which boy is naughtier, the subject is asked to explain his reasoning.

An advantage of this method of data gathering is that it is a more focused task than the first two methods. The contrasting features in the story pair enable the researcher to highlight a specific aspect of the situation. By systematically varying the elements in the story pair, the researcher can discover what attributes of a moral situation are important to a subject. Quite a bit of recent research has been devoted to exploring different story elements (c.f., page 56). Another advantage of this method is that it places less of a load on the subject's ability to organize his thoughts and verbally present them than the methods (a) and (b) above. There seem to be usable data in the subject's choice of the story itself even without the subject's explanation of the choice. In two studies (Bandura and McDonald 1963; Cowan et al. 1969) the correlation between simple story choice and the explanation data was in the high .80s. Since Piaget's procedure is a multiple-choice-task, the verbal load on the subject has been greatly minimized. In addition, with this technique researchers collect comparable information from subject to subject.

One variation of this method is to present several single stories and ask the subject to rate the naughtiness of each story character on a Likert scale (e.g., Buchanan and Thompson 1973). Another possibility is to present a moral dilemma (as for instance, the Heinz and the drug story), ask what ought to be done (e.g., should Heinz steal or not steal), and then systematically alter or add to the circumstances of the story to see what changes the subject's action choice (for instance, ask the subject to suppose that the druggist was holding on to the drug to save another person's life; should Heinz steal then? Suppose Heinz learned that his wife loved another man, should Heinz steal then? Suppose Heinz was a gifted artist whose work would be prohibited by a jail sentence; should Heinz steal then?). The aim here would be to identify those circumstances that weigh heavily enough in the subject's mind to change his choice. Such a procedure is somewhat similar to concept formation studies in which attributes are altered until the subject says the basic concept is changed.

A disadvantage with these procedures is that they are so structured that discoveries about new features of people's thinking are unlikely. To use these methods, the researcher must already have a good idea of what characteristics he is looking for. Another difficulty with these methods is that they are more applicable to the study of lower stage concepts. For instance, I cannot imagine how one could use story pairs to test the idea of social contract.

d) *Use of stage prototypic statements.* In this procedure, the researcher exemplifies the distinctive reasoning of a stage by using examples of clearly scored statements. The researcher presents these prototypic statements to a subject and can ask the subject to respond in one of several ways: for example, to rate or rank them in terms of preference, to recall them, to paraphrase or recapitulate them, to match them with other statements, or to group them. Each task has its peculiarities, as will be discussed below. But the use of prototypic stage statements enables the researcher to focus the subject's attention on specific forms of reasoning, and to go through an inventory of reasons systematically. Thus the stimulus conditions can be highly standardized and the points that are discussed are not left to the subject's predilections or the interviewer's clinical sense of what is important. The use of prototypic statements enables the researcher to study a subject's reactions to higher as well as lower stage concepts.

Subjects can be asked to react to prototypic statements in various ways:

1. The subject can be asked to *rate* or *rank* the statements in terms of which statement gives the best arguments, or which statement gives reasons most like the reasons the subject thought of. This preference task has been used in several studies (Rest, Turiel and Kohlberg, 1969; Rest, 1973). As variations, the instructions to a subject could ask him to rate or rank statements as he thinks he might have done when he was ten years old, or rank the statements as he thinks his mother would, or as executives at General Motors would, or as the subject perceives is typical of the general climate of thinking in his

school. Of course, all these alterations in instructions produce information about how a subject perceives *others'* moral thinking.

A serious difficulty with rating or ranking prototypic statements is that subjects may misinterpret a statement and rate their misinterpretation rather than the features the statement was designed to represent. In the 1969 and 1973 studies, almost all subjects tended to give high ratings to the high stage statements, and in fact little differentiation was shown among subjects. One subject had spontaneously produced mostly Stage 2 responses on the usual Kohlberg interview, but later in the procedure when he was shown Stage 6 statements, said that that was just what he himself had said before. Apparently this subject was projecting some of his own, more simple ideas, onto the higher stage statement, and regarded the higher stage statement as just a fancier way of stating his Stage 2 ideas. In Chapter 2, examples were given of distortions of a Stage 6 statement to Stages 4, 3, and 2 (page 38). Therefore, some subjects may give high ratings to Stage 6 statements because they understand the distinctive Stage 6 way of thinking and appreciate its greater adequacy, but other subjects may give high ratings to Stage 6 because they project their own thinking into the statement and like its fancier style. The problem with rating or ranking data is that one cannot always be certain of the basis on which a subject is judging the statement.

2. The subject can be asked to *recall* as many statements as possible after looking at the set. Presumably a subject will be able to recall with greater accuracy those statements that correspond to his own thinking (and thinking he used to have), but will not recall accurately statements that were beyond his grasp when presented. If a recall task is used, a scoring guide must be constructed, setting criteria for how much alteration or omission is allowable if the subject is to be credited with satisfactorily remembering the original statement. A recall task is every bit as time-consuming and difficult to score as scoring original justifications (as in "b" above). The task was used at least once, in Rest, Turiel, and Kohlberg (1969). Note that information about what a subject recalls is a measure of his *capacity* to use certain modes of reasoning rather than his actual reasoning in making decisions. In fact, the 1969 study suggested that reasoning at simple stages that a subject had outgrown were easiest to recall. Of course individual differences in memory and attention affect recall just as much as the availability of certain stages of thinking to the subject.

3. The subject can be asked to *paraphrase* or *recapitulate* the statement in his own words. The subject's recapitulation is then scored according to guides as to whether or not the subject understood the

distinctive point of the statement. Such information can be used to ascertain what stages or concepts a subject comprehends. This task has been used in Rest, Turiel, and Kohlberg (1969), and Rest (1973). Again, this is information about a subject's *capacity* to think in certain ways, not necessarily the way that a subject chooses to think. Excerpts of the scoring guide in the 1973 study are contained in Chapter 2. While this procedure enables a systematic and comprehensive inventory of concepts, the procedure is time-consuming and difficult. As mentioned in Chapter 2, the procedure sometimes involved as much as 13 hours of interviewing.

As a slight variation to the paraphrase task, I also asked subjects to criticize the prototypic statements, and to give a counterargument to each. This material was often useful in ascertaining whether a subject understood the statement, because if the subject rejected the statement by pointing out a limitation, one could be certain that the subject really understood the concept. On the other hand, if the subject argued against a statement by distorting it, that was a good indication that the subject didn't understand it. Future research might be devoted to studying the ways in which subjects refute statements typifying stages other than the ones they prefer. Subjects may have characteristic ways in which they "write off" or reject reasoning different from their own. If a person is entrenched in rejecting and distorting higher stage statements, he or she may be resistant to development or meaningful discussions with higher stage subjects.

4. A subject may be asked to *match* statements. One format that has been used as a multiple choice test of moral comprehension (Rest et al. 1974; Rest 1975) is to present a paragraph that uses reasoning at one stage and then, after that paragraph, four shorter statements; the subject's task is to pick from among the four statements the one that best summarizes the ideas in the paragraph. Note that the subject is not asked to give his own ideas here, but just asked to find the best match between the paragraph and statements. Again, this task gives information concerning a subject's *capacity* to think in certain ways rather than his tendency to use those ideas in making decisions. For example, the following item is used in the multiple-choice comprehension test:

HEINZ-4

> If Heinz steals, he is breaking his agreements with other members of society. In most countries, men have agreed not to steal because they see that not stealing is better for each one of them. Heinz himself would have to admit that a law against stealing is a good law to have. And so if

Heinz wants to have laws that he and other people think are good to have, he should abide by them.

| Good | Fair | Poor | a.) People consent to laws because they recognize that in the long run laws benefit each member of society. One's obligation to obey the law comes from this recognition. |

| Good | Fair | Poor | b.) Heinz should not steal because if he does, people will think he has broken his agreements with them, and they would regard him as untrustworthy. |

| Good | Fair | Poor | c.) Once the law is set, no one is right in breaking it. No matter what good intentions a person may have, if he breaks the law, he's in the wrong. |

| Good | Fair | Poor | d.) Heinz has a duty to obey the law because he helped to make the law. If he breaks his agreements, he will be setting an example that could lead to everyone's breaking the law. |

Rank the statements from best interpretation of the paragraph (1) to worst (4).
1. _____ 2. _____ 3. _____ 4. _____

Presumably subjects who understand the concepts embodied in the paragraph have a greater probability of making a "correct" match (in the example above, option "a"). In devising the distractor items for this test (the "wrong" statements that do not match the paragraph), I had interviewed subjects about what they thought the paragraph said, and chose as distractors the distortions and misinterpretations that the subjects had generated themselves.

5. Subjects may be presented a number of stage-prototypic statements and asked to *sort* the statements into *groups* that seem to reflect the same point of view. The goal here is to determine if subjects see the logical interconnectedness between statements at the same stage. Subjects might then be asked to explain how the statements in each group belong together. No study that I know of has used this procedure, but this possibility may be useful for studying subjects' sense of the logical interconnections among various stage concepts. Are subjects aware of the stage patterns discussed in Chapter 2? Or do subjects see very different logical connections, and would they sort statements into different groups from those according to our stage designations?

6. Subjects may be presented with arguments at a particular stage for one story (for instance, Stage 4 arguments on the Heinz story) and them given a new story (the Doctor's Dilemma) and asked to *extrapolate* what the counterpart arguments would be on the new story. The test here is to see if a subject can transfer arguments from one story into a new context. Presumably this ability would be good evidence that the subject understood the underlying reasoning as opposed to its situational specificity and context dependence. No study has used this technique, but it illustrates the diverse ways that prototypic statements can be used.

e) *Defining and judging the crucial issues in a moral dilemma.*The prototypic statements discussed in section (d) above are arguments or justifications for a course of action. A related but distinguishable cognitive process involved in making moral judgements is the determination of what the crucial and important issues are in a moral dilemma. For example, justification statements used in section (d) give reasons for stealing or not stealing the drug. But what does the subject see at stake or at issue in the Heinz dilemma? What is the crux of the problem for a subject? What is the most important question a subject thinks a person should ask himself or herself in making a decision in the Heinz story? Is the issue whether Heinz might get caught and sent to jail? Is the issue whether a loving husband would care so much for his wife that he'd stoop to do a dastardly deed? Is the issue how the law and order of a community are going to be maintained?

People perceive the crucial issues of moral problems in different ways. Take, for example, the problem of interracial relations in our country. Some people see this as primarily an issue of racial prejudices and equal opportunity, others as busing and neighborhood schools, or states' rights and creeping federalism, and so on. Not only do people differ in the course of action they prefer, but they differ in the basic categories and frameworks used to perceive and interpret the problem, in the transformations they make of bits of information into something of meaning and significance. Of course, people's definition and judgment of the crucial issues in a dilemma are often related to their favoring one course of action over another. But the definition of a problem is a significant activity and an important process to research. Quite often when people go to others for advice, they not only want to know the other's choice of action, but also want advice on how the other person "sees" the problem, what the important considerations are, and what is at stake. In public policy debate, much attention centers on defining the crucial issues involved in a situation.

An assumption of DIT research has been that developmental stages of moral judgment (as described in Chapters 2 and 3) involve distinctive ways of defining social-moral dilemmas and of evaluating the crucial issues in them. It is assumed that describing a person's moral stage is a shorthand way of characterizing his or her transformations of the incoherent bits and pieces of social situations into meaningful concepts. If we indulge in speculation about the subprocesses involved in making moral judgments, we might regard the process of defining a situation as in the earlier phases of the genesis of a moral judgment, and the process of justifying an action as in the later phase. I'm not sure how one could test this speculation, however, and it may be impossible to separate the defining activity from the justifying activity of moral judgment. In any case, I see the description of moral judgment stages as involving both the defining and the justifying processes.

Information on the way people define and judge the issues in moral dilemmas may be obtained in several ways. The most direct is to present a moral dilemma and ask the subject, "What are the important issues in this dilemma? What is the crux of the problem? What is the main thing at stake?" Curriculum writers for high school Social Studies (e.g. Newmann and Oliver, 1970) have suggested that teachers ask high school students to analyze dilemmas in this way. Indeed, a major element in the "New Social Studies" (Hunt and Metcalf 1968; Fenton 1967; Oliver and Shaver 1966) is the critical analysis of public policy issues. Teachers have found, however that high school students have great difficulty in doing this (c.f., Kohlberg and Lockwood 1970). Use of this technique in research is reported by Lockwood (1970), who found that students differing on their Kohlbergian stage also tended to differ in what they saw as the most important problem in social-moral dilemmas. This was quite an interesting finding. Some of my later unpublished pilot work, however, indicated that students (even at the college level) have great difficulty in explicating the crucial issues in dilemmas in an open-ended production task.

Another conceivable possibility for obtaining information on how people define issues would be to present a film clip of people acting and in dialogue, with a minimum of interpretation and categorization of their actions. For instance, one film clip could be of Heinz who learns of his wife's illness, of his conversations with the druggist, etc. Then after seeing a collection of Heinz's activities and conversations, ask a subject to describe Heinz's problem. The subject's interpretation of the raw activities depicted on film, the categories the subject uses, and the linkages he or she makes would then be used to make inferences about the subject's perceptive framework. For instance, does the subject even use the word "steal" to describe Heinz's dilemma? There might be striking differences in the way people describe Heinz's situation and dilemma. To my knowledge, no one has explored this possibility. Subject responses may be, however, heavily confounded with verbal expressiveness.

The DIT collects information by presenting a number of questions to the subject, and then asking the subject to rate and rank the questions in terms of the importance of each consideration in making a decision about what ought to be done. Whereas Lockwood asked subjects to produce spontaneously their views of the important issues, the DIT presents a number of alternatives and asks subjects to rate and rank these. Table 4.1 lists questions for the Heinz dilemma, along with the stages they represent and page numbers in Chapter 2 where those specific concepts are discussed. The various stages of moral judgment are exemplified in the twelve items, and the assumption is that a subject's developmental level will influence how he rates and ranks the items. As with all methods for obtaining information on moral judgment, this method has problems and peculiarities. The next section of this chapter will discuss these in some detail, and will give reasons why I chose this method for studying moral judgment over others.

Specific Characteristics of the DIT

In 1970 when I first began thinking about alternative ways of assession moral judgment, several problems with Kohlberg's interview-and-scoring method were of concern, as were also several problems with my dissertation research. One concern was the great inferential leaps that a scorer often has to make in linking interview material to features in the scoring guide. Most subjects just are not as articulate, clear, and differentiated as the criteria in the scoring guide or as the illustrative excerpts cited as examples. As an interviewer, I often found myself running out of nondirective probe questions, but still without a clear sense whether the subject's thinking should be categorized under one point in the scoring guide, or another. At times I was tempted to show the subject the two different points in the scoring guide and say, "Here, you score your own response — you might be able to tell better what you have in mind than I do sitting here listening to you." After thinking about that possibility for a while, I found it less ridiculous. Instead of having a subject talk about his moral thinking and then having a scorer categorize the response, why

Table 4.1. Defining Issues Test Format

On the left hand side of the page, check one of the spaces by each question to indicate its importance.

Great Importance	Much Importance	Some Importance	Little Importance	No Importance	
____	____	____	____	____	1. Whether a community's laws are going to be upheld. (Stage 4, page 29)
____	____	____	____	____	2. Isn't it only natural for a loving husband to care so much for his wife that he'd steal? (Stage 3, page 28)
____	____	____	____	____	3. Is Heinz willing to risk getting shot as a burglar or going to jail for the chance that stealing the drug might help? (Stage 2, page 26)
____	____	____	____	____	4. Whether Heinz is a professional wrestler, or has considerable influence with professional wrestlers. (Non-stage item — serves as a check on random responding)
____	____	____	____	____	5. Whether Heinz is stealing for himself or doing this solely to help someone else. (Stage 3, page 28)
____	____	____	____	____	6. Whether the druggist's rights to his invention have to be respected. (Stage 4, page 29)
____	____	____	____	____	7. Whether the essence of living is more encompassing than the termination dying, socially and individually. (Meaningless item used as a check on tendency to endorse complex items blindly)
____	____	____	____	____	8. What values are going to be the basis for governing how people act toward each other? (Stage 6, page 37)
____	____	____	____	____	9. Whether the druggist is going to be allowed to hide behind a worthless law which only protects the rich anyhow. (Stage 4½, antiauthoritarian rejection of the conventional order)
____	____	____	____	____	10. Whether the law in this case is getting in the way of the most basic claim of any member of society. (Stage 5A, page 34)
____	____	____	____	____	11. Whether the druggist deserves to be robbed for being so greedy and cruel. (Stage 3, page 28)
____	____	____	____	____	12. Would stealing in such a case bring about more total good for the whole society or not? (Stage 5A, page 34)

From the list of questions above, select the four most important:

Most important____ Second Most Important____ Third Most Important____

Fourth Most Important____

not present the subject with a set of standardized alternatives and have the subject sort out his own thinking? This shifts the burden of classification away from the trained scorer into the hands of the person who, although untrained, has the greatest access to his own thinking. It seemed worth a try.

Another concern was that the difference in the scoring system between a low stage and higher stage response often seems to involve elaborations and explications of a similar idea. Chapter 2, page 44 gives an example. How can we be certain that the subject who is scored at a lower stage did not miss the higher scoring because he is less articulate, or was not as stimulated as other subjects by the interviewer, or could not get interested in working to capacity in this task? Assessment less affected by a subject's verbal expressiveness seemed to be called for, standardized as much as possible so that noncomparability in the testing situation and test stimuli could be minimized.

Another concern is that the Kohlberg procedure essentially asks for justifications for a course of action. The procedure elicits *post hoc* reasoning. After making a decision, the subject then has to defend it. How do we know whether the subject's reasons had influenced his original decision or whether the procedure is forcing the subject to invent rationalizations for a previous commitment? The demand characteristics of the Kohlberg procedure prompt and probe the subject's *post hoc* judgments. But are these judgments representative of the considerations that tacitly guide his decision-making? Or are these judgments representative only of what a subject can explain and verbally defend afterwards? Is there some other way of getting information about moral judgments that isn't defending a decision *post hoc*?

Added to these problems, the 1969 study had pointed out some pitfalls with an objective format that had subjects ranking and rating prototypic statements, and paraphrasing them. The most serious is that subjects can project their own meanings into high stage statements, hence rankings and ratings cannot be unambiguously interpreted. We do not know how the subject views what he is rating. Related to this problem is that subjects may have been attracted to the more complex sentence construction, and to the more complex words in the higher stage statements rather than the stage-distinctive meaning of those statements. If objective test format were ever going to be useful, one must somehow overcome the problem of subjects projecting all sorts of interpretations onto stimuli statements, and one must somehow reduce nonstage cues such as sentence complexity and word usage.

Another lesson from the 1969 study was not to sacrifice psychological reality for tidiness of design. In the design of the 1969 study, statements had been written to exemplify each of the six stages, both for and against stealing, and for each of five moral issues (that is, life, law, intentions and consequences, guilt, and property). In other words, prototypic statements were written for each cell in a 6 by 2 by 5 matrix. The problem with it, however, is that the reality of people's thinking does not conform to this orthogonal, balanced design, nor is it always possible to find a pro and con statement at every stage. In regular interviews, people don't produce statements in every cell in the 6 by 2 by 5 matrix (see discussion in Chapter 2, pages 43-44). Nevertheless in the name of scientific rigor, prototypic statements concocted according to this design were used in the study. Such statements introduced rather farfetched arguments (although still codable at the designated stage), and sometimes presumed a change of circumstances in the dilemma. For example, one Stage 6 statement on the Heinz story reads:

> Heinz is faced with the decision of whether to consider the other people who need the drug just as badly as his wife. Heinz ought to act, not according to his particular feelings towards his wife, but considering the value of all the lives involved.

In this Stage 6 statement, the need of other people for the drug introduces an element that was not mentioned in the original story. When subjects saw this statement, they focused on the spurious assumption about other people needing the drug. It was very difficult to have them consider the structure of the reasoning. In interviews, subjects never make this type of argument. Therefore, the artificiality of the statement interfered with its usefulness in studying modes of reasoning. For the most part, information from these statements was useless and had to be eliminated from the analysis. Even if a researcher can concoct an item that logically represents certain characteristics, it does not follow that the item represents a psychological reality in people's thinking. Ironically, these counterbalanced sets of statements that contain some contrived statements have been frequently used to illustrate stage characteristics (e.g., Kohlberg 1969, pp. 379-382; Kohlberg 1971, pp. 170-171; and they also appear in a number of college textbooks), and some researchers still regard such orthogonally balanced, pro-and-con statements as a mark of design craftsmanship.

Another difficulty in any objective procedure (which has a subject responding by checking off something or writing a number, etc.) is that the researcher has no direct guarantee that the subject is really processing the test information: he may be randomly checking. A person can put check marks on a page (such as the DIT, page 87) without doing any moral judging at all. As discussed in Chapter 3 (page 61), the problem of false positives is serious in objective measures whereas the problem of false negatives is serious in production measures.

Given all these concerns, it was not clear at all in 1970 that a new means of assessment was feasible, much less that an objective test using ratings and rankings would work. Indeed, an objective test of cognitive structure might be impossible in principle, because a structured test has already predetermined the phenomenon that is of interest—namely, the structuring activity of the subject. Although this argument has some intuitive force, Piagetian researchers have devised objective methods for studying basic cognitive structures (see review by Miller 1976), and psycholinguists have devised objective methods for studying children's grammatical structures (e.g., Frazer, Bellugi, and Brown 1963).

While experimenting with various formats and techniques, I became aware of Lockwood's dissertation (1970) and its attention to differences in the way subjects construe the dilemma itself rather than their justifications for resolving it. It occurred to me that some of the difficulties in using prototypic stage statements (justifications for a course of action) could be ameliorated by using issue statements (different questions that pose different ways of construing the most important problem in a dilemma).

Issue questions could be short and cryptic (in constrast to prototypic statements that develop a line of argument advocating an action), and shorter statements might discourage spurious interpretations. In addition, issue questions can more easily be written to have comparable length, sentence complexity, and vocabulary at each stage than the longer prototypic statements of the 1969 study. Furthermore, issue questions need not build in an argument for one course of action or another. If a subject does not understand an issue question, nothing in the wording itself advocates one course of action over another; hence, it is less likely that subjects would prefer, because of its "fancier" wording, an issue question that they didn't understand. All these features seemed to offer hope for ameliorating the problem of subjects' projecting their own meanings into statements, or choosing them as fancier ways of advocating their choices. To illustrate, compare the Stage 6 prototypic statement in Chapter 2 (page 37) with a DIT Stage 6 item, below.

The prototypic statement: Where the choice must be made between dis-obeying a law and saving a human life, the higher principle of preserving life makes it morally right—not just understandable—to steal the drug. . . . If Heinz does not do everything he can to save his wife, then he is putting some value higher than the value of life. . . . By not acting in accordance with your sense of the value of human life, you would condemn yourself . . . you would know that you have betrayed your own moral integrity.

The DIT item: "What values are going to be the basis for governing how people act towards each other."

As can be seen, the DIT item gets to the distinctive feature of Stage 6 much more succinctly, without a lot of advocacy verbiage that might attract all subjects favoring the stealing choice, and with-out any more elegant language or more words than the other DIT items. Does the format difference between the DIT item and the proto-typic statement make a difference in the way subjects rate and rank items? In the Rest 1973 study, virtually all the subjects preferred the Stage 6 prototypic statement regardless of their Kohlberg stage—in short, there was no discrimination. However, in the Rest, et al. 1974 study using the DIT item above, only 10% of the junior high school subjects ranked the item as first or second most important; 25% of the senior high school subjects, 70% of the college subjects, and 87% of the doctoral students in political science or moral philosophy ranked it as first or second most important. In the 1974 study the opposite trend was true for the lower stage DIT items: In answering the Stage 2 item, "Is Heinz willing to risk getting shot as a burglar or going to jail for the chance that stealing the drug might help?", 48% of the junior high, 30% of the senior high, 10% of the college, and 0% of the doctoral students ranked that item as first or second most important. Hence, the change in format made a drastic difference in discriminability.

Another feature of the DIT is the inclusion of meaningless but complex-sounding items. For instance, item 7 in Table 4.1 is a mean-ingless (or "M") item: "Whether the essence of living is more encom-passing than the termination of dying, socially and individually." The M items were sprinkled throughout the questionnaire as a check on subjects who endorse items because of their apparent complexity and pretentiousness rather than because of their meaning. In the in-structions to the DIT, subjects are forewarned that there will be pretentious-sounding but meaningless items in the questionnaire, and when they come to such an item, to rate and rank it low. If a subject nevertheless endorses whatever items sound complex, chances are that that person will endorse many M items. If a subject accumulates too high an M score, that questionnaire is regarded as invalid and is discarded from the sample. In general, the tendency to endorse the Principled items (Stages 5 and 6) is *not* related to endorsing M items (the correlation is .00). Presumably, then, subjects who have high scores on Principled items because they have been endorsing items that they really don't understand also have high M scores, and thus are eliminated from the sample.

A third decision in constructing the DIT, also motivated by the concern to optimize discriminability, was not to order the items randomly but to place strong low stage items earlier in the list, followed by a mix of items. Items at Stages 5 and 6 usually come after the fourth item (but are mixed with items at Stages 3 and 4 in the last positions). My strategy here was to introduce lower stage ideas early in the list of items so that less advanced subjects could find their own ideas in a low stage item and would be less likely to project their thinking to a higher stage item. Presumably the less advanced subjects would already have read some items that they understood in the early items, and having a standard for what is comprehensible, would then reject the higher stage statements along with the M items. Presumably the more advanced subjects would also understand the early low stage items, but recognizing them as inadequate ways of construing the dilemma, would wade through until coming to the higher stage items. The more advanced subjects see the relevance and logic of the lower stage items (they too are concerned with Heinz's own self interest, with a husband's affection for his wife, with maintaining order in a community) but would regard each of these considerations in itself as an insufficient basis for making a decision. The more advanced subjects see that what is called for is a principle for establishing a hierarchy of claims, such as the higher stage items suggest without really spelling it out. The more advanced subjects recognize in the higher stage items a fragment of their own structuring of the dilemma, whereas the less advanced subjects do not see anything more in the high stage items than in the M items. In sum, the reason for placing high stage items later in the list of items was to minimize the problem of less advanced subjects distorting higher stage statements.

A dissertation by Lawrence (1978) investigated several of these assumptions about how subjects process DIT items. Lawrence interviewed subjects intensively about how they understood the DIT items, what they were thinking when they rated and ranked the items, and the basis for rating and ranking items. Her results indicate that subjects with high DIT scores do understand the Stage 2 and 3 items and also the Stage 5 and 6 items; in contrast, subjects with low DIT scores do not understand the high stage items as well. Lawrence measured "understanding" in several ways, including the subject's ability to present an accurate paraphrase of the sense of the item (somewhat similar to the comprehension test used in the 1969 study), and also in terms of the subject's report about how easy the item was to understand. Furthermore, Lawrence asked subjects to evaluate the items in terms of the items' adequacy in decision-making. Subjects with high DIT scores viewed the lower stage items as inadequate bases for making moral decisions; however, the subjects with low DIT scores saw many low stage items as more adequate. Lawrence's study therefore confirms that item selection on the DIT is largely governed by two processes: the ability to comprehend an item and the sense of an item's conceptual adequacy. Lack of comprehension limits the selection of high stage items by less advanced subjects; conceptual inadequacy limits the selection of lower stage items by more advanced subjects. Lawrence also showed that subjects tend to regard the M items as difficult to understand, but that advanced subjects treat them differently from high stage items.

What if a subject doesn't even read the items but just places check marks at random across the page? To detect random checking (and misunderstanding of the instructions) we use the Consistency Check.[1] The Consistency Check compares a subject's rankings at the bottom of the page with his ratings at the top of the page. If a subject has ranked an item in first place of importance, then the rating of that item should be as high or higher than the ratings of all other items. Similarly, if an item is ranked in second place, then only the item ranked in first place should have a higher rating. A count is made of the number of times a discrepancy occurs (e.g., the number of items that are rated higher than the item ranked as most important). If the number of inconsistencies exceeds a certain limit, we do not consider the questionnaire as furnishing reliable data, and it is eliminated from the sample. Typically the loss of questionnaires on the basis of the M score and the Consistency Check is in the 2 to 15% range; however, larger losses have occurred with disadvantaged or unmotivated groups. In studies that have analyzed data both with and without purging subjects, we have found that purging the subjects gives much clearer results and better reliability than leaving all the subjects in (see Panowitsch 1975).

A noticeable feature of the DIT is that there are not equal numbers of items for each stage of each story. The DIT uses six stories (such as the Heinz story), each with 12 items, for a total of 72 items. There are no Stage 1 items because the reading level and general sophistication required to take the questionnaire (about an eighth grade reading level) is so high that finding Stage 1 subjects at this age is unlikely (see McGeorge, 1975 for discussion of reading levels in the DIT). Likewise, there are few Stage 2 items, assuming that the subjects also are advanced beyond this stage. The three stages in which subject's thinking is expected to center are Stage 3, Stage 4, and the Principled stages (5A, 5B, and 6); these have roughly equal numbers of items, 17, 19, and 21, respectively.

The distribution of these items throughout the stories, however, is not balanced. Early in the development of the DIT, I decided that I had learned a lesson from my dissertation and that design considerations should not sacrifice psychological reality. Ideally, a set of items should represent the ways that subjects construe the important issues of a dilemma (at least the major and most frequent ways should be represented). The best clue to this construction is through extensive interviewing of subjects, noting the issues they raise and the ways that they express the issues. The DIT uses stories from Kohlberg's work (the Heinz, Prisoner, and Doctor dilemmas) and from Lockwood's work (the Student, Newspaper, and Webster dilemmas), for which extensive interviewing has been done. If subjects often raise five different Stage 4 issues on a dilemma, then there should be five Stage 4 items on that dilemma; if subjects raise only two Stage 4 issues, then there should be only two Stage 4 items. Our best estimate of the issues that have psychological reality for subjects, not some abstract notion of balance, should determine the number of items at a stage. Some commentators (e.g., Martin, Shafto, and Van Deinse, 1977) have contended that equal numbers of items for the DIT should be written pro and con, for each stage. But nothing in science guarantees us a completely counterbalanced, orthogonal psychological world. If items are contrived solely for the purpose of balancing the numbers of items for each stage, the test maker may have a sense of balance and proportion, but subjects are not attracted to artificial issues, and hence, psychologically speaking, the contrived items have no functional value — they are like distractor items in a multiple choice test that are so silly that no one ever picks them. In the future it may be possible to devise dilemmas in which subjects raise equal numbers of issues at each stage so that we can have psychological reality and tidy design, too. At present, we are reexamining the DIT items to see if any subjects were attracted to each item — if hardly anyone likes an item, then it should be replaced. Again, writing an item and placing it in the test is no guarantee that it has any psychological reality for any subject.

In summary, the DIT collects information about how people construe a dilemma rather than how they justify a course of action. Extensive interviewing preceded the writing of items; the issues that subjects raised spontaneously determined the items. Item analyses will indicate which ones did in fact attract high ratings and rankings and suggest future item revisions. Having twelve items per story seemed enough to cover the issues raised; however, future research may experiment with the number used. We took care to match items on word length, syntactic complexity, and use of technical or specialized terminology. Some meaningless but pretentious-sounding items were interspersed to check on subjects' test-taking set. Consistency between ratings and rankings served as a check on random responding. Research by Lawrence shows that more advanced subjects do understand the high stage items and regard them as more adequate ways of making a moral decision than the lower stage items; less advanced subjects have difficulty understanding the high stage items and are less discerning in choosing the lower stage items as adequate.

It can be seen, then, that the DIT employs one data source among many for collecting information about moral judgment. As with all methods for collecting information, there are problems, and the test maker's art is to devise ways that minimize the problems and optimize the advantages of that method.

Validating and Indexing

Having a method for producing ratings and rankings, what then do we do with all that information from 72 items? Chapter 3 discussed the desirability of collecting many bits of information so that idiosyncratic interactions of contexts and items with subjects could equal out to reveal underlying general trends. Indexing is the method of putting all that information together into some kind of score for each subject. The question of validity is what evidence determines whether the scores thus produced have any meaning and usefulness. The two questions are inextricably bound because there are many reasonable ways of indexing DIT data (the usual ones for indexing Kohlbergian tests of moral judgment were discussed in Chapter 3, pages 70-72) and the way to choose among alternative indices is to choose that one which gives the best validity (i.e., best demonstrates the properties empirically expected of the construct). In the pages that follow, the question of validity will be discussed first, then the question of choosing an index.

A Validating Strategy

What kinds of empirical studies can establish the validity of a test of moral judgment? The first possibility that commonly comes to mind is to ask how well the new test correlates with Kohlberg's. Why not simply establish the newcomer by piggybacking on the better known test? This strategy for validating the DIT was not adequate for several reasons. First, Kohlberg's test has been undergoing revision, changing almost every year since 1970. A correlation in 1972 could not establish what the correlation might be with the 1974 version, etc. A recent report cited a correlation of only .39 between the 1958 Kohlberg system and the 1978 (Kohlberg, Colby & Gibbs, 1978), so one cannot claim that results with one system hold true with another system. Second, although Kohlberg's test is the best known measure of moral judgment, its empirical properties have not been clearly demonstrated. The 1978 version is too recent for many studies to have been conducted with it: for instance, we do not know how well the invariant sequence findings with the group of Chicago boys will be replicated in other populations; we do not have convergent and discriminant validity studies; and only preliminary studies of test-retest stability, scorer reliability, and so on, are available. Therefore, linking the DIT with Kohlberg's test would not establish the DIT's empirical properties; at best it would provide an alternative. Third, to claim that one test is equivalent to another test, correlations are required at least in the .80s, and correlations of this magnitude are rare in this field.

It became clear that the DIT would have to be validated by its own program of studies. But what studies does one do?

Kohlberg has stated that his validating strategy is to demonstrate perfect invariant sequence in longitudinal data from subjects tested at three-year invervals over 20 years (Kohlberg 1976). Certainly a developmental variable should show directional change over time. But is this the only empirical test of moral judgment? Many variables show directional changes over time (weight, vocabulary, formal operations, number of dental fillings, shoe size, etc.) and the construct, moral judgment, surely has many more demonstrable and distinguishing properties than change over time. Furthermore, is a 20-year study required, so that there can be no contenders for assessing moral judgment other than Kohlberg's test until 1992? Is *perfect* invariant sequence in longitudinal sequence required?

Some psychologists propose that a test of moral judgment have "predictive validity" to moral behavior (e.g., Kurtines and Greif 1974). Subjects at each stage should behave differently in actual situations, otherwise what is the use of having *six* stages? This way of thinking about moral judgment has had a popular following for a long time, as the review by Pittel and Mendelsohn (1966) cited in Chapter 1 indicates. To Cognitive Developmentalists, however, the point of studying moral judgment has not been to find verbal behaviors that predict "real life" behaviors better than real life behaviors predict each other; nor is a test of moral judgment validated by direct linkages with variables like delinquency, cheating in a classroom, amount of candy shared with other children, and so on. The relation of moral judgment to such variables is bound to be complex, and moral judgment has to be studied first in its own right as a subjective phenomenon (see Chapter 6 for discussion).

As an analogy, let us consider another subjective construct, "knowledge of psychology"; by this, I mean an academic knowledge of the facts, theories, research strategies, controversies, and methods of the discipline of psychology. The variable presumably is increased when students take courses offered by a department of psychology. Students are regularly evaluated on their knowledge of psychology. How would one go about validating a test purporting to measure "knowledge of psychology"? Since some of the reasons for taking psychology courses are to help people live happier, richer lives and to help them relate to other people, we might imagine that some researchers will want to validate a test of knowledge of psychology by correlating the items with "real life" behaviors, like hospitalization for mental breakdowns, number of friends, ratings of "good life adjustment," income, divorce, compatibility with fellow workers. Surely such a validation procedure would be simple-minded. It would be ridiculous even to assume that a test of knowledge of psychology administered to professional academic psychologists would correlate highly with psychology career behaviors like number of publications in psychology journals, years to promotion to full professor, amount of dollars for research grants, perceived greatness by the A.P.A., annual income, and so on. Most of us would agree that a complex of factors determines these "real life" behaviors. For similar reasons, it is simple-minded to attempt to validate a test of moral judgment by correlating the items with delinquency, or cheating in a classroom.

How does one go about validating tests of subjective measures like moral judgment or knowledge of psychology? No single study or single empirical finding can validate such constructs, but a set of interlocking studies can build a case for the validity of each construct. A beginning round of studies for both constructs might employ strategies commonly used by researchers.

1. *Face validity or ecological validity.* This kind of validity is involved in the selection of a task to collect information, in the selection of characteristics of thinking that would be used as indicators, and in the rationale for scoring certain responses higher than others. For the DIT, I have attempted to explain the appropriateness of the DIT task for studying moral judgment and to discuss the stage characteristics used and why some of them are regarded as more advanced — all this is relevant to face validity. Had I used Rorschach inkblots and counted the number of bat responses as an index of moral judgment, this would have lacked face validity. For a test of knowledge of psychology, representative items from the domain of psychology would be essential to its face validity.

2. *Psychometric reliability.* Any test must produce variability in scores; different judges should be able to agree on what the response was; the various items should be internally consistent; and, test scores should be stable over short periods of time. In short, the test must have certain basic psychometric properties to be considered reliable.

3. *Criterion group validity.* Another kind of evidence typically used in psychological validation studies is to give the test to different groups of subjects who would ordinarily be expected to have different average scores. For instance, for knowledge of psychology, the test might be given to entering college freshmen on their first day of class in a psychology course, and to their instructors. Since ordinarily we expect the instructors to know more psychology than entering students, the "experts" should have higher scores. For moral judgment, we have contrasted the scores of doctoral students in moral philosophy and political science with younger, less educated subjects, expecting the more expert group to have higher scores than the less expert group.

4. *Longitudinal validity.* With any construct that postulates natural development, it is crucial to test the same subjects at successive points in time to determine if, in fact, the subjects do show upward movement. Kohlberg's twenty-year longitudinal study is the longest study in moral judgment of this kind, but longitudinal studies of shorter duration can test essentially the same point: Do subjects show upward movement over time?

5. *Convergent-divergent validity.* One might study the patterns of correlations of the test with other tests. A theoretical analysis of the construct gives some sense of what variables one would expect to be closely related and what variables are distantly related. In the case of the DIT, one would expect other tests of moral judgment

to be related, then other tests of cognitive development; least related should be such measures as socioeconomic status, sex, and IQ. Validity is strengthened when the correlations among the theoretically convergent variables is distinctly greater than correlations among the theoretically divergent variables.

6. *Validation through experimental enhancement studies.* The key idea here is that certain experiences ought to be more effective in changing scores than other experiences. For instance, if a test of psychology really taps knowledge of psychology and not general intelligence or test-taking skills, then we would expect that scores should increase more after a course in psychology than after a course in physics. If one can identify experiences or learning conditions that are especially enhancing to the construct in question, experimental or educational treatments that supply those experiences should produce greater "pre-post" gains than treatments that do not. In DIT research, we have used this strategy to contrast gains related to an ethics course to gains related to a formal logic course, religion course, or art course.

7. *Validation through experimental manipulation of test-taking sets.* Whereas the validity of a measure is supported if experimental treatments of the enhancing sort (as above) do in fact increase scores, in contrast, experimental manipulation of test-taking sets can undermine validity. For instance, if subjects are asked to "fake good" (that is, to pretend that they are taking a moral judgment test with "the highest principles of justice"), and if under this condition their scores dramatically rise, then this effect challenges the validity of the measure. We must then assume that an unknown portion of the variance of everybody's score under normal conditions is owing to a subject's willingness or unwillingness to "fake good". Subjects with the highest scores might not really view moral dilemmas any differently than subjects with average scores, but the high scorers might be more eager to please or to look good. Therefore, results of this kind of study support the validity of a measure when no treatment effects are found.

These seven criteria have been the basis for building a case for the construct validity of the DIT. Of course, this list of studies can be added to; but if a test of moral judgment produces the expected results in these many varied studies (and also if the studies are replicated), a measure has passed the first round of validation and merits further exploration and refinement. Eventually we want to explain complex phenomena like crime and delinquency, acts of heroism and altruism, why politicians act the way they do, and how world cooperation can be increased. But these phenomena are complex and moral judgment is one among many possible factors in interaction. Ways of identifying these other factors and assessing them must be developed before much progress can be made in explaining the more complex phenomena. In the meantime, we can build some assurance in the validity of a measure of moral judgment by doing the kinds of studies listed above, all of which are well within psychology's present state of technology.

Indexing

Having a list of validity criteria, here is our strategy for choosing an index: Calculate the various possibilities; then put them in competition with each other to see which one best fulfills the criteria above. If one index has better test-retest stability, stronger longitudinal trends, a better convergent-divergent pattern of correlations than another, then the first index is preferred.

Actually, we have compared various sets of DIT indices in three different studies. In the first two studies, various indices were compared, and the P index (i.e., the relative importance given to Stage 5 and 6, Principled Thinking—see discussion below) was the superior index in both sets of analyses. The third analysis by Mark Davison was recently completed, introducing scaling procedures based on a latent trait model, and has demonstrated the advantages of the "D" index (discussed in Chapter 8). Since all research to 1976 has used the P index, almost all of the research in this book reports DIT results in terms of the P index. In this chapter I will not report all the analyses that were carried out in the first and second studies of indices, which are superseded by Davison's work. In Davison's chapter, the P and D indices are compared; a summary of the validity properties of the P index, used primarily throughout the current studies, can be found there. I will, however, mention the types of indices investigated in the first and second studies, but were found to be less powerful than the P index.

In a dissertation by Douglas Cooper (1972) many types of indices were investigated. 1. The *P index* is calculated in this way: the item ranked as first importance in each story is given 4 points; the item ranked second, 3 points; the item ranked third, 2 points; and the item ranked fourth, 1 point. Since each dilemma has four ranks, each has 10 points to distribute among the stages. Points are totaled across the six stories for each stage. For instance, if a Stage 3 item was ranked in first place and another Stage 3 item was ranked in fourth place on the Heinz story, and if another Stage 3 item on the next story was ranked in second place, Stage 3 points would be 4 + 1 + 3. Total points would be calculated for each stage. There are 60 points in all, and the total number of points at each stage is divided by .60 to yield a percent score (for the convenience of having a base of 100 instead of 60). This procedure yields scores for Stage 2, 3, 4, 4½, 5A, 6, and M. The P index is calculated by adding together the scores of Stages 5A, 5B, and 6. The P index then represents the sum of weighted ranks given to "Principled" items, and is interpreted as the relative importance give to Principled moral considerations in making a moral decision. (See *Revised Manual*, 1979, for details.)

As mentioned before, when compared with other indices (except Davison's, Chapter 8), the P index showed better results in the validity studies. How can a continuous index based on only the highest stages possibly represent moral judgment development? At this point we can only guess, starting with the finding that the P index did in fact perform better than other indices. Perhaps the explanation is suggested in Figure 3.2 in Chapter 3. Note that in this hypothetical figure, the highest type shown has a steady gradual increase over much of the developmental continuum, despite the complex fluctuations in the other types. In this case, one could use the amount of the highest type as a fairly good indicator for locating a subject along the underlying developmental continuum. Perhaps the P index works as well as it does because, in general, principled thinking gradually increases over the course of development. We have no *a priori* reason for expecting this to be the case, since the more complex stage model does not predict beforehand what the shapes of the developmental curves will be, and developmental theory is generally noncommital about what kind of index will work best. Developmental theory supplies the criteria by which various indices can be checked out (that is, it tells us what kinds of studies are relevant to the construct and what trends are theoretically expected), but which particular index produces the clearest and strongest trends must be decided empirically, not theoretically.

Intuitively, at first consideration, the P index does not seem as though it would be the best performer in the validity studies. In fact, it might be challenged on the grounds that it throws away information on all the lower stages (Stages 2, 3 and 4). Would not this contradict the line of argument in Chapter 3 about preserving information? A qualification must be kept in mind: Information should be preserved until it is determined that it is not useful. The criticisms in Chapter 3 were directed at discarding information before any tests could be made about the importance of that information (for instance, scoring rules that discard information before getting on the scoring sheets, or stage typing indices which discard information before data analyses can be run). The cardinal rule is to bring information forward to the point of data analyses so that one can determine which information is important. Once one is at the point of choosing among various indices (in which the data of many studies have been computed with each index, and the strength of the trends can be compared), then one can see which information is useful. After all, summarizing a subject's performance with a score inevitably throws away some information and highlights other information; the question is which treatment of the information (which index) is most useful. Until Davison's index, we had tried many ways of using the information from Stages 2, 3, and 4 and found that none gave us any improvement over the P index; most were decidedly worse (had poorer test-retest stability, didn't produce as clear a pattern of convergent-divergent correlations, didn't differentiate expert from nonexpert groups).

In the following pages I will indicate the various indices that we have tried, grouped by general families. I will not present the comparison data on the indices because that information is much too voluminous; however, Chapter 8 gives the summaries on the P and Davison's indices.

2. Variations on the P index were also investigated by Cooper, for instance, by using only the first two or three ranks instead of the first four ranks. He also looked at different point weighting schemes; for instance, instead of using 4, 3, 2, 1, respectively, for the first four ranks, he used 6, 5, 4, 3, or 1, 1, 1, 1, etc. None of these variations showed an advantage.

3. Cooper also tried combination indices like Kohlberg's MMS (Chapter 3, page 72) in which Stages 2, 3, and 4 and P were combined according to different weights. For instance, deriving stage scores in the manner discussed in No. 1, above, then multiplying the Stage 2 score by 1, Stage 3 by 2, Stage 4 by 3, and Stage P by 4. Many weighting schemes were tried (1, 2, 3, 4; 1, 2, 3, 8; 1, 2, 4, 8; 1, 3, 4, 8; 1, 3, 7, 13; 1, 3, 5, 20, etc.). Some of these combination indices had empirical properties similar to the P index, but since such indices were so contrived, the relative simplicity of the P index was preferred.

4. Cooper then tried several families of indices based on the *rating* data instead of the *ranking* data. One was to simply look at the stage of predominantly high average ratings. Subjects, however, did not show that much discrimination between stages on average ratings — that is, the predominantly rated stage was not greatly predominant

over the other stages. One problem with this kind of index is that it assumes all items are working equally well in computing a stage's average rating. But a stage's average may be considerably lowered by having a few bad items, items that nobody likes. This was not a problem with the ranking data, since subjects pick only four items from twelve, and if there are a few bad items, these items are not averaged into stage scores. Furthermore the ranking task forces subjects to make distinctions because ties are not permitted: something has to be ranked first, then second, and so on, whereas in the rating task, fine discriminations are not forced because subjects can rate many items as "most important." Third, the failure of rating data to be as discriminating as the ranking data was thought to be attributed also to different response sets that subjects bring to the rating task. An examination of average ratings showed that some subjects use the high end of the rating scale for everything, and some subjects use the lower end. An examination of standard deviations showed that some subjects rate every item within a few points on the rating scale, others use the full range. These response sets were thought to so confound results as to obliterate the useful discriminations. Therefore the rating data did not seem as promising a basis for an index as the ranking data to Cooper.

5. Cooper, however, further experimented with several other kinds of indices based on the ratings. According to one idea, if some items throw the whole index off, perhaps an index based on good items, excluding bad items, would work. Cooper studied the intercorrelations of items and performed several factor analyses to identify those items not clustering with other items of their stage; these items were eliminated. Items that did not discriminate junior high school subjects from graduate subjects also were eliminated. New rating indices, based on the remaining items, were computed. Again many variations were possible, given the options of a P score based on ratings, or various combinations of stage scores involving different weightings. Twenty-two different indices based on ratings were calculated and analyzed. All rating indices showed disastrous test-retest reliability, no matter how items were selected or which set of weights were used.

After examining 88 different ways of indexing the DIT, Cooper recommended the P index. Computing each of these indices for several hundred subjects and checking each one's empirical properties on a set of validating criteria was an enormous amount of computer work. Ironically, the P index was the same index I had initially chosen in the pilot study of the DIT in 1971.

In the ensuing years, between 1972 and 1974, several other kinds of indices were examined. These studies are unpublished, but since the uniform conclusion has been that nothing does a better job than the P index (until Davison's D), I will only list the kinds of indices explored in this second set of analyses.

6. One index assigns subjects to the stage that they use an exceptional amount. "Exceptional amount" is defined as a standard deviation above the mean based on a heterogeneous sample (Rest, et al 1974). In other words, each subject's stage scores (computed on weighted ranks, as in No. 1 above) are converted to standardized scores and then assigned to that stage that has a score above +1.0; if two or more stages are high, the highest stage is used; if no stages are high, then the subject is unscorable. Subjects are thus stage typed, not according to *predominant* use (the usual basis for stage typing) but according to exceptional use. (See *Manual*, Rest 1974, for more details).

The theoretical interest in this index is that it does not assume a simple stage model, but is consistent with a more complicated one. Each stage is not assumed to go through a period of predominance; the index requires only that some subjects use more of a type than other subjects and that this difference is useful in locating subjects along a developmental continuum. Furthermore if some stories "pull" more of some stages than other, or if some items in some stages are bad, these biasing effects are adjusted by using deviations from group means for the stage score rather than the absolute scores (which may be inflated or deflated by special circumstances). Despite these theoretical advantages, the empirical properties of the index are extremely bad (especially test-retest stability; see Rest 1976 for brief discussion) and it should not be used.

7. Stage typing on the basis of the highest stage used substantially is another index that assigns subjects to a stage. Instead of predominant usage or exceptional usage, one looks for the highest stage on which the subject scores at the mean or higher. Again, such an index does not presuppose a simple stage model and also compensates for story pull and bad items. The index is used in Rest, 1975 in comparison with other ways of data analysis to illustrate its undesirable properties (less sensitive to longitudinal trends). As is the case for all indices that stage type (or assign subjects to a stage as the way of indicating where they are developmentally), this is not a preferred index.

8. Whereas Cooper formed new indices on the *rating* data by eliminating bad items, some further experiments were performed on indices on *ranking* data, eliminating bad items. Bad items were identified in a variety of ways (low test-retest, low correlations with other items of that stage, poor discriminability) and ten new indices were

formed on the ranking data. None of these were superior to the P index on the validity criteria.

9. A new series of *combination* indices were explored. Instead of combining different stages by differentially weighting them, as Cooper did in No. 3 above, the new strategy was simply to subtract low stage scores from high stage scores. The basic idea was that using a difference score would capitalize on a subject's discrimination of high stage items from low stage items, and in rating data would compensate for response sets (i.e., subjects who generally rated high or rated low would cancel out their own response set by a difference score). Some indices used stage scores based on rating data, others used stage scores based on ranking data. Some indices subtracted Stages 2 and 3 from 5A, 5B, and 6; others subtracted Stages 2,3, and 4 from 5A, 5B, and 6. Some indices used stage scales built on all the items written for that stage; others used a purged subset of items. None of these indices, despite their greater complexity, demonstrated better empirical trends than the P index, although some were nearly comparable.

In summary, a huge amount of analysis has gone into the examination of indices for the DIT. This has not been a waste because once a set of validation studies have been completed, and the data are computerized, obtaining the optimal index is the easiest way of improving the power of the instrument. The search for an index is not a process of trial and error, but rather a search for ways of minimizing confounding factors and highlighting the trends that are theoretically expected of the construct. This is likely to continue beyond Davison's new work. The claim that a new index is better cannot be based on a single piece of evidence (such as test-retest); rather, any new index must be examined across the many criteria for validity before its general superiority is established.

5

Cross-Sectional
and Longitudinal Studies

Nothing is more crucial to a cognitive-developmental construct than evidence of change over time from less advanced forms of thinking (as theoretically defined by logical analysis) to more advanced forms of thinking. If subjects do not change at all or change in every possible way, no grounds exist for claiming directional change (or sequentiality) — a basic claim of any developmental construct. Some researchers challenge the claim that directional change occurs in moral judgment. Kurtines and Greif (1974), in their vituperative review of Kohlbergian research, concluded that Kohlberg's model of moral stages gives no evidence for sequentiality. Hogan (1970; see also Kurtines and Greif 1974) has claimed on purely conjectural grounds that Kohlberg's Stages 5 and 6 are equivalent to his characterizations of "the ethics of social responsibility' and "the ethics of personal conscience," respectively, and that these two orientations are manifestations of different personality styles, not developmental stages in which one comes before the other. Bandura and McDonald (1963) demonstrated that experiments in modeling effects could shift children's use of intentionality upward (developmentally higher according to Piaget's stages of moral judgment) or downward, and hence "revealed that the developmental sequence proposed by Piaget is by no means predetermined or invariant" (Bandura and Walters, 1963, p. 207).[1]

Cross Sectional Studies — Age and Education

The data in Piaget's 1932 book consists almost exclusively of comparisons of older subjects with younger subjects, showing that the older subjects tend to display more advanced forms of reasoning. Similarly, Kohlberg's 1958 dissertation and his research for the next ten years emphasized cross-sectional age trends among boys 10 to 16 years in samples from several foreign countries. Historically, then, cross-sectional data (i.e., scores from subjects grouped by age) has been the first line of evidence offered in support of the developmental nature of moral judgment.

What is the relevance of cross-sectional data to the proposition that moral judgment follows a prescribable course of change? Cross-sectional age trends can be interpreted in two ways. The version making more stringent assumptions regards all the subjects as coming from the same population, so that the moral judgment scores of subjects at age 16 represent what the scores of the 10-year-olds will be in six years, etc. In other words, it is assumed that the between-subject scores represent what the within-subject scores would be if the same group of subjects were actually retested at several intervals over the years. This involves assuming that there are no selection biases in sampling from the various age groups, no differences in cohort groups born at different times, and no special historical events that affect the development of one group differently from the others. Sometimes it is reasonable to make these assumptions (as for instance, in sampling fourth, fifth, and sixth graders from the same school in a stable, fairly homogeneous community in times of no dramatic historical changes). Further assuming that chronological age is at least a rough indicator of development in this age group, with the oldest group having the most advanced scores, that data constitutes some support that moral judgment does change along a prescribable course. Sometimes, however, it is difficult to make these assumptions, but even then cross-sectional data can be relevant and useful, although in a weaker sense. Consider, for example, comparisons between high school and college students. The two groups differ on age but also very likely on variables like IQ, socioeconomic status (SES), intellectual interests, and so on. It would be problematic, however, to assume that the college scores represent what the high school sample's scores will be in several years. Many high school students will not go to college: therefore, the college sample is not from the same population. While this type of cross-sectional data can not be used to project longitudinal scores (as was assumed in the first case), there are predictions derived from cognitive developmental theory that we could make about the scores of these two groups. The differences of the college group in age, and probably in IQ, SES, and intellectual interests, suggest higher moral judgment scores for the college group: A higher age affords more time for development, higher IQ suggests faster learning and development, higher SES may indicate greater opportunities and richer stimulation, greater interest in intellectual matters would point to a greater motivation to attain adequate conceptualizations and a focus on cognitive processing of information. Therefore cognitive developmental theory would predict the *direction* of difference between the high school and college samples but can not use the *amount* of difference to estimate what the high school sample's scores will be in several years. Finding differences between the groups would be a weaker form of support for developmental theory, but support nevertheless (considering that we would regard it a partial disconfirmation of developmental theory to find no differences between the high school and college samples, or to find high school students more advanced than college students). The logic of using cross-sectional data in this weaker sense is somewhat similar to the use of criterion group differences as a validation strategy, a much-used strategy in psychological research. The strategy involves grouping subjects according to some presumed difference (creative versus noncreative architects, schizophrenic versus normal persons, different occupational groups) and then assessing the groups on the measure of interest to see if the scores differentiate the groups in the way predicted.

In DIT studies cross-sectional data have been used more according to the criterion group strategy than as a substitute for longitudinal data. The first studies (Rest et al. 1974) sought to identify a group of people who could be regarded as "experts" in moral judgment and to contrast their scores on the DIT with scores from less expert groups. For the expert group, a sample of world renowned moral philosophers would have been ideal since access to such a sample was lacking, a group of doctoral students in moral philosophy and political science served as the "experts." For the least expert group, the youngest group was sought that could fully understand the DIT, a group of students in the ninth grade (at the time, pretesting had shown that some subjects younger than the ninth grade had difficulty with the format of the DIT). Between these two extremes, a group of twelfth graders, a group of college juniors and seniors, and a group of seminarians were tested.

Table 5.1 presents the stage scores of the different student groups from the Rest et al. 1974 study.[2] The table shows that the more advanced groups attribute more importance to principled moral considerations (Stages 5 and 6) than the less advanced groups, and that the use of the lower stages decreases with the more advanced groups. One-way analysis of variance on the P score between the five groups produced an F of 34.5, highly significant statistically (an F of 2.8 is significant at the .01 level) and accounted for 48% of the variance. Another way of representing the group differences is in terms of the percentage of subjects in each group predominantly using principled thinking (that is, have P scores above 50%). Only 2.5% of the junior high students used principled thinking predominantly, 7.5% of the senior high students, 45% of the college students, 60% of the seminarians, and 93% of the doctoral students in political science or moral philosophy.

The differentiation of student groups on DIT scores has been replicated in three other studies. In Rest et al. (1974) there was a replication in Sample 2, $n = 65$, with P correlating .67 with age-education. Blackner (1975) reported significant age trends, $F (4, 155) = 3.50$, $p < .01$, for five groups of students (ninth-tenth grade, eleventh-twelfth grade, ages 18-20, 21-23, and above 24 years) in a Mormon religious education program. Yussen (1976) reported age-education trends also, $F (3, 116) = 20.16$, $p < .001$, among four groups of 30 subjects each at ninth, tenth, twelfth grades, and college sophomores and juniors (groups equated on IQ, sex, SES, race, and locale). Martin et al. (1977) reported significant differentiation among junior highs ($n = 60$), senior highs ($n = 200$), and college students ($n = 105$) on all six stage scores.

The largest study of group differentiation on the DIT (Rest 1976a, Technical Report No. 2) collated data from many studies conducted

Table 5.1. Student Group Averages on Stage Scores

Student Group	Stage			
	2	3	4	5 & 6(P)
Junior high				
n=40	10.7	19.0	32.6	30.3
Senior high				
n=40	8.7	20.2	27.7	33.8
College				
n=40	5.0	13.4	22.9	50.4
Seminarians				
n=25	4.2	13.9	16.0	55.5
Moral philosophy and political science Ph.D.s				
n=15	2.0	8.2	17.4	65.2

by researchers from all over the United States. Over 50 researchers had collected DIT data on 5,714 subjects in 136 different samples from diverse backgrounds and regions, and they shared their data with me. A detailed listing of DIT scores and sample characteristics is given for each sample in the 1976 Technical Report and in the 1979 *Revised Manual.* A summary of the DIT's P index is given in Table 5.2, grouping the various samples by student status and omitting the adult subjects.

As can be seen in Table 5.2, the average DIT score increases about 10 points with each increase in level of education. Examining the sample means that went into the combined mean, most sample means were within 5 points of the combined mean. An estimate of the standard deviation for individual subjects (not sample means) was calculated on the basis of those studies that reported standard deviations for their samples. Over half of the studies reported standard deviations and the means of the studies with complete information are close to the combined means for each student group, so presumably the standard deviations are representative as well. One-way analysis of variance of the four student groups indicated an extraordinarily strong trend: F (3, 2905) = 604.9, $p < .0001$. Using the omega-square statistic (Hays 1963), grouping the samples by age-education accounts for 38% of the variance.

Most of these student samples were collected in intact classrooms. The classroom is a much more homogeneous unit that the broad educational levels used in the above analyses (e.g., junior high, senior high, college, graduate students). A classroom usually has students from the same grade in contrast to the broad educational groupings. In addition, students in a classroom are all in the same geographical region, in the same school, taking the test under the same conditions, and are probably more nearly alike in IQ and SES than heterogeneous subjects grouped into the four educational levels. Therefore, grouping subjects by classroom rather than broad educational level reduces within-group differences due to IQ, SES or geographical region and heightens between-group differences. An analysis of vari-

Table 5.2. P Index Averages and S.D. for Combined Student Groups

Group	n	Average P%	Estimated S.D.
Junior high	1,322	21.9	8.5
Senior high	581	31.8	13.5
College	2,479	42.3	13.2
Graduates	183	53.3	10.9

ance grouping subjects by classroom yielded a significant differentiation: F (65, 2843) = 42.8, $p < .0001$, accounting for 49% of the
variance (using the omega-square statistic). Grouping by classroom
thus accounts for more variance than grouping by broad educational
level, but only increases it by about 11%.

There seems to be little doubt, therefore, that students at different educational levels show discriminate DIT scores. But in student
samples, age and education are confounded (and probably IQ, SES
and other variables). Students at higher levels of education are inevitably older; adult samples give us a chance to disentangle age and
education. In adults, older subjects need not have completed more
formal education than younger subjects. An interesting study by
Dortzbach (1975) analyzed the relation of age and education to
moral judgment in an adult sample, aged 25 to 74, randomly selected
from voter registration lists in Eugene, Oregon. The education trends
of Dortzbach's sample are given in Table 5.3. While Table 5.3 shows
that moral judgment increases in adults with education, Table 5.4
shows that moral judgment decreases in Dortzbach's sample when

Table 5.3. Adults' Education Level and Moral Judgment

Highest Attained Education Level	n	Average P%	S.D.
Grade school	5	10.0	9.7
Junior high	2	28.3	11.8
Some senior high	44	28.2	16.4
Senior high or vocational school graduate	24	33.6	20.2
2 or more years college	64	37.4	17.3
Graduate or professional school	46	47.3	19.3

Source: Adapted from Dortzbach (1975).

Table 5.4. Adult Age and Moral Judgment

Age	Average P%	S.D.	n
35-44	33.9	17.4	30
45-54	34.6	18.9	37
55-64	31.9	18.9	39
65-74	24.3	12.0	25

Source: Adapted from Dortzbach (1975).

the same subjects are grouped by age. Therefore, moral judgment seems to be more highly related to education than to age.

Similarly, in another study 87 adults in a religious education program, ages 24-50, Coder (1975) found a slightly negative relation of P with age, r (86) = −.10, while the P score was positively and significantly related to education, r (81) = .25, $p < .05$. In a third study of adults, this time of 70 volunteers from a Naval base, age 18-59, Crowder (1976) found that age correlated with P, r = −.05, whereas education correlated r = .25 (p < .05). In a fourth study, G. Rest (1977) found a correlation of .45 of education with P in a sample of 43 adults randomly selected from the Minneapolis telephone book. Therefore, consistently in adults, moral judgment is more positively related to education than to age. Cognitive restructuring of one's moral thinking seems to be more related to formal education than to the passage of years.

The argument might be made that the negative age trends in adults indicate regression in moral judgment, just as the positive age trends in students are used to indicate development. This argument is not valid, however, because the negative age trend in adults can be completely accounted for by differences in education: The older adults in the Dortzbach and Coder studies are not representative of what the younger adults will be like after the passage of years. The older adults having less education than the younger adults are a different cohort group and have a different life history. For instance, the adults in the 65-74 age group in Dortzbach's study were born in the period 1901-1910, and many of them had only a grade school education. Just as they were starting out as adults, 20 to 30 years old, the Depression hit, forcing them to be concerned with the most basic, practical issues of living. Their pattern of thinking is not indicative of that of adults now 25 to 30 after 35 to 50 years from now, because many younger adults have had college educations and their affluence has enabled them to develop far-ranging interests and viewpoints. In short, the differences in moral judgment in the adult groups are more likely to represent different developmental tracks than simply different points on the same developmental track. In related research, Schaie and LaBouvie-Vief (1974) have demonstrated that cross-sectional studies of adults on intelligence and other psychological tests have falsely suggested declines and regressions in test performance, since in longitudinal studies there is no such decrement.

Note that adult groups at various ages can not be used as criterion groups in validating the DIT. No clear theoretical or common-sense prediction is possible as to whether 30-year-olds as a group should be significantly different from 50-year-olds. We do not know whether adults continue to rework and restructure their thinking as students presumably are doing "in their formative years," or whether adults are "so settled in their ways" that there wouldn't be much change on moral judgment scores; further, historical and societal changes over 20 to 50 years are likely to complicate predictions also. Therefore, no clear expectation based on theory exists as to how various adult age groups will score on the DIT.

One value in examining adult groups, of course, is to gain some idea how far moral judgment development continues in adulthood. How high do moral judgment scores get? The evidence at hand suggests that adults in general do not show much advance beyond that accounted for by their level of education. If we group adults according to their highest level of completed education and compare this average with that of students who are currently at that level of education, there is not much difference between adults and students. Table 5.5 presents groups of adults and compares their average P% with that of the comparable average P% for students (from Table 5.2). Table 5.5 suggests the hypothesis that, generally speaking, development in moral judgment seems to advance dramatically as long as a person is in school, and that when a person discontinues formal education, his moral judgment development tends to stabilize. Longitudinal studies are needed to test this hypothesis and to disentangle cohort effects from ontological change. In Chapter 7 we shall see that adults can change who are in special educational programs (c.f. Coder 1975), but it appears from the cross-sectional data that most adults do not advance much after formal schooling. Combining all the adult samples (1,149 subjects from 29 samples),[3] the average P% is 40.0, with an estimated standard deviation of 16.7. Adults are more heterogeneous than the student groups, presumably because of their wide educational backgrounds, controlled in the student groups. Also, it is noteworthy that in this composite sample, relatively few adults choose mostly Principled moral considerations (Stages 5 and 6) in making moral decisions.

Cross-Sectional Studies — Other Demographic Characteristics

Region and Religion: The Effects of Intellectual Milieu

Age and education do not tell the whole story. If we look at the combined samples at the same educational level we see considerable variation. Now it is true that some of this within-group variation can be

Table 5.5. Comparison of DIT Scores of Current Students and Adults
with Comparable Educational Achievement

Current Students	P%	Adults with Comparable Educational Achievement	P%
Composite sample of junior high students, n = 1,322 (from Table 5.2)	21.9	Adults with only grade school or junior high education, n = 7 (Dortzbach 1975)	11.2
Composite sample of senior high students, n = 581 (from Table 5.2)	31.8	Composite of 44 adults with some high school and 24 adults with vocational school or high school completion (Dortzbach 1975), plus 17 young working adults (Rest 1975)	31.5
Composite sample of college students, n = 2,479 (from Table 5.2)	41.6	Composite of 64 adults with some college (Dortzbach 1975), 87 college-educated adults (Coder 1975), 60 women in continuing education program (Jacobs 1975), 124 Roman Catholic women (Moore 1975)	41.0
Composite of graduate students (mixed majors, not specifically medical or seminary): 82 Masters in education (Bloom 1976); 20 graduates at Oklahoma State U. (Ismail 1976); 10 graduates at U. of Toledo (Jacobs 1975); 20 graduates in Curriculum and Instruction, Oklahoma State U. (Deal 1978); 63 first-year law students plus 41 advanced law students (Willging 1979)	50.1	46 Adults with some graduate or professional education (Dortzbach 1975)	47.3
Graduate students in medical school: 94 students in first year in school in Midwest (Jacobs 1977); 283 in first year in Northeastern school, plus 205 third-year students (Husted 1978)	50.6	Practicing physicians: 157 doctors in Northeast (Sheehan 1979)	49.5
Seminarians in liberal Protestant seminary: 27 (Rest et al. 1974) and 29 (Schomberg and Nelson 1976)	57.8	Practicing clergy in liberal Protestant church: 4 (Ernsberger 1976)	62.5

attributed to grade level within the broad educational grouping, for example, freshmen in contrast to seniors. However, there is another factor: The samples having the lowest P scores are from the Southern United States, areas of the country usually noted for their conservative and traditional outlook. Two college samples from Georgia and Virginia have P% averages of 24.5 and 34.0 respectively, the two lowest averages in the combined college sample, with a mean of 41.6. Possibly the low scores from the South samples reflect the effects of a conservative intellectual milieu. Furthermore, Husted (1979) found that pediatric residents who have been trained in foreign countries (many from India) had an average P% of only 32.3 ($n = 58$, SD = 13.0), whereas American-born and educated pediatric residents averaged 57.2 ($n = 46$, SD = 14.0). Similarly, Ismail (1976) found that a group of foreign-born students at Oklahoma State University (from Saudi Arabia) averaged 28.3 ($n = 40$, SD = 9.4), whereas a group of American-born students at comparable levels of education averaged 42.6 ($n = 40$, SD = 14.5).

Some corroboration of the lowering effects on moral judgment of a conservative intellectual milieu comes from Ernsberger's 1976 study of different churches. Ernsberger analyzed the religious education materials, position statements, and creeds of four congregations in the same geographical area of Minneapolis and drawing from similar SES backgrounds. He found that a Methodist and a Unitarian Universalist church employed more principled moral thinking in their educational materials and official statements than a Baptist and a Missouri Synod Lutheran Church. In fact, these Baptist and Lutheran churches used materials that stated that anything not written in the scriptures was not morally binding. Then Ernsberger obtained a random sample of church members from each of these churches, the averages of which are presented in Table 5.6.

There are striking and statistically significant differences on the P index between the liberal and the conservative congregations. Ernsberger further studied subsamples of laity from each congregation who had been heavily involved in religious education and/or were active on a social policies board of the church (designated "teaching" or "social action" groups in Table 5.6). For the Unitarian and Methodist churches, the church lay leaders had significantly higher P scores than the members randomly chosen from the congregations. For the Baptist and Lutheran churches, the lay leaders had significantly lower P scores than the random samples from these congregations. In other words, the P scores of the congregations varied according to the "official thinking" of the congregations, and the lay leaders were even more extreme than the members chosen at random.

What are the theoretical implications of "milieu effects"? Many interesting possibilities are suggested from these findings, but we can't offer a complete or decisive interpretation at this point. It may be, as Social Learning theorists suggest, that subjects imitate the moral judgments of others in their milieu and that the difference between samples from a more conservative milieu versus a more liberal milieu simply reflects different modeling opportunities and reinforcement contingencies. On the other hand, one might interpret the differences between the high P groups and lower P groups in terms of "enriched" versus "impoverished" environments, where in the enriched environment, people are encouraged to examine their views more thoroughly and systematically, leading to more complex and advanced thinking, and higher DIT scores.

Unfortunately for tidy psychological theorizing, probably both kinds of processes play a part in determining a person's ideology. On the one hand, we can cite cases in which a person's espoused views are highly determined by situational and social pressures. An extreme example of the influence of social pressure is the case of Galileo in his conviction that the earth revolves around the sun, and in his recanting of that opinion. Following Copernicus, Galileo had

Table 5.6. Moral Judgment and Religious Affiliation

Samples and Subsamples	n	P% Mean	S.D.
United Methodist	49	46.6	13.0
Random	20	42.1	10.7
Social Action	13	48.0	12.7
Teaching	16	51.0	14.7
Unitarian-Universalist	41	52.6	15.2
Random	17	46.2	17.7
Social Action	13	52.7	12.0
Teaching	11	62.3	8.8
Missouri Synod Lutheran	38	34.9	12.5
Random	18	35.7	13.6
Social Action	9	36.6	12.5
Teaching	11	32.1	11.0
Conservative Baptist Association	41	30.1	11.1
Random	21	30.5	10.7
Social Action	10	30.7	14.1
Teaching	10	28.7	9.4

Source: Adapted from Ernsberger 1976

charted the movement of the stars and planets, and after extensive mathematical computation, concluded that the earth must not be the center of the universe as was generally accepted. In 1632, Galileo published the treatise, *Dialogue on the Great World Systems,* which laid out his arguments and evidence. In April of 1633 Galileo was brought before the Inquisition, charged with heresy against the Holy Catholic and Apostolic Roman Church, and threatened with torture on the rack. In June of 1633, Galileo recanted and signed a document stating that he would "abandon the false opinion that the sun is the centre of the world, and moves, and that I must not hold, defend, or teach in any way whatsoever, verbally or in writing, the said doctrine . . . ." (quoted in Bronowski 1973, p. 216). Galileo's views after 1633 were clearly affected by factors other than conceptual adequacy — at least his public views. On the other hand, we can cite cases in which no amount of modeling or reinforcement is sufficient to overcome dificiencies in cognitive development — for instance, repeated readings of Galileo's *Dialogue* are not going to influence the views of a 2-year-old child, with or without rewards. These cases are extreme, however, and the contributions of social pressure and conceptual adequacy are bound to be more subtle and complex in accounting for DIT scores in the samples studied. But we cannot rule out conceptual adequacy nor social influence as determinants in people's moral thinking.

A dissertation by Lawrence (1978) sheds additional light on how ideological commitments can override conceptual adequacy in making moral judgments. Although in the general American population, DIT scores seem to be highly related to conceptual adequacy — that is, people tend to make moral judgments on the basis of the highest stage of reasoning that they can comprehend (see Chapter 6 for discussion), nevertheless, some groups in American society require strict adherance to a codified set of beliefs as a condition of membership. In these groups, decision-making is not based on critical and independent thinking, but is based on prescribed and unquestioned beliefs. Lawrence tested and interviewed one such group composed of radically Fundamentalist seminarians, living in a close-knit, autocratic community. On the DIT, this group had extraordinarily high Stage 4 scores, and had a very low P score (22%), even lower than Ernsberger's conservatives, but not too different from scores from a college in Georgia. Lawrence intensively interviewed these subjects and compared them with two other groups — a group of doctoral students in philosophy in a major state university and a group of ninth-graders in a liberal, middle-class suburb. In contrast to the philosophy students and the ninth graders, the Fundamentalist seminarians reported that they responded to the DIT in terms of their religious beliefs. Many reported they saw the task of taking the DIT in terms of figuring out which religious precept applied to each dilemma, and then discounting all other considerations. Their low P scores were due to their refusal to consider any item that did not have a religious or law-and-order overtone. In an independent test of the *capacity* to understand moral concepts, Lawrence found that the Fundamentalist seminarians scored in between the philosophy graduate students and the ninth graders (as one might expect from their general educational background): The philosophers had a comprehension score of 79%, the seminarians 62%, and the ninth graders 46%. However, in *using* concepts in making moral decisions, the seminarians were lowest in use of principled concepts (Stages 5 and 6): The philosophers had a P% score of 57, the seminarians 22, and the ninth graders 31. Therefore, both from the pattern of test scores and from the interviews about the processes used to take the DIT, ideological commitments were overriding considerations of conceptual adequacy for the Fundamentalist seminarians in making moral judgments.

A number of empirical studies would be interesting to do on this issue. If longitudinal data were available on members of more traditional groups, would their development reflect slower advance, or average development up to a certain point, then a premature plateau; or would there be some "overshooting" in young adulthood (i.e., reaching high scores) then a return to the cultural norm? Do members of conservative groups have low P scores on all kinds of dilemmas, or only on those issues which their ideology addresses? Can closer specification be made of the effective environmental variables that constitute an "intellectual milieu," and can they be measured for individual subjects? Do college graduates from the South have lower P scores when they move out of the South and are compared with non-Southern college graduates?

Other research on the relation of religious affiliation to moral judgment has not studied subjects in a particular congregation and the educational materials used in that church, as did Ernsberger. Usually, such studies have examined a collection of subjects available through some other connection than their church affiliation, and asked the subjects about their denominational affiliation and perhaps their degree of participation.[4] Hence, in these studies, members of different congregations are pooled, and there is no assurance that these subjects are representative of their congregations. In contrast, Ernsberger obtained a random sample and a selection of highly involved lay leaders to represent the specific congregations, and he had specific information on the intellectual milieu of those congregations. Ernsberger's study shows clearly that church affiliation bears a complex relationship with DIT scores in that church affiliation may be associated with high or low DIT scores, depending on the intellectual milieu of a particular church. Rather than dismissing religious affiliation as not related to moral judgment, researchers may find many interesting studies in this area.

Socioeconomic Status

There is less information on SES than for other variables. Table 5.7 lists samples identified as one or another SES category. Among ninth and twelfth grade samples classified according to SES level, there seems to be a slight tendency for higher SES groups to have a higher average DIT score. These data are imprecise, however.

Several individual studies contained measures of SES for individual subjects, and report correlations with DIT scores. Cauble (1976) used Hollingshead's two-factor index of SES for the families of college stu-

Table 5.7. Average P% of Different SES Groups

Education Level	Lower Middle SES P% Sample		Middle SES P% Sample		Upper Middle SES P% Sample	
Ninth graders	23.6	(McColgan 1975)	23.5	(Morrison, Toews, Rest 1975)		
	17.2	(McColgan 1975)	20.3	(Morrison, Toews, Rest 1975)		
	19.9	(Rest, Ahlgren, Mackey 1973)	30.2	(Rest et al. 1974)		
	22.6	(Rest, Ahlgren, Mackey 1973)	20.5	(Yussen 1976)		
Twelfth graders	18.9	(McColgan 1975)	36.0	(Guttenberg 1975)	44.0	(Balfour 1975)
			25.0	(Yussen 1976)	37.7	(Balfour 1975)
					33.0	(Guttenberg 1975)
					39.7	(Masanz 1975)

dents and found a correlation of .35 (n = 90) with the DIT. Coder (1975) also used Hollingshead's index on an adult sample and obtained a correlation with the DIT of .38 (n = 21). However, since educational level is a major determinant of Hollingshead's index and the adult's own SES, and not that of their parents, was measured in the Coder study (as in the other studies), this correlation of SES with DIT indicates essentially the same thing as the relation of education and the DIT. Crowder (1976) found a correlation of −.09 with Hollingshead's index on 58 adult volunteers from a Naval base. McColgan (1975) used the Duncan Scale of father's occupation as an index of SES, and obtained a correlation of .11 for delinquent boys and .19 for pre-delinquent and control group boys. Since the range of SES was not very large in McColgan's samples, these correlations may be attenuated. Rest et al. (1974) found a correlation of .02 using the Duncan index for junior highs and a correlation of .17 with father's or mother's education.

In summary, SES has not been a consistent or powerful correlate of the DIT. However, the data have been only incidentally collected. Most studies try to control for SES. A thorough study has not been done in which the full range of SES is studied while other variables are controlled or treated as covariates.

Sex

Recently the charge of sex-bias in Kohlbergian moral judgment assessment (Holstein 1976) has drawn much attention to the sex variable. In DIT research, 22 studies assessing sex differences were reviewed in Rest 1976, and only two had a significant difference in P score between males and females. As Table 5.8 indicates, even in those two studies only about 6% of the variance is accounted for by the sex variable. In both of those studies, females had higher scores. In DIT research, sex differences are rarely significant in junior high, senior high, college, and graduate students or adults. So it is not even true that at one age one sex has an advantage and at another age the other sex does. Whenever sex differences do occur, the influence of other variables, such as IQ, education, or SES should be checked.

The current attention given to the sex variable in moral judgment research is less warranted by the evidence (sex is not a powerful variable) than by the current concern in society about sex discrimination. Nevertheless, the charge of sex bias in moral judgment assessment is based on not very cogent arguments and on ambiguous evidence.

One argument that Holstein (1976) makes is that studies show (e.g., Haan, Smith, and Block, 1968; Holstein 1976) that females

are disproportionately scored Stage 3 and males are disproportionately scored Stage 4, thus showing a bias in scoring males higher.
Three counterarguments address this point. The first is that even in
the studies cited, the sex differences are not that striking or consistent. Holstein states, "Haan et al. (1968) found, in a study of several
hundred university students, that the majority of females were mo-
dally Stage 3, with 4 the next largest category . . . . " But examining
the data in the tables reported by Haan, et al. shows that 41% of the
females were Stage 3 and 39% were Stage 4, in contrast to 22% males
at Stage 3 and 43% males at Stage 4 — this is hardly evidence that

Table 5.8. Relations of DIT to Sex of Subject

Study	Sample	Statistic	Significance	Male or Female Higher
Allen & Kickbush (1976)	430 ninth graders	$r = -.05$	NS	—
Blackner (1975)	160 youth and adults	$F = 1.6$	NS	—
Bransford (1973)	85 college freshmen, sophomores, juniors	NA	NS	—
	60 college seniors	NA	NS	—
Cauble (1976)	90 college students	$r = -.13$	NS	—
Coder (1975)	87 adults aged 24-49	$t = .82$	NS	—
Dortzbach (1976)	185 adults aged 25-75	$t = .62$	NS	—
Johnson (1974)	66 Lutheran high school subjects in Phila- delphia, Pa.	$F = .64$	NS	—
McGeorge (1975)	140 3 year teachers	NA	NS	—
Morrison, Toews, & Rest (1973)	72 ninth graders	$r = .17$	NS	—
Rest, et al. (1974)	73 ninth graders	$r = .25$	$p < .03$	F
	40 twelfth graders	$r = .16$	NS	—
	40 college students	$r = -.12$	NS	—
Rest (1975)	88 students ages 14-18 (1972 testing)	$t = 1.95$	NS	—
	88 students ages 16-20 (1974 testing)	$t = 1.12$	NS	—
Schneeweis (1974)	64 high school students	NA	NS	—
Schomberg (1978)	411 college students	$r = .25$	$p < .01$	F
Schomberg & Balkcum (1976)	63 college students at Univ. of Minnesota	$t = .90$	NS	—
Schomberg & Nelson (1976)	29 seminarians	$t = -.80$	NS	—
Troth (1974)	47 college students	$r = .12$	NS	—
Yussen (1976)	120 mixed students	NA	NS	—

NS = nonsignificant; NA = not available

Stage 3 is a "female" stage and Stage 4 is a "male" stage. In Holstein's own study, the fathers were significantly higher in moral maturity score than mothers at one time, but not significantly higher ($p < .10$) at another time.

Second, Holstein gives the false impression that sex differences are consistently found in studies using Kohlberg's measure ("the distribution of scores for our sample and the sex differences found are consistent with those found in earlier studies . . . , " p. 26, 57), but this is not the case. Keasey (1972), in an article entitled, "The lack of sex differences in moral judgments of preadolescents," found no differences, as was the case in other studies (Blatt and Kohlberg 1975; Weisbroth 1970). Holstein did not do a thorough literature review, but picked examples that seemed to fit her conclusion. To do a review of studies using the Kohlberg test on sex differences would be difficult, since most studies have not attended to the sex variable, and also since comparisons between studies are difficult in that the Kohlberg test has so many different versions. Nevertheless, the Kohlberg test does not show consistent sex differences, and it is clear that the DIT studies consistently show hardly any differences.

Third, let us examine the logic of inferring that an instrument is biased if sex differences are evident. If it is found that males as a group are taller than females, does this imply a sex bias in the foot ruler? Is the measurement instrument necessarily biased because of differences between groups? There may actually be differences between groups, and one cannot assume that the differences are due solely to measurement defects. In the case of moral judgment, it is possible that men in our society at the present time may be more sophisticated in moral thinking than women because the *biases in society* foster the difference. Currently, men earn more money than women, but this does not imply that the method of counting dollars is biased; it could, however, represent a bias elsewhere. In samples where differences between sexes do occur, differences in educational opportunities, intellectual milieu, and IQ should be checked before assuming that the moral judgment measurement is sex biased.

A second argument that Holstein makes is that Kohlbergian moral judgment assessment is biased because the *pattern of correlations* is different for males than for females. A counterargument resembles the counterargument above: Group differences don't necessarily imply instrument defects. If the correlation of physical height with age is different for females than for males, this does not prove a bias in the foot-ruler. It suggests a phenomenon to study—that is, why do females begin their growth spurt in adolescence before males? Similarly if Stage 3 females are more liberal than Stage 3 males, why is this so? Many causes are possible.

Another charge that Holstein makes (1976, p. 60) is that Kohlberg is a man, his dissertation and longitudinal studies have focused on men, and that all the decision makers in his dilemmas are men, hence creating a male bias. These observations can at most establish how a sex bias could have come into Kohlberg's system; they do not establish or prove a bias. One might point out, moreover, that Kohlberg's female colleagues have played a major role in redefining the scoring system for the past eight years, and that many studies have collected information from females.

Lastly, Holstein argues that Kohlberg's stages are sexist because they highlight the cognitive side of moral decision-making and not the sentiments of compassion, sympathy, and love. Holstein states:

> One of the hallmarks of Stage 3 reasoning is a stress on compassion, sympathy, or love as a reason for moral action. Another hallmark of Stage 3 is a concern for the approval of others, especially those in the primary group. This latter emphasis "catches" children's reasoning. But at the same time, the Stage 3 emphasis on sympathy, so stereotypically part of the female role, is characteristic of much female moral reasoning in the present study .... Emotional response to moral conflict which is exemplified by females more than males results in adult female reasoning being categorized with children's. (p. 60, 61)

There are two implications in this argument: One, that because so many female adults in our present society think in a certain way, such thinking ought to be considered mature; second, that a scale of moral judgment ought to reflect the degree of compassion, sympathy, or love that a person has. Both implications show fundamental misconceptions of the cognitive developmental approach. The higher stages of moral judgment are called "higher" not because they represent some kind of stereotypical norm for adults, but because they are better conceptual tools for solving social problems (See Chapter 2). The function of moral judgment is to provide direction for people's cooperative interaction. Certainly the sentiments of compassion, sympathy, and love are relevant, and the realization of their relevance is the distinctive accomplishment of Stage 3. However, other considerations are also relevant, and to solve some kinds of moral problems, one needs to have conceptions of to whom one owes how much sympathy and how to decide between unavoidable conflicts of sympathy. For these latter considerations, Stage 3 thinking does not provide very clear directives and it is Stage 4 and higher that provide direction. If, therefore, culturally stereotyped female thinking is indeed

Stage 3, this fact does not overcome the conceptual inadequacies of Stage 3 in dealing with problems that involve conflicts in sympathies (or any of the other problems that only higher stages can handle). Holstein's contention that Kohlberg's system scores some adult thinking as equivalent to children's thinking, therefore, misses the point about the basis for ordering the stages. What Holstein must do is to present a theoretical analysis on how stereotypical female thinking at Stage 3 provides a rationale for solving complex social and moral problems, a rationale that is better than children's thinking or the thinking currently scored as Stages 4, 5 and 6. This, of course, has not been done.

In addition to the misunderstanding of the basis for claiming one stage is more adequate than another, there is misunderstanding in Holstein's argument about the kind of construct or the psychological variable that moral judgment is. Moral judgment is not intended to be a rating scale of compassion or kindness, or self-sacrifice. It is an assessment of the adequacy of conceptualizing solutions to moral problems. Research has not yet established whether people with sophisticated moral judgment also contribute more to charity, are warmer and nicer to small children, volunteer more often for suicide missions, or show up on time for appointments. All these things go into our estimation of a person as a total human being, but they should not be confused with one's moral judgment development.

In summary, the possibility that a Kohlberg-type scheme is sexist certainly is worthy of exploration, but the evidence to date and the arguments put forward hardly make a case.

Other Sample Characteristics

Another characteristic that might account for some of the variance in the samples is vocation or academic major in school. The patterning of this variable with DIT scores is not clear. In a pilot study by Gallia (1976), humanities undergraduates were more advanced than science majors (and this was the only study attempted to equate the students on other variables); however, these trends are somewhat reversed in the Schomberg (1975) study (who found engineers higher than majors in liberal arts or agriculture), and there does not seem to be a clear pattern of academic major with DIT in Bransford's (1973) study (comparing music-art, social science, natural science, and religion majors). McGeorge (1976) found that the college major in his sample showed significant differences, $F(4, 139) = 25.4, p < .05$, with majors in physical education and the social sciences having lower DIT scores than English or science majors, with music and art majors in between.

Intuitively it makes sense that moral judgment development might be enhanced by certain college majors and professions and not enhanced by others in which attention is on other matters—but the evidence is unclear as yet and the patterns that have been obtained are difficult to interpret.

The criminality-delinquency dimension also seems to account for lower than average scores. McColgan (1975) compared delinquents, predelinquents, and matched controls, and found the nondelinquents to score higher than the delinquents on the P index (this study will be discussed in more detail in Chapter 6). Kantner (1975) reports an average P% of 23.5 in 78 adult prisoners (in general, the average for adults in 40.0); Armstrong (1975) reports P scores of 31.2 and 33.3 for prison inmates and prison parolees, respectively.

Another variable that has been considered is membership in a political party. Coder (1975) found nonsignificant differences between Democrats (P = 45), Independents (P = 48), and Republicans (P = 40); whereas Dortzbach (1975) found striking differences: Democrats (P = 40.1), Independents (P = 47.5), and Republicans (P = 30.9). Perhaps the inconsistency in the two studies can be explained by the fact that Coder's subjects constituted a self-selected group in a church, and their common membership in the church may have been more significant than their differences in political party affiliation. On the other hand, Dortzbach's subjects were chosen at random from voter registration lists of a community, and therefore all these subjects were not in a single organization providing a common intellectual milieu. Another consideration, however, when examining the impact of political party affiliation, is that both major political parties embrace a broad spectrum of points of view and that subgroup identification within a party (the liberal wing, conservative wing) may be more highly correlated with moral judgment than party affiliation itself. To add to the complexity, G. Rest (1977) found a significant *curvilinear* relationship of P with political party among 43 adults randomly selected from the Minneapolis phone book—that is, middle values of P were more closely related to affiliation with the Republican party, whereas low P scores and high P scores were more related to the Democratic Party. G. Rest did not find any relationship (linear or curvilinear) of political party with P in a group of 77 college freshmen at the University of Michigan, Ann Arbor.

Education shows the most consistent and powerful relationship to the DIT of the demographic variables examined here. Age is related to the DIT for student groups but not for adult groups. There is suggestive evidence that intellectual milieu, as indicated by region of the country and religious membership (assessed at the individual congregation level, not denomination), is associated with moral judgment. SES, political party, type of residence, profession, or college major do not have clear and consistent relationships, and more research is warranted. Sex has a consistent nonsignificant or low correlation with the DIT.

These are the variables that researchers in the social sciences typically attend to in selecting a sample for a study or in interpreting the study. The information in this review should be of help to researchers planning to use the DIT in future studies or in trying to compare one study with another.

Demographic variables have special value in the exploration of moral judgment because these measures are well known and their measurement operations are straightforward. It is well worth the effort to check out a measure of moral judgment against these more familiar variables. Theoretically, however, demographic variables are surrogate variables, representing some psychological process or construct indirectly. Age and education (as discussed here) are indirect indicators of general cognitive development. Sex, SES, political party, religious affiliation, college major, and so on, all indirectly represent different life experiences and opportunities or different individual traits (and, this review suggests, do not represent them very clearly). In order to advance our knowledge of moral judgment, other studies of psychological variables must be conducted. This necessitates theoretically identifying the psychological constructs and measuring them, but devising a new variable means leaving out the old reliable, easily collected variables. The discussion of these studies will be the topic of Chapter 6.

Longitudinal Studies

Following the same individuals over time and retesting them at periodic intervals provides the most direct evidence of whether there, is change in the direction postulated by the theory (as discussed in Chapter 2). Since the first studies on the DIT were conducted in 1971-72, we have been able to follow subjects for only a short time, but several groups have been tested over two-year and four-year intervals. A two-year interval is a rather short span in moral judgment research, considering that subjects on the average take over five and one-half years to move one full stage in Kohlberg's longitudinal data (1975), and that the youngest subjects in DIT research are 13 to 14 years old and hence have already moved through the years of most rapid development. Kohlberg has chosen a three- to four-year interval for his own longitudinal study, but a two-year interval seemed to me to be about the smallest time span likely to pick up change without doing so much testing that subjects would get tired of participating.

What kind of evidence counts for directional change? In Chapter 3 I argued at some length that it is inappropriate to regard subjects as "in" this stage or that stage: rather, the appropriate diagnostic question is "To what extent and under what conditions does a subject's thinking exhibit the various logical types of thinking?" Therefore the question of directional change should *not* be, "Did the subject move to the next stage?" This way of construing the question assumes that change can be described as a "step by step" phenomenon. Change is more appropriately construed as a shifting distribution of responses across the various stages, with some stages gaining and other stages diminishing in usage. Evidence of directional change, therefore, is based on whether or not the scores of the higher stage ("higher" defined in terms of the theoretical scheme of advancement) increase at the expense of the lower stages. For instance, if over time a subject's Stage 2 score decreases and his Stage 5 score increases, that counts as evidence for directional (upward) change. If, however, his Stage 5 score decreases and Stage 3 score increases, that is downward change, against the direction postulated by theory.

In the cross-sectional studies, it seemed that the P index was a good single score indicator for a subject's whole distribution of responses. For instance, examination of Table 5.1 shows that information about the whole distribution of scores is quite well reflected in the P index. For that reason (and others, discussed at length in Chapter 4), analyses for the past five years have used the P index alone. However, in the course of more detailed analyses of the whole distribution of stage scores on longitudinal data, and with Davison's analyses (discussed in Chapter 8), it has become evident that the P index sometimes underestimates developmental change. Therefore, our longitudinal results will be presented first in terms of P index changes (which is the simplest and most comparable with the cross-sectional data), and second in terms of distributional comparisons of each stage (which proves more sensitive to lower stage change). Third, in Chapter 8, Davison shows how his new index, D, combines the convenience of a single score with the sensitivity of the distributional analyses.

The junior high and senior high subjects presented in Table 5.1, first tested in 1972, were tested again in 1974 and 1976. These subjects were from schools in urban St. Paul; SES and IQ data showed the sample was in the middle range of both measures (Rest et al. 1974); there were equal numbers of males and females. The first testing included 59 junior high students (hereafter, "Group J") and 74 senior high students (hereafter, "Group S"); the second testing included 50 subjects from Group J and 38 from Group S; the third testing included 31 subjects in J and 23 in S.

Group and Subgroup Averages

A simple question to put to this longitudinal data is whether it corroborates the age trends in the cross-sectional data. The simple answer is, yes. Looking at the P scores over the four-year span (the most comparable interval to the four education levels used in the cross-sectional data), the average P score for the 54 subjects tested all three times in 1972, 1974, and 1976 was 33, 40, and 44, respectively. The 11 point gain over 4 years is comparable to that between high school and college in the cross-sectional study, Table 5.2. Analysis of variance produced an F-ratio of 20.1, $p < .0001$. Group J and S each increased significantly ($F = 11.1$ and 14.0, respectively). Over the four years, 72% of the subjects increased on the P index. Furthermore, as will be discussed in Chapter 6, subjects increased significantly also on other independent measures of moral comprehension and of moral-political values, corroborating a pervasive and systematic shift in moral thinking.

Preliminary analyses of 1978 testings (not yet completed) indicate that the fourth testing of Groups J and S continues the trends in the first three testings. P scores continue to increase for the 41 subjects tested in both 1976 and 1978: from an average of 42.6 to 47.3 ($t = 2.96$, $p < .005$). Over the 6 years between 1972 to 1978 these subjects increased on the P score at every two-year interval ($F = 17.6$, $p < .0001$).

All subjects, however, did not change in the same way or at the same time, and the remaining analyses of the longitudinal data give a more detailed and complex account of change over time. Breaking the sample down into subgroups at two year intervals, we have the five subgroups given in Figure 5.1. Group Ja comprises those subjects originally in Group J who were tested all three times in 1972, 1974, and 1976; whereas group Ja and b includes the additional subjects who were tested in 1972 and 1974 but were not available in 1976. The designations are similar for Groups Sa and Sa and b. Group W consists of subjects originally tested by Wilson (1975) as high school seniors in 1974 in a small upstate community in Minnesota. We re-

Subgroup Stages Changes Over Two Years

Group	Ages	n	STAGE CHANGE			
			2	3	4	P
Ja + b	14 - 16	50	↓	↓	↑	↑
Ja	16 - 18	31	—	—	↓	↑
Sa + b	17 - 19	38	↓	↓	↓	↑
Sa	19 - 21	23	—	—	—	—
W	18 - 20	21	↓	↓	↑	↑

Figure 5.1

tested them in 1976 to increase the size and diversity of our longitudinal information. The ages of each subgroup are given at the first and second testing. Changes in each stage are indicated: If scores of a stage increased significantly over the two-year period, a large upward arrow is shown; if the scores decreased significantly, a large downward arrow is shown; a small arrow indicates a trend that did not reach statistical significance; a dash indicates no trend upward or downward. Figure 5.1 shows that Group J between 14 and 16 years decreased significantly on Stages 2 and 3, and increased significantly on Stage 4 and P; then between 16 and 18 years it decreased on Stage 4 and increased on P.[5] Note that between ages 14 and 16, Group J is still shifting from the preconventional stages into the conventional stage; but between 16 and 18 years, Group J is shifting from conventional to principled moral thinking. Group S between the ages of 19 and 21 did not show any average movement in any stage. Group W showed only significant changes in Stage 3, with slight, but nonsignificant upward trends in Stage 4 and P. As Davison will detail in Chapter 8, the P index was insensitive to Group W changes (as it was also to some degree in Group J between ages 14 and 16), and these shifts are represented better by the D score.

Individual Patterns of Change

An even finer analysis can be done by looking at the stage distribution of individual subjects. That is, each subject has scores at Stages 2, 3, 4, and P—what shifts are there over the two-year periods in individual subjects? The analyses of group averages above do not convey information about how many subjects were involved in a group trend, or whether the lack of a group trend is due to several contradictory trends that cancel each other out. Analyses of individual subjects give this kind of information. In these analyses, two decisions were made: One was based on the recognition that the scores have a margin of measurement error in them, especially in interpreting individual scores, and therefore we should not overinterpret just *any* change in an individual's scores. Instead, we only count those changes that exceed the average margin of measurement error. We have an estimate of measurement error from test-retest correlations (given more fully in Chapter 8). Using these correlations for each stage score, the formula $s\sqrt{1-r^2}$ was used (where s is the standard deviation of the score at the first testing, and r^2 is the square of the test-retest correlation), giving the following margins: for Stage 2, the difference between longitudinal testing must exceed 6 points to be considered real change; for Stage 3, 8 points; for Stage 4, 10 points; and for P, 9 points.

The second decision was in analyzing individual change patterns into five basic types, namely, upward change, downward change, no change, ambiguous change, and bidirectional change. An upward change pattern is one that shows gains in higher stages at the expense of lower stages; for example, a gain in P, loss in Stage 4 (designated "P/4"—stages before the slash show gains, stages after the slash show losses). Other examples of upward patterns are gains in Stage 4, losses in Stage 2 (4/2); or a gain in P with nonsignificant losses in the lower stages (P/—); and also, P/4,2; 3/2; —/2; etc. (see Rest 1975 for list of change patterns in that study). A downward change pattern is the opposite, as for instance, 4/P; 4,2/P; 2/3; 2/—; etc. A no change pattern is, of course, one in which no stage change exceeded the minimum margin of measurement error (—/—). An ambiguous change pattern is one in which the middle stages either gain or lose without significant losses or gains in the higher or lower stages (4/—, 3/—, —/4, —/3). A bidirectional change pattern is one in which the high and low stage both show gains or losses (P, 2/4; 4, 2/3; —/P, 2; P, 3/4).

Table 5.9 shows the percentages of subjects in the upward and downward change groups over the two-year and four-year periods. There is a much greater trend upward than downward, and the trend over four years is greater than over two years. Whereas the ratio of upward movement to downward is about 3.5 to 1 over the two-year interval, the ratio over the four-year interval is about 9.4 to 1. (The percentages of upward and downward movement do not add up to

100% because there are some subjects with no change, bidirectional change, or ambiguous change patterns—see Rest 1975 for more complete description.) Clearly an upward trend is predominant in individual change patterns. In the subgroup Sa between 19 and 21 years, 39% of the subjects had upward movements and 39% had downward movements; however, the amounts of change in most of these cases was only barely above the minimum. Actually, there was more stability in Group Sa than the upward and downward percentages would suggest; the correlation of P scores over this two-year period was .74, and the means were not significantly different.

Another longitudinal study using the DIT by McGeorge (1977) reported nonsignificant gains over two years (average P% = 42.7 and 44.2, respectively) of subjects in a New Zealand teacher's certificate program. Since no other data are available, analyses of the type performed on samples J, S, and W are not possible (analyses of stage score shifts, individual change patterns, and D score changes). Furthermore, it may be that as subjects pass the adult average P score (40.0), development may be slower and more difficult, and a two-year interval may be too short to pick up development (as also suggested by sample Sa between ages 19 and 21). Although development in adulthood is less striking than in student populations, educational interventions by Coder (1975) and Panowitsch (1975) indicate development does occur in some adults.

Table 5.9. Individual Pattern Changes Within Subgroups

Group	Ages	n	Percent Subjects Moving Up	Percent Subjects Moving Down
		Two-Year Interval		
Ja & b	14-16	50	52	12
Ja	16-18	31	52	16
Sa & b	17-19	38	66	5
Sa	19-21	23	39	39
W	18-20	21	48	14
			Average up = 53%	Average down = 15%
		Four-Year Interval		
Ja	14-18	31	68	6
Sa	17-21	23	63	8
			Average up = 66%	Average down = 7%

Comparisons with Kohlbergian Studies

It is of interest to compare these results with longitudinal studies of moral judgment using Kohlberg's test. I am aware of five completed sets of longitudinal data that have used earlier versions (pre-1978) of Kohlberg's scoring system. These studies are summarized in Table 5.10. The table shows that results from Kohlberg's test and the DIT are comparable: The predominant trend is upward, with a few reversals in each case; the trends are stronger with longer time intervals between testings. The Kohlberg studies, most comparable to DIT studies, are the high school groups in the Kramer and Holstein studies, with 42% and 63% of the subjects moving up over three years, respectively, compared with 66% of Groups J and S on the DIT over four years. In the Kohlberg data, subjects at the adult level or in college seem to slow down or plateau in development, as is also suggested in the DIT data.

In addition to these studies, Colby (1979) has given a preliminary report of a longitudinal study using the recent scoring system (Kohlberg, et al. 1978). The data come from 58 cases of American boys originally tested in Kohlberg's dissertation (1958) and followed up since then at three- to four-year intervals. Ten longitudinal cases in

Table 5.10. Upward and Downward Movement in Kohlbergian Longitudinal Studies

Study	Time interval between testings	Age of Subjects	No. of cases	Percentage moving up	Percentage moving down	Ratio of Up to Down movement
Kramer (1968)	3 years	High School	24	42	17	2.5 to 1
	3 years	College	19	21	16	1.3 to 1
Blatt and Kohlberg (1975)	1 year*	12-13 years	10	20	60	1.0 to 3
Holstein (1976)	3 years	High school	52	63	6	10.5 to 1
	3 years	Adults	97	29	18	1.6 to 1
Kuhn (1976)	1/2 year	5-8 years	100	44	24	1.8 to 1
	1 year	5-8 years	50	64	10	6.4 to 1
White, et al. (1978)	1 year	8-17 years	242	47	21	2.2 to 1
	2 years	8-17 years	86	87	8	10.9 to 1
		Average:		50.2	17.7	

*Experimental subjects in Study 1; comparison between posttest and one-year follow-up.

the American sample and three cases in the Turkish sample were used to develop the 1978 scoring system, making adjustments in scoring criteria and scoring rules so as to minimize stage mixture and maximize the patterns of sequential movement through the stages. Then the remaining cases were scored blind (as to subject identification and the year of testing) using the scoring system as developed on the previous cases. The results are spectacular. Every subject shows some movement, and it is almost invariably upward. In 193 instances of retesting, there are only 16 instances of backward movement, and 133 instances of upward movement (69%). Almost always the change is not a full stage change (for example, Stage 2 to Stage 3; Stage 3 to Stage 4) but is rather a partial stage change (Stage 3[2] to Stage 3 [4]). Subjects do not ever skip a stage. The ratio of upward movement to downward movement is 8.3 to 1, comparable to that found in the DIT over a four-year interval (9.4 to 1). In all these longitudinal studies, a few subjects have moved backwards, but a few reversals seem to show up in any longitudinal study—for instance, reversals occur in longitudinal studies of Piagetian conservations (Almy, Chittenden and Miller 1966, p. 91; Benson 1966, Appendix B; Wohlwill, Devoe and Fusaro 1971), and in longitudinal studies of Formal Operations (Neimark, 1975).

Longitudinal Change and College Attendance. In examining the individuals tested on the DIT three times (in 1972, 1974, and 1976), subjects who showed upward patterns in one interval tended not to show upward patterns in the other. Only 17% of the subjects showed upward patterns both times, and 63% of the subjects showed upward patterns one time or the other, but not both times. Therefore the picture is not one of even, steady growth by all subjects each year, but one of more erratic growth. The question arises, can we account for the conditions in which growth occurs?

This question will be taken up at greater length in Chapter 7, dealing with experimental and educational interventions designed to bring about change. At this point we will consider the special condition of education (more specifically, going to college) as a factor associated with longitudinal change. Education has been such a strong correlate of DIT scores in the cross-sectional data that we would expect it to be a factor also in longitudinal data—but with this qualification: The range of educational variation in the cross-sectional data ran from grade school to graduate school, whereas the range of education assessed in the longitudinal data is much narrower.

In 1975 the picture seemed quite clear (see Rest 1975). Group S included subjects who had gone to college and those who had not. In high school (1972), both subgroups were indistinguishable on the P index. Two years later (1974), the college-bound subjects had increased twice as much as the noncollege group (see Table 5.11), producing a significant difference between the groups, $t(30) = 2.42$, $p < .022$. The effects of education seemed clear and dramatic. In group S at the third testing, the difference between the college group and the noncollege subgroup was even greater: $p = 52.1$ for the college group and $p = 35.9$ for the noncollege group, again statistically significant.

Other groups of subjects that we have studied since, however, have not followed the pattern of Group S. As Table 5.11 shows, Group J showed about equal gains between 1974 and 1976 in both college-bound and noncollege subjects. Although the Group J college group had had less than a year of college at this time (attenuating the contrast), nevertheless, the noncollege group was far ahead of the Group S noncollege group. Perhaps young people not going to college in 1975 (Group J) are different from those not going to college in 1972 (Group S). Some high school teachers say that by 1975 word had gotten around in the high schools that there was much unemployment among college graduates, and perhaps this shifted the type of student not going to college. But we cannot tell if there was anything special about the Group J noncollege group.

Group W showed still another pattern. As seniors in high school, the college-bound students had much higher P scores than the noncollege group. Then two years later, the college group had essentially remained at that level, but the noncollege group made up some of the difference between the groups but still were not up to the college level.

It now appears that students having one or two years of college do not always show more gains than subjects not going to college. Cer-

Table 5.11. Two-Year Changes in College and Noncollege Groups on the P Index

Group	n	College-bound		n	Noncollege	
		High School Testing	Two Years Later		High School Testing	Two Years Later
S	15	32.7	48.2	18	29.5	36.8
J	23	36.0	43.9	8	36.9	42.3
W	11	42.0	39.2	10	25.0	34.4
Average	49	36.3	44.2	36	29.9	37.4

tainly we will want to follow up our longitudinal groups to see if more years of college produce the effects that were evident in Group S. Then too, we must admit that the factor of "going to college' is a rough characterization of developmental conditions. Colleges differ, and student experiences within the same college differ. People not attending college have growth experiences, too. In Chapter 7 we will see that some educational experiences facilitate change in moral judgment and others do not. In future longitudinal studies, we will want a more fine-grained characterization of experiences than that a person attended or did not attend a college. Further, it may be that as subjects approach the adult average P score (around 40), increases may be slower and more difficult. It would be interesting to have in a longitudinal sample some subjects who eventually become moral philosophers or political scientists, so that we could chart the course by which they attained P scores in the 60s and 70s. With most subjects, however, we can probably expect a plateau effect as they reach the adult norm.

Problems with Cross-Sectional and Longitudinal Designs and Sequential, Bifactorial Analyses

Some authors, most notably Baltes (1968; Baltes and Nesselroade, 1972) and Schaie (1965; 1970; Schaie, Labouvie, and Buech 1973; Schaie and Labouvie-Vief, 1974) have pointed out inherent problems in all cross-sectional and longitudinal studies. The basic difficulty comes in inferring that *individual* or *ontogenetic* change has taken place when there appear to be age trends in cross-sectional or longitudinal data, because such trends can be caused by a variety of factors.

Problems in interpreting cross-sectional data were cited in relation to DIT studies (Chapter 5, pp. 107-8). Admittedly, the student groups probably differ from each other in terms of IQ, interests, and education as well as age, so we cannot claim that difference in moral judgment of the student groups are solely due to age differences. (Recall however that the groups could still be regarded as "criterion groups", expected to differ because of a number of factors.) In general the problem of inferring ontogenetic change from any cross-sectional study is the questionable comparability of the populations from which the age groups are sampled, for they may differ in respects other than age. Baltes and Schaie have been particularly concerned with noncomparability of samples due to generational differences; for instance, a group born in 1900 has had a different cultural and environmental history than a group born in 1950, and therefore the two groups differ not only in age but also in the developmental tracks along which they change. This complication was discussed (p. 111) in connection with Dortzbach's study, in which adults aged 65 to 74 had lower DIT scores than adults aged 30 to 34. The short-comings of cross-sectional studies have already been discussed.

In contrast to cross-sectional studies, longitudinal studies control for sample comparability by using the same subjects at different times, and longitudinal data are superior in this regard. However, longitudinal studies are not without problems. The difference in scores between testings cannot be interpreted as unambiguously reflecting ontogenetic change because of possible testing effects, sampling biases, and generational effects. Let us consider each of these problems, in turn. 1. *Testing effects* can influence scores in a variety of ways; for instance, subjects who take a test repeatedly may show higher scores owing to practice, or may show lower scores because of boredom with the test, or scores may fail to reflect true change owing to habituating to answering the test in a certain way. Testing effects seem to have been a problem in previous moral judgment research using Kohlberg's test, in that the control groups in several studies show a drop in test scores over a short period of time (Blatt and Kohlberg 1975; Turiel 1966), suggesting a boredom or fatigue effect with retesting. Another kind of testing effect to which an interview test is vulnerable is noncomparability of interviewing. For instance, if interviewers change over the duration of a longitudinal study, test scores may reflect interviewer change rather than ontogenetic change. While it is true that *scoring* of interview data can be checked for bias by arranging for all scoring after all data are in, there is no check on bias in the interview itself, except with dual independent interviewers (which has never been done). If interviewers push subjects harder for elaboration at one testing, chances are that the scores will be higher than at the other testings. In the longitudinal study by White et al. (1978), the average cross lag cohort difference was 1.4 moral judgment units (the difference in moral judgment scores between different samples of subjects at the same age—for example, 10-year-olds in 1974 compared with 10-year-olds in 1976), whereas the average longitudinal difference was only slightly greater than this, at 1.6 (the difference between 10-year-olds tested in 1974 and the same subjects retested in 1976 at 12 years old). The data show a huge time of testing effect and therefore we do not know to what degree the longitudinal change was actually due to systematic testing effects in interviewing style between 1974 and 1976.

2. *Sampling biases* can affect the interpretation of longitudinal studies also. Baltes (1968, p. 150) cites research that suggests that subjects who volunteer for longitudinal studies tend to be of higher average intelligence and of a higher socioeconomic class. Such selective sampling impairs the ability to generalize the longitudinal findings. Another related problem is that during the course of a longitudinal study, some subjects drop out. If the subjects who drop out are not random, but have some common characteristic that is correlated with moral judgment development (they are bored to talk or think about morality, or have such low scores to begin with that they have little investment in continuing to be tested), then the generalizability of results is also lessened.

3. *Generation effects* can affect the generalizability of a longitudinal study, just as it can invalidate a cross-sectional study. For instance, consider the subjects tested in Kohlberg's twenty-year longitudinal study initiated in the mid 1950s. Over the period in which these subjects have been assessed for moral judgment, Americans have experienced the Civil Rights struggle, the student protests, the Vietnam War, Watergate, and the Women's Movement. All of these events have raised issues of justice and have focused attention on moral concerns. It seems highly likely that these social events have had an impact on people's concepts of fairness. Changes in moral judgment scores over the past twenty years therefore reflect cultural change as well as individual ontogenesis. The pattern of longitudinal change in Kohlberg's sample probably would not be representative of 20-year-changes of subjects in drastically different cultural conditions—for instance of Americans living in an age of rabid Joe McCarthy conservatism. Whereas the internal validity of a longitudinal study is not challenged by generational or cultural effects (that is, the particular subjects studied really did move upward), its external validity is so challenged (possibly other subjects under different cultural circumstances would show downward movement, so that the longitudinal change is not conclusive evidence for individual ontogenetic change).

Even if we recognize these problems in cross-sectional and longitudinal studies, what can be done? Baltes and Schaie have been concerned primarily with generational effects; they recommend "sequential" designs that contain replications over time of longitudinal studies and/or cross-sectional studies, so that generational effects can be assessed along with age effects. In other words, they recommend two-factor analysis of variance designs in which the two factors are chosen from three factors: age of subject at testing, time of testing, year of birth of subject (see Baltes 1968; Schaie 1965; Wohlwill 1973, Chapter VII). The minimum sequential design consists of a 2 x 2 analysis of variance design in which two groups of subjects born in two different years are observed at two different age levels.

The basic strategy is to attempt to disentangle the separate effects of two factors through two-way analysis of variance. Recently critics of this strategy have challenged the adequacy of sequential designs. "The valuable contribution of Schaie and his colleagues in drawing attention to the effects of cohort must be realized, but it would seem that the sequential strategies recommended and employed by those researchers are incapable of yielding unequivocal interpretations of results." (Adam 1978, p. 1315; see also McCall 1977). Nevertheless, I shall report the results of several sequential analyses to show that even using the analyses recommended by Baltes and Schaie, there are no grounds for attributing longitudinal change in DIT data to generational effects.

Table 5.12 presents what Schaie calls a "cohort sequential" design, in which age of subject and cohort (year of birth) are the factors.

Table 5.12. Design for Cohort Sequential Analysis

Cohort (Year of birth)	16-18 years old	18-20 years old
1955	Sample S $n = 38$ (Tested in 1972)	Sample S $n = 38$ (Tested in 1974)
1956	Sample W $n = 21$ (Tested in 1974)	Sample W $n = 21$ (Tested in 1976)
1958	Sample J $n = 31$ (Tested in 1974)	Sample J $n = 31$ (Tested in 1976)

Table 5.13. F-Ratios for Cohort-Sequential Analysis.

	F-ratio	d.f.	p
Age effect	29.3	1,87	.0001
Cohort effect	1.2	2,87	.32,N.S.
Age X Cohort	3.6	2,87	.03

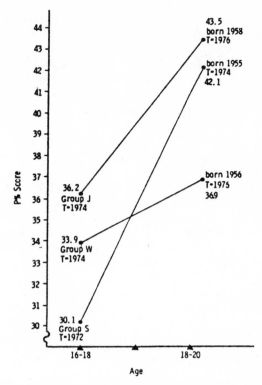

Figure 5.2. Cohort-sequential analysis. T = Time of testing.

Essentially, this design consists of three longitudinal studies (subjects first tested in high school, then two years later) of subjects born in three separate years. Of course testings at more ages is desirable, but this is the most data I have available for a two-factor design at present. Table 5.13 presents a summary of the analysis of variance.[6] As can be seen, a large significant main effect is present for age only, and no main effect for cohort. There is a weak interaction effect. Therefore, the age effect can hardly be construed as being caused by generational effects. Figure 5.2 shows that no systematic generational effects are present (i.e., neither the slopes of the lines nor their averages are systematically ordered by year of birth). Although generational effects may not be important, nevertheless, other sources of variability may be, since the three groups are not identical. The group differences could reflect individual differences in the makeup of these particular samples. Developmental theory does not predict that every individual at a particular age will have identical development, and we have seen from the composite samples (Table 5.2) that there is considerable individual variation. On the other hand, we note that all three groups show an increase over age. Whereas the average cohort difference is 4.1 (p% units), the average longitudinal change is 7.4 (p% units). In short, the cohort sequential analysis corroborates the cross-sectional data and the longitudinal data, that there is ontogenetic change on DIT, P scores.

Table 5.14 presents the design for what Schaie calls a "time sequential" analysis, in which age and time of testing are the two factors. This is essentially three cross-sectional studies reported previously as unifactorial analyses by Rest et al. (1974), Yussen (1976), and Martin et al. (1977). The actual times of testing were about two years prior to the publication dates given in Table 5.14. Table 5.15 presents a summary of the analysis of variance. As can be seen, there are significant main effects for both time of testing and age factors; nevertheless, the age factor is substantial on its own.

Table 5.14. Design for Time Sequential Analysis

Age	Rest et al. (1974)	Yussen (1976)	Martin et al. (1977)
		Time of Testing*	
14	Junior highs $n = 40$	Junior highs $n = 30$	Junior highs $n = 60$
17-18	Twelfth graders $n = 40$	Twelfth graders $n = 30$	Senior highs, average age = 17.8 $n = 200$
20-22	College juniors and seniors $n = 40$	College sophomores and juniors $n = 30$	College undergraduates average age = 20 $n = 105$

*Time of testing given in terms of the author of the study and publication dates when reported as unifactorial, cross-sectional studies. Actual time of testing was about two years before publication date for each study.

Table 5.15. F-Ratios for Time-Sequential Analysis

	F-ratio	d.f.	p
Age effect	80.1	2	.0001
Time of testing effect	10.6	2	.01
Age x time interaction	1.3	4	N.S.

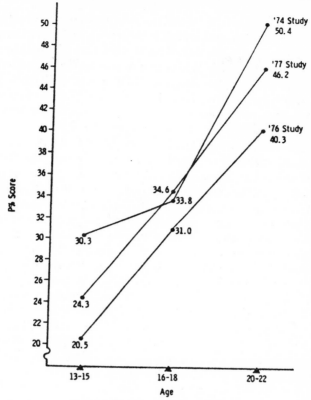

Figure 5.3. Time sequential analysis.

Figure 5.3 shows no systematic Time of Testing effects (i.e., neither the slopes of the lines nor their averages are systematically ordered by year of testing). Again, there are important cohort differences, but there is nothing to suggest that the age trends are due to generational effects.

In summary, the two sequential analyses (the cohort sequential and the time sequential) suggest that the age trends are not accountable in terms of generational effects but that true ontogenetic change is taking place, just as the cross-sectional and longitudinal studies themselves suggested.

The problem of *testing effects* in longitudinal studies is most adequately checked by drawing new samples from the cohort groups who have never been tested before and comparing their scores with the scores of the longitudinal subjects. This procedure was not possible with Group S and J, because all subjects who volunteered for the project were tested, and records are not available from the schools for subjects who did not volunteer. However, other evidence shows that testing effects are nonsignificant for the DIT. First, in short-term studies (one to three weeks), test-retest averages remain virtually the same: Nonsignificant differences with only one-point or two-point shifts in mean score were found in four studies (Bloom 1977; Geis 1977; McGeorge 1975; Rest et al. 1974). Second, in educational intervention studies lasting three to four months, the control groups show nonsignificant gains (see Chapter 7). All of these short-term shifts are so much less than the amount of change in the longitudinal studies that the longitudinal increases cannot be explained as a practice effect of retaking the DIT. Third, Panowitsch (1975) tested subjects three times over an eight-month period and found only a two-point gain (38.2 to 40.2), whereas group J and S subjects were tested three times over a four-year period and showed an eleven-point gain. The amount of change is not related to testings but to time elapsed. Fourth, Geis (1977) studied the effect of testing in a Solomon Four Group Design (Campbell and Stanley 1963) — that is, a design that has some subjects pretested and others not, and then compares their posttests. He found no main testing effect ($F = .18$, nonsignificant) and no interaction of testing with other effects ($F = .17$, nonsignificant). Therefore from the evidence available, there is no indication that longitudinal changes are due to testing effects, or even that there is any testing effect at all.

The possibility of sampling bias was investigated by comparing subjects who continued in the study with those who dropped out. The 1974 scores of both Group J and Group S were subdivided into subjects retested in 1976 ("ins") versus those who were not ("outs"). Comparisons were made on the P as well as the D score, comprehension and "law and order" (see Chapter Six and Eight for discussion of these variables). None of the eight comparisons (ins versus outs on four variables for Group J and S) were significant on 1974 data. Possible differences between the 1976 ins and outs were traced to the 1972 testing for Group J and S. In this analysis four years previous to subjects' staying in or dropping out, Group J showed no significant differences between ins and outs on IQ (Differential Abilities Test, Composite Verbal and Non-verbal score), or on indicators of socioeconomic status (gather's highest level of education, and status rating of father's occupation). (These data were not available for Group S.) Furthermore, comparisons on P and D were nonsignificant for both groups, as was also law and order attitudes. Only on comprehension was there a significant difference ($p < .04$ for Group J,

$p < .02$ for Group S.) In addition, comparisons were conducted on Group J on 1972 data, dividing subjects into those retested in 1974 ("1974 ins") versus those not retested in 1974 ("1974 outs").[7] No significant differences were found on the moral judgment indices P and D, nor on IQ or comprehension. There was a significant difference on father's occupation ($p < .002$), but not on father's education. There was a significant difference on law and order attitudes ($p < .02$). In summary, no evidence exists that subject attrition is correlated with moral judgment or IQ and only inconsistent evidence that subject attrition is related to socioeconomic status, law and order attitudes, or comprehension. In 23 of 27 comparisons, the differences between subjects who stayed in the study versus those who did not was nonsignificant.

Conclusions

As assessed by the Defining Issues Test, the number of years in school and the number of years since birth are related to the way subjects judge moral issues. Change over time in the direction postulated by theory is evident in the cross-sectional, longitudinal, and sequential studies. Students moving through high school and into college show the most dramatic change. Adults in general seem to slow down in moral judgment development in their 20s and to plateau after leaving school; however, those continuing their education in specialties that emphasize moral thinking (doctoral students in moral philosophy or political science, seminarians) attain much higher DIT scores than the average adult.

The particular strength of the cross-sectional data is the large number of subjects tested (several thousand) and the diversity of the samples (from all regions of the United States). The particular strength of the longitudinal and sequential data is the greater control of factors and finer-grained analyses that are possible. Analyses of individual subjects over time show a tendency for decreases in lower stages of moral thinking and increases in higher stages. Analyses on the possible contaminating factors of generational effects, sampling biases, and testing effects indicated that the age trends could not be explained in terms of these artifacts.

Kohlberg regards the demonstration of age trends in a moral judgment measure as sufficient validation of the measure and the construct (Kohlberg 1976, p. 46). While I regard the demonstration of age trends as crucial, I do not regard it as sufficient. For one, many other aspects of human behavior and experience change with development—for instance, verbal facility—and the demonstration of age trends in moral judgment assessments may be simply reflecting other developmental changes, in which case the postulation of sequential transformations in moral thinking of the kind described in Chapter 2 would not be required. Second, a cognitive developmental view asserts more than that moral judgment develops over time; it asserts that the development is due to *cognitive* changes, that is, to changes in a person's understanding of the social world. Other psychological theories can accord with the demonstration of general age trends in moral judgment, but they ascribe the changes to other causes than to the cognitive transformations in the service of better understanding of and equilibrium with the world.

For instance, in recent years Social Learning theory has accomodated to the facts of age trends in moral judgment development. Whereas in the early 1960s, Bandura was doing studies to disprove age trends in moral judgment (Bandura and McDonald 1963), recently Bandura states that "evidence of age trends" is something "which most every theory predicts" (Bandura 1977, p. 44). The way that Social Learning theory explains age trends in moral judgment is as follows:

> According to the social learning view, people vary in what they teach, model and reinforce with children of differing ages. At first, control is necessarily external. In attempting to discourage hazardous conduct in children who have not yet learned to talk, parents must resort to physical intervention. As children mature, social sanctions increasingly replace physical ones. Parents cannot always be present to guide their children's behavior. Successful socialization requires gradual substitution of symbolic and internal controls for external sanctions and demands. After moral standards of conduct are established by tuition and modeling, self-evaluative consequences serve as deterrents to transgressive acts. As the nature and seriousness of possible transgressions by children change with age, parents alter their moral reasoning. For example, they do not appeal to legal arguments in handling misconduct of preschoolers, but they explain legal codes and penalties to preadolescents in efforts to influence future behavior that can have serious consequences. (Bandura 1977, p. 43)

Instead of explaining the changes as due to internal cognitive processes as cognitive developmentalists do, Bandura explains the changes in moral judgment as reflecting changes in the influences of external socializing agents; changes in socializing practices trigger changes in moral judgment. To my knowledge, Social Learning theorists have not actually done naturalistic longitudinal studies of the socializing influences brought to bear on children, nor have they demonstrated that changes in these practices cause changes in moral judgment. This position is therefore more of a theoretical conjecture than one backed up by evidence. However, since this theory is a plausible explanation of age trends in moral judgment, cognitive developmentalists need additional evidence to bolster their own interpretation—particularly evidence linking moral judgment with internal cognitive processes rather than external influences. It is to these issues that we now turn.

6

The Relation of Moral Judgment to Cognition, Attitudes, and Personality

This chapter summarizes hundreds of correlations of the DIT with other psychological tests. The findings will be considered in terms of six main questions: (1) What is the evidence that moral judgment (as measured by the DIT) is related to cognitive processes? (2) What is the relationship between the DIT and Kohlberg's test? How closely do they compare and how can differences be accounted for? (3) What is the evidence that moral judgment as measured by the DIT is anything more than intellectual gamesmanship or sophistry? How do DIT scores relate to people's values and attitudes? (4) How do DIT scores relate to people's actual behavior, as assessed in naturalistic and experimental situations? (5) Given that moral judgment is only one component of a person's personality, how do DIT scores relate to other aspects of personality? (6) Is moral judgment a distinct construct? Would it be more parsimonious to explain moral judgment phenomena in terms of other already established constructs?

Cognitive Correlates[1]

IQ and Achievement Tests. Many people regard morality (and all questions of values) as in the "affective" domain; hence an emphasis on cognition may seem a strange way to approach the psychology of morality. Since both the psychoanalytic and behavioristic approaches emphasize noncognitive processes in accounting for morality, some of the earlier cognitive developmental articles (Kohlberg 1964, pp. 390 ff) emphasized the correlations of IQ with measures of moral behavior and with moral judgment (in the .20s to .50s), using these findings to argue for a cognitive component in morality. In more recent articles, Kohlberg (1969 p. 391) has cited replications of these findings (correlations from .30 to .50 between moral judgment and IQ), emphasizing that moral judgment is not reducible to IQ. What cognitive developmentalists want to argue is that there is a *moderate* relation of IQ with moral judgment, since moral judgment is one aspect of general intellecutal development; however, moral judgment is a *distinct* aspect of intellectual development and not simply the application of general cognitive and linguistic skills to moral content.

At this point, let us consider the evidence that moral judgment is related to cognitive processes, leaving until later the question of whether moral judgment is a distinct construct. Studies correlating the DIT with various tests of intellectual aptitude and achievement generally bear out Kohlberg's findings with his test. Table 6.1 presents 52 correlations, 83% of which are in the .20s to .50s range, confirming the claim of a moderate correlation. It is interesting to note that whenever subtests are given, the verbal subtest is not consistently more highly correlated with the DIT than the nonverbal subtest (in only three out of seven comparisons, verbal is more highly correlated than nonverbal) and that the composite indices (verbal plus nonverbal) are consistently more highly correlated than just the verbal subtests alone. This suggests that the linkage between intellectual aptitude and the DIT is not just verbal fluency or knowledge of special vocabulary, but the linkage is in a common general factor of intelligence.

Moral Comprehension. The philosopher, William Alston (1971), has presented a specific challenge to the claim that moral judgment development represents conceptual development:

> A careful scrutiny of the descriptions of Kohlberg's stages, and of the basis on which a subject is assigned to a stage, will reveal that what is being so classified is what might be called a person's habitual style of moral reasoning—the kind of moral judgments he is inclined to make and the way in which he is inclined to support such judgments.... But can we also construe these stages, as so described and so identified, as stages of conceptual development? Certainly the assignment of a person to a given stage has some implications as to his conceptual repertoire. That is, if a person utilizes certain concepts in a piece of reasoning, whether this is habitual or not, it follows without more ado that he has those concepts. Thus, a stage 3 person will necessarily have the concepts, for example, the concept of disapproval, that are essentially involved in stage 3 reasoning. However, this is not sufficient to make these into stages of conceptual development. It would also have to be the case that a person's habitual mode of moral reasoning

Table 6.1. Relations of DIT with IQ, Aptitude, and Achievement Measures

Study	Sample	Measure	Corre-lation
Allen and Kickbush (1976)	430 9th graders	Iowa Test of Basic Skills (used percentiles rather than raw scores)	.01
Coder (1975)	58 adults	Quick Word Test (Nunnally, 1972)	.42
Cooper (1972)	40 junior highs	Iowa Test of Basic Skills-verbal	.28
		-nonverbal	.14
		Differential Abilities Test	
		-verbal subtotal	.37
		-nonverbal subtotal	.37
		-abstract reasoning	.29
		-spatial reasoning	.27
		-mechanical reasoning	.25
		-clerical skills and spelling	.10
		-composite verbal and nonverbal	.41
Dispoto (1977)	87 Science-major undergraduates	College Board Exams	N.S.
	51 Humanities-major undergraduates		.57
Froming and Cooper (1976)	35 college students U. of Texas	S.A.T.	
		-total	.58
		-verbal	.58
		-quantitative	.43
Gallia (1976)	10 college science majors	S.A.T.	
		-verbal	.55
		-quantitative	.36
	10 college humanities majors	S.A.T.	
		-verbal	.16
		-quantitative	.52
Johnson (1974)	66 students in 8th to 11th grade in private Lutheran school, Philadelphia, Pa.	Otis IQ Test	.24
Masanz (1975)	34 high school girls	Lorge Thorndike IQ	.51
		American College Testing Program	
		-English	.38
		-Mathematics	.47
		-Social Studies	.36
		-Natural Sciences	.35
		-Composite	.44
		Minnesota Scholastic Aptitude Test	.44

Table 6.1 (Continued)

Study	Sample	Measure	Corre-lation
Masanz (1975)		Iowa Test of Basic Skills	
(continued)		Composite	.47
		-Reading comprehension	.30
		-Vocabulary	.36
		-Language word usage	.34
		-Language total	.36
		-Work study	.32
		-Mathematics I	.46
		-Mathematics II	.37
		Class rank	.47
		Grades (from last semester junior year)	
		-Natural sciences	.60
		-Social studies	.46
		-English	.56
		-Mathematics	.55
		-Sociology	.48
McColgan (1975)	29 delinquents	IQ (Shipley-Hartford)	.20
		Wide Range Achievement Test	
		-Reading	.16
		-Spelling	.09
		-Arithmetic	.25
McColgan (1975)	52 junior highs	IQ (Shipley-Hartford)	.33
Morrison, Toews, and Rest (1975)	67 9th graders	Differential Abilities Test Composite verbal and nonverbal	.22
Sanders (1976)	49 junior highs	SCAT: verbal reasoning	.16
Sprecher (1976)	33 7th graders	CTP (Educational Records Bureau)	
		-verbal aptitude	.30
		-total aptitude	.43
Walker (1974)	98 8th graders	IQ (Lorge Thorndike)	.29

embodies his highest or latest conceptual acquisitions in the moral sphere; that is, that he does not possess any concepts that are distinctive of higher stages of reasoning. And this we cannot infer just from the fact that he habitually or typically reasons about moral problems in a way that features stage 3 concepts. He might conceivably possess the concepts of stage 4, 5, or 6, even though he does not habitually employ them in his moral thinking. This conclusion is simply a particular application of a fundamental conceptual point about the concepts of having a concept, on the one hand, and of using a concept (or habitually or typically using a concept) on the other.

One cannot use a concept in a given situation without having it, but one can have a concept without using it in a given situation (or perhaps without using it at all, though this is more controversial). Possession of a concept is something more latent than a habit, trait, or tendency, and all the more latent than an actual performance, whether covert or overt . . . . It would obviously be desirable to have some more direct way of showing a developmental sequence in concept acquisition. A more direct demonstration would require the development of a test for *possession* of moral concepts, analogous to the test of typical mode of moral reasoning . . . .Here we are not tapping tendencies, we are not simply trying to determine what is most likely to emerge under certain institutable conditions; rather we are trying to determine what latent capacities a person does, and, most difficult, does not have. (Alston 1971, pp. 269-72)

The problem that Alston raises applies equally to the DIT. It is a logical possibility that age trends on the DIT as well as on Kohlberg's test reflect age trends in *preference* for certain forms of moral judgment (an "affective" matter), rather than age trends in capacity to think in new ways. Precisely for the reasons Alston gives, a series of studies had been begun in 1967 to inventory people's *comprehension* of moral concepts at various stages independently of their use or preference for certain moral concepts. The comprehension test used in the 1969 and 1973 studies has been extensively described in Chapter 2 (testing the subject's ability to recapitulate or paraphrase prototypic statements); the comprehension test used since 1974 was described in Chapter 4 (pages 82-83), involving a multiple choice matching of alternative interpretations with a paragraph.

In eleven studies, using either measure of moral comprehension, moral judgment scores have almost always been significantly correlated with moral comprehension. Table 6.2 summarizes studies of the DIT with the multiple-choice test of comprehension. For the nine studies using the full version Comprehension test, the average correlation is .51. Therefore, to answer the question raised by Alston, there is evidence that the way subjects judge moral issues is related to their cognitive comprehension. Subjects who have lower moral judgment scores tend to be subjects with lower comprehension; subjects with high comprehension tend to have high DIT scores.

The high correlations between the DIT and Comprehension Test are more impressive once the poor reliability of the Comprehension Test is taken into account. Its test-retest over two weeks was only $r = .51$ with 24 ninth graders, and the Kuder Richardson consistency coefficient was .56 on a sample of 160 subjects (Rest et al. 1974). Its two-year stability was only slightly less for 54 subjects ($r = .51$ and .45). It is likely that a more reliable test would have shown higher correlations with the DIT. In the McColgan 1975 study, a shorter form of the Comprehension Test was used because the subjects were poor readers; but the shorter Comprehension Test has questionable value, given the poor reliability of the full 11-item form, and this may explain the lower correlations in the McColgan 1975 study.

Strong corroboration of these correlations in cross-sectional studies comes from longitudinal studies of moral comprehension along with the DIT. Just as DIT scores increased from 1972 to 1974 and 1976 in the 54 subjects (page 128), so also comprehension scores increased. Mean scores over 1972, 1974, and 1976 were 5.1, 6.7, and 7.3, respectively (F = 10.3, p < .001); the difference between 1972 and 1976 gives a t of 7.3, p < .0001. Of the subjects who showed upward patterns of movement on the DIT between 1972 and 1976, 81% showed upward change in comprehension. Therefore moral comprehension is developmental, and is related to development as shown on the DIT.

The findings by Ernsberger (1976) and Lawrence (1978) that were cited earlier (Chapter 5, pages 115-118), qualify the comprehension findings, since they indicate that ideological commitments can override conceptual understanding in making moral judgments. People sometimes put aside their best conceptual understanding of a situation and make decisions on another basis. However, the subjects involved in the comprehension studies were not known to have any particular ideological bias (except perhaps the volunteers from the Naval base), and the findings did show a significant relation between comprehension and the DIT.

Table 6.2. Correlations of DIT with Moral Comprehension

Study	Sample	r
Alozie (1976)	91 junior highs and college students	.68*
	(37 college students only	.63)
Rest et al. (1974)	67 students, ages 14 to adulthood	.67
	160 students, junior high to graduate school	.62
	(9th graders only, n = 73	.58)
Rest, Davison, Robbins (1977)	54 subjects, age 19-22	.51
Coder (1975)	87 adults (age 24 to 49)	.49†
Rest (1975)	88 subjects, age 17-20	.42
Masanz (1975)	34 high school girls	.37†
McColgan (1975)	52 junior high predelinquents and controls	.34*
	29 delinquents	.19*
Crowder (1976)	53 volunteers from Naval base	.32

*Used shorter six item form of Comprehension Test.
†Used shorter form of DIT with four stories.

Is moral comprehension anything more than IQ or verbal aptitude? In the 73 ninth graders reported in Rest et al. (1974), moral comprehension correlated .41 with the DAT composite score and only .18 with the Iowa Test of Basic Skills (subscales of these tests produced even lower correlations). In the same sample, the correlation of comprehension with the DIT was .58, and the ITBS correlated with the DAT at .54. The partial correlation between the DIT and comprehension was .50 after removing DAT, socio-economic class, sex and controlling for age and education. Moral comprehension therefore seems to be distinct from general aptitude although related to it; it is more related to moral judgment.

The Mischels (1976 p. 88) cite a second research strategy for determining whether moral judgment is tapping conceptual capacity or merely preference:

> Unfortunately, the Kohlberg measure of maturity in reasoning about moral dilemmas does not permit one to separate the type of moral reasoning of which the respondent is capable from the moral reasoning which he favors (or which he prefers to use). To separate *competence* in moral reasoning from *performance* (or preference) it would be necessary for the test to encourage all subjects to display the "best" (highest, most mature) moral reasoning that they are capable of generating. This could be achieved by offering incentives for maximum performance (as on other achievement tests). Without such a procedure one cannot determine whether a subject's performance reflects the most mature moral reasoning that he *can* generate or the degree to which he uses (prefers) different types of moral reasoning in the dilemmas sampled or (as most likely occurs) some indeterminate mix of both.

Unfortunately the Mischels were not aware of a study completed by McGeorge in 1973 and recently replicated by Bloom that carried out exactly what is suggested. McGeorge and Bloom found that subjects decrease their DIT scores when instructed to take the DIT as "someone with no sense of justice," but subjects do *not* increase their scores when instructed to take the DIT when instructed to take the DIT as someone "with the highest principles of justice." These findings are exactly what one would predict if measures of moral judgment were reflecting conceptual capacity. These studies will be discussed further in Chapter 7; however, they are mentioned here as corroboration to the correlational studies with comprehension.

Correlations with Other Tests of Development. Table 6.3 presents correlations of the DIT P score with several other measures usually considered to be related to cognitive development. As can be seen, the correlations are generally positive and significant, but of a magnitude less than that for Comprehension. Taking these correlations together with the IQ correlations, and comprehension correlations, the DIT does seem to be related to cognitive developmental processes.

Comparisons with Kohlberg's Test

The relation of the DIT to Kohlberg's test is of special interest since the DIT is derived from Kohlberg's general approach and stage scheme. Can one test be substituted for the other? Do the different methods of assessment show close agreement? If not, why not? Table 6.4 shows several correlational studies of the DIT with various versions of Kohlberg's test. For the heterogeneous samples, the correlations are around .70, which along with those for comprehension are the highest correlations of the DIT yet reported. However, the correlations of the DIT in more homogeneous groups is much lower (average r = .43), indicating that the two tests are far from equivalent. Of course in homogeneous samples, the range of scores tends to be restricted, thus attenuating the correlations of variables. In discussing the degree of correlation of the DIT with Kohlberg's test, it is important

Table 6.3. Correlations of DIT with Other Cognitive Developmental Measures

Study	Sample	Measure	r
Briskin (1975)	32 college students	Leveling-Sharpening	.49
Meyer (1975)	40 male college students	Perry's Intellectual and Ethical Development	.45
Panowitsch (1976)	82 college students	Cornell Critical Thinking Test	.41
Cauble (1976)	90 college students	Piaget's Formal Operations	.40
McColgan (1975)	29 delinquents	Piaget's Golden Rule Task	.30
	52 predelinquents	Piaget's Golden Rule Task	.31
	52 predelinquents	Chandler's Cartoon Role-Taking	-.18
Copa (1975)	127 college women in home economics classes	Harvey's Conceptual Systems	.13
Chiosso (1976)	15 high school students, aged 16-18	Loevinger's Ego Development	.42
Satterstrom	56 high school students, white, middle class (18 7th graders, separately	Loevinger's Ego Development	.38
	ately (17 9th graders, separ-	Loevinger's Ego Development	.36)
	ately (21 12th graders,	Loevinger's Ego Development	.24)
	separately	Loevinger's Ego Development	.13)

to note the degree of correlation between different versions of Kohlberg's test itself. Data scored by Kohlberg's 1958 system and the same data rescored by the 1978 system correlated only .39 (Kohlberg, Colby and Damon 1978). Therefore, although the DIT is not equivalent to Kohlberg's test, it is more highly correlated than some versions of Kohlberg's test are with each other. Therefore, some of the variation in correlations with Kohlbergian measures may be due to variations in the Kohlbergian measures themselves, in addition to sample differences.

Alozie (1976) has made the most intensive study of the differences of Kohlberg's test with the DIT. Four design differences may account for the nonequivalence of the tests: (1) use of different methods of indexing (whereas Kohlberg's test uses stage typing and the MMS, the DIT uses the P index and, more recently, the D index); (2) use of different dilemmas (three of the DIT stories use Kohlberg's dilemmas, but the other three DIT stories have no parallel in Kohlberg's test); (3) use of different stage characterizations (for example, what Kohlberg's system calls Stage 3 may be keyed Stage 4 on the DIT; see

Table 6.4. Correlations of DIT with Kohlbergian Tests of Moral Judgment

Study	Sample	Measure	r
Sheehan (1979)	45 physicians	Kohlberg's 1976 Scoring System	.78
Alozie (1976)	91 students, combined college and high school	Kohlberg's 1972 Issue Scoring	.75
	(37 college students		
	(52 junior highs—see Froming and McColgan)		.28)
Gibbs and Fedoruk (1975)	41 college students	Gibbs' scale of principled moral thinking	.70
Rest et al. (1974)	47 students and adults	Kohlberg's 1958 Scoring System	.68
Froming and McColgan (1977)	213 students, combined college and high school	Kohlberg's 1972 Issue Scoring	.68
	(139 college students		.35)
	(74 junior high students of very low academic ability		.17)
Carroll and Rest (1977)	88 subjects, 18 to 22 yrs.	Short, written modification of Kohlberg's 1972 system*	.34
	55 subjects, 20 to 24 yrs.	Short, written modification of Kohlberg's 1972 system*	.41
Bode and Page (1978)	52 college students	Written version, Kohlberg Test (no year given)	.41

Chapter 2); (4) use of different tasks (whereas Kohlberg's test asks subjects to spontaneously produce justifications for a course of action the DIT asks subjects to evaluate the defining issues of the dilemmas provided).

To study the relationship between Kohlberg's test and the DIT, Alozie gave both tests to 91 subjects, including 37 college subjects and 52 junior high school subjects of low academic ability who had been tested by McColgan (1975) previously. Kohlberg tests of the junior high students were scored at Harvard by Kohlberg's group according to the 1972 scoring system (which is more similar to the 1978 than to the 1958 system, and Kohlberg tests of the college subjects were scored by Alozie himself, who had been trained at a Harvard workshop and who had established an interjudge agreement of 92.5% on a sample of 45 protocols with the Harvard group.

First, the effect of different indices was investigated by computing three indices for each test and intercorrelating the DIT's indices with the three indices from Kohlberg's test. That is, for each test, a stage typing index was computed, a MMS (weighted average of percent usage at each stage), and a P score (the percent of usage of Stages 5 and 6). Stage typing for the DIT was done according to an exceptional usage algorithm (see Chapter 4, page 104). A P index for the Kohlberg test was calculated by adding together the percent usage of Stages 5 and 6 for each subject, but since so little material is scored at Stages 5 and 6 with Kohlberg's test, the score of most subjects was 0%. Davison's index was not yet available at the time of this study and it could not be included. Table 6.5 presents the means and standard deviations of each index for each test. As can be seen, the DIT credited subjects with more advanced development on every index, a point we shall return to. Table 6.6 gives the intercorrelations of the indices.

Table 6.6 shows no gain in the correlation of the DIT with Kohlberg's Test by equating the type of index (p with P, MMS with MMS, and stage-typing with stage-typing). The highest correlation between the tests turns out to be between the indices recommended for each

Table 6.5. Means and Standard Deviations of Each Index
on the DIT and Kohlberg's Test

	Index		
	P% score	MMS	Stage-type
DIT	31 (17.2)	400 (43.8)	4.1 (.5)
Kohlberg's Test	2 (4.0)	248 (74.2)	2.2 (1.1)

Source: Adapted from Alozie 1976, p. 47.
*Standard deviation in parentheses.

test (DIT's P score and Kohlberg's MMS); thus the differences between the DIT and Kohlberg's test are not due to indexing differences.

Second, the effect of using different dilemmas was investigated by examining correlations for matching dilemmas. Both the DIT and Kohlberg's test have three comparable dilemmas in Heinz and the Drug, Escaped Prisoner, and the Doctor and Euthanasia dilemmas. The correlation of DIT P score and Kohlberg MMS on these three matched dilemmas was .73. Correcting for shortened test length brings the correlation to .75, which is exactly the correlation of the full version DIT with the full version Kohlberg test. Therefore, equating dilemmas does not seem to show any gain in correlations. Inspection of the correlations of other combinations of indices showed the same results—matching dilemmas does not increase the correlation between the DIT and the Kohlberg test. Furthermore, correlations at the level of individual dilemmas were examined (DIT-Heinz with Kohlberg test-Heinz, etc.). The average correlation of matched dilemmas ($r = .54$) was no higher than the average correlation of unmatched dilemmas ($r = .56$)—e.g., correlating DIT-Heinz with Kohlberg test-Doctor.

Third, the effect of scoring differences in stage characteristics was examined by keying the DIT items to conform more closely with Kohlberg's 1972 scoring scheme. For instance, since Kohlberg's scoring guides do not have any entries for Stage 6, all DIT items that were keyed as Stage 6 were reassigned to Stage 5 or 4, wherever they fit best in Kohlberg's scheme. (See Alozie 1976, Appendix C for details on rescoring of DIT items to fit Kohlberg's 1972 scoring guides.) After items were rekeyed, new indices for the DIT were calculated (new P score, MMS, and stage-typing). The overall effect of rekeying was to shift DIT scores downward: The average P% dropped by 1.4 points, the MMS dropped by 39 points, and the average stage-typing score dropped by .4 of a stage. However, the average scores on the rekeyed DIT are still much higher than comparable scores on the Kohlberg test (see Table 6.5). Therefore stage rekeying does not ac-

Table 6.6. Correlations of Three DIT Indices with Three Indices of
Kohlberg's Test ($n = 91$)

DIT Indices	Kohlberg's Test Indices		
	P	MMS	Stage-typing
P	.45	.75	.64
MMS	.42	.72	.66
Stage-typing	.33	.61	.55

Source: Adapted from Alozie, 1976, p. 47.

count for most of the difference between the Kohlberg test and the DIT. Even after adjusting for stage rekeying and after matching on comparable stories, the DIT is still 12 points higher on the average P%, 112 points higher on the average MMS, and 1.4 points higher on the average stage-type. Similarly, the correlations between the DIT and the Kohlberg test are not increased by stage rekeying: The correlation is .69 (actually lower than the correlation of .75 without rekeying). Therefore, differences in stage-keying of items does not account for much of the difference in scores.

The fourth difference between the tests is in the type of task used, and this difference is considerable. Alozie examined the three dilemmas that the tests have in common, looking at the stage that a subject was scored for that dilemma on the Kohlberg test and comparing that stage with the stage of the item ranked as most important on the DIT. For instance, if a subject was scored at Stage 3 on the Heinz dilemma on Kohlberg's test, Stage 3 would be compared with the item ranked in first place on the DIT's Heinz dilemma. In general Alozie found that subjects consistently preferred a higher stage item on the DIT; subjects scored at Stage 3 on the Kohlberg test tended to choose Stage 4 or 5 items on the DIT on the same dilemma. Table 6.7 presents a summary of these findings. Rubin and Trotter (1977) report a similar result using items taken directly from Kohlberg's scoring guides rather than DIT items: Subjects produced responses on the interview at a lower stage than the items they picked when presented with a selection of statements.

Subjects choose items on the DIT at higher stages than the stage at which they produce statements on the Kohlberg Test. This should not be too surprising, if the DIT is regarded as essentially a *recognition* task and the Kohlberg test a *production* task. As discussed at length in Chapter 3 (pages 60-62) a production task places a greater cognitive and linguistic load on subjects than a recognition task. In moral

Table 6.7. Percentage of Subjects Scoring Higher, Same, or Lower on DIT than on the Kohlberg Test ($n = 91$)

Story	Higher on DIT	Same on DIT and Kohlberg	Higher on Kohlberg
Heinz	64	27	9
Doctor	71	14	7
Prisoner	87	6	8
Total	77	16	8

Source: From Alozie 1976.

judgment research (Breznitz and Kugelmass, 1967) as well as in cognitive developmental research in general (c.f. Flavell 1970 and 1971), task differences such as that between the DIT and the Kohlberg test are responsible for differences in the organizational structures that subjects display on the tests. The DIT can be regarded as tapping the earlier and more tacit moral understanding of a subject while the Kohlberg test taps the more consolidated understanding and that which the subject can put into words.

It is interesting to note the greater discrepancy between the DIT and the Kohlberg test in the junior high sample than in the college sample. The junior high difference in terms of MMS was 179, whereas the college difference was 114; the junior high difference in terms of stage typing was 1.9 stages, whereas the college difference was 1.3 stages; the junior high sample was higher on the DIT in 86% of the comparisons, whereas the college sample was higher on the DIT in 64% of the comparisons. The college students probably are relatively more adept at putting their ideas into words; hence the discrepancy between a recognition task and a production task is less for them than for the low academic ability junior high students.

Attitude and Value Correlates

Form-Content Distinction. So far evidence has been presented regarding the developmental nature of DIT scores and their relation to cognitive processes. Now we shift to the question of whether or not moral judgment is sophistry—that is, more or less elaborate ways of presenting arguments for whatever one wants to do. If moral judgment is merely an intellectual style in presenting an argument, then it is a value-free skill, independent of any particular commitments or attitudes.

Two kinds of argument are advanced for the position that moral judgment has nothing to do with values. One argument dismisses the distinction between structure and content, and the second overexaggerates the distinction. The first argument asserts that moral judgment is a matter of "fine words," and fine words to not have a necessary connection with fine deeds. Mischel and Mischel (1976) state:

> People tend to be facile about justifying their own diverse actions and commitments—no matter how reprehensible these acts may seem to others. A wide variety of self-deceptive mechanisms may be used to facilitate and excuse the most horrendous acts. . . . History is replete with atrocities that were justified by invoking the highest principles. . . . In the name of justice, of the common welfare, of universal ethics, and of God, millions of people

have been killed and whole cultures destroyed. In recent history, concepts of universal right, equality, freedom, and social equity have been used to justify every variety of murder including genocide. (p. 107)

The Mischels thus imply that the "highest principles" can be invoked for virtually any action; hence there need be no connection between moral judgment and action or values. Indeed, the Mischels suggest there might even be a negation correlation! This argument, however, confuses the use of pious language or empty invocation of verbal garnish with constructing an argument that satisfies the logical requirements of justice. As discussed in Chapter 2, moral judgment has to do with the logic of cooperative arrangements, and with establishing a balance of interests among the participants in social interaction. What distinguishes Stage 5 and 6 from the other Stages is not the incantation of certain words. To equate fancy words with the logical structure of moral thinking is to deny that moral reasoning has any logical structure. I would be very curious to see a Stage 6 argument for the Nazi program of genocide against the Jews. It may be that Nazi proponents used the word, "justice," in talking about their program, but merely using the word is not equivalent to constructing an argument that satisfies the conditions of justice. The Mischels' argument is similar to stating that some of the most colossal mistakes and errors in human judgment have been justified in the name of science; therefore science has nothing to do with truth. Since the distinction between structure and content is confused, the argument implies that moral judgment has nothing to do with values.

The second kind of argument for maintaining that moral judgment has no relation to values does make the structure-content distinction, but exaggerates the distinction. This view claims that form is completely independent of content, that the structure of moral reasoning has nothing to do with one's moral choices. For example, a recent article by Martin et al. (1977) argues that "the Defining Issues Test, in its present form, does not achieve this distinction between form and content" because the P score was moderately correlated with the decisions of what to do in the dilemmas (e.g., the P score was related to whether Heinz should steal the drug). Martin et al. advocate trying to devise a P index that doesn't correlate with action choice.

It is surely a curiosity to argue that moral reasoning should be completely independent of moral decision. In contrast, Candee (1976) states:

But why should we be interested in studying the structure of reasoning? It is because, ultimately, structure *is* related to choice. . . . Any set of cognitive developmental stages. . . . would be of little interest if they did not lead to specific types of decisions. Piaget's discovery of formal operations as a set of structures would be of less interest were it not for the fact that having achieved formal operations an individual is able to solve multivariate problems that were unsolvable earlier. Likewise, in the social realm, we would be less interested in the structure of moral reasoning were it not for the prospect that the development of such reasoning leads one to make decisions that are more just. (p. 1293)

A conceptual and operational distinction between two constructs does not necessitate that the two be empirically uncorrelated, however. For example, human height and weight are conceptually independent and assessed by independent operations, but this does not entail that the two are empirically uncorrelated. So also is the case with moral reasoning and moral choice. The relation of reasoning with decision is not a simple one, however. In Kohlberg's earliest work (1958), he studied the relation of action choice with mode of moral reasoning. For example in the Heinz story, he found that Stage 1 reasoning was associated with advocating *not* stealing the drug, Stage 2 with stealing, Stage 3 with ambiguity of decision, Stage 4 with ambiguity, Stage 5 with stealing, Stage 6 with definitely stealing (Appendix B, Kohlberg, 1958). Therefore the choice decision flip-flops as we move through the stages, and the structure of some stages does not yield a clear basis for decision. In later work, Kohlberg, myself, and others attempted to emphasize the conceptual independence of stage of reasoning from choice by writing for every stage a reason for stealing and a reason for not stealing. Such "pro" and "con" statements at every stage did dramatize the difference between reasoning and choice, but generating the full set of statements nevertheless involved some contortions (see Chapter 4, page 89). Unfortunately, this has led some people to postulate that there should be *no* empirical relationship between moral judgment and moral decision.

Why should there be any connection? A moral judgment score is supposed to be an indication of the basic concepts of fairness generally used in construing a complex social situation. The presumption is that the way a person interprets a dilemma is going to have some bearing on the way he resolves it. Therefore form is related to content, but is not reducible to content.

The following sections report and elaborate studies of this relationship.

Action Choice. Cooper (1972) studied action-choice of the stories on the DIT. He determined that moral philosophy and political science doctoral students tended to make the same action choices in the six DIT dilemmas: For the Heinz and the Drug dilemma, they advocated *steal*; for the Student Protest Dilemma, they advocated *takeover*; for Escaped Prisoner, *not report*; for Doctor's Dilemma, *euthanasia*; for Webster, *equal opportunity hiring*; and for Newspaper, *not stop printing*. These six action-choices might be characterized as "humanitarian-liberal." Consequently, each subject was given a choice score that represented the degree to which their action choices lined up with the "humanitarian-liberal" pattern, ranging from 0 to 6.

Cooper found that choice was indeed correlated with moral reasoning: *r* with the DIT's P score was .34 on 160 subjects (Rest et al. 1974). As Kohlberg and colleagues have been finding since 1958, and as Martin et al. (1977) also reported, moderate and significant relationships exist between type of moral reasoning and type of decision.

Although choice and reasoning are correlated, evidence shows that the two are distinct, and as variables behave differently. Table 6.8 below compares some correlates of reasoning (the P index) with correlates of action-choice. As can be seen, the P index correlates much more highly with comprehension and Law and Order than does action choice, and therefore, the two variables behave rather differently.

Action choice in these cases is not more highly correlated with the P index because the relationship is not strictly linear. As Kohlberg reported in his dissertation, as one moves up the stages of reasoning, no consistent linear movement occurs towards the "humanitarian-liberal" choice, but the different ways of interpreting the dilemma sometimes favor one action, then the other.

Law and Order Attitude Test.[2] An attempt was made to devise a set of value choices that would be linearly related to the P index. This involves choosing value issues in which one alternative makes most sense from a Principled moral perspective (Stages 5 and 6) and the opposite alternative makes most sense from a Conventional moral perspective (Stages 3 and 4). A set of 15 political items called the "Law and Order" attitude test was devised to have these characteristics, as exemplified in Table 6.9, below.

The Law and Order questionnaire is scored by counting the number of items on which a subject gives almost limitless power to au-

Table 6.8. Comparison of Correlates of P Index with Correlates of Action Choice

	Correlate		
	Age	Comprehension	Law and Order Attitude
P index	.62	.60	-.60
Action choice	.29	.20	-.31

Table 6.9. Examples of Law and Order Items

1. Under what conditions do you think people should be prevented from speaking their opinions? (Check one)
   a. Those criticizing the President
   _____Prevented from speaking or punished for speaking
   _____Prevented in some cases
   _____Not prevented
   b. Those teaching Communism in schools or colleges
   _____Prevented from speaking or punished for speaking
   _____Prevented in some cases
   _____Not prevented
   c. Those speaking of overthrowing our government by force or violence
   _____Prevented from speaking or punished for speaking
   _____Prevented in some cases
   _____Not prevented

2. Under present laws it is possible for someone to escape punishment on the grounds of legal technicalities even though the person may have confessed to performing the crime. Are you in favor of a tougher policy for treating criminals?
   _____strongly agree with tougher policy
   _____mildly agree
   _____mixed agreement and disagreement
   _____mildly disagree
   _____strongly disagree

3. If a person is against a war that his country is engaged in, is it right to do things which disrupt the war effort (like destroying government records, disrupting government buildings, demonstrating at army installations, etc.)?
   _____never right
   _____sometimes right
   _____right most of the time
   _____don't know

4. Under what conditions might it be right to break a law?
   (Check one space for each statement.)

Usually right to break the law	Sometimes right to break the law	Never right to break the law	
_____	_____	_____	a. When one could break the law without detection or punishment
_____	_____	_____	b. When the law puts some people at a disadvantage
_____	_____	_____	c. When following the law would directly kill or harm innocent people

thorities or advocates that existing social institutions be maintained even at high cost to individual welfare and freedom. In Table 6.9, the first alternative to items 1a, 1b, 1c, 2, and 3, and the last position in items 4a, 4b, and 4c, were keyed "Law and Order."

Why should scores on the Law and Order test be correlated with scores on the DIT? Let's take as an example item 1b, whether or not those teaching Communism ought to be prevented from speaking. At the Conventional moral stages, one is oriented towards maintaining the social system and one's existing relationships. Therefore item 1b tends to be interpreted as asking whether you should give your avowed enemy the opportunity to stir up trouble against you and the established order. This way of interpreting the situation leads to the answer, "prevented from speaking or punished for speaking". At the Principled moral stages, one is aware of the possibility of many alternative ways of organizing society and that the competition of ideas and struggle for balanced solutions does in the long run contribute to government responsive to the welfare of its constituents. Therefore a "Principled" interpretation of the situation leads to a different response, "not prevented" or "prevented in some cases."

In general, the greater complexity of Principled thinking leads to advocating answers that are sometimes paradoxical to Conventional thinking. The design of the Law and Order test was to select items of this nature regarding controversial public policy issues.

Internal reliability and test-retest stability of the Law and Order test has been fairly good. Split-half reliability on a heterogeneous sample of 65 students was .89 (with Spearman-Brown correction), and the test-retest correlation over two weeks for 24 ninth graders was .74. Test-retest stability over two years for 88 junior and senior high students was .60.

Table 6.10 shows the correlations of the Law and Order test with the DIT P index.

The correlation of -.60 in the Rest et al. study is much higher than the correlation of .34 between the P index and Action-Choice on the same sample of 160 subjects. Therefore the Law and Order test did show a greater relationship with moral reasoning when the items were designed to be sensitive to the Conventional versus Principled morality destinction. Other studies (shown in Table 6.10) confirm that moral reasoning (as indexed by the DIT P index) has a significant relation with value stances on controversial political issues (of the nine correlations, only one is nonsignificant). Furthermore, in the four-year longitudinal study, as DIT scores showed a significant increase, Law and Order scores showed a significant decrease, $t(53) =$

4.2, $p < .001$. Of the subjects who increased on the DIT, 84% decreased on the Law and Order test. Therefore as cognitive development in moral reasoning progresses (as measured by the DIT and Comprehension tests), values shift.

Studies using Kohlberg's test have also generally found significant relationships between political ideology and moral judgment when Law and Order issues were used in measuring political ideology. Candee (1976) found a correlation of .57 between moral judgment and a questionnaire based on the Watergate and Lt. Calley situations, scoring answers as either consistent with human rights or with maintenance of conventions and institutions (for instance, "Should American officers be convicted for war crimes ordered by their superiors"?). Fishkin, Keniston, and Mackinnon (1973) found that Stage 4 thinking was correlated (.68) with approval of conservative slogans, whereas preconventional thinking favored violent radical slogans (.34) and postconventional thinking was negatively correlated with Conservatism (-.40 and -.35). Similarly, Fontana and Noel (1973) found that Stage 4 correlated negatively ($r = -.35$) with "leftist" ideology, Stage 2 correlated .23, although correlations of Stages 5 and 6 were nonsignificant. Kohlberg and Elfenbein (1975) found a biserial correlation of .76 between moral stage and opposition to capital punishment.

Studies of political ideology have long recognized the important distinction between a maintenance-of-society view and a human-rights-and-equalitarian view. Discussion of "left" versus "right" politics (Tomkins 1963), Liberalism-Conservatism (Keniston 1968) and Authoritarianism (Adorno et al. 1950) have all noted this dimension of political ideology. The claim of moral judgment research is that such differences in political ideology in part reflect a *developmental* difference. Instead of explaining political ideology in terms of person-

Table 6.10. Correlations of DIT with Law and Order Attitude Test

Study	Sample	r
Rest et al. (1974)	160 students—junior high to graduate students	-.60
	(73 junior high students	-.23)
	65 students—junior high to adults	-.48
Rest (1975)	88 subjects, 16 to 20 years	-.52
Coder (1975)	87 adults	-.49
Rest, Davison and		
Robbins (1978)	55 subjects, 18 to 22 years	-.47
Panowitsch (1975)	44 college students	-.27
Crowder (1976)	70 adult volunteers from a Naval base	-.25
Masanz (1975)	34 high school girls	-.19*

*nonsignificant

ality dynamics or in terms of social learning of the norms of one's subculture, moral judgment research attributes a Law and Order political stance to Stage 4 concepts of fairness—coming after preconventional thinking, but developmentally prior to principled thinking. Adorno and colleagues in *The Authoritarian Personality* explicitly denied that differences in authoritarianism reflected a difference in maturity. Hence the substantial correlations of the F-scale with IQ and education (Christie 1954, estimates them to be as high as -.50 or -.60) were something of an embarassment to them. Such high correlations were not easily explicable by psychoanalytic theory. Loevinger (1962; Loevinger and Sweet 1961; Ernhart and Loevinger 1969) was one of the first to propose that the conservative-authoritarian syndrome was a phase of development, that this syndrome has a curvilinear relationship with development, and to demonstrate age trends in authoritarianism. Subsequent work in moral judgment offers a reconceptualization for the consistent finding that IQ correlates with measures of conservative-authoritarian attitudes: IQ tests indirectly tap conceptual development; one aspect of conceptual development is moral judgment development; with higher levels of moral judgment development, social norms and maintenance of order are viewed more critically in assessing their value in fostering human welfare and liberty; with greater criticality, authoritarianism and conservatism decline. In other words, a possible explanation of the IQ-authoritarian linkage is to be found in the mediation of moral judgment development. (More will be discussed on this issue in the last section of this chapter).

Other Political Attitudes. Table 6.11 presents correlations of the DIT with other measures of political attitudes. As can be seen, the correlations here are generally lower and more inconsistent than in Table 6.10. In the Rest et al. 1974 study, Political toleration was highly correlated with P in the 160 sample, but in other studies the correlations were .04, -.08, .21, and .12—therefore, not consistently significant. Similarly, Rokeach's scale of Dogmatism was inconsistently correlated (-.75, -.03, -.21). Scales of liberalism-conservatism in Coder (1974) and G. Rest (1977) were nonsignificant.

The studies by Gutkin and Suls, and Nardi and Tsujimoto are especially interesting in relating the DIT to Hogan's Survey of Ethical Attitudes (1970, 1975a). Hogan has claimed that differences in moral judgment are not to be understood in terms of cognitive development but rather in terms of personality differences. According to Hogan, some people are oriented to an "ethics of personal conscience" and others are oriented to an "ethics of social responsibility."

Table 6.11. Political Attitude Correlated of DIT's Index

Study and Sample	Attitude Test and Variable	Correlation
Allen and Kickbush (1976) 410 ninth graders	Dean alienation scale:	
	-Powerlessness	.04
	-Normlessness	.18
	-Social isolation	.06
	Political efficacy	.16
	Political trust	-.03
	Salience (interest in political courses)	-.08
	Political aspiration	.01
Crowder (1976) 70 volunteers from a Naval base	Political toleration	.04
Coder (1974) 58 adults	Radical-conservatism scale (Nettler and Huffman)	.13
Gallia (1976) 10 college science majors 10 college humanities majors	Rokeach dogmatism Rokeach dogmatism	-.75 -.03
Gutkin and Suls (1977) 68 college students, 114 college students	Hogan's Survey of Ethical Attitudes Stage 4	-.27 -.23 .26*
Morrison, Toews, Rest (1973) 71 junior highs in Canada	Portune's Attitudes Towards Police	-.13
	Political toleration	-.08
	Political efficacy (I)	-.13
	Participation	.12
	Political trust	.07
	Political efficacy (II)	.17
	Civic tolerance	.10
	Political interest	.11
	Rokeach Dogmatism	-.28
Nardi and Tsujimoto (1977) 179 college students	Hogan's Survey of Ethical Attitudes	
	Stage 4	.46*
	Stage 5A	-.26*
	Stage 5B	-.32*
	Stage 6	-.03*
Rest (1975) 88 high school students	Political toleration	.21
Rest G. (1977) 120 voters (combined students and random adults)	Liberalism-Conservatism	.10

Table 6.11. (Continued)

Study and Sample	Attitude Test and Variable	Correlation
Rest, Ahlgren, and Mackey (1972) 61 junior high students	Portune's Attitudes Toward	
	Police	-.37
	Political toleration	.12
	Political efficacy	-.17
	Copo-Polo Scale	
	-View police as helpful	.23
	-Angry feelings toward police	.15
	-Attribute concern to police	-.10
Rest and Feldman (1973) 160 students	Political efficacy	.04
	Political activity	-.19
	Political positiveness	-.34
Rest et al. (1974) 160 students	Political toleration	.63
	(73 ninth graders	.37)

*Correlations not with P, but with another stage.

This is not a developmental difference whereby one view is more mature than the other, but both are equally mature alternatives, reflecting different personality structures. Kurtines and Greif (1974), students of Hogan, claim that Kohlberg's stages 5 and 6 correspond to Hogan's ethics of responsibility and personal conscience, respectively.

Quite contrary to Hogan's view, the data support the following inferences: (1) Hogan's Survey of Ethical Attitudes is not closely related to any moral judgment stage, but concerns something different from moral judgment as defined here; (2) Hogan's "ethics of responsibility" is more highly related to Stage 4 than to Stage 5; and, (3) the ethics of personal conscience as measured by the Survey of Ethical Attitudes is positively correlated with *both* the general welfare orientation of Stage 5A and the personal autonomy orientation of 5B, but not at all with Stage 6; (4) since the DIT does show age trends, is related to developmental measures, and is related to intelligence, Hogan's assertion that moral judgment is not developmental seems to be empty. Therefore, the "ethics of responsibility" and "ethics of personal conscience" as defined by the Survey of Ethical Attitudes are not equivalent to Stage 5 and 6 and seem to have little relevance to moral judgment theory and phenomena.

Why doesn't the DIT show significant correlations with all measures of political attitudes? If one examines the items contained in many of the political attitude scales reported in Table 6.11, it is difficult to imagine why moral judgment should have any such relationship. For instance, a measure of political trust contains the item, "Congress does a good job representing the people"; a measure of political interest contains the item, "How often do you read about public affairs or politics in magazines?"; the Portune scale of Attitudes Towards Police contains the item, "Police are mean." As described in Chapter 2, the DIT assesses different generalized concepts of fairness; it does not follow that one stage would lead a person to agree that "police are mean" and another stage would disagree. These items are different from the Law and Order items because, for instance, denying free speech to Communists is inconsistent with Stage 5's concepts of basic human rights. Moral judgment scores also may not correlate with political attitudes, because people perceive the facts differently or have had different personal experiences. The experiences of inner city youth with police in contrast to those of suburban youth are likely to have a greater bearing on the item, "Police are mean" than is their moral judgment stage. Two people at the same stage who have a different understanding of the facts in a moral problem are likely to disagree about attitudes or actions. We cannot claim that moral judgment scores will predict all kinds of political attitudes, because some attitudes have no direct logical relation with stage orientations.

A second reason why moral judgment scores may not correlate with political attitudes is that the relationship may not be linear. As already cited in connection with the "action choices," if the choice favored by a stage tends to flip back and forth as we move up the stages, these inconsistencies will attenuate a correlation of DIT with action choice. A correlation will show up clearest if the lower stages favor one action and the later stages favor the other. Also, moral judgment scores will not correlate if virtually all the stages favor one action. In short, correlations indicate only one type of relationship; a nonsignificant correlation does not rule out other possible relations of moral judgment with attitudes and values.

Third, it must be recognized that an assessment of moral stage is not a full characterization of a person's moral ideology. Moral stage only characterizes abstract, basic conceptual structure. A Nazi stormtrooper, a Christian monk, a Communist Party boss, and an Israeli farmer can all be at Stage 4 (by virtue of basing moral obligation upon the laws and norms of their respective groups), yet the ideologies and attitudes of these individuals are bound to be radically different. Therefore we should not expect moral judgment to predict every moral attitude and choice, because much is determined by a person's culture and subculture, and by other aspects of one's ideology. A moral judgment score at best represents only the basic structure of a moral ideology, not its full content.

Behavior and Moral Judgment

Granting that moral judgment is not fully representative of moral ideology, what relation *does* moral ideology have to moral behavior? Moral judgment and various attitude measures are based on subjects' reports about what they think in a research context, not in an actual decision-making situation. For instance, subjects are questioned about the Heinz story as a hypothetical dilemma; is the reasoning that they report anything like the reasoning that they would actually go through if they were in that dilemma, and would it have anything to do with whether they would actually steal the drug?

What theoretically can we say about the relation of verbally espoused moral statements and the way a person lives his life? This issue is exceedingly complex, and a discussion of it is necessarily involved. Two ancient traditions exist on this matter, and they conflict. The Socratic tradition links ideology and behavior closely:

> First, virtue is ultimately one, not many, and it is always the same ideal form regardless of climate or culture. Second, the name of this ideal form is justice. Third, not only is the good one, but virtue is knowledge of the good. He who knows the good chooses the good. Fourth, the kind of knowledge of the good which is virtue is philosophical knowledge or intuition of the ideal form of the good, not correct opinion or acceptance of conventional beliefs. (quoted in Kohlberg 1971, p. 232)

On the other hand, the tradition of the New Testament views "knowledge of the good" as a very different matter from "choosing the good." Paul the Apostle says, "The good that I would, I do not; but the evil which I would not, that I do" (Romans, 7:19). Throughout the Gospels, it is a common observation that "the spirit is willing but the flesh is weak", and that there are many who "do not practice what they preach."

The Socratic view is most plausible when we think of great moral leaders: Socrates, Sir Thomas More, Albert Schweitzer, Eleanor Roosevelt, Mahatma Gandhi, Martin Luther King. The lives of these individuals are inseparable from their espoused moral ideologies. Each of these individuals spent much time and effort working out their views and reflecting upon "the good." Correct thinking was important to them. The central passion of their lives seems to have been carrying out their vision of "the good," and they were willing to endure hardship and sacrifice on its behalf. The pattern of their activities is coherent in terms of their moral thinking, which they were eager to make known; ideology, behavior, and motivation are united.

What, however, of the rest of us? As Paul says, "weakness of the flesh" creates a slippage between professed ideals and actions. A psychology that applies to human beings who haven't yet attained the integration of these great moral leaders must account for the discrepancy between professed ideals and actions.

An overall picture of the psychological processes presumably involved in acting morally may help to explain this discrepancy especially if we identify the particular set of functions that moral judgment involves within the total set of psychological functions. Moral judgment as a psychological variable has a limited role in the explanation of moral action—it may be a star role but it is only one player in a large cast. As discussed in Chapter 2, moral judgment is concerned with people's concepts of fairness. The psychological processes involved in making a moral judgment already presuppose that a dilemma has been detected, facts have been established, and that the situation is not urgent or immediate, so that the person has at least a little time to reflect. Once a moral judgment is made, many further psychological processes remain in determining the plan of action to be —whether it strictly follows from notions of fairness or not. Describing more precisely these other psychological processes that accompany the processes of moral judgment is speculative, but many clues and suggestions come from the psychological literature. Each one of these other processes or factors acts either as a mediating variable between moral judgment and behavior, or as a complicating factor in the relationship, hence each variable provides part of the explanation for discrepancies between moral judgment and action.

The list of factors and processes given below are presented in an order representing roughly that of their microgenesis—that is, approximately the temporal order in which the processes might follow one another from initial detection of a moral dilemma through final execution of action in response to the dilemma:

1. *Initial detection of a moral dilemma—differences in moral sensitivity.* Great individual differences are apparent in people's threshold for noticing moral dilemmas in the flux of social interaction. Some people seem to find a moral dilemma almost everywhere; others recognize a *moral* issue only after the most blatant signs of human suffering. Although moral sensitivity may be correlated with moral

judgment stage (people who are always seeing moral dilemmas tending to have developed more sophisticated forms of moral reasoning), no necessary connection exists, and current moral judgment measures only test directly for different conceptualizations of fairness, not directly for moral sensitivity. For example, "bleeding heart liberals" may be morally sensitive but not conceptually sophisticated, and "hard hearted lawyers" may be conceptually sophisticated but not morally sensitive. Moral sensitivity seems to be a property of the early recognition processes in perceiving situations and events, whereas moral conceptualization (that most clearly tapped in the DIT and Kohlberg's test) seems to be more concerned with the organization and interpretation of elements once a moral dilemma is recognized (defining the crucial issues, justifying one alternative over another). If one is morally insensitive, not even aware of a moral dilemma, then one's moral conceptualization and moral character do not matter in determining one's behavior.

In research in social role-taking, Flavell (1970, p. 1029 ff) has pointed out the distinction between *noticing* that a particular situation calls for a particular kind of analysis (for example, the situation calls for a role-taking analysis, or calls for a moral analysis) and actually *carrying out* that analysis (drawing inferences about others, or deciding what is fair). Applying this distinction in the morality domain, differences in moral sensitivity can complicate the relation between moral judgment and action.

2. *Differences in the role of reflective thought in organizing behavior.* Once a moral dilemma is recognized, do a person's concepts of fairness take over and determine the person's behavior? Not necessarily, it seems. Moral judgment tests obtain information about conscious-reflective thinking, but a person's behavior may be organized in ways that do not reflect his conscious-reflective thinking at all. Piaget in 1932 distinguished different "planes of mental life" (p. 85) —a reflective-conscious plane and an operative one. For instance, he reported that the actual pattern of cooperation in the children's marble playing was more advanced than the children's verbal reflections about cooperation. In actual play, children's activity was much more coordinated and structured according to the rules than would have been surmised from interviewing the children about rules. Piaget says, "Thought always lags behind action and cooperation has to be practiced for a very long time before its consequences can be brought fully to light by reflective thought" (p. 64). Piaget asserts that a structure of "rulefulness" in practical activity will appear before the person has a conscious realization of that structure that can be verbal-

ized. Another convincing example of this phenomenon is that children's speech at 2 years of age displays an operative knowledge of many grammatical rules, yet children are much older before they consciously realize and can discuss the rules of grammar that govern their speech patterns. There are immensely important implications to the view that different "planes of mental life" can have different structures and characteristics. One implication is that a person simply might not be conscious of his own operative structures, and hence self-report and verbalization may be an unreliable source of information about underlying organizational structures. Once one allows the possibility that the structure of human conduct may be organized by a different "program" than the program that a researcher would infer from a subject's verbalizations, then Aronfreed's view must be acknowledged:

> Common observation as well as introspection can raise some very serious questions about whether any significant amount of moral decision-making [such as that assessed in verbalization justifications] enters into the internalized control of conduct for most human beings (despite the fact that various states of moral knowledge may be available to them) .... Accordingly, the conception of the child as a miniaturized moral philosopher leaves something to be desired when one takes a larger psychological view of the full range of manifestations of the conscience. (Aronfreed 1976, p. 56—insert in brackets added).

Aronfreed's research (1976; 1968) clearly supports the view that at least some social behavior is controlled by conditioning that is largely independent of rational conscious decision. Aronfreed also goes on to show that the behavior *can* come under the control of rational, conscious decisions. However, "human beings are highly conditionable animals, whose social habits often assume an autonomy and permanence unburdened by any evaluative [i.e., conscious moral reasoning] thought processes." (Aronfreed, 1976, p. 59—insert in brackets added).

Thus, information coming from the verbalized "plane of mental life" need not tell us much about the "operative" plane. Acceptance of this proposition obliterates the necessity of there being a high correlation between ideology (assessed from verbal self-reports) and behavior; it renders the relationship as a matter of empirical study, in which nothing can be assumed. Piaget's own work, ironically, provides one of the chief reasons for doubting a *necessary* relation between organizational structures manifested in verbalization and the organization of behavior.

Furthermore, once one allows the possibility of different "planes" of organization, each a system with its own structure, why limit them to just two? Why not more than two? Much of moral judgment research seems to have assumed that only one program can be in a person's head at a given time; that the aim of assessment is to find out which one (of two or six or whatever); and that the problem of development is to account for the reason a person moves out of one program and into another (see especially Turiel, 1977, 1974, 1973). Piaget's notion of different planes of mental life contradicts the single track, "monaural" picture of morality and introduces two-track "stereo"—but why not "quad- or polyphonic? Is it not possible that there may be a verbal-production "plane," a recognition-tacit understanding plane, a plane of unreflective, automatized activity, and so forth; Each plane may be structured in different ways (or be at different stages, as Piaget suggests). Note, however, that actual decision-making may be governed by any plane; that is to say, behavior need not always be carried out by unreflective, automatized structures, but can be under the governance of consciously symbolized concepts.

Note that Piaget's distinction of planes is not simply the distinction between "thought" and "behavior." Cognitive functioning must be present to integrate and organize all activity not purely reflexive (a knee-jerk or eyelid closing). Piaget's distinction has to do with the extent of conscious symbolism of the cognitive structure and its amenability to manipulation by deliberate thought processes. Therefore the conscious plane is not necessarily empty rhetoric. For instance, much that we do in professional life I believe is primarily governed by reflective, conscious conceptualization that a person can verbally describe and defend.

Saying that verbalized judgments on the conscious-reflective plane is not necessarily related to behavior might appear to negate completely the importance of moral judgment research. On the contrary, I believe moral judgment research is crucial to a psychology of morality for two reasons: For one, asking people how they would solve hypothetical dilemmas has been the most effective way to discover the complex ways that people interpret and organize activity in complex social situations. Verbal responses to hypothetical dilemmas can provide information regarding what stimuli a subject is attending to, what interpretations he gives these and how they relate to past experiences, how a chain of activity is to be sequenced, and what goal of the activity is envisioned. A psychology of morality must take all these components into account. Moral judgment research has attempted to encode information about all these elements. Simply looking at a behavior, such as whether or not a person cheats on an exam, does not contain information about how the person interpreted the situation. Did it even occur to the subject to cheat? Was the whole situation so artificial that it didn't really seem like cheating? The behavior doesn't indicate what the person's intentions were: Was the person trying to gain acceptance within the group? Has the person in the past been taught that achievement is all important, regardless of the means? When studying morality, the whole complex of interacting factors is important, and a subject's verbalizations have thus far been the most useful method for discovering how these factors co-occur and interact. Other methods, such as naturalistic observation of actual behavior, may be developed whereby the full complex of factors can be appraised; however, gaining ideas about how to define these complexes to date has come primarily from subjects' verbalization.

Second, verbalized judgments are important because they do sometimes reflect the structures governing actual conduct. Further, action arising from reflective, conscious judgment is likely to be more morally defensible than action arising from preconscious, unexamined structures: Behavior governed by structures at the conscious, reflective plane is more likely to be coordinated with long-range goals, to take more factors into account, and to be more amenable to coordination with the plans of others. As Brown has stated (1965), one of the aspects of moral development is for behavior to come under the governance of reflective, conscious judgments.

3. *Superficial information about reflective thought.* Even if a person's behavior is primarily governed by reflective, conscious judgments, the information elicited in an interview or questionnaire may not be representative of a person's true thoughts, but may reflect more the subject's response to characteristics in the testing situation. In response to a researcher's questionnaire, a subject may be expressing high-sounding ideas that he or she believes would favorably impress the researcher, rather than the conceptual tools he or she actually uses in decision-making. Hence, a person espousing the ideals of love or justice, when put in an actual situation, vividly aware of the conflicting pulls and claims, may not be able even to figure out what the loving or just thing would be. In such cases, the person's action may hardly seem loving or just, in striking contrast to the espoused beliefs. This type of discrepancy may be most typical of people we call hypocrites. A person may be chic liberal or Sunday-morn-

ing Christian, and publicly affirm allegiance to ideals, yet may live out life hardly aware of the day by day implications of these ideals.

This kind of discrepancy may be most pronounced, however, between *superficially* held beliefs and actual behavior. No doubt many tests of ideology only assess beliefs held at a superficial level; but this is a failure to fully assess a person's ideology. Tests of ideology should go beyond slogans and a person's presentation of his public "face." The discrepancy, therefore, is more a matter of superficial and incomplete assessment of true thinking (also discussed in Chapter 4) than the theoretical problem of people's thinking not being more highly correlated with behavior.

Research by Bem and Allen (1974) and Markus (1977) indicates that the relation is stronger between verbal reports (as in interviews and on questionnaires) and externally observed behavior if the verbal information given by subjects represents a consciously thought-out position. If a moral judgment score represents only what came to mind to the subject when pressed by the interviewer or questionnaire, the chance of a strong relation between this information and behavioral assessments is lessened.

4. *Deliberate misinformation about reflective thought.* Closely related to the above complication is that people sometimes deliberately misrepresent their true thinking. A politician may hire a speech writer to give him something that appeals to voters, but the speech writer's way of thinking may be window dressing. Someone in the business of persuading other people may sometimes sense that his listeners would be influenced by a bit of moral talk; however, it may be that moral values hardly affect his actual decision making. One of the distressing contradictions in the Nixon administration was Nixon's moralistic public presentations and his installation of Billy Graham in the White House, as contrasted with the apparent absence of moral reasoning in the White House Transcripts (New York Times, 1974).

Although it may be easy to misrepresent the importance of moral values in one's value system, it apparently is not so easy to "fake upward" the stage of moral judgment reasoning. Several studies reviewed in the next chapter indicate the difficulty of faking high on the DIT. Regardless of one's stage, however, a person can fake great concern for moral values.

5. *Breakdown in cognitive processing.* Even if our information about a person's reflective thought is accurate, and even if he generally tries to govern his behavior according to consciously chosen ideals, nevertheless, the situation may be so electrifying and abrupt that he

is unable to pull his thoughts together. One of the most striking findings coming from research on bystander reactions to emergencies is that people fail to help others not because of general apathy or evil intent but because of confusion. In emergencies, people are often uncertain about what the situation is and whether one's personal action is called for (Huston and Korte 1976; Latane and Darley 1968). In this case, the discrepancy between verbally espoused ideals and actual behavior is due to the inability to perform a rational appraisal of the situation—the mental processing short-circuits before computing what action would follow from one's ideals. Subjects typically report that they did not know what to do, were not sure about what was happening, or did not know what they should do.

Since most moral judgment research has studied how people think under relaxed conditions, most of our information about moral judgment in hypothetical dilemmas has not involved highly charged situations. But performance "in the heat of battle" may fall short of intended performance or of performance under practice conditions. Practice situations are likely to differ from actual situations, because the latter "are for real"—that is, one feels the pressure of having something at stake. Real situations are likely to present more distractions and pressures than hypothetical ones, with actual people arguing and threatening, with the contagion of others' actions, with the real difficulty of carrying out a line of action, rather than just intending it. Real situations are likely to be more ambiguous and confusing, because hypothetical situations often present the basic facts as established, whereas in real situations one must ascertain and interpret the situation as well as devise a plan in response to it.

Whereas the research on bystanders' reactions to emergencies suggests that many people in such situations are confused and have difficulty with moral decision-making, other research in less intense or less abrupt situations suggests that reasoning in real situations may be fairly similar to that in hypothetical situations. The most careful study of this kind was by Damon (1977), who found that children's reasoning in a hypothetical distributive justice situation was similar ($r = .85$) to their reasoning in a real situation. Haan (1975), on the other hand, found only a rough similarity between reasoning about the Kohlberg dilemmas and reasoning about a real instance of student protest, but instrumentation problems abound in that study. In another study, Haan (1978) found a few significant relationships between reasoning about hypothetical situations and reasoning used by adolescent participants in five social games. The discrepancy between real and hypothetical situation is most likely related to the extent of pressure and the speed with which a person must make a decision, as well as to contextual similarities of the dilemmas.

6. *Differences in "ego strength" in executing a plan of action.* In an actual situation even when a person has determined what ought to be done, despite the distractions and pressures, he still may falter in the execution. Two people may have the same understanding of a situation and the same plan of action, but one may have iron will, courage, and resolve, whereas the other person may fail to carry through. The two people differ in "ego strength." A considerable amount of research has investigated ego strength as a component in self regulation. For instance, research on delay of gratification (Mischel 1974) contrasts subjects able to endure and work for a greater goal, as opposed to subjects who cannot endure. Krebs (1967) and Kohlberg (1969) report a study in which subjects at Stage 4 with low ego strength cheat more than subjects at Stage 4 with high ego strength— presumably the subjects with low ego strength were less able to carry out their beliefs than those with high ego strength. Low ego strength makes a person more vulnerable to situational pressures and distractions, and less able to carry out one's highest ideals.

Sometimes the term "moral character" is used to depict a person's ability to "live up to his convictions." According to the present analysis, moral character defined as ego strength is distinguishable from moral sensitivity and from adequacy in moral judgment. Strictly speaking, ego strength is amoral, since it is a feature of executing plans, whatever the plan may be. For instance, high ego strength might be manifested in practicing the piano for 10 hours a day, administering an injection into a child's arm, carrying out a bombing mission over enemy territory, or pulling off a bank robbery according to plan. Although ego strength is often crucial for the performance of moral action, in and of itself, it is amoral.

7. *Interplay of moral values with other values.* Another reason that verbalized moral judgments may not predict behavior is that behavior reflects the interplay of many kinds of values, moral values being only one kind. Damon's research (1977) is illuminating on this point. Children were asked how to divide ten candy bars as rewards for bracelets they had made. Under one condition, children actually made bracelets and were asked to discuss the basis for dividing the candy bars ("real life reasoning"). Under another condition, the problem was described as a hypothetical situation and each child was asked how the candy bars should be divided ("hypothetical reasoning"). In addition, the children were given a chance to actually divide the candy bars ("actual social conduct"). As suggested earlier, the real

life *reasoning* was similar to the hypothetical reasoning. However, neither of these related well to the actual social *conduct*. Damon states, "We must conclude from the present set of findings that predicting a child's social conduct from his or her reasoning remains a complex and risky task" (1977, p. 116). However, the discrepancy between reasoning (hypothetical or real) and conduct was owing to the children abandoning their concept of what is fair to give themselves more candy bars. The discrepancy between moral reasoning and conduct in Damon's study was due to another competing value operating in behavior, self interest, which had been suppressed in the discussions of fairness.

Moral judgment tests tell us something about a person's concepts of fairness. Moral judgment tests, however, do not measure the relative strength or moral values compared with other values a person may have. Sometimes moral values can be compromised by other values (success in a career, the promotion of the Third Reich, etc.), and sometimes moral values are completely set aside. For instance, John Dean in his book, *Blind Ambition*, recounts that his nefarious activities as Special Counsel to President Nixon were motivated by unquestioning loyalty to that administration and by his own ambitions within it. Dean says that he constantly put aside the larger questions of morality—such thinking was completely preempted by more pressing practical concerns. It is inappropriate to seek an explanation of Dean's behavior in terms of low moral judgment scores, because the whole process of thinking about fairness was short-circuited. The most flagrantly cruel people of the world (Hitler, Goering, Stalin, Idi Amin, the Munich Terrorists, Mafia chieftains) are not to be understood in terms of low moral judgment scores. They talk about being "beyond good and evil," and not encumbered by "mere morality." Therefore, expecting a high correlation of moral reasoning with social conduct assumes that moral values are the only operative values in decision-making.

Above, in the section on attitudes, it was stated that the assessment of moral judgment is not a full characterization of moral ideology. The Stage 4 Nazi stormtrooper presumably has a different ideology from the Stage 4 Christian monk. Different ideologies have different values. Moreover, people have different values that are not expressed in ideological statements (or sometimes even acknowledged). Nevertheless, these values can influence decision-making along with moral values. Typically in moral judgment research, no assessment is made of other values and their relevance to a subject in a particular situation. Until we start doing this, we can hardly expect to find very high predictability of behavior, nor much cross-situational consistency (when different values may be salient in different ways to subjects).

In summary, a moral judgment test only gives us information about a subject's concepts of fairness; however, many other psychological processes are involved in interpreting situations and organizing one's actions. If we try to identify some of these processes, we can see how each one complicates the relationship between moral judgment and behavior, and each one provides an explanation for the attenuated relationship between moral judgment and behavior. On the other hand, this discussion also gives us a basis for predicting the conditions under which the correlation between moral judgment should be higher: (1) if the subjects see a *moral* dilemma in the situation; (2) if all subjects have the same facts and information; (3) if the behavior in question does not occur in a high-pressure situation (for instance, under battlefield conditions); (4) if the behavior in question is governed by structures on the conscious-reflective plane rather than by preconscious, operative structures; (5) if the information on moral judgment reflects well-thought-out positions rather than ideas "off the top of the head;" (6) if the information on moral judgment is not a deliberate misrepresentation; (7) if the ideology of subjects differs more in terms of stage differentiators (some subjects are Stage 2, some are Stage 4) than in terms of other aspects of ideology (a Stage 4 Nazi versus a Stage 4 Israeli); (8) if the characteristics used as stage differentiators are logically related differentially to courses of action (e.g., Stage 2 logically favors action X, whereas Stage 4 logically favors action Y); (9) if all subjects are high in ego strength (will carry out their plans of action); and (10) if moral values are predominant over other values for the subjects.

These ten conditions are derived from the previous discussion regarding what other mental processes and situational variables influence moral judgment. In addition, recall that previously mentioned were two statistical or methodological conditions that affect the strength of a correlation. (11) A correlation will be highest if the lower stages of thinking interpret the situation so that one course of action is strongly favored while the higher stages strongly favor the opposite course of action. If, for instance, a Stage 2 interpretation favors action A, Stage 3 favors B, Stage 4 favors A, and Stage 5 favors B, then a linear correlation will not show up, even though the interpretive framework of each stage logically favors one action over another. Furthermore, if action choice flip-flops back and forth through the order of stages, then the fact that subjects show considerable stage mixture (especially for adjacent stages) will further blur the correlation between moral judgment and behavior. The strongest correlations therefore will be for situations in which Stage 2 favors one action, Stages 5 and 6 the opposite action, with Stages 3 and 4 in between. Obviously not all situations will be patterned this neatly (for example, the Heinz dilemma). (12) A correlation between moral judgment and behavior will probably be higher if some redundancy is built into each measure. In Chapter 3 it was argued that a moral judgment measure should contain several dilemmas, so that idiosyncratic reactions would not obfuscate the general patterns of thinking. Likewise, such redundancy is desirable in behavioral measures too, for the same reason (see Fishbein and Acjzen 1974, Burton 1976 for more discussion that behavioral measures with more than one bit of information show stronger correlations with ideology). To date, almost without exception, moral behavior has been indexed by a single act or bit of information; this practice may be as limiting as trying to index IQ by a one-item test.

With all these qualifications and complications, it is a wonder that any studies have found any significant correlations between moral judgment and behavior. It is to these studies that we now turn.

DIT Studies

Many studies have related one or another version of Kohlberg's test to behavior: Froming and Cooper 1976; Fodor 1972; Haan, Smith and Block 1968; Harris, Mussen and Rutherford 1973; Hudgins and Prentice 1973; Kohlberg and Freundlich 1973; Krebs 1967; McNamee 1973; Milgram 1963; Podd 1972; Rothman 1976; Saltstein, Diamond, and Balenky 1972; Schwartz et al. 1969; Turiel and Rothman 1972. I will not attempt to summarize these studies since a different measure of moral judgment was used and they are being reviewed elsewhere by Blasi (1978). By and large the studies show positive and significant correlations. However, the strength of the correlations are low, suggesting that many of the factors discussed in the previous section may be attenuating the relationship.

There are nine DIT studies to report: five using experimental measures of behavior (promise-keeping in the Prisoner-dilemma game, susceptibility to group pressure in an Asch-type situation, distributive justice, and two tests of cheating), and four using naturalistic measures of behavior (delinquency-nondelinquency, behavioral ratings in school, job performance ratings of medical doctors, and voting in the 1976 Presidential Election).

Jacobs' Study[3]

Jacobs (1975, 1977) studied behavior in the Prisoner's Dilemma game, a simulation game widely used in the study of conflict resolution (Rapaport and Chammah 1965). In this game a subject and a partner play a given number of trials in an effort to accumulate points having monetary value. In each trial, the subject and partner indicate whether they want to compete or cooperate. Each does not know the other's choice until after that specific trial. If the subject and a partner both indicate cooperation, both win a modest gain; if one competes and the other cooperates, the competing one wins double and the cooperating one loses double; if both compete, both lose moderately. The game therefore presents an interpersonal conflict situation whereby two people can win very unequal amounts, both lose, or both win a modest amount. The experimental situation furthermore employs a confederate of the experimenter as the partner, who agrees with the subject early in the procedures that they will cooperate throughout all the trials so that both the alleged partner and the actual subject will win a modest amount. The behavior of interest is whether the subject will maintain the agreement and continue to indicate cooperation on all the ensuing trials.

Subjects were assigned to one of three different experimental conditions. In one condition ("Defect" condition) the confederate partner broke the promise to cooperate and started competing with the subject, thus making the subject sustain double losses as long as the subject cooperated and kept the previous agreement. In a second condition, the confederate partner broke the agreement only 50% of the time ("Partial Defect" condition). In a third control condition, the partner maintained the agreement ("Cooperative" condition). Thus subjects' promise-keeping behavior could be examined as a function of the provocation of the confederate partner's deviance from the original agreement.

Subjects had been tested previously on the DIT and divided into a "Conventional" morality group (subjects whose P% scores were lower than 50% or who chose Stage 3 or 4 predominantly) or a "Principled" morality group (subjects whose P% scores were greater than 50%). In order to obtain 30 subjects for each morality group, 127 adult women volunteers ranging in age from 20 to 55 were tested. All subjects and partners were women.

The design of the experiment, therefore, consisted of randomly assigning subjects into one of three treatment groups, blocking on moral judgment (Principled versus Conventional). The dependent

variable was the number of times the subject indicated the cooperation response. The "Cooperation" condition was seen as a control;
the "Defect" and "Partial Defect" conditions were seen as creating a
moral dilemma in the subject whether to keep the original promise or
not, despite the partner's pledge.

Jacobs hypothesized that Conventional subjects would break their
promises whereas Principled subjects would keep theirs. Jacobs linked
moral judgment to this behavior in the following way:

> Conventional Level: While stage 3 and 4 reasoning recognizes the impor-
> tance of keeping one's word, such behavior is based on a commitment to
> role obligation as defined by society, e.g., being a cooperative game part-
> ner or a compliant experimental subject. Faced with a promise-breaking
> partner, stage 3 subjects were expected to try to minimize their losses and
> to rationalize this behavior as being 'natural', particularly in a situation
> where the partner was being 'not nice'. Stage 4 subjects were expected to
> break their promise for similar reasons and in addition perhaps to punish
> the promise breaker.

> Principled Level: Stage 5 subjects were expected to keep the promise re-
> gardless of losses, because for them free agreement and contract is the bind-
> ing element of obligation outside of the legal realm. The Golden Rule was
> expected to guide the behavior of stage 6 subjects. In addition, the agree-
> ment to behave cooperatively reflects the stage 6 valuing of human beings
> as ends and not means (Jacobs, 1977, p. 50).

Having derived a behavioral prediction from a logical analysis of
how different stages would differentially interpret the situation,
Jacobs then continued to trace the linkage of thought to behavior.
As a check on whether subjects took the situation seriously or just regarded it as a silly, nonconsequential laboratory game, Jacobs obtained
ratings on State anxiety at various points in the procedure (Spielburger, Goruch, and Lushene 1970), that is subjects' report on how both-
ered and anxious they felt at those particular times. Subjects in the
control cooperative condition experienced low levels of anxiety, while
subjects in the Defect and Partial Defect conditions experienced significantly more anxiety, $F(2,50) = 23.57$, $p < .001$, indicating that
both Conventional and Principled subjects whose partners broke the
agreement did experience the situation as nontrivial and real.

In addition to the State anxiety measure (anxiety felt at a particular time), Jacobs also tested subjects on Trait anxiety (Spielburger
1970), that is, habitual or chronic anxiety. Conventional subjects
were no different from Principled subjects. This lack of difference
between the groups provides a control for the possible contention

that Principled subjects are more thin-skinned, compliant, and neu-
rotically moral than Conventional subjects. Therefore it cannot be
maintained that Principled subjects are apt to be more cooperative
because they are more anxious people who dare not offend anyone.

Subjects were asked in a debriefing session the following questions
about their subjective experience in the Prisoner's Dilemma Game:

1. When you and your partner agreed to cooperate, how committed did
you feel to that agreement?
2. During the experiment, how much conflict did you feel about keeping
the agreement?
3. How much of the conflict was due to your partner's behavior?
4. How much of that conflict was due to a desire to earn the largest payoff?
5. During the last five trials, how committed did you feel to your original
cooperative agreement? (Jacobs 1977, p. 53)

Subjects responded to each question on a five-point scale ranging
from "none" to "a great deal."

Responses to Question 1 indicate that both Principled and Conventional subjects felt equally committed to the agreement at the beginning. Responses to Question 5 indicate that Principled subjects remained more committed to their promise than Conventional subjects
at the end of the trials, $F(1,50) = 12.79, p < .005$. Responses to Question 2 indicate that subjects in the Defect and Partial Defect conditions felt more conflict about keeping the promise than subjects in
the Cooperate condition, $F(2,50) = 11.57, p < .001$, and attributed
their sense of conflict to the partner's behavior (Question 3). In Question 4, Conventional subjects indicated they were more concerned
with the desire for a large payoff, $F(1,50) = 11.65, p < .005$.

In addition to the above questions, the informal debriefing session
after the experiment provided interesting information. Principled
subjects more often than Conventional subjects spontaneously cited
keeping the agreement as the rationale for their behavior, $\chi^2 = 9.27$;
$p < .01$.

Thus Jacobs showed an association between the generalized framework for interpreting moral dilemmas (as assessed by the DIT) and
the moral interpretation given to this specific situation. Furthermore,
she showed that this laboratory situation was perceived and felt as a
real moral dilemma for subjects whose partners broke their agreement.

This much of the study demonstrates consistency in verbalized subjective report. What about the actual behavior as measured by the
cooperative or competitive response on the trial? Table 6.12 gives the
behavioral data. The three treatment conditions (varying the behavior
of the partner) are each subdivided by Principled and Conventional

Table 6.12. Means and Standard Deviations of Cooperative Responses

Group	Practice Trials	Total Post-Agreement Trials	Individual Trial Sets Post-Agreement			
			1-20	21-40	41-60	61-80
Cooperative						
Principled $\overline{X}$	12.00	80.00	20.00	20.00	20.00	20.00
SD	3.91	0.00	0.00	0.00	0.00	0.00
Conventional $\overline{X}$	10.10	79.89	19.89	20.00	20.00	20.00
SD	4.65	0.31	0.31	0.00	0.00	0.00
Partial Defect						
Principled $\overline{X}$	10.00	64.70	18.00	16.60	14.20	15.90
SD	5.67	17.25	3.49	4.78	6.01	5.36
Conventional $\overline{X}$	10.20	59.40	16.70	15.70	13.20	13.80
SD	1.98	15.45	3.36	3.91	4.89	5.63
Defect						
Principled $\overline{X}$	10.70	52.89	14.50	12.70	12.30	13.40
SD	2.49	22.37	3.20	6.65	7.63	8.89
Conventional $\overline{X}$	8.50	23.50	12.60	4.60	3.20	3.10
SD	2.55	18.39	4.22	5.58	4.44	6.02

Source: From Jacobs 1977.

moral judgment groups ($N = 10$ in each of the six groups). The practice trials occurred before the subject and partner agreed to cooperate, and show that the Principled subjects were no more cooperative by nature than Conventional women. Following the agreement, however, the nature of the situation changed. In the control group, the Cooperative treatment, both Conventional and Principled subjects cooperated just as their partners cooperated throughout all 80 trials. However in the Defect conditions, in which the partner was competing when she had promised to cooperate, subjects showed some competing responses too. But the Principled subjects kept their promise significantly more often than the Conventional subjects, $F(1,50) = 31.71$, $p < .001$. The major hypothesis of the study was therefore confirmed: Principled subjects kept the promise more often even in the face of a promise-breaking partner and monetary loss. Thus, a generalized measure of moral reasoning (DIT) was related to moral reasoning in an actual specific situation, and both were related to behavior.

Comparing the three treatment conditions, a main effect was also found for partner's behavior; as common sense would predict, the more the partner deviated, the more the subject deviated, $F(2,50) = 137.87$, $p < .001$. Post hoc analysis of the interaction of moral judgment by partner's behavior shows that the partner's promise-breaking affected Conventional subjects more, $F(2,50) = 19.2$, $p < .001$.

Furthermore, the interaction of moral judgment level with trials was significant, $F(3,5) = 2.82$, $p < .05$, indicating that Conventional subjects with defecting partners got progressively more competitive, whereas Principled subjects showed an initial dip in cooperation followed by a slight increase in cooperation.

Jacobs' study is important not only for demonstrating a relationship between the DIT and behavior, but more so for conceptualizing what the mediating processes might be and building in ways to check out these linkages. It is the type of study that promises to advance our understanding of verbalized moral judgment's relation to behavior. One last interesting observation: After the debriefing, Jacobs reports that significantly more Principled subjects refused payment for participation than Conventional subjects, $\chi^2 = 9.29$, $p < .01$.

Other Studies

Froming and Cooper (1976) studied compliance behavior in an Asch-type situation. The subject listened to very rapid clicks in earphones and was asked to count the number of clicks. The subject was in a group of confederates of the experimenter, and the group was asked to report the number of clicks. The real subject heard the other participants' estimates on each trial. On some trials the confederates overestimated or underestimated the number of clicks, and the behavior of interest was to see if the subject would go along with the group when they were wrong. The measure of compliance was the frequency with which the subject went along with the incorrect estimation of the group, and the extent of deviance that the subject would go along with. The subjects were 91 male undergraduates in an introductory psychology course. The authors report a significant negative correlation of compliance scores with the DIT P score ($r = -.33, p <$ .03). On a subset of 35 subjects for whom SAT scores were available, the correlation between compliance and the SAT was nonsignificant; the partial correlation between the DIT and compliance with SAT scores *partialled out* was still significant ($r = -.31, p < .05$).

Gunzberger, Wegner, and Anooshian (1977) studied the distributive justice behavior in 44 male subjects aged 13-18 who believed they were a member of a group of four students to be rewarded for their work. After working for one hour on a questionnaire the subject was asked to distribute money among four people. The subject (designated "A") had worked for one hour. He was told that a second person (designated "B") had also worked for one hour. A third person (designated "C") had worked only 25 minutes because supposedly that was the extent of time that would be profitable for him to work. A fourth subject (designated "D") could have profitably worked for an hour, but had been called back to a class after 25 minutes. The subject's distribution of money was classified into one of five patterns, as follows:

> (1) a *self-interest* distribution was one in which a subject allocated more money to himself than to any other group member (A $>$ B = C = D); (2) a *parity* distribution was one in which money was allocated equally to all group members (A = B = C = D); (3) an *equity* distribution was one in which money was allocated on the basis of the actual input of time worked (A = B $>$ C = D); (4) a *social responsibility* distribution was one in which additional money was allocated to the constrained individual (person D) from all other group members (A = B = D $>$C); (5) an *individual responsibility* distribution was one in which the conditions of equity (above were met, and in which additional money was allocated to the constrained individual (person D) from the reward allocation (person A) alone (C $<$ A = D $<$B). (Gunzburger, Wegner, and Anooshian 1977, p. 165-66).

Subjects given the DIT were divided into stage groups on the basis of endorsing to an exceptional degree one of the stages. Analysis of variance indicated that the way subjects distributed the rewards was significantly different among the moral judgment groups, $F(3,39) =$

5.10, $p < .05$. The *equity* pattern was highest for the Stage 3 group; the *social responsibility* pattern was higher for the Stage 4, 5, and 6 than the Stage 2 and 3 groups; and the *individual responsibility* pattern was highest for the Stage 6 group.

Leming (1978) studied cheating behavior with the Hartshorne and May "circles test." In this test, subjects are asked to attempt to memorize the location of nine circles on a page of paper, and are then instructed to close their eyes and write the numbers 1 through 9 in the circles. Subjects then report their scores. Since it is virtually impossible to place more than a few numbers in the circles, high scores presumably represent peeking while instructed not to do so. Of 152 college undergraduates tested, Leming found that subjects with low DIT scores cheated more ($\chi^2 = 10.4, p < .01$). When the results were analyzed separately for a high supervision condition versus a low supervision condition, not significant differences in cheating were noted between low DIT scorers and high DIT scorers in the low supervision condition; however, significant differences were seen in the high supervision condition.

Malinowski (1978) studied cheating behavior in terms of the fidelity with which subjects reported their scores when left alone to work on a pursuit tracker (a physical coordination task). The subjects were 53 male college undergraduates. Subjects low in DIT scores cheated to a greater extent (Mann-Whitney U test, $z = 2.75, p < .006$), were more likely to cheat sooner ($\chi^2 = 6.14, p < .025$), and cheated on more test trials ($t = 2.64, p < .05$).

McColgan's Study of Antisocial Behavior

The classification of youth as delinquents, predelinquents, or nondelinquents can be regarded as a naturalistic measure of antisocial behavior, in that the behavior is not elicited in a laboratory or contrived situation but has occurred in the normal course of events. In other words, no intervention on the part of the researcher occurred to produce the behavior. Also delinquency, in and of itself, is of tremendous interest and importance, and need not generalize beyond itself (as do most laboratory measures to be of social significance). However, "delinquency" is a legal, not a psychological term; many factors influence the designation of "delinquent" besides the behavior of the youth, and many behaviors are subsumed under that label. This makes research on delinquency difficult and imprecise, but not impossible nor uninterpretable.

No one can seriously claim that low moral judgment *causes* delinquency, or is related to delinquency in a one-to-one manner. If low moral judgment caused delinquency, all young children early in their development would be delinquents. Rather, low moral judgment is seen as a contributing factor to antisocial behavior. All things being equal, a youth who understands and appreciates the fairness of certain laws and codes of behavior is less likely to break those codes and laws than one who does not understand their fairness. Young people who understand the fairness of laws are more likely to see their stake in the social order. Of course, all things are not equal, and some young people have strong situational pressures that provoke antisocial behavior. But add to these factors a view of the social world in which "playing it straight" does not make any sense, and the disposition to delinquency is overwhelming.

Several previous studies have reported significant relationships of delinquency with measures of social cognitive development (Chandler 1973; Fodor 1972; Hickey 1972; Kohlberg and Freundlich 1973; Selman 1973). In these studies, delinquents were found to have retarded development on Kohlberg's test, role taking skills, and Piaget's Golden Rule task (interpreting the meaning of the Golden Rule). In addition, using the DIT, Kantner (1975) found that a sample of 60 male prison inmates had very low DIT scores, averaging 23.5 (compared with the general adult average of 40.0). Similarly, Armstrong (1975) found that 20 prison inmates in Illinois had average DIT scores of 31.2, and 15 prison parolees with IQs slightly above average had a DIT average of 33.3. Furthermore, McColgan (1975) studied a group of 29 incarcerated delinquents, average age 16 years, and found their P% score to average 18.8 (significantly lower than a "normal" group averaging 28.7 that was roughly comparable on age, sex, race and IQ). McColgan also found the delinquent group to be low on Kohlberg's test (mean MMS = 233) and low on Piaget's Golden Rule task (most subjects failed to interpret the Golden Rule in terms of ideal reciprocity but answered in terms of concrete reciprocity).

A serious problem in interpreting such findings is that although prisoners or delinquents may have lower than average social cognitive development, prisoners and delinquents disproportionately come from disadvantaged backgrounds, and so lower social cognition scores may simply be part of a general picture of disadvantage rather than being something distinctively associated with antisocial behavior. The crucial test is whether delinquents have lower scores than people from the same backgrounds who do not engage in antisocial behavior. In short, finding the appropriate comparison group is crucial.

McColgan (1975, 1977) has made the most impressive attempt to find an appropriate comparison group. Sensitive to the possibility that incarceration itself may have an effect on test taking, McColgan identified a group of youths designated "predelinquent" with records of flagrant antisocial behavior, but who had not been isolated and institutionalized but were kept as much as possible in the mainstream of school and social life. Thus a comparison group from the same current milieu could be picked. Twenty-six predelinquents were identified in three junior high schools in Minnesota who had been described by their teachers in the following ways: "aggressive, inadequate impulse control, acts without forethought, poor self-image, excessive variations in mood, poor interactions with peers, poor work habits" (McColgan 1977, p. 62). Many of these subjects would have gone through juvenile court proceedings rather than be maintained in school if they had been in a different state or dealt with at a different time. But an experimental program had been devised by the state Community Corrections and the local Department of Special Education to keep these youths in the community. After gathering background information on the 26 predelinquents, a search was undertaken to find 26 nondelinquent subjects who were closely matched individually with the predelinquents. Each predelinquent was matched with a control on 14 dimensions: age, IQ, SES, race, sex, test instruments (same measures and same order of presentation), interviewer, evironmental conditions for all interviews, time of testing, scoring system, residential locale (same city and neighborhood), school, school grades, family with one parent. Table 6.13 compares the two groups on age, SES, and IQ; note the high correlation of predelinquents with their matched controls, and note that none of the differences are significant on these control variables.

Table 6.14 presents the comparison of the groups on the dependent variables, five measures of social-cognitive development. As can be seen, the predelinquent group was most strikingly different from the controls on the DIT and, surprisingly, not significantly different on the Kohlberg test or on Chandler's role taking measure. Apparently,

Table 6.13. Predelinquents and Controls Compared on Age, SES, IQ

Variable	Predelinquent		Control				
	M	SD	M	SD	r	t-test	p value
Age (months)	168.7	11.4	170.3	8.3	.79	−1.16	.26
SES*	37.8	27.5	38.0	27.3	.95	− .11	.92
IQ†	94.0	13.7	95.1	14.3	.91	− .91	.37

Source: Adapted from McColgan, 1975, p. 40.

*Duncan Scale

†Shipley-Hartford Intelligence Test

when subjects with records of antisocial behavior are matched with controls who do not show such antisocial behavior, the DIT statistically discriminates the groups, and does so notably better than several other measures of social cognitive development.

It may seem paradoxical that the amount of "principled" moral thinking should be a discriminator between subjects showing antisocial behavior and those showing conventional behavior—would not we expect the differences between the groups to show up more on the amount of Stage 3 and 4? Recall, however, that previous studies (discussed in Chapter 4) have shown that the P index is the most useful general indicator of moral judgment development of DIT responses. Possibly Stages 3 and 4 are not discriminating because of low reliabilities on these scales.

McColgan speculated on why the DIT might be working better than the Kohlberg test with these subjects:

the DIT, as a recognition/comprehension task, is not as heavily loaded on verbal expressive skills as are the other instruments, particularly the Kohlberg instrument . . . . I believe the data support the suggestion that a person's tacit awareness of principled arguments has a lot to do with one's decision regarding overt action. I'm less convinced that being able to verbally explain arguments has much to do with people's actions. (McColgan 1977, p. 64)

Marston (1978) followed up McColgan's subjects three years after they were originally tested. Marston obtained behavioral ratings on the subjects from assistant principals ("School Behavior Profile," Balow and Rubin, 1974), and found that the original P scores of the DIT were still significantly correlated to the behavior of these subjects, even after three years (r = .34). Statistically partialling out IQ

Table 6.14. Antisocial Subjects and Comparison Subjects:
Means, Standard Deviations, and Matched Pair t Tests on Dependent Measures
(n = 26 in both groups)

Variables	Antisocial Subjects		Comparison Subjects		t-test	p value
	M	SD	M	SD		
DIT P Index	16.9	4.6	23.7	7.0	3.58	<.001
Kohlberg Moral Maturity Score	189.3	14.0	196.1	30.6	1.13	.27
Piaget Golden Rule Task	223.1	32.3	228.9	37.9	0.72	.48
Chandler Role Taking Task	12.8	4.1	12.1	5.1	−0.54	.59

and SES had no appreciable effect on DIT predictability. The DIT, therefore, had a significant concomitant relationship with behavior (in McColgan's study) but also had a significant predictive relationship with the rating scale and in predicting school dropouts ($t = 2.3$, $p < .025$).

Sheehan and his associates (1979) related DIT scores of 348 medical doctors in residency programs to ratings of their professional performance as doctors. Each resident was rated by three to eight medical faculty members, and a performance score was calculated for each resident by averaging the ratings and weighting the score by the national prestige of the institution. This professional performance score correlated .57 with the DIT. A canonical correlation between the DIT stage scores and 18 components of the professional ratings for 257 pediatric house officers was .68, $p < .0001$.

G. Rest's Study of the 1976 Presidential Election

Psychologists researching morality have long neglected a very important type of behavior, one that might be called "advocacy behavior." Psychologists have tended to think of moral behavior in terms of cheating, hurting, helping, donating, resisting authority, sharing, and so on. Measures of these actions are "behavioral" in that they are based on publicly observable events and have impact on the flow of events in the world; that is, they are not merely signs of inner, private events that may only affect the subjective experience of a single person. But consider also advocacy behavior; for example, a jury member arguing with other jury members for acquittal of a defendent; a nurse proposing in a staff conference that some crisis be handled in a particular way; a citizen casting a vote for a particular candidate; a faculty member circulating a petition for stronger Affirmative Action policy; a former employer writing a very cautious letter of recommendation. All these activities are public and have impact on the flow of events (and so are "behavioral" in that sense); however, they are primarily verbal or quasiverbal, and are deliberate expressions of subjective preferences or decisions. Advocacy behavior is an extremely important aspect of all decision making in which preferences of individuals are taken into account. Advocacy behavior may be formalized in terms of elections or may be more informal, such as speaking up in a group for or against a position. "Advocacy behavior" is expressing an attitude in order to influence decision making.

To the degree that issues of fairness are involved in advocating one position over another, we may expect moral judgment to be related to different advocacy positions. Moral judgment might be highly correlated with voting in some elections, but not in others, in which, for instance, interpretation of facts or the candidates personalities, or different predictions of future events was the salient ingredient. As Reinhold Niebuhr (1960, p. 171) wrote, "The realm of politics is a twilight zone where ethical and technical issues meet," but some political questions may involve a different mix than others.

Advocacy behavior can profoundly influence the course of events, but not always in straightforward ways. For instance, suppose many people speak out for protecting the environment, and public opinion in a particular locality is mobilized to elect an "environmentalist" candidate to public office. Then the environmentalist candidate, in following what he believes to be his public mandate, proposes legislation to ban the use of disposable metal cans for beverages. The legislation passes and prohibits the sale of beverages in cans. Consequently, the behavior of the locale is changed; no one uses metal cans because the merchants do not sell them under penalty of stiff fines. In this case, the attitudes and advocacy behavior of people is related to "ban the can" behavior not directly, but is mediated through social structures responsive to public opinion and through legal structures that carry the weight of powerful sanctions. Psychologists have usually only considered the relation of an individual's attitudes to his behavior by direct linkages within the individual, that is, they would test for proenvironmental attitudes and test for voluntary restraint from buying beverages in cans, then correlate the two measures within individuals. But even if this correlation were zero, it would be wrong to conclude that attitudes had nothing to do with "real" behavior. Not limiting the possible mediation to within-the-skin linkages, another type of attitude-behavior linkage may occur: Attitudes lead to advocacy behavior that influences social or political structures that in turn create a system of norms and sanctions governing people's behavior. This type of mediation starts at the level of individual processes, jumps to the level of group processes and social structures, then returns to the level of individual behavior. "Advocacy behavior" is at the first interface of the two levels: It is individual behavior that when aggregated has impact at the societal or group level.

G. Rest (1977) studied the relation of moral judgment to "advocacy behavior" in the 1976 Presidential election. Subjects were asked which candidate they voted for, and were also asked about their attitudes regarding election issues and the personalities of Ford and Carter. More specifically, subjects were asked to indicate a preference for either Ford's or Carter's stand on nine issues: defense spending, abortion, amnesty for draft evaders, health insurance, welfare reform, inflation, jobs, big government, and the Nixon pardon. Quotes from party platforms and the candidates' speeches were used to represent the candidates' stands. Subjects also indicated which of the issues were more important to them personally. Interestingly, subjects' preferances on the nine issues were highly intercorrelated (Crohbach's alpha in the 80s), and a summary index was devised (Overall Issue Orientation) that reflected a general preference for Ford or Carter on the issues, weighted by the importance that the subject gave to each issue. Similarly, subjects rated items on the personalities of the candidates (e.g., "Ford is not very intelligent for a President," "Carter would spend too much of the taxpayer's money if elected President"). Subjects indicated degree of agreement and importance on 43 such items, pro and con both candidates. Responses to these 43 items were also highly intercorrelated (alphas at about the same level), and thus were represented by a single index, the "Total Personality Preference Score."

In addition, G. Rest collected information on party affiliation, liberalism-conservatism, demographics (race, sex, religion, family income, geographical region, residential setting), IQ (SAT verbal scores from students), and other political attitudes. One sample consisted of 77 college undergraduates at the University of Michigan, Ann Arbor. A second sample consisted of a sample of 43 adults selected at random from the Minneapolis telephone directory.

Examining linear relationships of the DIT with the election attitude measures, a trend was found that people with higher Stage 4 preferred Ford's Issue stands over Carter's $r(120) = .22, p < .01$, and also regarded themselves as more conservative, $r(120) = .25, p < .01$. Examining curvilinear relationships of the DIT with the election measures, stronger relationships were found with Overall Issue Orientation and Candidates Personality Preference (significant at the .001 level). Subjects in the middle range of the DIT tended to favor Ford's stance on the issues and his personality, whereas subjects in the upper and lower ranges of the DIT favored Carter. A logical connection between moral judgment and political attitudes in this specific election is that Ford seemed to represent the maintenance of the existing social system, hence linking Stage 4 with his stands on issues and his personality; Carter was perceived by both low and high stage subjects as more oriented to the underprivileged. A curvilinear relation between moral judgment and political attitudes has also been found by Haan et al. (1968) and Fishkin et al. (1973).

A curvilinear relation was also found between DIT scores and the actual vote of subjects. Dividing subjects into low, medium, and high ranges of the DIT, 85% of the subjects in the low range voted for Carter, 43% of the subjects in the middle range voted for Carter, and 54% in the high range voted for Carter. As with the attitude measure, Carter's strength drew from the extremes and Ford's strength was in the middle. A Chi-square test was significant, $x^2 (4) = 10.90, p < .028$. The voting pattern was almost identical to the attitude pattern; one could predict the vote from the attitude information with 91% accuracy of those who voted.

It is reasonable to ask whether the relationship of moral judgment with political attitudes and voting might be due to some other variable. Accordingly, G. Rest carried out extensive multiple-regression analyses to determine the unique contribution of moral judgment, after partialling out its covariance with other variables. Using moral judgment, party affiliation, liberalism-conservatism, and demographics to predict to Issue Orientation, it was found that dropping moral judgment from the regression significantly lowered the variance accounted for ($F = 2.56, p < .025$). (The most powerful single variable was party affiliation; demographics and liberalism-conservatism did not lower the R^2 significantly, if dropped from the regression). Almost identical results were obtained in predicting to Candidate's Personality—dropping moral judgment from the regression was significant, $F = 3.24, p < .025$.

Multiple regression performed on the student sample included the IQ measure, the SAT Verbal scores, along with liberalism-conservatism, family's income, and moral judgment. Predicting to issue orientation, the effect of dropping moral judgment from the regression significantly lowered the variance accounted for, $F = 8.0, p < .01$. Predicting to Candidate Personality, moral judgment also was seen to have a contribution, $F = 5.9, p < .025$.

Thus there were significant relationships of moral judgment to political attitudes in a real, not hypothetical, situation (the Presidential Election of 1976), and to advocacy behavior (the actual vote). Of course, it is not suggested that Democrats always draw from people in the high and low ranges of moral judgment, and Republicans from the middle range. The type of election, the candidates, and the issues are likely to vary the way in which moral judgment relates to attitudes and voting. G. Rest's study demonstrated that moral judgment was a significant factor among others, in this instance of advocacy behavior.

Other areas of advocacy behavior, besides national politics, are worth exploring, for instance, advocacy behavior in professional or home life where issues of fairness are involved. Certainly group decision-making in many arenas is responsive to the attitudes and views of its participants, and clarifying the role of moral judgment in these processes is worth further research.

Personality Correlates

Moral judgment development is only one aspect of personality, and many interesting questions remain about the relation and interaction of moral judgment with other aspects of personality. Do certain personality traits, such as empathy, sociability, or ambition, hinder or facilitate moral judgment development? Is moral development a component of general personality development, as theorists like Loevinger (1976) and Erikson (1950) suggest? Do certain personality traits accompany moral judgment stages (Stage 2 and Machiavellianism, Stage 3 and conformity, Stage 4 and authoritarianism)? How closely correlated is moral judgment to other aspects of personality (self-concept, mental health)? Can we improve the predictability of behavior by combining information about moral judgment with information about other personality characteristics as ego strength, autonomy, or various value structures?

Some discussion of these questions has already taken place. For instance, moderate positive correlations were shown between the DIT and cognitive development measures, including IQ, achievement tests, and Loevinger ego development. Also, the interaction of moral judgment with various other factors was discussed in the section on behavioral correlates.

Most of the discussion below deals with the question of the degree of overlap between moral judgment and other personality variables. In other words, the studies correlated the DIT's P score with various other measures. While simple correlational studies cannot answer many of the questions of interest, they do give us a picture of how the DIT maps onto existing measures.

Eight studies have correlated the DIT with measures of Locus of Control. It might seem as though internal Locus of Control should be related to the increasing autonomy of moral judgment development. Table 6.15 shows that the relationship is weak, if existent at all. Upon closer logical examination, however, the constructs are really quite distinct. Locus of Control has to do with believing or not believing that one's own behavior is the cause of reinforcement. As discussed in Chapter 2, this concept is operative at Stage 2, and higher stages of moral judgment are not marked by increasing strength in this belief. The increased "autonomy" of the higher stages has nothing to do with believing in luck, chance or fate (the crucial dimension of Locus of Control) but rather has to do with conceptualizing cooperation in broader terms than one's own personal interests, friendships, and established laws. Hence the two constructs may interact in interesting ways (as in the production of behavior), but are not equivalent.

Several studies have correlated the DIT with value measures. Two studies using the Allport-Vernon-Lindzey Study of Values are reported in Table 6.16, and do not show consistent or strong relationships. The differences could be a function of the different samples. Two studies have used Rokeach's Value Survey (1973) which consists of simply ranking a list of abstract words, given in Table 6.17, according to the perceived importance of the value represented by the word. The Standring study produced much higher correlations although the smaller sample size warrants caution in interpreting the study. The Lockley study reported only two values with significant correlations

Table 6.15. DIT Correlates with Locus of Control

Study	Sample	Measure	Correlation
Bloomberg (1974)	53 undergraduates	Rotter's IE scale	-.06
Dortzbach (1975)	185 adults	Rotter's IE scale	-.17
Goldman (1977)	40 undergraduates	Rotter's IE scale	NS
		IAR (Positive events)	NS
		IAR (Negative events)	.28
		IAR (Total)	.26
		NPI (Good events)	.30
		NPI (Bad events)	NS
		NPI (Total)	.27
Gutkin & Suls (1977)	70 college undergraduates	Rotter's IE scale (Collin's revision)	.09
Medairy (1976)	44 college freshmen	Rotter's IE scale	-.14
	40 college seniors	Rotter's IE scale	-.06
Sanders (1976)	49 junior high students	Norwicki-Strickland's Locus of Control	.30
Troth (1974)	47 undergraduates	Gurin's Internal-External Control	
		Total	.12
		Control Ideology	.02
		Personal Control	.21
		System Modifiability	.15
Winocur & Rogers (1975)	87 undergraduates	Rotter's IE scale	-.14

If the authors of these studies gave the actual correlations, those are shown in this table. If they simply reported that the correlation was nonsignificant, "NS" is given in this table.

in the same direction as the Standring study: "Inner Harmony," and "Salvation." Lockley also correlated Rokeach's "Instrumental Values" with the DIT, and only one ("Broadminded") produced a correlation reaching the .20s. The inconsistency between the two studies may be in part that these abstract words have different meanings in New Zealand than in New Jersey—but it is also likely that subjects within the same geographical region interpret these abstract words differently, rendering any generalization problematic.

Table 6.18 presents correlations of the DIT with personality variable from 14 other studies, each using different measures. There are a number of noteworthy points. First, various self-concept measures do not seem to be related to the DIT. Second, Hartwick's study is interesting in that it uses a well researched personality scale, the California Personality Inventory, and has a good sample size. The scales with the most powerful correlates ("Achievement via independence" and "Intellectual efficiency") are aspects of personality that might be viewed as related to general cognitive development. The other correlations in the .30s seem as though they would be related to moral judgment ("Responsibility", "Tolerance", and "Psychological mindedness"); however "Capacity for status" requires a little ingenuity in interpretation. Schomberg's study uses the Omnibus Personality Inventory, another well researched scale with many items similar to the CPI, and produces significant positive correlations at the .01 level with "Complexity," "Autonomy," and a negative correlation with "Practical outlook." Third, of the approximately 150 correlations between the DIT and personality variables, most are nonsignificant and only rarely are any in the .50s and .60s range, whereas the converse was true with the correlations of the DIT with cognitive and de-

Table 6.16. DIT Correlations with
Allport-Vernon-Lindzey Value Test

Allport-Vernon-Lindzey	Study	
	Schneeweis 1974	Constantian & McAdams 1977
Theoretical	−.04	.34
Economic	−.07	−.17
Aesthetic	−.03	−.18
Social	−.02	.10
Political	.05	−.21
Religious	.07	.08
Sample	64 Minnesota high school students	52 Harvard graduate students

velopmental measures; most of the cognitive measures were significant and many were in the .50s and .60s range. This difference may be for at least two reasons: One, the DIT is more related to cognitive processes than to personality traits; also, personality traits do not exhibit developmental trends, whereas the DIT does.

Distinctiveness of Moral Judgment

Having discussed the convergence of moral judgment with many other variables, what is the divergent validity, or distinctiveness, of the DIT? Granted that the DIT gives us information about a person, couldn't we do just as well using some other test? Do DIT scores give unique information?

The two most likely variables under which moral judgment might be subsumed are liberal social attitudes and general intelligence. If we were to do away with the moral judgment construct, could we explain all the obtained findings through the use of the constructs of liberalism and general intelligence?

Table 6.17. DIT Correlations with Rokeach Value Survey

Value Word	Study	
	Standring, 1976	Lockley, 1976
Comfortable life	.05	−.17
Exciting	.38	NS
Sense of accomplishment	.23	NS
World at peace	.30	NS
World of beauty	.16	NS
Equality	.36	NS
Family security	−.37	NS
Freedom	.50	NS
Happiness	−.24	NS
Inner harmony	.34	.18
Mature love	−.05	NS
National security	−.52	NS
Pleasure	.63	NS
Salvation	−.60	−.29
Self-respect	.18	NS
Social recognition	−.13	NS
True friendship	.04	NS
Wisdom	.12	NS
Sample	33 college students in New Zealand	190 college students in New Jersey

Table 6.18. Personality Correlates of DIT

Study and Sample	Personality Test and Variable	Correlation
Allen and Kickbush (1976) 430 ninth graders	Rosenberg scale of self esteem	.02
	Rosenberg scale of faith in people	.02
	Jourard: self disclosure	
	-on attitude and value	-.06
	-on personality	-.02
	Sense of power in school	.01
	Generalized attitudes toward	.04
Blackner (1975) 80 high school students	Tennessee Self Concept Scale	
	-positive total scale (self-esteem)	.15
	-moral ethical self	.19
	-personality integration	-.03
Blackner (1975) 80 adults	Tennessee Self Concept Scale	
	-positive total scale (self-esteem)	-.20
	-moral ethical self	-.12
	-personality integration	.05
Cauble (1976) 90 college students	Constantinople's Inventory of Personality Development	.01
	Marcia's Ego Identity Statuses	NS
Hartwick (1975) 98 undergraduates	California Personality Inventory	
	-Dominance	.11
	-Capacity for Status	.32
	-Sociability	.11
	-Social presence	.17
	-Self acceptance	.20
	-Sense of well-being	.20
	-Responsibility	.33
	-Socialization	-.05
	-Self-control	.18
	-Tolerance	.39
	-Good impression	.09
	-Communality	.15
	-Achievement via conformance	.25
	-Achievement via independence	.48
	-Intellectual efficiency	.42
	-Psychological mindedness	.32
	-Flexibility	.11
	-Femininity	.03
Jacobs (1975) 60 adult women	Trait Anxiety (Spielburger, 1970)	NS
Johnson (1974) 66 high school students	Intrinsic-extrinsic religious orientation	NS
Masanz (1975) 33 high school students	Teachers ratings	
	-Initiative, industry	.40
	-Motivation	.35
	-Cooperation	NS
	-Emotional stability	NS

Table 6.18 (Continued)

Study and Sample	Personality Test and Variable	Correlation
Masanz (continued)	-Common sense	NS
	-Leadership	NS
	-Personality	NS
	-Reliability	NS
	-Concern for others	NS
	-Honesty	NS
	-Respect for authority	NS
	-Work effort	NS
McColgan (1975)	Jesness Test	
29 delinquent boys,	-Social maladjustment	.20
age 16, in Minnesota	-Value orientation	.28
	-Immaturity	-.18
	-Autism: distort reality	-.03
	-Alienation: distrust of others	.36
	-Manifest aggression	.06
	-Withdrawal	.17
	-Social anxiety	.29
	-Repression	-.34
	-Denial to acknowledge conflict	-.33
	-Antisocial index	.14
	I-Level	NS
Morrison, Toews and Rest	Minnesota Affect Assessment	
(1973)	-General school interest	.16
73 junior high students	-Autonomy	-.11
	-Self-expression	-.21
	-Academic set	-.05
	-Fine arts	-.03
	-School personnel	.00
	-Importance of affect	-.15
	-Intrinsic motivation	.13
	-External locus of control	.21
	-Need for direction	.09
Schomberg (1975)	Omnibus Personality Inventory	
35 college students	-Thinking introversion	.36
	-Complexity	.45
	-Autonomy	.47
	-Practical outlook	-.51
	-Masculinity/femininity	-.11
	-Theoretical orientation	.29
	-Estheticism	.32
	-Religious orientation	.10
	-Social extraversion	.11
	-Impulse expression	.19
	-Personal integration	.31
	-Anxiety level	.39
	-Altruism	.26

Table 6.18 (Continued)

Study and Sample	Personality Test and Variable	Correlation
Tsujimoto and Lucas (1977) 49 10th-12th graders	Wrightman's Trust Scale	.13
	POI (Shostrum) Inner-Directedness	.24
	POI (Shostrum) Time Competence	.24
Tsujimoto and Nardi (1977) 172 undergraduate and graduate students	Hogan's Empathy X Stage 5B	.27*
	Hogan's Autonomy X Stage 6	.18*
	CPI Socialization X Stage 4	.25*
Winocur and Rogers (1975) 87 undergraduates	Machiavellianism (Mach V)	.01
	Rotter's IE scale	-.14
	Ring and Wallston's Performance Style Typology	
	-P: wants to be own person	-.11
	-T: enjoys interpersonal games	.20
	-C: "social chameleon"	-.31

*Note that these correlations are not with P Index but with another stage score from the DIT.

Considering liberal-conservative attitudes, we have seen that measures which purport to measure this dimension do not uniformly correlate highly with the DIT. Coder (1974) cited a correlation of .13 with Nettler and Huffman's measure, and G. Rest in his multiple regression analyses found very little shared variance between the DIT and self-reported liberalism-conservatism. Also, meager correlations were found between Hogan's SEA and the DIT. Therefore, it is unlikely that the DIT functions as it does because it indirectly taps into the construct of liberalism-conservatism; the DIT just does not consistently correlate with these political attitudes. In those instances when it does (as with Law and Order Attitudes, Table 6.10), the explanation is clearer from moral judgment theory than from an explanation that supposes a powerful and unitary dimension of liberalism-conservatism.

The DIT does correlate with measures of general intelligence fairly consistently. Of course moral judgment is theoretically presumed to be one aspect of general cognitive development, so we would expect these correlations. The question here, however, is whether it is useful to regard moral judgment as distinct from *general* intellectual development. The crucial test is whether DIT scores "behave" any differently than measures of general intelligence. Three kinds of evidence are relevant: correlations, multiple regression analyses, and experimentally induced change.

Table 6.19 presents intercorrelations between six measures: two measures of moral reasoning, two measures of general intelligence, and two measures of liberal political attitudes. The sample consists of 73 junior high subjects from the same school (reported in Rest et al. 1974). Note that the two measures of moral reasoning (DIT and Comprehension) correlate most closely with themselves, the two measures of general intelligence correlate most closely with themselves, (Differential Aptitude Test and Iowa Test of Basic Skills), and the two attitude tests correlate most closely with themselves. Note also that the general intelligence measures correlate next best with the moral reasoning measure. The correlation of DIT with Comprehension remains statistically significant even after partialling out the IQ and attitude measures. Moral reasoning cannot be reduced to either general intelligence or to liberal attitudes; it is distinct from both, yet serves as a bridge between them (as discussed above on page 165).

The pattern of correlations in this one study is consistent with the pattern of correlations from the general review of studies: The average correlation of the DIT with measures of general intelligence in 51 studies (Table 6.1) was $r = .36$; whereas the average correlation of the DIT with other measures of moral reasoning was .49 in 23 correlations from various studies (Tables 6.2 and 6.4).

For the second line of evidence for the distinctiveness of moral judgment, recall that in the multiple regression analyses by G. Rest, the DIT was found to have a unique and significant predictability to election attitudes, beyond that shared in common with SAT scores and liberalism-conservatism scores. In other words, even after taking out the DIT's common variance with IQ and liberalism, the DIT produced significant predictability to people's election positions. Furthermore, recall that McColgan first controlled for IQ differences, then found a relationship between DIT and anti-social behavior. Similarly, Froming and Cooper found that the relation between DIT and compliance behavior was little affected by partialling out their common variance with SAT scores; and Marston also found that partialling out

Table 6.19. Intercorrelations of Moral Reasoning,
General Intelligence, and Attitude
($n = 73$)

	1	2	3	4	5
DIT					
Comprehension	.58				
DAT (Composite)	.35	.41			
ITBS (Composite)	.02	.18	.54		
Law and Order	−.23	.12	−.06	.10	
Libertarianism	.37	.08	.11	−.18	−.41

IQ and SES did not significantly diminish the DIT's predictability to behavior. Therefore the DIT adds different predictability from that accounted for by liberal attitudes or IQ variables.

The third line of evidence for the distinctiveness of moral judgment comes from studies of experimentally induced change, namely, that the experiences that lead to increases on the DIT are focused on *moral* content, not on *general logical* content. But the discussion of these studies is the topic of Chapter 7.

7

Experimentally Inducing Change in Moral Judgment

> Most modern psychologists have been taught that it is only by the experimental method that direct cause-effect conclusions can be specified with confidence and that such statements constitute the principal goal of our discipline (McCall 1977, p. 334.)

Experimental studies in which subjects are randomly assigned to treatment and control conditions are of great scientific interest, and are considered by some psychologists to be the only method of obtaining "hard" evidence. A second interest in experimental studies is the practical one: can moral judgment development be affected or improved by deliberate intervention? Is there some way that all this theory and research about moral judgment development can be used to improve people's lives?

Of the two interests in experimental studies—the scientific and the practical—the practical has fared better in moral judgment research. In fact, the experimental method has not been the sharp decisive tool in developmental research that it has in other fields. A number of writers recently have given several reasons for the difficulties of the experimental method in developmental research (Wohlwill 1973, Chapter XI; also Flavell 1977; Kuhn 1976; McCall 1977):

1. Diagnosis of developmental level is often hopelessly complicated by intervention. Developmental diagnosis is problematic enough without interventions, since what is being assessed is supposedly a person's underlying mental operations. But interventions often make even more questionable the signs used as evidence of underlying operations

of structures. For instance, in assessing the development of conservation, one sign that researchers use is if the child says, "It's the same because I can put them back the way they were." This utterance is taken to index the underlying operation of reversibility. But suppose that a nonconserving subject is put in a training session in which the teacher constantly points out that two objects (e.g., two rods, two balls of clay, two beakers of liquid) are the same because the deformed one can always be changed back to the way it was and be the same as the other object. In other words, the treatment consists of verbalizing what natural (nontreated) conservers say. In this case, how can one test for conservation in the treated subject? One can't use the same criteria as with natural conservers, because the child may simply parrot the teacher without fully understanding. Hence the intervention itself undermines the inference process by which developmental level is assessed. In moral judgment interventions, this is especially a problem when part of the intervention is to read and discuss Kohlberg's writings on morality. A course that states that Stage 6 thinking is better than other stages, and which furnished examples of "superior" thinking cannot then assess course participants in the same way as naive subjects, because we have no way of knowing whether the participants' responses on the posttest reflect underlying thought processes or memorized surface responses.

2. The short-term, one-session treatment is inappropriate for studying the reorganization of basic cognitive structures. In long-term interventions the power of the experimental method to control confounding variables is compromised.

Experimental studies provide elegant evidence when the treatment variable can be clearly isolated and exactly manipulated while every other variable is held constant. This ideal might be approximated in the short-term, one-session study. But there is no reason to believe that the reorganization of basic cognitive structures can take place instantaneously or even overnight. It takes time to reflect upon various experiences and coordinate their many implications before one can arrive at a new way of construing a problem. In Kohlberg's longitudinal data (1978), an individual takes on the average over twelve years to move a full stage. The basic phenomenon that a developmentalist is studying cannot be expected to change in a short period of time; hence longer term interventions are necessary. However, the longer the intervention, the more difficult it is to control the extraneous factors and the more complex the treatment becomes. The particular virtue of the experimental methodology becomes compromised.

The claim could be made that significant change induced in a short-term intervention is evidence *against* a structural-development theory. If for instance, significant stage change occurs after a 20-minute intervention, several interpretations are possible. A plausible argument is that the original assessment was faulty, grossly underestimating the subject's real capacities, and the 20-minute intervention made it clear to the subject what the experimenter was really after. In this case, the intervention did not cause structural change, but acted as a condition for bringing out the true capacity of the subject. It could also be argued that change after a 20-minute intervention signifies that the phenomenon being studied is really not a basic, underlying structure, but a specific piece of information or response learned quite easily. If supposedly "basic cognitive structures" can be moved around so easily, one wonders how "basic" they are, or if the means of assessing them are adequate.

3. Strictly speaking, the most that can be concluded from a treatment condition that enhances developmental change is that the condition is one *possible* way of enhancing development; it cannot be concluded that it is the only condition that facilitates change or is the effective condition operating *naturally* that facilitates development. In order to establish the sufficient and *necessary* conditions for development, deprivation treatments would be necessary, which of course ethical considerations do not allow. Furthermore, in conservation training studies (as well as in moral judgment intervention studies), many difficult kinds of interventions apparently produce change, therefore indicating that the paths to development are many. The classical experimental goal to determine whether X or Y leads to Z is therefore frustrated because a lot of different Xs and Ys seem to lead to Z. Wohlwill (1973) and others have suggested that development need not be tied to specific environmental events or stimuli, but that a variety of stimuli and environmental conditions can furnish the basic material upon which the child operates to construct the basic cognitive structures of meaning. In this case it is beside the point to do studies in the classic experimental tradition, manipulating X and Y, looking for the unique cause of Z. Instead, McCall (1977) urges developmental researchers to spend more effort at describing change in complex naturalistic environments.

In summary, there are great problems in using the experimental method to ascertain the necessary and sufficient conditions for development; nevertheless the practical issue remains: Can moral judgment development be facilitated at all?

Intervention Studies

The Panowitsch-Balkcum Study

One of the most interesting education studies was of philosophy courses taught by Elvin Balkcum and evaluated by Henry Panowitsch. The chief interest of the study was double-edged: On the one hand, an interest was expressed in seeing what kind of philosophical education was most conducive to development in moral judgment—would a course specifically focused on ethics, or a course focused on logical thinking in general, be most conducive to moral judgment development? On the other hand, there was an interest in addressing the discriminant construct validity of the DIT—can scores on the DIT be as easily affected by general cognitive stimulation as by educational experiences specifically focused on the moral domain? Of course an underlying question is whether moral judgment as measured by the DIT can be affected by any educational intervention.

A cognitive developmental view of these matters focuses on the familiar Piagetian processes of assimilation and accomodation to account for development in moral judgment. New schemes or structures evolve from the person's interaction with experiences that do not quite fit the old schemes. New moral schemes are successive transformations of old moral schemes in the light of new moral experience. Therefore, one needs to actively confront moral problems in order for moral judgment to develop. Moral schemes (such as ideas of social contract, legitimated authority, the institution of law, balancing moral claims in terms of value hierarchies) deal distinctively with moral problems and are not simply direct applications of more formal logical schemes (Formal Operations, reversibility) to moral content, although the more formal logical schemes may be constituent parts of the moral schemes. Complete mastery of Formal Operations does not necessarily include the ability to construct a Stage 5 or Stage 6 interpretation of a moral dilemma, although Formal Operations may be a necessary prerequisite. The cognitive developmental view is in agreement with the commonsensical view portrayed in Stanley Kubrick's film *Dr. Strangelove*. Both assert that it is possible for a person to be advanced in general cognitive development—in fact, to be a genius in technical matters—but to be obtuse when it comes to moral thinking.

The Mischels, coming from a Social Learning approach, take a different view. They contend that it is "not parsimonious" to distinguish moral judgment development from general intellectual development:

The increasing cognitive and verbal competencies of the child follow an age-related sequence which in turn is reflected in age-related changes in moral reasoning. But it would not be parsimonious to believe that the latter reflects more than the growth of cognitive competencies interacting with socialization practices (1976, p. 96-97)

The Mischels therefore discount the specialness of moral concepts and that they develop with regard to special kinds of problems. Instead, there is cognitive and verbal development in general, and these competencies can be applied as well to moral problems as to any other kind of problem. If Dr. Strangelove is good at math, he also should be good at morality.

In Chapter 6, correlational and multiple regression evidence was reviewed concerning the distinctiveness of moral judgment from general intellectual development. An intervention study provides another test. If we assume along with the Mischels that moral judgment development is not distinct from general intellectual development, then any intervention that stimulates general intellectual development should be effective in stimulating moral judgment development. If a philosophy class in *logic* is successful in stimulating general intellectual development, then scores on the DIT should increase as much as in a philosophy course in *ethics* that is successful in stimulating general intellectual development. In other words, to the degree that either course is successful in stimulating intellectual development, increases on the DIT should reflect general cognitive stimulation in either course.

On the other hand, if we subscribe to the cognitive developmental view that the courses are dealing with distinct conceptual domains (ethics and logic), that development in one is distinct from development in the other, and that the DIT is selectively sensitive to moral judgment development rather than to intellectual and verbal development in general, then we would predict a more specific effect from the two courses. To the degree that the ethics course was successful, we would expect increases on the DIT but not necessarily on a test of logic ability; to the degree that the logic course was successful, we would expect increases on a logic test but not necessarily on the DIT. In short then, the Social Learning view predicts general effects and the Cognitive Developmental view predicts specific effects.

Subjects were undergraduates aged 17 to 44, in a two-year general arts and sciences college in Minneapolis, 73 had enrolled in sections of the ethics course and 28 had enrolled in sections of the logic course. The DIT was administered before and after the courses. As a test of logic ability, the Cornell Critical Thinking Test (CCTT) was used; this test, developed by Robert Ennis and Jason Millman (1971), measures a person's judgment of whether a simple generalization of the hypothesis is warranted or whether a reason is relevant, whether information is reliable on the basis of its source and the condition under which it was secured, and whether a statement follows from premises.

The ethics course taught by Balkcum first acquainted students with the basic ideas of several moral philosophers (Kant, Neitzche, the Stoics, Utilitarians), and then applied these ideas to contemporary moral problems (abortion, civil disobedience, suicide) using peer discussion as the primary mode of classroom activity. Students were required to demonstrate first that they could approach the contemporary problems from the point of view of the various classical philosophers, and then they were directed to develop the most cogent line of reasoning about the problems that they could, using whatever sources seemed helpful. Thus the course gave students a concentrated experience in solving complex moral dilemmas, and an exposure to classical moral thinkers as well as interaction with their peers.

The logic class, also taught by Balkcum, was aimed at developing rigorous and systematic thinking, not specifically centered on *moral* thinking. The contents of the logic course included hypothetical syllogisms, propositional logic, truth tables, and formal proofs. Thus the logic course emphasized formal thought in abstract symbols as applied to generalized content areas. In contrast, the ethics course emphasized analysis of specifically *moral* situations, and problem solving in a specific content area.

Table 7.1 presents the group averages of the pre and post tests for both groups on both measures. As can be seen, the ethics class went up on the DIT but not on the logic test, whereas the logic class went up on the logic test but not on the DIT.

Table 7.1. Averages on Pre and Post Tests of the DIT and CCTT
in the Ethics and Logic Class

	DIT			CCTT		
	Pre	Post	*t*-Test Significance	Pre	Post	*t*-Test Significance
Ethics class	41.6	46.5	$p < .03$	43.8	44.7	NS
Logic class	40.1	40.5	NS	44.8	47.5	$p < .04$

An analysis of the interaction of type of test with type of intervention can be computed by counting the number of subjects in each class that gained on each test.[1] Table 7.2 shows the percentages of gainers in each group. From the marginal probabilities, a set of expected frequencies can be calculated for each cell, and a Chi-square "goodness of fit" test applied to the comparison of expected frequencies with obtained frequencies. The Chi-square was significantly greater than chance ($p < .01$), indicating an interaction of type of treatment with type of test. Therefore, both analyses from Table 7.1 and 7.2 support the specific effect view and not the general effect view.

A subsample of subjects from each group were available for a five-month followup testing on the DIT. For the ethics class, a group of 26 subjects had a pretest mean of 40.2, a posttest mean of 46.7, and a follow-up mean of 46.4. For the logic class ($n = 15$), the respective group means were 38.2, 42.1, and 40.2. In other words the ethics class maintained the gains of the posttest in the five-month follow-up and the logic class did not catch up.

One caution to give about this study is that subjects were not randomly assigned to the treatment groups, and therefore subjects selecting an ethics course may be more disposed and "ripe" for change on the DIT than subjects not selecting an ethics course. We cannot infer from this study that all students would have gained as much on the DIT had they been placed in the ethics course. We cannot determine to what degree the change effects are due to the educational program and to what degree due to a special interest in ethics. However, if the groups were different in some way, it did not show up on either the DIT or the CCTT pretest, or on a questionnaire designed by Panowitsch that asked reasons for taking the courses.

The nonrandomness of the two groups, however, does not undermine the two major conclusions of the study: One, that significant changes can show up on the DIT from an educational program sever-

Table 7.2. Percent of Subjects Who Gained
on the DIT or CCTT

	Percent Gainers on DIT	Percent Gainers on CCTT
Ethics class	32	22
Logic class	14	50

$\chi^2 = 6.9, p < .01$

al months long; and two, that the DIT is selectively sensitive to ethical thinking rather than to logical thinking in general.

Review of Intervention Studies[2]

Table 7.3 presents a summary of 16 intervention studies using the DIT. Following Lawrence (1977), the studies have been grouped into four types of interventions: brief, short-term interventions; interventions predominantly focused on social studies or civics curriculum; interventions intended to promote general personality and social development, including "Deliberate Psychological Education" programs (see *The Counseling Psychologist*, 1977) and "Confluent Education" programs; and interventions primarily focused on moral problems, moral philosophy, or moral discussion (see Lawrence 1977 for more discussion of the treatments).

Problems in the designs of the studies make conclusions and generalizations difficult. Eight problems are recurrent in these studies, and the last column of Table 7.3 indicates which studies have which problems. (1) Only four studies (1, 2, 11, and 15) randomly assigned subjects to treatment groups, the rest used intact groups. (2) Some studies did not have control or comparison groups (3, 6, and 10). Of the 13 studies with comparison groups, only eight made statistical comparisons between the gains in the experimental group and those of the control group. Such comparisons were done either by use of a series of t tests, as in the Panowitsch-Balkcum study reported above, or by analysis of covariance of the posttests with the pretests as covariate. (3) Some studies included exposure to and discussion of Kohlberg's stage theory, thereby making it difficult to interpret the posttest gains (6, 10, 12, 14.) Other interventions might have taught the Kohlberg stages, but this was difficult to determine from the project descriptions. (4) Some studies reported that many subjects did not understand the test, or were too young to take it, or were given so many tests that motivating the subjects to work on the DIT was difficult (2, 3, 4, 9). (5) Most studies did not include follow-up testing to determine if the gains on the posttest were maintained (only 4 and 13 had follow-ups). Stability of gains in a follow-up has been one of the usual criteria of cognitive developmentalists for claiming that true structural change, rather than just superficial, transitory change, has taken place (see Kuhn, 1976). (6) Two of the studies had extremely brief interventions (1 and 2). (7) Most of the interventions were taught by inexperienced teachers or were trying out the program for the first time without previous trial runs (all but No. 13). Therefore, the full power of the programs are yet to be tested. (8) A num-

Table 7.3. Summary of Intervention Studies

Study and Sample	Characteristics of Treatment	Change of Main Experimental Group	Comparison of Experimental Group Gains with Control Gains	Problems with study (see key, below)
Short-Term Studies				
1. Geis (1977) 90 college students	4 hour-long class periods over 2 weeks in group discussion of moral dilemmas	Nonsignificant	No difference	F, B, N
2. Walker (1974) 70 8th graders	Short, one-time exposure to different levels of moral reasoning	Nonsignificant	No difference	M, F, B, N
Social Studies Programs				
3. Rest, Ahlgren, Mackey (1972) 61 9th graders	12-week social studies unit to change attitudes towards police	Nonsignificant	No control group	R, A, M, F, N
4. Morrison, Toews, and Rest (1975) 103 9th graders	Half-year course in civics and social studies, involving discussion and projects	Nonsignificant	No difference	R, M, N
Psychological Development Programs				
5. Balfour (1974) 84 senior high students	Semester-long course with seminar and	3.3 point gain $t(53) = 2.01$, involvement in a community	No comparison reported	R, A, F, N
6. Erickson et al. (1975) 19 junior highs	Semester-long DPE Curriculum for personal development, in elective school class	6.84 point gain $t(18) = 2.27$, $p < .05$	No control group	R, A, C, F, N, S
7. French (1977) 117 senior highs	Quarter-long classes in English and History with values clarification	3.43 and .4 point gains t tests not available	No difference	R, F, N
8. Hurt (1975)	Quarter-long training in	Nonsignificant	No comparison reported	R, A, F, N, S

	Treatment	Results	Comparison	
	a semester unit on moral education			
10. Sprinthall and Bernier (1977) 18 in-service teachers	6 weeks summer workshop in DPE plus one quarter of consultation	9.0 point gain $t(17) = 2.91$, $p <.01$	No control group	R, A, C, F, N, S
11. Whitely and Nelson (1976) 77 college freshmen	8-month experience in special residential college and course work in psychological growth	5.14 point gain $t(34) = 2.37$ $p <.024$	No comparison reported	A, F, N
Moral Education Programs				
12. Coder (1975) 87 adult church members	6 weeks, 2 hours per week, moral education program	10.0 and 11.0 point gains t test values not reported	Posttests significant difference $F = 5.69$, $p <.005$	R, C, F, N
13. Panowitsch (1975) 152 college students	Quarter-long applied ethics course (see section above)	4.9 point gain $t(72) = 3.21$, $p <.002$	Significant difference in post tests, $t = 2.56$, $p <.03$; no difference in pretests	R
14. Piwko (1975) 68 college students	10 two-hour sessions in quarter-long course on moral values and commitments	8.1 point gain $F = 6.89$, $p <.05$	No comparison reported	R, A, C, F, N
15. Siegal (1974) 252 high schools	Semester-long course on moral discussion	No test of pre/post significance	No difference	F, N
16. Troth (1974) 42 college students	Semester elective course on moral values (to integrate personal values and behavior)	Nonsignificant	No comparison reported	R, A, F, N, S

Key: R = subjects not randomly assigned to treatments

A = inadequate statistical comparison of experimental gains with gains of control group

C = contamination of post testing by exposure to Kohlberg stage descriptions

M = subjects not motivated to take test or too young to understand it

F = no followup testing to determine if posttest gains are stable

B = treatment was too brief

N = treatment was conducted for first time or taught by inexperienced teacher

S = sample was too small (experimental group less than 30)

All tests of significance are two-tailed.

ber of studies had such small sample sizes that inferences are very hard to make (6, 8, 10, 16).

The 16 studies suggest that DIT scores (group averages, at least) are not easily changed. In none of these studies did the control group show significant change. As Table 7.3 shows, only two studies (12 and 13) showed that gains of the experimental group exceeded gains of the control groups, although seven studies reported significant pre to post gains of the experimental groups by themselves. If the studies are excluded that directly taught the Kohlberg stages and thus contaminated the posttesting (these studies are discussed below), the amount of change in the experimental groups in the remaining studies is only about 5 points. Recall that in Chapter 5, the longitudinal subjects had moved an average of 11 points over four years, and that the average difference between the academic groups in the cross-sectional studies (Table 5.2) was 10 to 11 points. Therefore even when interventions do shift DIT scores upward, they do not shift much (see the next section for discussion of the "contaminated" studies).

The Panowitsch-Balkcum study remains the most convincing evidence that deliberate interventions can change DIT scores, since that study has the fewest design problems, produced significant change, and maintained the gains in a five-month follow-up. Even so the intervention consisted of an extremely concentrated dose of moral problem solving and yet the average gain was less than 5 points. I believe the recalcitrance and the stability of the control groups lends credence to the claim that the DIT is measuring basic structures of moral thinking.

Manipulation of Test-taking Sets

The effects of repeatedly taking the DIT were discussed in Chapter 5 (p. 141ff), and the conclusion was that testing effects do not seem to be appreciable. The question of interest here is whether changing the instructions to the subject (and presumably changing the subject's test-taking set) has an effect on DIT scores. One theoretical issue is whether subjects under the usual conditions are giving the most advanced thinking of which they are capable on the DIT, or whether DIT scores represent a level of performance that they are comfortable with or that they prefer. This issue was discussed in Chapter 6 (p. 147ff); the Mischels suggested (1976) the procedure of urging subjects to work to their highest capacity. Therefore, one interesting manipulation of test instructions is to ask subjects to "fake high" on the DIT. If it happens that subjects significantly boost their DIT scores when instructed to fake high, it would be difficult to claim that the age trends of the DIT found in longitudinal and cross-sectional studies are solely due to increases in cognitive capacity; some of the changes could be attributed to changes in preference or performance factors (see Chapter 2 for discussion of "performance factors"). Furthermore, if a large portion of the variance in DIT scores is due to preference or performance factors, the interpretation of education intervention studies is also complicated: A pre-post gain in DIT scores may not be due to structural development but to changing the subject's willingness to work harder on the posttest than on the pretest; or the subject's wanting to help out the friendly experimenter by giving higher scores on the posttest; or the subject coming to realize in the course of the intervention that the experimenter values complicated thinking; and so on.

McGeorge (1975) did the first study in this area. He set up three treatment conditions: In one condition, subjects were asked to take the DIT with the usual instructions. He asked subjects, "Fill in the questionnaire to show what you yourself really think about the problems raised." In a second condition, he instructed subjects to "fake good":

> Please assist us by trying to fill in the questionnaire so that it records the highest, most mature level of social and ethical judgment possible. Fill in the questionnaire as someone concerned only with the very highest principles of justice would fill it in. (McGeorge 1975)

In a third condition, he instructed subjects to "fake bad":

> Please assist us by trying to fill in the questionnaire so that it records the lowest, most immature level of social and ethical judgment possible. Fill in the questionnaire as someone with no sense of justice and no concern for other people would fill it in. (McGeorge 1975)

McGeorge formed five experimental groups of subjects. Each group was asked to take the DIT twice—one group under the fake good condition first, then under standard conditions; another group under the fake bad condition first, then under standard conditions; and so on, as indicated in Table 7.4.

As McGeorge's study shows, subjects did not significantly increase their P% scores when instructed to fake high; however, they did decrease significantly when instructed to fake bad. Also subjects did not increase their M scores (meaningless scores—see Chapter 4, pp. 91, 92). These findings are what would be expected if the DIT under standard conditions taps the upper levels of a subject's capacity, for then the subject does not really know how to increase his score. Also assuming that moral judgment is developmental, the subject can easily fake downward because he is aware of simpler, less adequate ways of thinking now discarded but still understood.

The second study in the area was by Yussen (1976). This study was not conceived as a fakability study but rather as a role-taking study; yet it is relevant to a consideration of test-taking instructions. Instead of asking subjects to fake good or fake bad, Yussen instructed subjects to take the DIT (1) as they themselves would, (2) as an average policeman would, and (3) as an average philosopher would. Yussen's interest was in seeing if subjects would differentiate these moral perspectives, and further, if the amount of differentiation was a function of the subject's age and education. Thirty subjects each at the ninth, tenth, twelfth, and college grades were tested. Table 7.5 shows the P% means for four groups for the three perspectives: At the ninth grade level, none of the differences between social role (i.e., taking the DIT as self, as a policeman, as a philosopher) was significant. At tenth grade, a significant difference was shown between the policeman and philosopher roles. At twelfth grade, the policeman-philosopher difference was significant, and the self-philosopher difference was significant. For the college group, all three comparisons were significant. There the older groups show more differentiation of social

Table 7.4. McGeorge's Fakability Study

Group	Testing 1	Testing 2	t Test
Good-Standard ($n = 22$)	41.3	45.6	1.29
Standard-Good ($n = 23$)	44.0	40.0	1.98
Bad-Standard ($n = 29$)	27.0	43.5	5.28*
Standard-Bad ($n = 25$)	44.3	16.7	11.64*
Standard-Standard ($n = 47$)	40.9	42.5	1.13

*$p < .001$

Table 7.5. Yussen's Moral Role-Taking Study

Social Role	9th Graders	10th Graders	12th Graders	College
Self	20.5	25.0	31.0	40.3
Policeman	24.8	22.1	24.8	24.2
Philosopher	25.4	26.2	42.7	48.8

roles than the younger group; and furthermore, the twelfth graders and the college groups significantly increased the "philosopher" scores over their "self" scores.

Yussen's study appears to contradict that of McGeorge. Yussen offered this distinction: McGeorge's instructions leave the subject to decide for himself what constitutes a "good" or "bad" set of ratings on the DIT, whereas Yussen's instructions to take the test as a philosopher gives the subject more specific information about how to rate the DIT issues, namely, to look for issues that a philosopher would choose as important. But how can a subject whose own DIT score is very much lower than that of a philosopher's (averaging 65.2, see Table 5.1) distinguish those issues that philosophers would choose? Do subjects have an apprehension of issues that are philosophically more adequate? Or are subjects simply choosing issues that sound incomprehensible because philosophers sound incomprehensible to them? This issue could be illuminated by determining if subjects who significantly increased their P scores also increased their M scores. If increases in M go along with increases in P, then the instruction to take the test like a philosopher is in effect an instruction to choose the incomprehensible items. Then subjects really have not demonstrated any higher capacity than their own DIT scores, but in fact their high M scores would invalidate the questionnaire.

Unfortunately Yussen did not analyze his data for M scores and has not made the data available for analysis of M scores, so we cannot really determine what the significance of his finding is. It is, therefore, unclear whether the increase in P scores under the philosopher condition means that subjects can fake high, given some clues, or whether the increase in P scores indicates a test-taking set (picking the incomprehensible items) that would invalidate the questionnaire.

In order to clarify the ambiguity raised by Yussen's study, Bloom (1977) designed a third study. Bloom assigned 132 college students to one of six groups: Group 1 subjects were instructed to take the DIT twice, first under "fake good" instructions such as McGeorge used, then under normal conditions; Group 2 subjects, first under normal conditions, then under fake good conditions; Group 3 subjects, first fake good, then inder instructions to take the test as a philosopher, such as Yussen had used; Group 4, philosopher, then fake good; Group 5, philosopher, then normal; Group 6, normal, then philosopher.

P scores were analyzed in a 6 x 2 (treatments by order) two-way ANOVA design. Bloom found no significant order or interaction effects ($F = 1.92$, $p < .09$), and the "P scores were essentially identical under standard, fake good, and philosopher instructions" (Bloom 1977, page 4). M scores were analyzed in the same way, with no order or treatment effects ($F = .69, p = .63$).

These three studies indicate that DIT scores cannot be significantly increased by instructions to fake good without an increase in M score invalidating the questionnaire. Subjects do not seem to have more advanced concepts of justice than the ones given on the usual DIT. Subjects seem to use the highest concepts they have. This corroborates the findings that DIT scores are highly correlated with measures of moral comprehension, and that longitudinal change in DIT scores are accompanied by longitudinal change in comprehension scores. Furthermore, the fakability studies are consistent with the intervention studies in finding that group averages on the DIT are recalcitrant to deliberate change (especially the studies without exposure to Kohlberg's stage description).

Now let us consider the intervention studies that directly taught Kohlberg stages as part of the learning experience (studies 6, 10, 12 and 14 in Table 7.3). Some of these studies had pretest to posttest gains around 10 points, nearly twice as much as in the Panowitsch-Balkcum study (13), which did not teach the Kohlberg stages but which seems to me to be one of the most concentrated, powerful interventions to facilitate development in moral thinking. Possibly the studies that directly teach Kohlberg stages are powerful interventions in facilitating real development in moral judgment, and studying developmental theory may be the most effective way to promote structural development. On the other hand, teaching Kohlberg stages may, in effect, instruct subjects specifically how to fake high on the posttest. Simply instructing subjects to fake high (as in the McGeorge study) does not give them any clues as to which items are higher than the ones the subjects have already chosen. Instructing subjects to "fake high like a philosopher" (as in the Yussen study) may give subjects a cue to choose the complicated, incomprehensible DIT items; however, both P and M items may then be chosen. But teaching the subjects how Kohlberg's stages 5 and 6 are defined may give subjects useful clues for distinguishing the P items from other DIT items without necessarily having the whole network of thinking that the P items reflect. Thus these interventions may be only successful in instructing subjects how to fake high on the DIT posttest without invalidating the questionnaire by the M score. At this time we cannot say for sure why the highest pre to post gains in experimental groups are obtained in "contaminated" studies.

Several lines of further research would be helpful. Future intervention studies may include measures of moral comprehension as well as the DIT. Also, short-term studies may be designed to determine how subjects can use information about Kohlberg stage descriptions to sort and select DIT items (for instance, if a subject is given a five-minute description of Stages 5 and 6, can the subject select P items on the DIT at a higher rate than his P score under standard conditions?). Further studies may examine more intensively the conditions under which subjects pick M items, and the conditions under which subjects avoid picking M items.

Before leaving the topic of test conditions, several other studies deserve mention. Graham, Turnbull, and La Rocque (1977), and also Fincham (1977) investigated the effects of alcohol on taking the DIT. Both studies found that subjects who are moderately intoxicated do not differ on the P score than sober subjects. Guttenberg (1975) found that presenting the DIT dilemmas in the form of videotaped dramas did not significantly alter DIT scores from the usual presentation via written paragraphs.

Experiences Associated with Change

What kinds of experience promote development in moral judgment?

Theoretical discussions by cognitive developmentalists about how life experiences affect moral judgment (Kohlberg 1969; Turiel 1969, 1972) have usually treated the issue at a high level of abstraction, using the concepts of "disequilibrium," "cognitive conflict," "assimilation and accommodation," or "hierarchical reintegration." The general notion is that existing cognitive structures change when new experiences cannot be assimilated to existing structures, thus inducing a state of cognitive conflict or disequilibrium and accommodating or changing the cognitive structures so that the new structures can assimilate the experience. The new structures are said to reintegrate the past structures into a new hierarchical organization. Research on these ideas is set up to induce cognitive disequilibrium in a subject by presenting moral arguments at different stages of development, to model the next stage's structures; then change from pretest to posttest is analyzed (Turiel 1966, 1969, 1972). The studies have attempted to rule out a simple modeling explanation of change and to argue for a "disequilibrium" explanation by showing that the most effective model is the stage directly above the subject's own.

Cognitive conflict research has been useful in suggesting differences between modeling processes and the processes of structural change. However, several problems in the basic research paradigm have prevented conclusive findings. For one, the paradigm has used short-term interventions (sometimes only 10 to 20 minutes) and the resulting changes between pretests and posttests have not been great, generalized, or enduring. Also, the paradigm assumes a simple stage model of development (see Chapter 3) in which subjects are "in" one stage and statements are said to be in one stage above, two stages above, and so on. Such a design does not recognize the stage mix in subjects nor the many kinds of decalage. Third, the paradigm has assumed that the presentation of statements at different stages is a treatment that induced cognitive conflict in subjects; however, theoretically cognitive conflict is an inner, subjective condition of a subject, not something that can be manipulated by external treatment conditions. That statements at different stages or advocating different actions are presented does not mean that the subject will see the conflict or any necessity for changing his ideas, nor does it guarantee that the subject will search for ideas at the "next" stage rather than regard the discrepancy as "one of those differences of opinion." Fourth, the research on cognitive conflict is too abstract to specify the concrete experiences in naturalistic situations that are pivotal in promoting development. Even if cognitive conflict were crucial to the process of structural change, we would want to know what concrete experiences in real life occasion cognitive conflict.

A number of suggestions about crucial experiences come from correlational, not experimental studies. In the cross-sectional studies reported in Chapter 5, the number of years of formal education was more highly correlated than chronological years in adults with the DIT. Certainly it is not an outlandish proposition that formal education should have an effect on people's basic concepts of fairness— the promotional material of many colleges and universities claim that this is so. Yet the variable, "years of formal education," is a gross and imprecise variable, in which many kinds of experiences are involved, curricular and extra-curricular. The short-term longitudinal studies contrasting college-bound people with non-college attending people have been ambiguous so far (see Chapter 5), but the range of education assessed in the longitudinal studies is much restricted compared with the cross-sectional studies. Perhaps clearer findings will emerge when wider range studies are completed. Several studies (Bransford 1973; Dispoto 1974; Gallia 1976; McGeorge 1977; Schomberg 1978) have contrasted college academic majors (natural science majors contrasted with humanities majors), looking for relationships to moral judgment but no clear patterns have emerged as yet.

Biggs, Schomberg, and Brown (1977) conducted a large scale study on 767 freshmen at the University of Minnesota. Different precollege experiences were assessed by a checklist that contained five sections. The first section, *Literary*, listed 73 authors and 27 books, and subjects were asked to report their level of acquaintance with the authors and books; similarly the *Artistic* section listed 65 painters, sculptors and musical composers; the *Academic-Conceptual* section listed 35 concepts or topics in science and mathematics; the *Contemporary-Cultural* section listed 59 individuals whose names had appeared in the popular press in the last ten years; and the *Jobs* section listed a variety of jobs, asking subjects if they had ever held any of them. A subject's precollege experience score in each of these five areas was computed by simply counting the number of items with which the subject indicated an acquaintance. Biggs, Schomberg and Brown report that higher acquaintance scores in the Literary, Artisitic, Academic-Conceptual, and Contemporary-Cultural lists, but not number of jobs, were significantly associated with P scores (the highest was Literary, correlating .31).

In the Rest (1975) study, subjects were asked to reflect upon their experiences of the previous two years and to speculate about what had influenced their moral thinking. Subjects cited a variety of experiences in the four lines provided for that purpose on the questionnaire. Their answers were categorized under six kinds of life experience: (1) formal instruction, reading, or study which lead to expanded knowledge of world events, world affairs, etc.; (2) new "real-world" responsibilities—for example, a new job, marriage, birth of children, managing money for the first time; (3) maturation, a sense of "just growing up"; (4) new social contacts, new friends, an expanding world; (5) religious experience and/or instruction; (6) direct involvement in community or world affairs, political involvement, assumption of leadership roles.

The 1975 study found that those subjects who cited the first two kinds of experiences (formal instruction and reading, new "real world" responsibilities) did in fact show more change than subjects who had not cited those experiences. Unfortunately, in a subsequent follow-up study (retesting the subjects again in 1976), this pattern was not replicated, nor was it replicated in a similar study by McGeorge (1976), testing New Zealand college students. The information obtained on life experiences in this way has been brief and unelaborated. Perhaps more thorough interviewing of subjects would yield less ambiguous results. However, it is also quite possible that people's moral judgment is influenced by many different kinds of experiences, and that there is no single path by which people arrive at the same place.

In the literature, there is speculation on the kinds of experiences that might facilitate development in the basic structure of moral judgment: (1) discussing with others controversial moral problems, and in the process gaining practice and insight in making moral judgments; (2) exposure to better moral thinking than one's own; (3) recognition of conflicts in one's own values, or in the inadequacy of one's own assumptions and decision-making strategies, thus setting off the search for more adequate forms of thinking; (4) the assumption of new responsibilities for taking care of others which require a new perspective for integrating their perspectives with one's own interests; (5) the press to make important life decisions (e.g., career, marriage, style of life) that creates the need for a conceptual framework for sorting out the issues involved in these decisions and for making the decisions consistent; (6) experience of personal tragedy or being profoundly touched by another's tragedy which shocks one into reflecting about what is important in life; or being shocked into reflection by experiencing brutality, suffering, or evil; (7) "broadening" experiences like travel, art, reading, a move to a new city, etc., in which new breadth of experiences prompt new thinking; (8) meeting new people who have a drastically different perspective, and who draw out new attitudes in oneself.

This list is not exhaustive, but very little descriptive, longitudinal work has been done relating such life experiences to change in moral judgment. Many kinds of experiences may provide the impetus and material on which people reflect and construct the fundamental structures of their moral thinking. Obviously, much work remains to be done both in charting out the influential life experiences that promote development naturally, and in determining what kinds of educational programs can be effective.

8

The Internal Structure
and the Psychometric Properties
of the Defining Issues Test

by Mark L. Davison

This chapter reports two studies (Davison, Robbins, and Swanson, 1977; Davison and Robbins, 1977). In the first study, scaling and factor analytic techniques were applied to DIT responses to test the stage structure hypothesis, the hypothesis that moral judgment stages comprise a definite order. In the second study, I compared several new indices derived from scaling techniques with the P index. Investigations of longitudinal trends, internal consistency reliability, and concurrent validity, particularly the correlation with Kohlberg's own interview measure of moral development, indicate a new index to replace P as an overall index of moral development.

Stage Structure in DIT Responses

Kohlberg's (1969) theory of moral development asserts a six-stage sequence in which persons progress from lower to higher stages by a series of transformations. Each transformation produces qualitative changes that move the person toward more comprehensive, complex modes of reasoning about moral issues. This developmental progression is marked by the replacement of lower stage, less comprehensive modes of reasoning by higher stage, more comprehensive modes.

Wohlwill (1973, p. 198) has suggested applying what he calls a disjunctive scaling technique to moral judgment data in order to obtain more direct evidence on the sequentiality of the stages. As Wohlwill applies the term to developmental research, a set of responses are said to form a disjunctive scale if "each behavior, as it appears, dis-

223

places the preceding one," (p. 104). Moral judgment stages would be said to form a disjunctive scale if, as development proceeds, modes of reasoning characterizing higher stages successively displace modes of reasoning characterizing lower stages. The disjunctive scaling models considered by Wohlwill are designed to test for the unidimensional, hierarchical ordering of responses (or response types) assumed to form a disjunctive scale. For purposes of this paper, a set of responses will be said to form a disjunctive, developmental scale if (1) the responses are ordered along a single developmental sequence, and (2) each response is related to that sequence by a single-peaked, non-monotone function; that is, each response at first tends to increase in strength (frequency) as it replaces preceding responses, but later decreases in strength (frequency) as it is replaced by subsequent responses in the ordering. The response types of interest in this study are the different modes of moral reasoning derived from the six stages in Kohlberg's theory. Figure 8.1 depicts the kind of nonmonotone functions that might be assumed to relate ordered response types to a latent developmental dimension when those response types are part of a disjunctive, developmental scale.

Note that a model of development in which higher stage usages replace lower stage usages does not imply that the lower stages are obliterated from the subject's mind. It only implies that the subject prefers to use the higher stages as they become possible, not that the

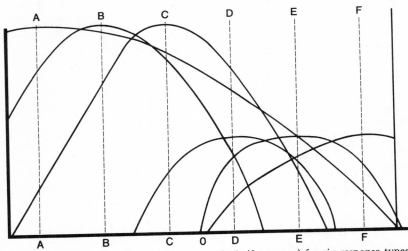

Figure 8.1. Expected observed response strength (frequency) for six response types expressed as a function of the respondent's position along the latent developmental dimension presumed to underly the disjunctive scale formed by the six response types.

subject is incapable of using the lower stages. Indeed, the fakability study by McGeorge (Chapter 7) indicates that the lower stages are readily available for use, and the comprehension studies (Chapter 6) indicate that the *capacity* to use stages of moral thinking is cumulative (i.e., understanding the higher entails understanding the lower). However, the *use* of the various stages in making decisions about moral dilemmas is disjunctive (the higher replaces the lower). Moreover, a disjunctive pattern of usage does not imply that a subject may also not continue to develop in understanding the lower stages as systems of ideas (c.f. Chapter 3, p. 66). Nevertheless, the main interest in moral judgment research has been in the kinds of thinking used to make moral decisions; and since both Kohlberg's test and the DIT are concerned with usage, this discussion will focus on usage rather than comprehension.

Besides asserting that higher stage reasoning displaces lower stage reasoning, Kohlberg's theory asserts that reasoning of adjacent stages is structurally more similar than the reasoning of nonadjacent stages. Consequently, a person who scores higher than others on a given stage is more likely to score higher than others on stages adjacent to the given stage than on stages nonadjacent to the given stage. That is, the person with the highest score on Stage 4 should have high scores on stages adjacent to Stage 4, Stages 3 and 5, but not on nonadjacent stages, such as Stages 1 and 6. Because the reasoning of adjacent stages is more similar than the reasoning of nonadjacent stages, a disjunctive scaling technique should reveal whether an ordering to the stages is present, and whether the ordering is the one theoretically predicted.

Wohlwill (1973) suggests several disjunctive scaling techniques (Coombs 1964; Coombs and Smith 1973; Leik and Mathews 1968; Torgerson 1958; and Wohlwill 1963). Three of these techniques (Coombs 1964; Coombs and Smith 1973; and Torgerson 1958) specify assumptions that can be satisfied only by error-free responses (i.e., scores with perfect reliability and validity) and that no fallible data could possibly meet. All of the above procedures except Coombs' (1964) assume dichotomous data (e.g., responses scored as either "yes" or "no") and could be applied to our data only if the variables were first artificially dichotomized. Because the results of any dichotomous procedure can vary as a function of the method by which the continuous variables are dichotomized, however, I have chosen to base the analyses on procedures associated with the metric unfolding model (Coombs and Kao 1960; Davison 1977; Ross and Cliff 1964; and Schönemann 1970). Those procedures assume continuous response variables, do not require error-free data, and include a number of testable data predictions.

As applied to moral development, the metric, unidimensional unfolding model assumes (1) that stage scores are expressed on an interval scale, (2) that both persons and stage score variables can be assigned scale values on an underlying continuum, and (3) that for a given stage, persons with the highest score will be those whose level of development is nearest that stage. Or in other words, subject i's score on stage j, s_{ij}, will be a linear function of the squared difference between the scale value for stage j (x_j) and person i (y_i):

$$s_{ij} = a_j (y_i - x_j)^2 + b_j + e_{ij} \qquad\qquad 1$$

Here a_j and b_j are constants associated with variable j, and e_{ij} is an error term. The second assumption, which asserts a developmental continuum, may at first seem inconsistent with Kohlberg's (1969) discrete stage theory. Kohlberg, however, recommends scoring moral development interviews on a continuum from 100 to 600. In this scoring system, pure stage types are represented by scores of 100, 200, 300, 400, 500, and 600. Thus Kohlberg himself seems to treat moral development as a continuous dimension along which persons and stages (pure stage types) can be assigned scores or scale values. Loevinger's (1966, 1976) ego development, a construct closely related to Kohlberg's moral development, is explicitly described as a dimension of individual differences along which the stages serve as markers or milestones. Therefore, it is theoretically plausible to think of moral development as a continuum along which persons and stages can be placed. As the authors are using the term, moral development refers to a continuous process marked by gradual, qualitative change in moral reasoning.

In effect, the third assumption asserts that scores on stage variables are related to developmental level by single-peaked, nonmonotone functions of the sort depicted in Figure 8.1. Higher stage variables peak at higher points along the continuum. The scale value associated with each variable represents the point along the developmental continuum at which that variable reaches its maximal expression. Loevinger (1966, p. 202) suggests just such a form for the major indicators of ego development, which she calls milestone variables and which she describes as

> observable behaviors that tend to rise and then fall off in prominence as one ascends the scale of ego maturity. For example, conformity to generally accepted social standards becomes increasingly characteristic of behavior up to a point, but beyond that point with increasing maturity becomes progressively less compelling, though not necessarily turning into nonconformity.

For the reasons cited above, metric unfolding assumptions (2) and (3) are consistent with those embodied in the related theories of moral and ego development. The interval data assumption, while debatable, receives some support from the work of Anderson (1975).

As applied to moral development data, the predictions of the metric unfolding model all involve the structure of stage score variables each of which reflects the subject's tendency to respond with statements characteristic of a given moral judgment stage. One example of such a variable is the rated importance a subject attaches to moral reasons typical of a given stage in the theory. Another is the frequency with which a subject spontaneously responds to a moral dilemma with statements typical of a given stage. The predictions, which are derived by Davison (1977) and Schönemann (1970), can be briefly summarized as follows:

1. The correlations of the stage score variables should display a simplex-like structure. To test this prediction, one first orders the rows and columns of the correlation matrix so row and column one correspond to the first stage score, row and column two correspond to the second stage score, row and column three correspond to the third stage score, and so on. Once the rows and columns have been so rearranged, the correlations should display the distinctive simplical structure in which the correlations in any row consistently decrease as one moves away from the diagonal element in either direction. As an example, the third row of a simplex correlation matrix might contain elements .28, .61, 1.00, .76, .57, and .47. If one begins with the diagonal element (the third element 1.00) and moves right along the row, the values steadily decrease from .76 to .47. Or if one moves left from the diagonal value, the elements steadily decrease from .61 to .28.

2. A principal components factoring of the variable correlations should yield two factors. The two-factor space should contain one factor along which intermediate stages have the highest loadings. Along another factor, variable loadings should be arrayed in stage order. Along this factor, the first stage should have the lowest loading, the second stage should have the second lowest loading, the third stage should have the third lowest loading. If the two-factor loadings are plotted, the points representing variables should fall along a semicircle in stage order (Coombs and Kao 1960; Davison 1977; Ross and Cliff 1964).

3. A metric unfolding analysis (Schönemann, 1970) of the response variables should yield one dimension. Along that dimension, persons should be ordered by age and variables by stage.[1] Schöne-

mann's analysis provides a method of estimating the scale values for stages and the developmental scores for persons described in Equation 1. According to the theory, older persons should have higher scores and higher stages should have higher scale values. Readers interested in the derivation of these predictions should consult Davison (1977) and Schönemann (1970), since they are too complex to discuss in detail here.

The research reported below was designed to test these three predictions. Should the predictions be supported, results would confirm the assertions (1) that the reasoning of adjacent stages is more similar than the reasoning of nonadjacent stages, (2) that there is an ordering of the stages, and (3) that the ordering corresponds to the theoretically predicted sequence.

Method

Subjects. The data reported in this research were obtained from 160 subjects: 40 junior high, 40 senior high, 40 college undergraduate, and 40 graduate students. The graduate students consisted of 25 male seminary students and 15 male doctoral students in moral philosophy. The remaining 120 subjects were approximately evenly divided between males and females. Rest et al. (1974) failed to find significant sex differences in moral judgment. Consequently, there is no reason to believe that any differences between the 40 graduate students and the 120 other students can be attributed to the all male composition of the older group. For a more complete description of the sample, see Rest et al. (1974).

Instruments. Subjects responded to a number of questionnaires, but only data from Rest's Defining Issues Test were analyzed in this study. Six stage scores were derived for each person by computing the average *rating* given by the subject to items keyed to each of the six stages: Stages 2, 3, 4, 5A, 5B, and 6.

Results

Table 8.1 gives the intercorrelations of the six stage scores. As one moves away (either left or right) from the diagonal element in any row, the values do tend to decrease. If the order of variables 5A and 5B were reversed, there would be no violations of the simplex pattern in this matrix. Generally, the stage score intercorrelations do display the predicted simplex-like structure.

Tables 8.2 and 8.3 show the factor analytic results which bear on hypothesis two. As shown in Table 8.2, principal components factor analysis of the stage score correlations produced two large characteristic roots greater than 1.00 and four small roots less than 1.00. These roots support the prediction of two factors. Along the second factor, the variables are ordered by stage, except for a minor reversal involving Stage Scores 5A and 5B. If points representing variable loadings, plotted in Figure 8.2, were connected by a smooth curve, that curve would be concave with respect to the origin and would approximate a semicircle. Points would generally fall along that curve in stage order.

Tables 8.2 and 8.3 show the results of the metric multidimensional scaling (Schönemann, 1970). Visual inspection of the roots shown in Table 8.2 suggests two dimensions. However, a plot of the dimension numbers (shown in column 1) against the actual roots (shown in column 3) would reveal that the situation is somewhat ambiguous. Either one or two dimensions might be retained. The most reasonable interpretation of these roots is that they suggest one major and one minor dimension.[2] Along the first dimension, the scale values for variables, shown in Table 8.3, are ordered by stage.

The metric unfolding analysis also provides estimates of scale values for persons. These scale values can be interpreted as estimates of subjects' moral development levels. Along Dimension 1, the mean scale value estimate was -1.22 for junior high students, -.21 for senior high students, .59 for college undergraduate students, and .84 for graduate

Table 8.1. Stage Score Correlations

Stage	2	3	4	5A	5B	6
2	1.00	.59	.59	.15	.18	−.05
3	.59	1.00	.59	.29	.33	.19
4	.59	.59	1.00	.36	.37	.32
5A	.15	.29	.36	1.00	.69	.54
5B	.18	.33	.37	.69	1.00	.47
6	−.05	.19	.32	.54	.47	1.00

Table 8.2. Characteristic Roots

Vector	Principal Components	Metric Scaling
1	2.80	3.00
2	1.52	1.23
3	.60	.69
4	.40	.66
5	.39	.28
6	.29	.14
	6.00	6.00

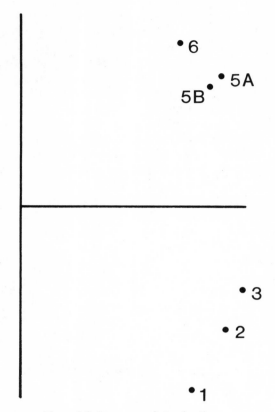

Figure 8.2. Stage score factor loadings.

students. The differences between these group means were statistically significant ($F = 23.50$, $p < .001$, $df = 3, 156$), and the order of these means is as predicted by the theory. Contrary to hypothesis four, the metric multidimensional scaling did not unambiguously yield one dimension. However, along the first dimension, both stage score variables and persons were ordered as predicted.

Scaling analyses were also performed on single statements. The top of Table 8.4 gives the mean scale value estimates for statements keyed to each stage. Stages 2, 3, and 4 are ordered as expected, but not Stages 5A, 5B, and 6. However, both Stages 5A and 6 include one statement with a highly deviant scale value, which partially accounts for the finding that the standard deviations for these two stages are higher than those for any others. Removing these two statements yielded the adjusted means given in parentheses. Taking these adjusted means as more accurate measures of central tendency, then the stages are ordered as predicted, except for another reversal involving Stages 5A and 5B. Even without removing these two deviant statements, the differences between the means are statistically significant ($F = 24.13$, $p < .01$, $df = 5, 56$). Hays' (1963) $\omega^2 = .65$ indicates that 65% of the variance in the scale values can be accounted for by the stages to which the items are keyed. The mean scale values for items keyed to each stage were also ordered as predicted by theory in a second, much larger sample. These replicated means are shown at the bottom of Table 8.4 and will be discussed later in more detail.

Care must be exercised in interpreting the intervals between scale values in Tables 8.3 and 8.4 because they depend upon two confounded sources of variation, the distribution of persons over the latent developmental continuum and the magnitude of differences in response patterns for the various statements. However, certain trends are worth noting. The largest interval between theoretically adjacent stages occurs between Stages 4 and 5A; this interval corre-

Table 8.3. Stage Score Factor Loadings and Scale Values

Stage	Unrotated Loadings		Scale Values
	Factor 1	Factor 2	
2	.61	−.67	−6.94
3	.73	−.45	−3.17
4	.79	−.30	−2.59
5A	.71	.48	2.27
5B	.67	.44	3.05
6	.57	.60	4.12

Table 8.4. Means and Standard Deviations of Scale Values
for Items Keyed to Each Stage

	Stage					
	2	3	4	5A	5B	6
Sample 1						
$\bar{x}$	−.34	−.17	−.13	.34	.35	.31
				(.40)		(.42)
s	.10	.19	.15	.25	.09	.27
Sample 2						
$\bar{x}$	−.33	−.26	−.03	.29	.40	.31
						(.42)
s	.12	.16	.21	.22	.05	.23

sponds to the transition from Conventional to Principled Thinking in Kohlberg's theory. The second largest interval occurs between Stages 2 and 3; it corresponds to the transition between Preconventional and Conventional Thinking in Kohlberg's theory. In short, the major distinctions between Preconventional, Conventional, and Principled Levels were drawn more clearly in the scale values than were the distinctions between stages within levels.

In contrast to the scale values of Tables 8.3 and 8.4, the intervals between factor loadings in Table 8.3 have no significance. The stage loadings along Factor 2 can be expected to reproduce the order of the stages, but not the size of the intervals between them (Ross and Cliff, 1964).

The notable inconsistencies between Tables 8.1, 8.3, and 8.4 involve Stages 5A and 5B. In Table 8.3, for instance, 5A has the higher scale value, but not in Table 8.4. These seemingly inconsistent results probably represent chance fluctuations in scale value estimates for stages (statements) that represent approximately the same developmental level. There may be two paths out of Conventional, Stage 4 reasoning, with one path leading toward the individualistic orientation of Stage 5B and the other leading to the social contract orientation of Stage 5A.

Taken as a whole, the results of the analyses suggest the following interpretation. In general, the theory seems to account for the importance that subjects attach to moral reasons associated with different stages. Subjects attaching the most importance to higher stages tend to attach less importance to lower stages and vice versa. As a result, stage scores give rise to a simplex-like correlation matrix; a stage-ordered, semicircular factor structure; and stage-ordered scale values. These findings indicate (1) that the thought structures of adjacent stages are more similar than those of nonadjacent stages, (2) that there is an ordering of the stages, and (3) that the ordering corresponds to the theoretically predicted sequence.

Discussion

The correlations of stage scores reported by Kohlberg (1958) displayed a simplex-like structure. Both Kurtines and Greif (1974) and Loevinger (1966) have challenged Kohlberg's evidence. Kurtines and Greif (1974) argued that Kohlberg's evidence was weak because the same sample was used to derive scoring rules and to estimate the correlations. The simplex-like correlation matrix observed in this study is not subject to the same criticism. Kurtines and Greif also point out that Kohlberg's data do not unambiguously determine stage order because the order of adjacent stages can be interchanged without destroying the simplex-like structure of Kohlberg's matrix. However, even Kurtines and Greif's rearranged matrix supports the ordering of Preconventional (Stages 1 and 2), Conventional (Stages 3 and 4), and Principled (Stages 5 and 6) thinking in Kohlberg's theory. In any case, the results of this study clearly support the ordering of Stages 2, 3, 4, 5A, and 6. Further, they provide little reason for concluding that either Stage 5A or 5B represents a higher level of development than the other. Moral judgment theory has been unclear about whether Stages 5A and 5B are two alternate pathways between Stages 4 and 6 or whether they are ordered in the sense that Stage 5A precedes 5B. The present data indicate that they are not ordered and that Stages 5A and 5B are alternate pathways.

Loevinger (1966) has dismissed Kohlberg's correlations and presumably would dismiss the correlations reported in this study as a mere confusion of models. Guttman (1954b) proposed a simplex model of abilities in which ability variables are hierarchically ordered by their factorial complexity because each successive variable loads on one more ability factor than the variable that precedes it. Since the factorial structure of adjacent ability variables in the model will be more similar than that of nonadjacent variables, the simplex model can and has been used to account for simplex correlations among ability variables. As a result, simplex correlation matrices have usually been interpreted as evidence for an ability development process quite unlike moral development. By showing that the metric unfolding model predicts a simplex-like structure, Davison (1977) has shown that observed, correlational structures can be accounted for by a model of moral judgment usage. But since a simplex correlation matrix can be explained by Guttman's (1954b) ability model, which is inconsistent with theories of moral judgment usage, or by the unfolding model, which is consistent with such theories, is there any evidence that the sequencing of moral judgment stages reflects anything other than a Guttman sequence of cognitive abilities?

Note first that at issue is the *usage* of different moral judgment stages rather than the ability to *comprehend* different moral judgment stages. Comprehension of lower stages is not lost as subjects come to use higher stages, and comprehension of lower stages may even continue to improve as subjects use yet higher stages (see Chapter 3).

However, at issue here is whether Guttman's ability model can account for usage data of the sort produced by Kohlberg's test and the DIT.

The evidence on this question is indirect but tends to disconfirm Guttman's ability model as an explanation of our data. First, our basic data are 5-point rating scales, a highly unusual medium for tapping human abilities. Second, cognitive ability models (Guttman, 1954b) posit $n - 1$ factors to account for the simplex correlations among n variables. Guttman's (1954a) criterion clearly indicated that only two factors were required to account for the correlations between the six stage scores. Finally, ability models typically assume that all correlations and partial correlations between ability variables are positive. Although we have not presented such data, when we correlated stage scores 2 and 6, after partialling out stage scores 3, 4, 5A, or 5B, the partial correlation was always significantly less than zero ($p < .05$). The presence of these significant, negative partial correlations contradicts the ability model. Though the evidence is indirect, it tends to disconfirm a cognitive abilities interpretation of the simplex correlations between the stage scores.

Kohlberg presented his theory to account for developmental trends in subjects' responses to open-ended questions about moral dilemmas, and most of the support for his theory has come from such interviews. Our data suggest that his stage ordering can also account for trends in objective moral judgments elicited by the Defining Issues Test. The simplex-like correlations of stage scores—the semicircular, two-factor configuration of stage score variables, and the ordering of persons and variables along the first scaling dimension—all provide support for a developmental sequence that is similar in major respects to Kohlberg's. Specifically, these findings indicate that (1) the reasoning of adjacent stages is more similar than the reasoning of nonadjacent stages, (2) there is an ordering to the stages, and (3) the stage ordering is the theoretically predicted sequence. To the evidence on the hierarchical structure of stages provided by previous studies of longitudinal trends, cross-sectional trends, and intervention studies, the present research provides a fourth kind of evidence. The data indicate that the patterning of stage scores within and across subjects is consistent with the hypothesis that moral judgment development proceeds by the gradual replacement of lower stage reasoning with higher stage modes of thought.

The Reliability and Validity of the DIT

Having examined the structure of DIT stage scores, Stephen Robbins and I then turned to an examination of the P score as an index of overall development. Loevinger (1976, p. 223) points out that P lacks intuitive appeal as a measure of overall development because it incorporates no information from issues keyed to the Stages 2, 3, or 4. Several unexplored alternatives to P are a sum of responses to all items or possibly a weighted sum of item responses. In a series of studies, the reliability and validity of Rest's P score were compared with those of a simple sum of item responses, a theoretically weighted sum of responses, and an empirically weighted sum of responses. Besides indicating an alternative to replace P, the research updates the available information on the reliability and validity of the Defining Issues Test.

Method

Subjects. In evaluating the reliability and validity of the DIT, seven samples were used. Each will be described below.

Sample 1 consisted of the 160 subjects described above whose data were used to investigate the ordering of stage scores. This sample was used to estimate the test's internal consistency reliability, its correlation with a measure of cognitive ability (*DAT Manual*, 1966), its correlation with a measure of comprehension of moral issues, and its correlation with two measures of attitudes related to moral development.

Sample 2 contained 1,080 subjects ranging in age from 15 to 82. The sample was equally split between those with a junior high school, a senior high school, a college, and a graduate education. Of these subjects, 424 were male and 452 were female. The sex of 203 was unknown. The data from this sample were used solely to estimate the empirical weights for the empirically weighted sum. As I shall show, these weights are of theoretical interest in their own right.

Sample 3 consisted of 123 subjects. All were subjects in moral education programs, and all had taken the DIT twice over an interval of from one week to five months. Evaluations of the individual moral education programs showed no significant change in DIT scores as a result of any project. These subjects ranged in age from

16 to 56. Of the 88 for whom sex information was available, 43 were males and 45 were females. Thirty-eight had a junior high school education, 24 a senior high education, 34 a college education, and 27 some type of graduate training. These data were used to estimate test-retest reliability.

Sample 4 was used to obtain a second test-retest reliability estimate. This sample contained 19 ninth graders, called sample 4a, and 33 Australian, college-age students from a study by McGeorge (1973), called sample 4b.

Sample 5 was used to estimate the correlation between scores on Kohlberg's interview measure and scores on Rest's paper-pencil measure. This sample contained a total of 213 subjects. Seventy-four were ninth grade males living in Minnesota. The remaining 139 were college students, about half male and half female, enrolled in an introductory psychology course at the University of Texas (Froming and McColgan, 1977). Rest (1976) reports that only two of 22 studies have found significant sex differences on the DIT. Consequently, the fact that the ninth grade sample contains only males is probably unimportant.

Sample 6 contained 54 subjects, 21 subjects who were ninth graders when first tested in 1972 and 33 who were eleventh graders when first tested in 1972. Their ages ranged from 14 to 18. All 54 were retested in 1974 and again in 1976. The sample, more completely described in Chapter 5, included 21 males and 33 females. Their data were used to study longitudinal changes as assessed by each moral judgment index.

Sample 7 contained 21 subjects, nine male and 12 female, who were high school juniors and seniors when first tested in 1974 by Elaine Wilson. All were retested in 1976. Like the data from Sample 6, the data from Sample 7 were used to study longitudinal changes as assessed by each moral judgment index.

Indices. As stated above, four indices were compared; Rest's P score, a simple sum of item responses (SS), a theoretically weighted sum of item responses (TS), and an empirically weighted sum (ES— explanations of weighting are below). P has been described above, but the remaining three are described here.

The simple sum (SS) is a sum of the 5-point importance ratings for each item (5 = most importance and 1 = least importance) after reverse scoring items keyed to the lowest stages; 2, 3, and 4.

Both weighted sums (e.g., TS and ES) are weighted sums of double centered item ratings. The double centered rating of person i for item j, x_{ij} is defined as:

$$\tilde{x}_{ij} = x_{ij} - x_{i.} - x_{.j} + x_{..}$$

where

x_{ij} = the importance rating given by person i to item j.

$x_{i.} = (1/n) \sum_{j} x_{ij}$, the mean importance rating given by person i to the n items.

$x_{.j} = (1/N) \sum_{i} x_{ij}$, the mean response to item j in the standardization sample of 1,080, and

$x_{..} = [1/(Nn)] \sum_{ij} x_{ij}$, the grand mean of responses in the standardization sample.

The double centering has two appealing features. First, by removing the term $x_{i.}$, double centering adjusts for the tendency of some subjects to give higher importance ratings to all items no matter what their content. Secondly, by removing the term $x_{.j}$, double centering adjusts for the fact that some items are simply more popular regardless of their stage content. As Chapter 3 explains, not all items keyed to the same stage will seem equally important to subjects at a given developmental level. Subtracting the mean of responses to that item compensates for this phenomenon and thus makes an adjustment for "item pull" (see Chapter 3, p. 56).

Both the theoretically and empirically weighted sums have the form:

$$s_i = \sum_{j} w_j \tilde{x}_{ij}$$

where

s_i = the sum for person i,

w_j = a weight for item j, and

$\tilde{x}_{ij}$ = subject i's double centered response to item j.

For the theoretically weighted sum (TS), the weight w_j was simply the number of the stage to which the item is keyed. Because the theoretically weighted sum is analogous to the Moral Maturity Score successfully used by Kohlberg, it was investigated as one scoring option.

For the empirically weighted sum (ES), the weight was proportional to the item's projection onto the first principal component of the double centered response matrix in the standardization sample of 1,080. The rationale for choosing the empirical weighting scheme lies in the work on the ordering of stages (Davison, 1977; Davison, Robbins, and Swanson 1977), which seems to support a unidimensional, metric unfolding model for objective moral judgments, as discussed in the previous section of this chapter. According to the model, each person can be characterized by a scale value or score representing his or her level of moral reasoning. Each item can be characterized by a scale value representing the level of moral reasoning expressed by the statement. Persons are assumed to attach the most importance to statements expressing levels of reasoning nearest their own. Given the model, Schönemann (1970) has shown that least squares estimates of person scores are a weighted sum of double centered responses to items, where the weights are proportional to the projections of items onto the first principal component of the double centered response matrix.

The empirical weight estimation scheme represents empiricism at its blindest. If it had turned out that higher stage items did not have higher scale values, we would have had no logical basis for arguing that the empirical sum reflected a stage-ordered moral development sequence. On the average, however, higher stage issues did have higher scale values, as we shall report below.

In the following section, I will first report empirical item scale values. Then I will compare the four scoring schemes in terms of their internal consistency reliabilities, test-retest reliabilities, correlations with other measures, and sensitivities to longitudinal trends.

Results

Empirical Item Scale Values. Table 8.4 shows that in Sample 2, consisting of 1,080 subjects, the scale values for Stages 2, 3, 4, 5A, 5B and 6 as estimated by Schönemann's (1970) algorithm were -.33, -.26, -.03, .29, .40, and .31. As in the scale value estimates from Sample 1, Stage 6 has one item whose deviance is reflected in the large standard deviation of scale values for that stage. Also as in Sample 1, it is larger than for any other stage. Removing the deviant item yields the Stage 6 mean weight shown in parentheses. Taking the adjusted mean as a more accurate measure of central tendency, the stages are again ordered as predicted.

The mean scale values in Table 8.4 provide clear support for the hierarchical ordering of Kohlberg's Stages 2, 3, and 4 and somewhat more ambiguous support for the ordering of Stages 5 and 6, which are unambiguously higher than Stages 2 through 4. The ordering of weights (or scale values) suggests that the reasoning of adjacent stages is more similar than that of nonadjacent stages. Consequently, the ordering of the items corresponds to the theoretically predicted stage sequence. Because the empirical weights mirror Kohlberg's hierarchically ordered moral development sequence, grounds exist for believing that the sum based on those weights reflects a subject's level along a stage-ordered moral development sequence. The weights provide clear evidence for the sequentiality of the stages, a hypothesis for which Kurtines and Greif (1974) assert that evidence has been lacking.

Reliability. Table 8.5 shows reliability data for the four scoring schemes and for Rest's six stage scores. Since a number of researchers (Dortzbach 1975; Erickson et al. 1976; Guttenberg 1975; Morrison, Toews and Rest 1973; Sanders 1976; and Troth 1974) have used a three-story version of the DIT to save subject time, Table 8.5 also contains reliability data on the shorter version as well. For those who wish to compute standard errors of measurement, as did Rest (1975), Table 8.6 reports standard deviations for test and retest scores. The discussion, however, will focus on the indices of overall development derived from the full six-story version of the DIT.

Table 8.5. Internal Consistency and Test-Retest Reliabilities

Score	Internal Consistency	Test-Retest Sample			
		Six Stories			
	1	3	4	4a	4b
P	.77	.82	.76	.81	.71
SS	.70	.75	.72	.52	.73
TS	.90	.67	.77	.90	.67
ES	.79	.87	.76	.92	.27
Stage 2	.50	.44	.62	.78	.67
Stage 3	.51	.55	.66	.66	.67
Stage 4	.52	.61	.76	.66	.80
Stage 5A	.60	.65	.66	.57	.68
Stage 5B	.28	.60	.51	.49	.56
Stage 6	.43	.72	.54	.57	.49
		Three Stories			
	1	3	4	4a	4b
P	.76	.77	.65	.58	.67
ES	.71	.83	.71	.81	.63
Stage 2	.30	.32	.69	.70	.42
Stage 3	.32	.48	.52	.54	.50
Stage 4	.27	.56	.66	.47	.74
Stage 5A	.53	.69	.63	.60	.64
Stage 5B	--	.58	.41	.45	.39
Stage 6	.00	.50	.47	.26	.52

All four indices of overall development exhibit fair to good reliabilities in these samples. The two scores most commonly employed by users of the DIT, P and the empirically weighted sum, generally have reliabilities in the upper .70s and .80s. Two trends in this table are worth noting. First, the empirically weighted sum is superior to the simple sum in all but one case. It is significantly more reliable in Samples 3 and 4a ($p < .05$). In the one case where the reliability of the simple sum is higher than that of the empirically weighted sum, it is not significantly higher ($p > .05$). Second, the reliability of P and the empirically weighted sum are generally about .80 for the six-story DIT. For the shorter, three-story version, the reliabilities more commonly drop to about .70.

Table 8.7 shows the test and retest means for the test-retest samples. The evidence for retesting effects is not appreciable. Only the theoretically weighted sum changes significantly in samples 4, 4A, or 4B. No one has recommended use of this index, and it is included here only for comparative purposes. All measures change in Sample 3, but these are pre-post data from several moral education studies,

Table 8.6. Standard Deviations in Test and Retest Samples
for Three and Six Story DIT Data

	Sample 3		Sample 4	
	s_{pre}	s_{post}	s_{pre}	s_{post}
Six Stories				
P	18.53	19.90	13.40	12.70
ES	10.76	10.90	5.86	5.53
Stage 2	2.91	2.78	3.19	3.49
Stage 3	6.12	6.31	5.29	5.35
Stage 4	7.13	6.97	7.21	7.73
Stage 5A	7.48	7.40	6.18	5.75
Stage 5B	3.65	3.67	3.27	3.23
Stage 6	3.90	4.33	2.60	2.79
Three Stories				
P	20.43	22.83	15.86	14.63
ES	6.20	6.16	3.91	3.40
Stage 2	3.56	3.51	4.55	4.19
Stage 3	7.83	8.58	6.77	6.12
Stage 4	8.72	8.06	7.92	9.25
Stage 5A	9.51	10.43	8.03	7.78
Stage 5B	3.18	3.24	3.00	2.69
Stage 6	3.53	3.82	3.11	3.36

some of which lasted five months. While none of the individual studies reported significant change from pre-test to post-test, when we combined the data from the several studies, a significant t-statistic resulted. Because the data come from moral education studies, the sample 3 test-retest reliabilities in Table 8.7 provide a measure of the stability for the relative standing of individuals, but the sample 3 mean difference in Table 8.7 is not simply a measure of retesting effect. Only samples 4, 4a, and 4b mean differences reflect the effect of retesting alone. P, the empirically weighted sum, and the simple sum did not change significantly in these samples nor in the two other test-retest studies cited in Chapter 5, p. 142).

Validity. Table 8.7 shows the correlations of scores on the DIT with scores on several measures of constructs thought to be related to moral development. Sample 1 was used to estimate the correlations between the DIT and measures of Comprehension of Moral Issues, Law and Order Orientation, and Political Tolerance. Chapter 6 describes these measures and explains their relationship to moral development. The correlations between scores on the DIT and scores on the Differential Aptitude Test (*DAT Manual*, 1966) were computed on the 40 ninth graders in sample 1, the only people for whom DAT data were available. Sample 5 data were used to estimate the correlations between the DIT and Kohlberg's interview scores.

The theoretically weighted sum did not correlate significantly with the Comprehension of Moral Concepts measure. Using a .05 level of significance, both P and the empirically weighted sum correlated sig-

Table 8.7. Mean Scores for Test and Retest Samples

	P	SS	TS	ES
Sample 3				
Test	40.78[*]	62.14[†]	49.76[†]	22.00[*]
Retest	44.93	66.36	49.12	23.05
Sample 4				
Test	39.58	66.29	47.44	22.94
Retest	39.58	67.69	46.19	23.65
Sample 4a				
Test	36.48	59.74	46.62	20.26
Retest	35.78	62.16	46.60	22.05
Sample 4b				
Test	41.37	70.06	47.91[*]	24.48
Retest	41.77	70.88	45.95	24.58

[*]$p < .05$

[†]$p < .01$

nificantly better than did the theoretically weighted sum with measures of Comprehension of Moral Concepts, Law and Order Orientation, and Political Tolerance. But most important, the theoretically weighted sum was not significantly correlated with Kohlberg's interview measure of moral development in the total Sample 5 or in either subsample. In Sample 5 as a whole, P, the simple sum, and the empirically weighted sum all had significantly ($p < .05$) larger correlations with Kohlberg interview scores than did the theoretically weighted sum. Table 8.8 points to a serious weakness in the theoretically weighted sum; it does not correlate as highly as one would expect with measures that should be related to one's level of moral development.

While three of the moral development indices are highly and significantly correlated with Kohlberg's measure in sample 5 as a whole, all have modest to low correlations with Kohlberg's measure in the junior high school sample, sample 5a, and the college subsample, sample 5b. Prior research (Rest 1975; Holstein 1976; and Kuhn 1976) indicates that older subjects score higher than do younger subjects on both Rest's and Kohlberg's tests. The fact that the two measures correlate only modestly in age homogeneous samples, however, suggests that the majority of their common variance in the total sample can be accounted for by the measures' common age trends. The modest correlations in age homogeneous samples further indicate that Rest's and Kohlberg's test cannot be considered equivalent measures which differ only in format.

Longitudinal Studies. Table 8.9 shows the longitudinal trends ob-

Table 8.8. Correlations of Four Moral Development Indices with
Measures of Cognitive Ability (DATVN), Comprehension of
Moral Issues (COMP), Law and Order Orientation (LO),
Political Tolerance (PT), and Kohlberg's Interview Scores

	P	SS	TS	ES
DATVN	.43[†]	.23	.12	.47[†]
COMP	.65[†]	.54[†]	.12	.63[†]
LO	−.59[†]	−.50[†]	−.14[*]	−.49[†]
PT	.62[†]	.50[†]	.16[*]	.55[†]
Kohlberg Interview				
Sample 5	.68[†]	.63[†]	.07	.70[†]
Sample 5a	.17	−.12	.22[*]	.20[*]
Sample 5b	.35[†]	.32[†]	.14	.37[†]

[*]$p < .05$

[†]$p < .01$

served in samples 6 and 7. Over the four years in which sample 6 subjects were studied, there was a significant decrease in their Stage 2 and 3 scores and a significant increase in their stage 5A and 5B thinking. All four indices, P, the simple sum, the theoretically weighted sum, and the empirically weighted sum increased significantly over the period studied. As indicated by the size of the F statistics, the strongest longitudinal trend occurred for the empirically weighted sum, followed by P, the simple sum, and the theoretically weighted sum.

A different pattern was observed in sample 7 (see Chapter 5, page 128). Of the stage scores, only Stage 3 scores changed significantly, and Stage 3 is not reflected by Rest's P. Not surprisingly, P displays no significant upward shift. Applying the conventional .05 level of significance, only the empirically weighted sum changed significantly, although the significance level for the theoretically weighted sum al-

Table 8.9. Means of Moral Development Measures by Year
in Two Longitudinal Studies

	Sample 6			
	1972	1974	1976	F
P	32.87	39.78	44.15	20.06[†]
SS	59.85	62.72	67.31	7.70[†]
TS	45.90	48.87	48.05	4.18[*]
ES	20.26	23.26	24.06	24.86[†]
Stage 2	6.30	5.00	4.62	6.60[†]
Stage 3	11.30	8.04	7.56	12.50[†]
Stage 4	18.15	18.61	17.16	1.30
Stage 5A	12.44	16.48	17.82	18.20[†]
Stage 5B	4.26	4.83	5.46	3.50[*]
Stage 6	2.85	2.72	3.20	.60

	Sample 7		
	1974	1976	t
P	33.88	36.92	− .97
SS	58.62	58.05	.22
TS	50.11	52.86	−2.00
ES	20.46	22.96	−2.64[*]
Stage 2	5.00	3.59	1.60
Stage 3	12.38	9.17	2.90[†]
Stage 4	18.10	19.98	−1.12
Stage 5A	14.29	14.42	− .08
Stage 5B	3.76	3.88	− .15
Stage 6	2.29	3.86	−2.25

[*]$p < .05$
[†]$p < .01$

most reached the .05 level ($p = .06$). As indicated by the t statistics, the empirically weighted sum again showed the strongest longitudinal trend.

Loevinger (1976) expressed concern that Rest is using P as an index of overall development when P reflects only the upper stages. The longitudinal data in this study serve to amplify her concern. In sample 6, the longitudinal trend in P was weaker than that for the empirically weighted sum because P does not reflect the observed changes in Stages 3 and 4. The results are more dramatic in Sample 7, where the only significant changes were in lower stage scores not reflected by P. As an index of overall development, P appears insensitive to change occurring in lower stages. Such insensitivity should be of particular concern to researchers using the DIT to evaluate outcomes of clinical and educational programs.

The simple sum was even more inferior than P to the empirically weighted sum in its sensitivity to longitudinal trends. In both samples 6 and 7, the longitudinal trend as reflected in the simple sum was weaker than the trend as reflected in any of the other three indices. On two counts, reliability and sensitivity to longitudinal trends, the simple sum has proven inferior to the empirically weighted sum and P.

Discussion

One conclusion suggested by this research is that the empirically weighted sum provides the most desirable measure of overall development. It takes into account information from all stages, and as a result, it is more sensitive to longitudinal change than is P, particularly when the change occurs in lower stages. The empirically weighted sum yielded generally higher reliabilities and greater sensitivity to longitudinal change than did the simple sum. As compared to the theoretically weighted sum, the empirically weighted sum yielded a significantly higher correlation with Kohlberg's measure and stronger longitudinal trends. Davison, Robbins, and Swanson (1977) list a program that uses DIT responses to compute stage scores, P, and the empirically weighted sum. The program is available from the author and makes tedious hand scoring unnecessary.

To summarize the reliability data from these samples, the overall indices of reliability (P and the empirically weighted sum) based on six stories generally have internal consistency and test-retest reliabilities in the high .70s and low .80s for age heterogeneous samples. For age homogeneous samples, the test-retest reliability of P stayed in the .70s, but for the empirically weighted sum it fell to .67 in one sample. For the three-story DIT, reliabilities of the overall indices generally seemed to fall about .10 points. Stage score reliabilities, either test-retest or internal consistency, seldom surpassed .70. Most were in the .50s and .60s.

As for concurrent validity, the overall indices seemed to correlate in the .40s with a measure of general aptitude, in the .60s with a measure of comprehending moral concepts, in the high .40s or .50s with a measure of law-and-order orientation, and in the .50s or .60s with a measure of political tolerance. Correlations with Kohlberg's measure were about .70 in an age heterogeneous sample but only about .20 in a sample of ninth graders and about .35 in a sample of college students.

The reliability data in Table 8.5 indicate that using the shorter three-story DIT should have little effect in studies where the group means are the focus. In studies of group means, one need only have precise estimates of means; that is, estimates that have low standard errors. Regardless of a measure's reliability, mean estimates can be made as precise as desired by a sufficiently large sample size. In correlational studies, the drop in reliability associated with the shorter version cannot be overcome by an increase in sample size. According to classical reliability theory, the net effect should be a drop in the correlation between the DIT and any outside variable. The drop should be proportional to the square root of the three-story DIT reliability divided by the square root of the six-story reliability. For example, imagine that the six-story version correlates about .40 with some variable, and it has a reliability of .80 in the population of interest, whereas the shorter version has a reliability of .70. The shorter version would be expected to have a correlation of $(\sqrt{.70}/\sqrt{.80})(.40) = .37$. Using the shorter version would always reduce the observed correlation somewhat and may even reduce it to nonsignificance, but the reduction should usually be small.

Rest (1975) has stressed the importance of examining each subject's stage score profile as well as some overall index of development such as P or the empirically weighted sum. Even with the full six stories, Table 8.5 shows that none of the stage scores have an internal consistency reliability above .60, and seldom do test-retest reliabilities rise above .70. Because stage scores have modest reliabilities, researchers must be careful about overinterpreting small differences between the same stage score assessed on two occasions. Rest (1975) shows how the standard error of prediction, which can be estimated from data in Tables 8.5 and 8.6, can be used to avoid overinterpreting small differences.[3]

9

DIT Research: Conclusions, Options, and Future Directions

This book was written with four objectives in mind: (1) One objective was to review the substantial data now accumulated on the moral judgment construct as measured by the DIT. Previous to DIT research, speculation about the nature of moral judgment had far outrun its data base. The foregoing chapters review over 100 studies conducted in different parts of the country and based on information given by thousands of subjects. Now interlocking and replicated studies confirm the fundamental features of the moral judgment construct, namely, its developmental and cognitive nature. However, there are also some surprises in these studies. (2) Another objective has been to examine the usefulness of the DIT as an assessment instrument. No single study establishes the validity of a test of moral judgment, but in this "first round" of validation studies, the DIT has performed well. (3) Another objective has been to highlight the crucial decisions about research strategy that anyone doing programmatic research in moral judgment must face. Each decision point has many options. I have presented the rationale for the set of options chosen for DIT research, but it remains to be seen how other options will work. (4) Within each chapter, suggestions for further research have been made. The current body of research gives us confidence that we are studying a meaningful and important phenomenon, and that our present research strategies are moving us along. Yet research in moral thinking has to go an immense distance to explain and predict more complex human interactions, such as political behavior, decisions of fairness in work and in private life, and so on.

The preceding chapters have discussed these objectives in some detail, however, at this point a summary may help put them in perspective and point out their interconnectedness.

Major Findings

An exploration of the theory of moral judgment and the process of validating a particular measure of moral judgment go hand in hand. A theory can be tested only in terms of some specific measurement instrument; the validation of specific measures of moral judgment can only be done by "construct validation," that is, determining the degree to which the test scores exhibit the properties implied by the theoretical construct. Therefore, Objectives 1 and 2 will be discussed together.

The most fundamental claims about moral judgment asserted by a cognitive developmental approach are (1) that moral judgment is developmental, (2) that it is primarily governed by cognitive processes, and (3) that it has a role in real life decision-making. Each of these claims is complex and requires various kinds of studies.

To claim that moral judgment is developmental entails having a theoretical description that identifies the markers of development and how they are sequenced, and a rationale for claiming that one type of moral judgment is more "advanced" or conceptually adequate than another. Chapter 2 presented the conceptual scheme presupposed in DIT research. On the empirical side, one line of evidence for the ordering of the stages came from Davison's work on the internal structure of the DIT (Chapter 8). Using techniques derived from multidimensional scaling, he found that the average scale values of the stages are empirically ordered according to their theoretical order; the finding on a sample of 160 subjects was cross-validated on a sample of 1,080 subjects. A second line of evidence came from cross-sectional studies of different student groups (Chapter 5). A composite sample from all regions of the United States, totalling over 4,500 students, showed that grouping the subjects by their age-education (junior highs, senior highs, college, and graduate students) accounted for 38% of the variance of moral judgment scores; grouping the subjects at the individual classroom level accounted for almost 50% of the variance. Older, educationally advanced students have higher moral judgment scores. Doctoral students in moral philosophy and political science have the highest DIT scores of any student groups. The cross-sectional studies thus support the claim that moral judgment is developmental, since the groups expected to have the highest scores do in fact have the highest scores. A third line of evidence came from the longitudinal studies (Chapter 5). Retesting the same subjects at two-year intervals over four years showed mean scores (the P% index of the DIT) of 33 in 1972, 40 in 1974, and 44 in 1976 ($F = 20.1$, $p < .0001$). Analyses of individual cases showed that 66% of the subjects went up ond only 7% went down. The predominant trend in the longitudinal studies is for change in the direction postulated by theory. Bifactorial sequential analyses, and analyses of testing effects and of possible sample bias, indicated that the age trends obtained in the cross-sectional and longitudinal studies could not be attributed to generational change or the other artifacts. A fourth line of evidence that moral judgment is developmental comes from its correlations with other developmental measures; with other measures of moral thinking, the DIT correlates as high as the .60s and .70s; with measures of IQ, aptitude, and achievement, the correlations are generally in the .20 to .50 range (Chapter 6). A fifth line of evidence comes from intervention studies (Chapter 7). In educational studies designed to stimulate more rigorous and more defensible moral thinking, whenever a significant change occurred in group averages between pretest and posttest, it was always upward. These diverse kinds of studies, taken as a whole, give substantial support to the claim that moral judgment as measured by the DIT is developmental.

The claim that moral judgment scores are governed by underlying general *cognitive* organizations is also supported by several lines of research. One line of research relates moral *judging* (DIT scores) to a measure of the *capacity* to comprehend high stage moral concepts (see Chapter 6). Significant correlations (up to the .60s) suggest that subjects who can comprehend high stage concepts do tend to make judgments using those concepts, whereas subjects who do not make high stage judgments cannot understand the concepts. Second, in longitudinal studies, as moral judgment increases, so also does comprehension. Third, the DIT has consistently significant correlations with other cognitive measures. A fourth line of evidence that moral judgment scores represent a subject's upper levels of cognitive ability comes from several "fakability" studies (Chapter 7). When subjects are encouraged to raise their moral judgment scores above their "natural" levels (obtained under normal test conditions), no significant increase is shown (at least, it seems, without invalidating the protocol by the "M" score check). However, when subjects are asked to "fake bad," their scores are significantly decreased. This suggests that DIT scores usually represent a subject's highest cognitive capacity in moral thinking. Fifth, some suggestive support for the notion that moral judgment is governed by deep-seated cognitive processes comes from educational intervention studies, which indicate that moral judgment is very slow to change and difficult to manipulate. Even after weeks and months of intervention, the moral judgment scores of students are nowhere near those of doctoral students in moral philosophy or political science. If moral judgment reflected more simply a person's *preference* for certain concepts (rather than capacity for concepts), it is difficult to explain why the interventions don't produce more dramatic shifts.

Although cognitive developmentalists claim that moral judgment is primarily governed by cognitive processes, they also want to claim that something distinct about moral thinking separates it from other aspects of general cognitive development. It is argued that more advanced moral concepts evolve from less advanced moral concepts, rather than that higher moral concepts are derived from the application to moral content of more generalized forms of intellectual development. Three kinds of evidence address the distinctiveness of moral judgment development from general intellectual development. In one study, an ethics class and a logic class were given the DIT and a logic test before and after the courses (Chapter 7). It was found that the ethics class moved subjects up on the DIT and the logic class moved subjects up on the logic test, but not vice versa, thus demonstrating a specific effect of specific kinds of cognitive stimulation rather than an effect common to any kind of intellectual stimulation. A second line of evidence about the distinctiveness (not total independence) of moral judgment comes from correlational studies (Chapter 6). One study showed intercorrelations among six variables: two measures of moral thinking, two measures of intellectual aptitude, and two measures of political attitudes. Although all six measures were intercorrelated to some degree, the moral thinking measures correlated best with each other, the intellectual aptitude measures correlated best with each other, and the political attitude measures correlated best with each other. Although general intelligence variables share common variance with moral thinking variables, there is a specific factor too. Third, studies using multiple regression techniques show that moral judgment has unique predictability to criterion variables beyond that accounted for by IQ or other variables (Chapter 6).

Cognitive developmentalists want to claim that moral judgment is related to real life decision making, and is not value-neutral, purely cerebral sophistry or intellectualism. How to conceptualize the relation between moral judgment and "real life" decision-making is complex, some psychologists have asserted that the relationship has to be a straight-line linear one, while others assert that there is no relationship. This conceptual issue will be further discussed below, but the evidence in Chapter 6 is that the DIT is significantly related to people's value stances on controversial public policy issues, and is related to experimental and naturalistic measures of behavior. Generally, moral judgment is no less correlated to behavior than behavioral measures are correlated with each other. At this point in the discussion, I want to claim that evidence shows that moral judgment is related to real life decision making.

All of this research supports the basic tenets of the cognitive developmental notion of moral judgment, and since the DIT was the measure used, the research supports the validity of the DIT as an assessment tool. Davison's Chapter 8 summarizes some of the reliability properties of the DIT: The internal consistency in various studies gives an alpha in the high .70s and the average test-retest reliability is in the .80s. The DIT does not seem to have appreciable testing effects from repeated testing. In short, both the validity and reliability data confirm the usefulness of the DIT and warrant further development of the instrument.

While the DIT research has provided much needed substantiation for basic tenets of the cognitive developmental approach, other findings have broken new ground, and in some cases, produced some surprises. While these are too numerous to list completely, a number of instances can be cited:

1. In adults, years of education is much more predictive of moral judgment scores than age.

2. Subjects from the conservative South and from conservative religious groups have lower DIT scores than subjects from other regions or who are affiliated with more liberal religious groups.

3. There are no consistent sex differences on the DIT.

4. Development seems to slow down after a P% score of 40 or after leaving school. Adults seem to plateau in moral judgment development after leaving school.

5. The DIT is no more highly correlated with verbal subtests than with nonverbal subtests on general aptitude tests.

6. The moral judgments that subjects produce on the Kohlberg interview are consistently scored at lower stages than the stages of items picked on the DIT. Much of the discrepancy seems attributable to the difference between a production task and a recognition task.

7. Many political attitude and personality tests have nonsignificant correlations with the DIT, attributable at least in part to the lack of any logical relationship between the DIT and the other variable. For instance, Rotter's I-E scale, Allport-Vernon-Lindzey's Study of Values, Hogan's SEA scale, various-self concept measures, and Rokeach's Value Survey have low or inconsistent correlations with the DIT; whereas several subscales of the CPI and Omnibus Personality Inventory seem to have significant correlations. There is no support for the notion that moral judgment is more related to personality than to cognitive development.

8. Some educational interventions seem capable of facilitating development, but movement is not great in any study.

9. Experimentation on dozens of ways of indexing the DIT have shown that the "P" index and Davison's index, "ES," have the best overall qualities, with the ES index showing an advantage in change studies with less advanced subjects.

10. The DIT discriminates predelinquents from nondelinquents better than several other measures of social cognition (Kohlberg's test, Chandler's Role Taking Test, Piaget's Golden Rule Test).

Future Directions in Research Strategy

Objectives 3 and 4 will be summarized together.

Once a research program is initiated, it becomes apparent that many options for constructing studies are available, and that some questions and some methods have to be neglected to move ahead on others. Working on the DIT has highlighted six kinds of crucial decision points.

Model of Development

Recognizing that children have different patterns of thought from those of adults, how should the course of psychological development be modeled? Following Piaget, many developmental psychologists have described the various patterns of thinking in terms of logical typologies, each type being portrayed as a coherent system of thought in use at a particular time. The notion of "stage" implies the use of typological concepts as well as the implication that one particular type of thinking is characteristic of a particular span in a person's life. Development, therefore, is portrayed in terms of moving through a series of stages, one step at a time. While this model of development is useful for calling attention to qualitatively different systems of thinking and to the logical interrelations of various ideas, nevertheless the stage model assumes that human beings have only one organization of thinking at their disposal at a time (or two, if the subject is in transition between stages). The stage model has been misleading in many respects as a model of the psychological functioning of actual subjects, and in its simple form does not fit well with the data from cognitive developmental research (discussed in Chapter 3).

Researchers in moral judgment, therefore, have three basic options. One option is to use the simple stage model anyway, disregarding the empirical problems and shrugging off the disconfirmations as so much "noise." But to conduct research, questionable practices are adopted in developmental assessment (such as discarding discrepant data); questionable data analyses are performed (such as matching stages on one measure with stages on another measure in order to see which construct is prerequisite to the other); and questionable research designs are used (such as assigning subjects to "+1," "+2," "-1" treatment groups).

The second option is to modify the simple stage model—and this is the option taken in DIT research. The "stages" still represent qualitatively different logical systems of thinking, but a subject is not assigned one-for-one to a stage. This view acknowledges that people use various organizations of thinking, are somewhat inconsistent, and that the kind of logical organization they bring to a problem is considerably influenced by the particular content and properties of the problem. Accordingly, developmental diagnosis is only relativistic and probabilistic; change is viewed in terms of shifts in distributions of responses rather than step by step; and certain research designs are abandoned (those that require subjects to be designated as "in" one stage). The second option is conceptually less tidy than the simple stage model but is workable and has a better fit with the data.

The third option is to regard the notion of stage as only a useful fiction in the early phases of developmental research, but to move as quickly as possible to less global characterizations of people's thinking and on to more specific features (see Flavell 1977 for endorsement of this view for cognitive development). Instead of talking about a subject's Stage 4 thinking, for instance, one would make statements about his concept of obligatory public law, or his concept of authority as occupying a role position in a formal system of social organization. In option three, the specific concepts become the focus of developmental description rather than the more global terms, the stages. Piaget's own work in moral judgment was more in accord with this option, as he describes intentionality, immanent justice, or objective responsibility. Furthermore, Davison's scaling procedures (Chapter 8) have provided a means for allocating specific concepts along a general continuum of development independent of an *a priori* designation of that concept into a stage. In fact, Davison's new index does not require the postulation of stages at all. (Note, however, that Davison's scaling procedures are not inimical to the postulation of stages, and have been used, in fact, to explore stage structure of the DIT items, as Chapter 8 discusses.)

The choice between Option 2 (a modified stage model) and Option 3 (no stage model) depends on finding evidence that various concepts have some sort of psychological unity or cohesiveness. What is at stake is whether a typological approach or more atomistic approach will better represent people's thinking. I have favored Option 2 because the interview material produced by Kohlberg suggests that subjects themselves see the linkages between various concepts. That is, interviewing subjects with Kohlberg's interview procedure, I have been struck by instances in which a subject mentions one "Law and Order" Stage 4 idea, which in turn seemed logically to lead the subject into another Law and Order idea. In such cases, it seems more accurate to represent that subject's thinking in terms of a generalized Law and Order orientation instead of as the co-occurrence of independent concepts. Certainly the thinking of philosophers (and graduate philosophy students) has to be viewed in terms of organized systems, not isolated, disconnected concepts. Yet how typical is it of people (especially young subjects) to be aware and concerned about the logical interconnectedness of their ideas? Perhaps organizing one's moral ideas into an interconnected system of thinking is a kind of development in its own right, and we ought not to assume that everyone (including young children) have *systems* of thinking until evidence appears of a logical connectedness between concepts. Obviously much research is needed on the degree of interconnectedness among concepts, and whether the interconnections are always those assumed in our stage descriptions.

Abandoning the simple stage model (as I think we must do) means giving up many convenient assumption about the course of development. For instance, if stages do not neatly rise, peak, and decline in turn over development, but overlap and mix in complicated ways, then one goal of research should be to chart this complex course, messy as it may be. Another goal of future research should be to assess the influence of content, task, and performance factors on the organization of a person's thinking. Current research has done little more than demonstrate abstractly that such an influence exists. Now what is needed is an encompassing model that identifies all these factors and predicts how much and when each influences a person's organization of thinking. Another area of needed research is to reconsider the notion that subjects episodically pass alternately through a phase of consolidation of a stage, in which the world is generally understandable, and a phase of transition, in which the world is generally confusing. It is likely that consolidation and transition are occurring together all through development rather than alternating.

Developmental Features

Discussion of the first issue has led to the second crucial research decision that any researcher must make: What features of people's thinking are to be considered in a developmental analysis? What concepts or kinds of things that people say are to be used as markers of development?

Piaget in his 1932 book identified about a dozen developmental features (for example, intentionality, immanent justice, objective responsibility). A number of alternative sets of features have been proposed (Bull 1969; Damon 1977; Eisenberg-Berg in press; Lee 1971; Hoffman and Saltzstein 1967; Hogan 1970) but by far, Kohlberg and his associates have done the most extensive and impressive work in identifying developmental features. While brief descriptions of Kohlberg's six stages are well known (often presented as a one page table), much less known are the approximately 100 features (or "criterion judgments") by which scoring is actually done. Becoming familiar with the specific features has been difficult for many researchers because this work is too long and involved for journal article-length presentations and because the work has been undergoing revision for the past ten years. A close look at the recent scoring guides is necessary to appreciate the scope and depth of this work in identifying developmental features.

The researcher must choose some set of features (or devise one's own) by which to analyze people's thinking. The set of features employed in the DIT are based on Kohlberg's features. As Chapter 2 discusses, Kohlberg's 1958 formulations were used in my 1969 dissertation study, and that in turn led to the specific characterizations of moral judgment development used in writing the DIT in 1971. Some differences of DIT features with Kohlberg's 1978 features are discussed in Chapter 2.

A considerable amount of theoretical work needs to accompany one's choice of a set of developmental features: (1) the features must be specific enough to have clear application to what people actually say; (2) each feature needs to be logically placed within some organization of thinking; and (3) there should be a rationale for claiming that some features are more advanced or more highly developed than others. In Chapter 2 the thesis is proposed that development in concepts of fairness depends on two factors: (1) conceptions of how people can establish mutual expectations about each other's behavior (ranging from knowing what is expected by simply being told what to do, to knowing what is expected by a logical analysis of the prerequisites of nonarbitrary cooperation); (2) conceptions of how the interests of people can be balanced so as to optimize welfare and ensure that everyone feels a stake in supporting the system of cooperation (ranging from rudimentary notions of reciprocity to notions involving ongoing social structures and preconditions for accepting a set of social arrangements). Admittedly models of the "deep structure" of moral thinking are speculative and highly inferential. However, without such models, a researcher does not have an explicit statement of what is meant by the construct or by development. Clarity on these points is necessary for predicting the relationship of moral judgment to other constructs, its role in general personality functioning, and what experiences should affect it.

Much research is needed to identify many new features of moral judgment. To date, little attention has been given to questions of the distribution of wealth (should garbage collectors earn less than baseball players or professors?), of the distribution of power (should communities have the right to dictate curriculum to their local schools?), and of the distribution of opportunity (should Blacks be given preferential treatment in admission to colleges?). Studies of people's moral judgments on these and other issues should identify new conceptions and new features of thinking for developmental analysis. How these new studies will affect our present notions of stages is unpredictable. Then, too, future research will also inform us about the usefulness and empirical validity of some of our present ideas about developmental features. One of the main activities of Kohlberg's group at Harvard for the past 10 years has been the reconceptualization of developmental features in light of new longitudinal data. The process of identifying developmental features has only begun and requires continuing redefinition.

Sources of Information

What information about people does a researcher collect so as to say something about their moral judgment? Kohlberg's information

source has been interviewing subjects about their solutions to hypothetical dilemmas. One of Piaget's main information sources was to
present story pairs with contrasting action sequences, and to ask
subjects which actor was naughtier. The DIT asks subjects to rate and
rank the importance of a list of issues in a moral dilemma. In Chapter
4, over a dozen ways to get information about a person's moral judgment are discussed, some of which have not been tried as yet. I make
two general assumptions about data sources. One is that there ought
to be a variety of ways that moral judgment is manifested *if* moral
judgment is an important and pervasive variable in how people function. If there were only one way to collect information about moral
judgment, then we would have to question how important it is as a
psychological variable. A second assumption is that every method of
collecting information has problems; however, some methods have
advantages as well. The test-maker's art is to find ways for minimizing
the problems while maximizing the advantages.

The particular *advantages* of the DIT are its ease of administration,
its objective scoring, its standardization, and its minimal dependence
on verbal expressiveness. In addition, the way that subjects define issues in moral problems is of interest in its own right. The particular
problems with any objective test like the DIT are the possibility of
subjects' filling out the test in random fashion, the problem of mis-
interpreting the items or projecting their own thinking idiosyncrati-
cally onto stage-prototypic statements, and the problem of selecting
items on the basis of irrelevant cues, such as the apparent complexity
of an item or its lofty language. For each of these potential difficulties, I devised some means to minimize the problem—namely, constructing the "Consistency Check," and the "M" items; using short
items that did not advocate a course of action; maximizing the "psychological reality" of the set of items rather than artificially keeping
the number of items at each stage constant; and ordering the items
(Chapter 4). A limitation of the DIT is that it cannot be used with
subjects who have lower than 12-year-old reading level.

Rather than regarding the DIT as the ultimate solution to moral
judgment assessment, I regard it as having illustrated a general approach that other researchers may want to use in exploring new
sources of information. Nothing is magical about rating or ranking
twelve items, and certainly other formats deserve exploration.

In addition to exploring new data sources and new formats, further
work in developing the DIT itself is warranted. Some preliminary
item analyses indicate that not every item on the DIT is working well
(not surprisingly). Some research should determine what differenti-

ates "good" items from "bad." Research has begun on the test taking processes, by interviewing subjects as they fill out the questionnaire, asking them to speak out loud what they are thinking, how they are perceiving the items and the task, what associations come to mind and so on.

Indexing

Indexing addresses the issue of how to put together many pieces of information about a subject into a single score. If we ask a subject to respond to several dilemmas or if a subject rates many items, we want to be able to make a general statement about the subject rather than just reproducing the subject's ratings. But how do we combine the information into a single score?

Note that indexing would not be a problem if development really actually proceeded according to the simple stage model (Chapter 2, p. 50ff), because every item or question put to a subject would yield the same stage answer. For instance, if a subject gave a Stage 4 answer to one dilemma, all the answers would be Stage 4 regardless of content, format, text situation, or the subject's mood. If the simple stage model were true, it would be pointless to ask a subject more than one question—any question—since the information would be the same. We know, however, that subjects are inconsistent and are affected by test content and performance factors. Hence enough questions have to be asked that a subject's organization of thinking will stand out against these other background factors.

Once we have many bits of information on a subject, a single score can be derived in many ways. The most frequently used methods of indexing are to assign the subject to the stage of predominant use, or to assign a subject to the highest stage that he or she uses, or to index a subject by a weighted average (such as the Moral Maturity Score). Many other types of indices can be devised that have a plausible theoretical rationale. Developmental theory isn't decisive on the selection of an index, and developmentalists typically have simply picked one arbitrarily, without checking its properties as compared with other indexes. In DIT research, we have noticed that different indexes have different properties, and so it has been important to check them out.

In DIT research, our strategy in choosing an index has been to compute many possibilities and then determine which has the best set of properties (Chapter 4 and Chapter 8). After trying out over a hundred indices, we found that the "P" and "ES" indices have the best set (i.e., have given the strongest trends theoretically expected in empirical studies of the moral judgment construct). People have asked why we prefer a continuous index to a stage typing index, or why it makes sense to look at principled moral thinking at all in young subjects. The answer is simply that these indices work better.

Validation

What are the criteria of "working better"? In other words, how does one establish the validity of a test of moral judgment? What kinds of studies must one do and what kinds of results must one obtain to say that the moral judgment construct is valid as assessed by a particular instrument? It is certainly not "dust bowl" empiricism to ask that a measure demonstrate some empirical properties before assuming it is valid.

My position has been that moral judgment is not validated by "face validity" (intensively interviewing subjects about their moral judgments does not guarantee that the inferences are valid), nor by "predictive validity" (linear correlations with behavior), nor by "concurrent validity" (showing the DIT is equivalent to Kohlberg's Test), but by "construct validity" (Cronbach and Meehl 1955), which involves a number of different kinds of studies. The previous section of this chapter summarized the set of studies addressing the DIT's reliability and validity (evidence regarding developmental trends, cognitive processes, and relatedness to value decisions). No single study can test the validity of a measure of moral judgment, but a convincing case can be built from a variety of interlocking studies. To my knowledge, no other single measure of social cognitive or moral judgment has been put through as complete a round of studies as the DIT. To be sure, none of the DIT studies are unique, but this research is unique in the area of social cognition, in that the same measure has been used throughout all the studies, enabling comparisons of results and the accumulation of a data base. That many different researchers have been involved and have tested different populations also adds to the DIT's case.

Yet, all this work must be regarded as only "one round" in moral judgment research. This work has been devoted to "studying moral judgment as a subjective phenomenon in its own right," as discussed in Chapter 1. While certainly much remains to do in studying moral judgment as a subjective phenomenon, eventually the most convincing case of the usefulness of the moral judgment construct is the demonstration of its crucial role in explaining real life decision-making. Such studies have only just begun and are difficult, because many other variables are involved. For the next round of studies, measures of other constructs have to be developed and new, more complex designs are necessary. The difficulty in moving from the study of subjective internal processes to studying complex "real life" phenomena is demonstrated by the lack of such successful instances in all of psychology. For instance, in surveying the literature in cognition, information-processing, and memory research, one cannot be impressed by the number of instances in which this research furnishes powerful predictions about important, real-life, naturalistic behaviors. Even intelligence tests have been shown to have limited usefulness beyond predicting school grades, and certainly the experimental study of moral behavior has a long way to go in explaining and accounting for "real life" behavior. Moral judgment research, along with the rest of psychology, has yet to produce its dramatic equivalent of putting a man on the moon, or wiping out polio.

Validation therefore, is a continuing enterprise, moving from more gross, preliminary tests to more exacting tests. For Piaget in 1932, validation in moral judgment research amounted to finding cross-sectional age trends in a sample of Swiss students, plus making a conceptual argument explaining why one type of thinking is more advanced than another. Nowadays, the criteria are tougher. As we move into new rounds of research, the basic concepts are redefined (as for instance, in the concept of "stage," and in the identification of features); the complexity of design increases (as for instance in sequential designs, contrasted to cross-sectional); and the number of variables that have to be considered increases.

The Relation of Moral Judgment to Behavior

The sixth crucial decision faced by anyone doing programmatic research in moral judgment concerns how to view the relation of moral judgment to behavior. As mentioned in Chapter 1, some researchers view the relationship as a simple, linear one. For instance, Kurtines and Greif (1974) faulted moral judgment research for not demonstrating "predictive validity." According to them, if there are six stages of moral judgment, there ought to be six different behaviors in every moral situation, corresponding one-for-one to the different moral judgment stages; otherwise, why have six stages? Also, some researchers have believed so completely in a simple, linear relationship between moral judgment and moral behavior that they do item analyses according to which items have the highest correlations with behavior (keeping the items with higher correlations, discarding those with low correlations).

At the other extreme, some psychologists have stated that no relation exists between the structure of thinking and decision-making.

Indeed, some have argued that finding a relationship is a sign of invalidity of the measure of moral judgment (for example, Martin et al. 1977). According to this view, the distinction between structure and content implies complete empirical independence. Other psychologists (for example, Mischel and Mischel 1976) claim there is no relation between moral judgment and behavior, because words do not predict to deeds, and assume that advanced moral judgment is indistinguishable from the invocation of fancy language.

Between these extreme views, my own view (not a unique one) is that moral judgment is an important factor in real life decision-making, but that the interaction with other factors (Chapter 6 discusses such factors) complicates the relationship so that simple, linear correlations cannot be expected. In the first rounds of validation studies, therefore, it is appropriate to study moral judgment as a subjective phenomenon in its own right, not validated by "predictive validity." Moral judgment scores tell us something about the general interpretive frameworks that a person brings to a moral problem, and presumably the way a person interprets a problem has a bearing on his decision-making. However, the postulation of six different stages does not imply that there will be six different decisions, because the same decision can be reached for different reasons. Furthermore, the developmental order of moral judgment stages need not correspond in a linear way to the justification of any one kind of decision; for instance, the concepts of Stage 2 may favor one decision, concepts of Stages 3 and 4 may favor the opposite, and Stage 5 may favor the same as Stage 2. To predict the relation of moral judgment to behavior, one must do a logical analysis of the particular interpretive framework of a given stage, and how that framework is likely to interact with features of a particular moral problem in disposing to an action.

Given the complications in the relationship between moral judgment and behavior, additional simple correlational studies are not likely to add much to our current understanding. Enough studies of this kind have been done to indicate that moral judgment has "something" to do with behavior. However, some other kinds of studies do look promising. Jacobs' study (in Chapter 6) illustrates one type: The researcher begins by asking *why* different stages would have any bearing on decision-making in a particular situation. Hypotheses should be formulated about what the mediating linkages might be. Then the researcher builds into the study ways of empirically checking out whether the assumptions about each mediating linkage are confirmed. This kind of study attempts to examine the chain of mediating linkages between moral judgment and behavior, not simply to correlate the two end points. Second, Chapter 6 suggests that future research pay more attention to "advocacy behavior," i.e., a person's public expression of a preference in situations where public opinion influences social institutions. Moral judgment may be closely related to advocacy behavior, which in turn influences social institutions, which in turn creates a system of norms and sanctions that influences people's behavior. In this case, the connection between moral judgment and behavior is not purely intrapsychic, but is mediated by group processes and social structures. A third approach is to do multivariate studies in which various factors are controlled (as in the McColgan study) or measured and entered as variables in multiple regression studies (as by G. Rest's study).

Finale

DIT research has come from someplace and is going somewhere. The legacy of Piaget and especially of Kohlberg is apparent throughout the book. DIT research has built on this work and extended it; and although this book has called attention to departures from previous work, by and large this research confirms the validity and usefulness of the basic ideas. Yet each DIT study seems to point to the need for many more studies, and throughout the book I have tried to be specific in suggestions for future lines of research. In addition to these suggestions are several large areas of inquiry that have been neglected because of the particular priorities of DIT researchers. One area of neglect concerns the mechanisms and specific conditions for change in moral judgment development. Related to this area is research on the effects of specific aspects of educational programs (what program influences whom, and under what conditions?) Cross-cultural research receives no mention in this book, as well as research devoted to the role of affect in moral judging. There is much to do. Considering what futurists tell us about the difficult moral problems that lie ahead, and of the necessity for attaining unprecedented levels of cooperation, there is an urgency to move ahead.

NOTES

Notes

Chapter 2

1. I refer to "Kohlberg's scheme," but the reference is really a short-hand to refer to the group at Harvard headed by Kohlberg, which includes Anne Colby, John Gibbs, Marc Lieberman, Clark Power, and Betsy Speicher-Dubin. Their efforts and contributions have been considerable, but it is impossible to separate the credits. Plans are under way to publish the new scoring system plus reliability and validity data (Colby, Gibbs, Kohlberg, in preparation).

Chapter 3

1. In discussing Figure 3.2., to dramatize a point I have used the word "type" rather than "stage," but after this discussion I adopt the customary usage of "stage" to designate a logical organization of thinking (as opposed to the mix of patterns that actually occurs in individuals).

2. Note that I am not discussing here the situation in which an earlier idea becomes incorporated into a more advanced and larger system of ideas, as for instance when the Stage 2 recognition of cause-consequent relationships is incorporated into higher stage thinking. Rather, I refer to greater clarity and facility in understanding the Stage 2 system of thinking itself as a way of making moral judgments. For instance, see the "rejection-hit" of Stage 2c cited in Chapter 2: "He is only worried about what will happen to Heinz . . . . He doesn't care about his wife—he's saying that for all the troubles Heinz has to go through, it isn't worth it." This example shows that the subject clearly understands the inner logic of Stage 2 thinking and clearly sees its limits. I would speculate that this subject did not understand Stage 2 quite so clearly when he was using a lot of Stage 2 thinking himself in making decisions.

Chapter 4

1. A debt is owed to George Bass, Andrew Ahlgren, Henry Panowitsch, Douglas Anderson, and Steve Robbins for developing the Consistency Check, testing it, and writing computer programs for it.

Chapter 5

1. Portions of this chapter first appeared in *Child Development*, 1978.
2. The P values in Table 5.1 are slightly different from the values in Cooper 1972 and in Rest et al. 1974, even though the data come from the same subjects, because Cooper adjusted the P score upward for M and A items (so that the stage scores would total 100% without M and A), but this practice has been discontinued in subsequent analyses. The two procedures give nearly identical results, however.
3. See Rest 1976, "Moral Judgment Related to Sample Characteristics," for listing of each sample's characteristics that went into the adult combined sample.
4. Ernsberger's and Lawrence's findings are in contrast with Kohlberg's statement (1967, pp. 180-181):

> Our evidence of culturally universal moral stages, then, is also direct evidence against the view that the development of moral ideologies depends upon the teachings of particular religious belief systems. No differences in moral development due to religious belief have yet been found. Protestant, Catholic, Moslem, and Buddist children go through the same stages at much the same rate when social class and village-urban differences are held constant. Although we should not conclude from these and other findings that there is no relation between religious experience and moral character, we can conclude that religion is not a necessary or highly important condition for the development or moral judgment and conduct.

5. Subgroup Ja (without Jb) also showed these trends between 14 and 16 years. Figure 5.1 uses as many subjects as we have over two years, and therefore combines Ja and Jb.
6. Since the age factor was based on longitudinal data, a repeated measures design was utilized on this factor but not on the cohort factor.
7. Comparisons on Group S on 1974 "ins" and "outs" was inappropriate, due to the different age compositions of the groups.

Chapter 6

1. This section adapted some material previously cited in Carroll 1977.
2. *Ibid.*
3. This discussion draws heavily from Jacobs (1977a).

Chapter 7

1. Mark Davison performed these analyses.
2. This review borrows from a review from Lawrence (1977).

Chapter 8

1. Schönemann's (1970) algorithm requires the assumption that the multiplicative constant, a_j, be the same for every variable j. Schönemann assumes that $b_j = 0$ for all variables. For the purpose of ordering stage variables, however, b_j need not be zero nor even equal for every variable.
2. Guttman's (1945a) suggestion—retaining all dimensions associated with roots greater than 1.00—cannot be applied in this situation, because his suggestion applies only to principal components analyses of correlation matrices.
3. I wish to thank William J. Froming, Edgar B. McColgan, Collin McGeorge, James R. Rest, and Elaine Wilson for the use of their data.

REFERENCES

References

Adam, J. Sequential Strategies and the separation of age, cohort and time of measurement contributions to developmental data. *Psychological Bulletin*, 1978, 85, (6), 1309-1316.

Adorno, T.W., Frenkel-Brunswik, E., Levinson, D.J. & Sanford, R.N. *The Authoritarian Personality*. New York: Harper, 1950.

Allen, R. & Kickbush, K. An evaluation of the Nicolet High School Confluent Education project for the second year, 1974-75. Unpublished manuscript, Nicolet High School, Glendale, Wisconsin, 1976.

Almy, M., Chittenden, E. & Miller, P. *Young children's thinking: Studies of some aspects of Piaget's theory*. New York: Teacher's College, Columbia University, 1966.

Alozie, C.F. An analysis of the interrelationship of two measures used in the measurement of moral judgment development: The Kohlberg Moral Judgment Interview and the Rest Defining Issues Test. Unpublished doctoral dissertation, University of Minnesota, 1976.

Alston, W.P. Comments on Kohlberg's "From is to ought." In T. Mischel (Ed.), *Cognitive development and epistemology*. New York: Academic Press, 1971, 269-284.

Anderson, S.M. The assessment of moral judgment development for dental hygiene education. Unpublished Master's Plan B Paper, University of Minnesota, 1975.

Armsby, R.E. A reexamination of the development of moral judgments in children. *Child Development*, 1971, 42, 1241-1248.

Armstrong, P.M. Psychological comparison of prison inmates and parolees. Unpublished doctoral dissertation, Southern Illinois University, 1975.

Aronfreed, J. *Conduct and Conscience*. New York: Academic Press, 1968.

Aronfreed, J. Moral development from the standpoint of a general psychological theory. In T. Lickona (Ed.), *Moral Development and Behavior*. New York: Holt, Rinehart, & Winston, 1976, 54-69.

Baldwin, C.P. & Baldwin, A.L. Children's judgment of kindness. *Child Development*, 1970, 41, 30-47.

Baldwin, J.M. *Social and Ethical Interpretations in Mental Development*. New York: Macmillan, 1906.

269

Balfour, M.J. An investigation of a school-community involvement program's effect on the moral development of its participants. Unpublished master's paper, University of Minnesota, 1975.

Balow, B. & Rubin, R.A. *Manual of Directions for the School Behavior Profile.* Department of Special Education, University of Minnesota, 1974.

Baltes, P.B. Longitudinal and cross-sectional sequences in the study of age and generation effects. *Human Development,* 1968, 11, 145-171.

Baltes, P.B. & Nesselroade, J.R. Cultural change and adolescent personality development: An application of longitudinal sequences. *Developmental Psychology,* 1972, 7, 244-256.

Bandura, A. *Social learning theory.* New Jersey: Prentice-Hall, 1977.

Bandura, A., & McDonald, F.J. The influence of social reinforcement and the behavior of models in shaping children's moral judgments. *Journal of Abnormal and Social Psychology,* 1963, 67, 274-281.

Bandura, A., & Walters, R.H. *Social learning and personality development.* New York: Holt, Rinehart & Winston, 1963.

Bar Yam, M., Reimer, J., & Kohlberg, L. Development of moral reasoning in the kibbutz. Unpublished manuscript, Harvard University, 1974.

Bem, D.J. & Allen, A. On predicting some of the people some of the time: The search for cross-situational consistencies in behavior. *Psychology Review,* 1974, 81, 506-520.

Benson, F.A.M. An examination over an eight-month period of Piaget's concept of number development and the presence or absence of certain interrelated tasks in a group of first grade children. Unpublished Ed.D. dissertation, University of Oregon, 1966.

Berg-Cross, L.G. Intentionality, degree of damage, and moral judgments. *Child Development,* 1975, 46, 970-974.

Berndt, T.J. & Berndt, E.G. Children's use of intentionality in person perception and moral judgment. *Child Development,* 1975, 46, 904-912.

Biggs, D.A., Schomberg, S.F., & Brown, J. Moral judgment development of freshmen and their pre-college experiences. *OSA Research Bulletin,* 17(6), University of Minnesota, 1977.

Biskin, D. Personal Communication, August 28, 1974.

Blackner, G.L. Moral development of young adults involved in weekday religious education and self concept relationships. Unpublished doctoral dissertation, Brigham Young University, 1975.

Blasi, A. A developmental approach to responsibility training. Unpublished doctoral dissertation, Washington University, 1971.

Blasi, A. Bridging moral cognition and moral action: a review of the literature and a functional-developmental model. Unpublished manuscript, University of Massachusetts at Boston, 1978.

Blatt, M. Studies on the effects of classroom discussion upon children's moral development. Unpublished doctoral dissertation, University of Chicago, 1969.

Blatt, M. & Kohlberg, L. The effects of classroom moral discussion upon children's level of moral judgment. *Journal of Moral Education,* 1975, 4, 2, 129-161.

Bloom, R.B. Resistance to faking on the Defining Issues Test of moral development. Unpublished manuscript, College of William and Mary, 1977.

Bloom, R.B. Morally speaking, who are today's teachers? *Phi Delta Kappan,* 1976, 57, 624-625.

Bloomberg, M. On the relationship between internal-external control and morality. *Psychological Reports,* 1974, 35, 1077-1078.

Bode, J. & Page, J. Comparison of measures of moral judgment, *Psychological Reports,* 1978, 43, 307-312.

Bortner, M. & Birch, H.G. Cognitive capacity and cognitive competence. *American Journal of Mental Deficiency, 1970, 74, 735-744.*

Bracht, G.H. and Glass, G.V. The external validity of experiments. *American Educational Research Journal,* 1968, 5, 437-474.

Brainerd, C.J. Judgments and explanations as criteria for the presence of cognitive structures. *Psychological Bulletin,* 1973, 79, 172-179.

Brainerd, C.J. Response criteria in concept development research. *Child Development,* 1977, 48, 360-366.

Braine, M.D.S. The ontogeny of certain logical operations: Piaget's formulation examined by nonverbal methods. *Psychological Monographs,* 1959, 73, (5 Whole No. 475).

Bransford, C. Moral development in college students. Unpublished manuscript, St. Olaf College, 1973.

Breznitz, S. & Kugelmass, S. Intentionality in moral judgment: development stages. *Child Development,* 1967, 38, 469-479.

Briskin, A.S. Relationships between three stage-level models of development. Unpublished paper, University of Minnesota, 1975.

Bronowski, J. *The Ascent of Man.* Boston: Little, Brown & Co., 1973.

Brown, R. *Social Psychology.* New York: Free Press, 1965.

Bruner, J.S. The course of cognitive growth. *American Psychologist,* 1964, 19, 1-14.

Bryan, J.H. You will be well advised to watch what we do instead of what we say. In D.J. DePalma & J.M. Foley (Eds.), *Moral Development: Current Theory and Research.* Hillsdale, N.J.: Lawrence Erlbaum Associates, 1975, 95-112.

Buchanan, J.P. & Thompson, S.K. A quantitative methodology to examine the development of moral judgment. *Child Development,* 1973, 44, 186-189.

Bull, N.J. *Moral Judgment from Childhood to Adolescence.* Beverly Hills, California: Sage Publications, 1969.

Burton, R. Honesty and dishonesty. In T. Lickona (Ed.), *Moral development and Behavior,* New York: Holt, Rinehart & Winston, 1976, 173-197.

Campbell, D.T. and Stanley, J.C. Experimental and Quasi-experimental research on teaching. In N.L. Gage, *Handbook of Research on Teaching.* Chicago: Rand McNally, 1963, 171-246.

Candee, D. Structure and choice in moral reasoning. *Journal of Personality and Social Psychology,* 1976, 34, 1293-1301.

Carroll, J.L. Cognitive and political attitude correlates of the Defining Issues Test. In J. Rest (Ed.), *Development in Judging Moral Issues, Technical Report #3,* University of Minnesota, 1977.

Carroll, J. & Rest, J.R. Study in progress, University of Minnesota, 1977.

Cauble, M.A. Formal operations, ego identity, and principled morality: are they related? *Developmental Psychology,* 1976, 12, 363-364.

Chandler, M.J. Egocentrism and antisocial behavior: The assessment and training of social perspective-taking skills. *Developmental Psychology,* 1973, 9(1), 1-6.

Chandler, M.J., Greenspan, S., & Barenboim, C. Judgment of intentionality in response to video taped and verbally presented moral dilemmas: the medium is the message. *Child Development,* 1973, 44, 315-320.

Chiosso, E.T. A high school curriculum in interpersonal relations: A deliberate psychological education intervention. Unpublished doctoral dissertation, University of Minnesota, 1976.

Chomsky, N. *Syntactic Structures.* The Hague: Mouton, 1957.

Chomsky, N. *Cartesian Linguistics.* New York: Harper & Row, 1966.

Christie, R. & Jahoda, M. (Eds.), *Studies in the Scope and Method of "The Authoritarian Personality."* New York: Free Press, 1954.

Coder, R. Moral judgment in adults. Unpublished doctoral dissertation, University of Minnesota, 1975.

Colby, A. Logical operational limitations on the development of moral judgment. Unpublished doctoral dissertation, Columbia University, 1972.

Colby, A. Evolution of a moral-development theory. In W. Damon (Ed.), *New Directions for Child Development*, 1978, 2, 89-104.

Colby, A. A longitudinal study of moral judgment. Paper presented at the 1979 Convention of the Society for Research in Child Development, San Francisco.

Colby, A., Gibbs, J., Kohlberg, L. *The Assessment of Moral Judgment: Standard Form Moral Judgment Scoring*. In preparation.

Collins, W.A., Berndt, T.J., & Hess, V.L. Observational learning of motives and consequences for television aggression: a developmental study. *Child Development*, 1974, 45, 799-802.

Constantian, C.A. & McAdams, D. The relationship between values and principled moral reasoning. Unpublished manuscript, Harvard University, 1977.

Contreras, P. A structural analysis of cognitive processes underlying college students' judgments on social issues. Dissertation proposal, University of Minnesota, 1976.

Coombs, C.H. *A Theory of Data*. New York: Wiley, 1964.

Coombs, C.H. & Kao, R.C. On a connection between factor analysis and multidimensional unfolding. *Psychometrika*, 1960, 25, 219-231.

Coombs, C.H. & Smith, J.E.K. On the detection of structure in attitude and developmental processes. *Psychological Review*, 1973, 80, 337-351.

Cooper, D. The analysis of an objective measure of moral development. Unpublished doctoral dissertation, University of Minnesota, 1972.

Copa, B.A. Relationships between theories of conceptual and moral development. Unpublished master's dissertation, University of Minnesota, 1975.

Costanzo, P.R., Coie, J.D., Grumet, J.F. & Farnill, D. A reexamination of the effects of intent and consequences on children's moral judgments. *Child Development*, 1973, 44, 154-161.

Cowan, P., Langer, J., Heavenrich, J. & Nathanson, M. Social learning and Piaget's cognitive theory of moral development. *Journal of Personality and Social Psychology*, 1969, 11, 261-274.

Crockenberg, S. & Nicolayev, M. Stage transition in moral reasoning as related to conflict experienced in naturalistic settings. Unpublished manuscript, University of California at Davis, 1977.

Cronbach, L.J. & Meehl, P.E. Construct validity in psychological tests. *Psychology Bulletin*, 1955, 52, 281-302.

Crowder, J.W. The Defining Issues Test and correlates of moral judgment. Unpublished Master's thesis, University of Maryland, 1976.

Crowley, P.M. Effects of training upon objectivity of moral judgment in grade-school children. *Journal of Personality and Social Psychology*, 1968, 8, 228-232.

Damon, W. *The Social World of the Child*. San Francisco: Jossey-Bass, 1977.

Daniels, N. (Ed.), *Reading Rawls: Critical Studies on Rawls' "A Theory of Justice."* New York: Basic Books, 1974.

DAT Manual (4th Ed.). New York: The Psychological Corporation, 1966.

Davison, M.L. On a unidimensional, metric unfolding model for attitudinal and developmental data. *Psychometrika*, 1977, 42, 523-548.

Davison, M.L. & Robbins, S. Indexing moral development. Unpublished manuscript, University of Minnesota, 1977.

Davison, M.L. & Robbins, S. The reliability and validity of objective indices of moral development. *Applied Psychological Measurement*, 1978, 2(3), 391-403.

Davison, M.L., Robbins, S. & Swanson, D. Stage structure in objective moral judgments. *Developmental Psychology*, 1978, 14(2), 137-146.

Davison, M.L., Robbins, S., & Swanson, D. A Fortrand Program for scoring the Defining Issues Test. Unpublished manuscript, University of Minnesota, 1977.

Deal, M.D. The relationship of philosophy of human nature, level of cognitive moral reasoning and pupil control ideology of graduate students in a Department of Curriculum and Instruction. Doctoral dissertation, Oklahoma State University, 1978.

Developmental counseling psychology. *The Counseling Psychologist*, 6(4), 1977.

Dewey, J. Selected writings. In R.D. Archambault (Ed.), *John Dewey on Education: Selected Writings*. New York: Random House, 1964 (a posthumously published collection; original writings in 1895).

Dispoto, R.G. Moral valuing and environmental variables. *Journal and Research in Science Teaching*, 1977, 14(4), 273-280.

Dispoto, R. Socio-moral reasoning and environmental activity, emotionality and knowledge. Unpublished doctoral dissertation, Rutgers University, 1974.

Dortzbach, J.R. Moral judgment and perceived locus of control: a cross-sectional developmental study of adults, aged 25-74. Unpublished doctoral dissertation, University of Oregon, 1975.

Edwards, C.P. The effects of experience on moral development: Results from Kenya. (Doctoral dissertation, Harvard University, 1974). *Dissertation Abstracts International*, 1975, 36, 776-A. (University Microfilms No. 75-16, 860, 301).

Ehrlich, P. & Ehrlich, A. *The End of Affluence*. New York: Ballantine Paperback, 1974.

Eisenberg-Berg, N. The development of children's prosocial moral judgment. *Developmental Psychology*, in press.

Ennis, R.H. & Millman, J. *Manual for Cornell Critical Thinking Test, Level X*. Urbana, Illinois: University of Illinois, 1971.

Erickson, V.L., Colby, S., Libbey, P., & Lohman, G. The young adolescent: a curriculum to promote psychological growth. In G.D. Miller (Ed.), *Developmental Education*. St. Paul, Minnesota: Minnesota Department of Education, 1976.

Erikson, E.H. Childhood and society. New York: Norton, 1950.

Ernhart, C.B. and Loevinger, J. Authoritarian family ideology: a measure, its correlates, and its robustness. *Multivariate Behavioral Research Monographs*, 1969, No. 69-1.

Ernsberger, D.J. Intrinsic-extrinsic religious identification and level of moral development. Unpublished doctoral dissertation, University of Texas, 1976.

Eysenck, H.J. The biology of morality. In T. Lickona (Ed.), *Moral development and Behavior*. New York: Holt, Rinehart & Winston, 1976, 108-123.

Fenton, E. *The New Social Studies*. New York: Holt, Rinehart & Winston, 1967.

Fincham, F.D. Prototypic stage statements in moral judgment assessment. Unpublished manuscript, University of Witwatersrand, South Africa, 1977.

Fincham, F.D. & Barling, J. Effects of alcohol on moral functioning in male social drinkers. Unpublished manuscript, University of Witwatersrand, South Africa, 1977.

Fish, D. Personal communication, 1976.

Fishbein, M. & Acjzen, I. Attitudes towards objects as predictors of single and multiple behavioral criteria. *Psychological Review*, 1974, 81(1), 59-74.

Fishkin, J., Keniston, K., & MacKinnon, C. Moral development and political ideology. *Journal of Personality and Social Psychology*, 1973, 27, 109-119.

Flavell, J. *The Developmental Psychology of Jean Piaget*. Princeton, N.J.: Van Nostrand, 1963.

Flavell, J.H. Concept development. In P.H. Mussen (Ed.), *Carmichael's Manual of Child Psychology*. New York: Wiley, 1970. Pp. 983-1059.

Flavell, J.H. Stage-related properties of cognitive development. *Cognitive Psychology*, 1971, 2, 421-453.

Flavell, J. *Cognitive Development*, Englewood Cliffs, N.J.: Prentice-Hall, 1977.

Flavell, J.H., Botkin, P., Fry, C., Wright, J., & Jarvis, P. *The Development of Role-taking and Communication Skills in Children*. New York: Wiley, 1968.

Flavell, J.H. & Wohlwill, J.F. Formal and functional aspects of cognitive development. In D. Elkind & J.H. Flavell (Eds.), *Studies in Cognitive Development: Essays in Honor of Jean Piaget*. New York: Oxford University Press, 1969, 60-120.

Fodor, E. Delinquency and susceptibility to social influences among adolescents as a function of level of moral development. *Journal of Social Psychology*, 1972, 86, 257-260.

Fontana, A., & Noel, B. Moral reasoning at the university. *Journal of Personality and Social Psychology*, 1973, 3, 419-429.

Fraser, C., Belliugi, U., & Brown, R. Control of grammar in imitation, comprehension, and production. *Journal of Verbal Learning and Verbal Learning and Verbal Behavior*, 1963, 2, 121-135.

French, M.D. A study of Kohlbergian moral development and selected behaviors among high school students in classes using values clarification and other teaching methods. Unpublished doctoral dissertation, Auburn University, 1977.

Froming, W. & Cooper, R.G. Predicting compliance behavior from moral judgment scales. Unpublished manuscript, University of Texas, 1976.

Froming, W.J. & McColgan, E. A comparison of two measures of moral judgment. Unpublished manuscript, University of Texas at Austin, 1977.

Fromm, E. *The Art of Loving*. New York: Harper, 1956.

Gallia, T.J. Moral reasoning in college science and humanities students: summary of a pilot study. Unpublished manuscript, Glassboro State College, 1976.

Geis, G. The relationship between type of peer interaction and development in moral judgment. Unpublished manuscript, Ambassador College, 1977.

Gelman, R. Logical capacity of very young children: number of invariance rules. *Child Development*, 1972, 43, 75-90.

Gibbs, J.C. & Fedoruk, C.J. Experimentally induced change in moral judgment. Paper presented at the Symposium of the Jean Piaget Society, Philadelphia, 1975.

Gilligan, C. In a different voice: Women's conceptions of the self and of morality. *Harvard Educational Review*, 1977, 47(4), 481-517.

Goldiamond, I. Moral development: A functional analysis. *Psychology Today*, 1968, 2(4), 31ff.

Goldman, S. Locus of control in relationship to moral judgment, ethical behavior, and religious motivation. Unpublished master's dissertation, Loyola University, 1977.

Gorsuch, R. & Barnes, M. Stages of ethical reasoning and moral norms of Carib youths. *Journal of Cross-Cultural Psychology*, 1973, 4, 283-301.

Graham, K., Turnbull, W., & LaRocque, L. Alcohol and moral judgment. Unpublished manuscript, Simon Fraser University, 1977.

Grim, P.F., Kohlberg, L. & White, S.H. Some relationships between conscience and attentional processes. *Journal of Personality and Social Psychology*, 1968, 8, 239-252.

Gunzburger, D.W., Wegner, D.M., & Anooshian, L. Moral judgment and distributive justice. *Human Development*, 1977, 20, 160-170.

Gutkin, D.C. The effect of systematic story changes on intentionality in children's moral judgments. *Child Development*, 1972, 43, 187-195.

Gutkin, D.C. & Suls, J.M. Relationship between principled moral reasoning, internal-external control, and the ethics of personal conscience. Unpublished manuscript in preparation, State University of New York at Albany, 1976.

Gutkin, D.C. & Suls, J. The relation between the ethics of personal conscience—social responsibility and principled moral reasoning. Unpublished manuscript, State University of New York at Albany, 1977.

Guttenberg, R. Videotaped moral dilemmas: altering the presentation of the stimuli in the Defining Issues Test. Unpublished manuscript, Brown University, 1975.

Guttman, L. Some necessary conditions for common-factor analysis. *Psychometrika*, 1954a, 19, 149-162.

Guttman, L. A new approach to factor analysis: The radex. In P.F. Lazarsfeld (Ed.), *Mathematical Thinking in the Social Sciences*. Glencoe, Illinois: Free Press, 1954b.

Haan, N. Hypothetical and actual moral reasoning in a situation of civil disobedience. *Journal of Personality and Social Psychology*, 1975, 32, 2, 255-270.

Haan, N. Two moralities in action contexts: Relationships to thought, ego regulation, and development. *Journal of Personality and Social Psychology*, 1978, 30, 286-305.

Haan, N., Smith, M.B., & Block, J.H. The moral reasoning of young adults: political-social behavior, family background, and personality correlates. *Journal of Personality and Social Psychology*, 1968, 10, 183-201.

Harris, S., Mussen, P., & Rutherford, E. Some cognitive, behavioral, and personality correlates of maturity of moral judgment. Unpublished manuscript, University of California at Berkeley, 1973.

Hartwick, R. Personal Communication, June 6, 1975.

Hays, W.L. *Statistics for Psychologists*. New York: Holt, Rinehart & Winston, 1963.

Hebble, P.W. The development of elementary school children's judgment of intent. *Child Development*, 1971, 42, 1203-1215.

Hewitt, L.S. The effects of provocation, intentions, and consequences on children's moral judgments. *Child Development*, 1975, 46, 540-544.

Hickey, J. The effects of guided moral discussion upon offenders' level of moral judgment. Unpublished doctoral dissertation, Boston University, 1972.

Hickey, J. The prison and the inmate's conception of legal justice. (1972) In L. Kohlberg & Colleagues, moral stage scoring manual. Cambridge: Center for moral education, Harvard Graduate School of Education, 1976.

Hoffman, M.L. & Saltzstein, H.D. Parent discipline and the child's moral development. *Journal of Personality and Social Psychology*, 1967, 5, 45-47.

Hoffman, M. Moral development. In P. Mussen (Ed.), *Carmichael's manual of child psychology*. Vol. II. New York: Wiley, 1970, 261-359.

Hogan, R. A dimension of moral judgment. *Journal of Consulting and Clinical Psychology*, 1970, 35, 205-212.

Hogan, R. Moral development and the structure of personality. In D.J. DePalma & J.M. Foley (Eds.), *Moral Development: Current Theory and Research*, Hillsdale, N.J.: Lawrence Erlbaum, 1975, 153-168.

Hogan, R. Theoretical egocentrism and the problem of compliance. *American Psychologist*, 1975b, 30, 533-540.

Holstein, C. The relation of children's moral judgment level to that of their parents and to communication patterns in the family. In R. Smart & M. Smart (Eds.), *Readings in Child Development*. New York: MacMillan, 1972, 484-494.

Holstein, C. Moral judgment change in early adolescence and middle age: A longitudinal study. Paper presented at the biennial meeting of the Society for Research in Child Development, Philadelphia, Pennsylvania, March, 1973.

Holstein, C.B. Irreversible, stepwise sequence in the development of moral judgment: a longitudinal study of males and females. *Child Development*, 1976, 47, 51-61.

Hubart, L. Problems of seriation using a subject by item response matrix. *Psychological Bulletin*, 1974, 81, 976-983.

Hudgins, W., & Prentice, N.M. Moral judgment in delinquent and nondelinquent adolescents and their mothers. *Journal of Abnormal Psychology*, 1973, 82(1), 145-152.

Hunt, M.P. & Metcalf, L.E. *Teaching High School Social Studies*. New York: Harper & Row, 1968.

Hurt, B.L. Psychological Education for college students: a cognitive-developmental curriculum. Unpublished doctoral dissertation, University of Minnesota, 1974.

Husted, S.D. Using a stage profile to assess judgment of moral issues: examining the development of moral reasoning in pediatric faculty, house officers, and medical students. Unpublished manuscript, University of Connecticut Health Center, Farmington, 1978.

Huston, T.L. & Korte, C. The responsive bystander: why he helps. In T. Lickona (Ed.), *Moral Development and Behavior*, New York: Holt, Rinehart, & Winston, 1976, 269-283.

Imamoglue, E.O. Children's awareness and usage of intention cues. *Child Development*, 1975, 46, 39-45.

Irwin, D.M. & Moore, S.G. The young child's understanding of social justice. *Developmental Psychology*, 1971, 5, 406-410.

Ismail, M.A. A cross-cultural study of moral judgments: the relationships between American and Saudi Arabian university students on the Defining Issues Test. Unpublished doctoral dissertation, Oklahoma State University, 1976.

Jacobs, M.K. Women's moral reasoning and behavior in a contractual form of prisoners' dilemma. Unpublished doctoral dissertation, Toledo University, 1975.

Jacobs, M.K. The DIT related to behavior in an experimental setting: Promise keeping in the Prisoner's Dilemma Game. In J. Rest (Ed.), Development in Judging Moral Issues—a summary of research using the Defining Issues Test, Minnesota Moral Research Projects, Technical Report #3, 1977a.

Jacobs, M.K. Personal communication, 1977b.

Jenson, J. & Hughston, K. The effect of training children to make moral judgments that are independent of sanctions. *Developmental Psychology*, 1971, 5, 367.

Johnson, M.A. A study of relationships between religious knowledge, moral judgment and personal religious orientations. Unpublished manuscript, Temple University, 1974.

Johnson, R.C. A study of children's moral judgments. *Child Development*, 1972, 33, 327-354.

Kantner, K. Personal communication, 1975.

Keasey, C.B. The lack of sex differences in moral judgments of preadolescents. *The Journal of Social Psychology*, 1972, 86, 157-158.

Keasey, C.B. Implicators of cognitive development for moral reasoning. In D.J. DePalma & J.M. Foley (Eds.), *Moral Development: Current Theory and Research*, 1975, 39-56.

Keller, B.B. Verbal communication characteristics of couples at principled, conventional or mixed levels of moral development. Unpublished Master's dissertation, College of William and Mary, 1975.

Keniston, K. *Young Radicals*. New York: Harcourt, 1968.

Kickbush, K. Personal communication, 1975.

King, M. The development of some intention concepts in young children. *Child Development*, 1971, 42, 1145-1152.

Kirchenbaum, H. Recent research in values education. In J. Meyer, B. Burnham, J. Cholvat (Eds.), *Values Education: Theory, Practice, Problems, Prospects*. Waterloo, Ontario, Canada: Wilfrid Laurier University Press, 1975, 71-78.

Kohlberg, L. The development of modes of moral thinking and choice in the years 10 to 16. Unpublished doctoral dissertation, University of Chicago, 1958.

Kohlberg, L. Development of moral character and moral ideology. In M. Hoffman (Ed.), *Review of Child Development Research*. Volume 1, New York: Russell Sage Foundation, 1964.

Kohlberg, L. Moral and religious education and the public schools: a developmental view. In T. Sizer (Ed.), *Religion and Public Education*. Boston: Houghton-Mifflin, 1967.

Kohlberg, L. Stage and sequence: the cognitive-developmental approach to socialization. In D. Goslin (Ed.) *Handbook of Socialization Theory and Research*. Chicago: Rand McNally, 1969, 347-480.

Kohlberg, L. The concepts of developmental psychology as the central guide to education: examples from cognitive, moral and psychological education. In M. Reynolds (Ed.), *Psychology and the Process of Schooling in the Next Decade: Alternative Conceptions*. Minneapolis: Department of Audio-visual Extension (University of Minnesota), 1971a.

Kohlberg, L. From is to ought: How to commit the naturalistic fallacy and get away with it in the study of moral development. In T. Mischel (Ed.), *Cognitive Development and Epistemology*. New York: Academic Press, 1971b.

Kohlberg L. Stages of moral development as a basis for moral education. In C.M. Beck, B.S. Crittenden, & E.V. Sullivan (Eds.), *Moral Education: Interdisciplinary Approaches*. Toronto: University of Toronto Press, 1971c.

Kohlberg, L. *Collected Papers on Moral Development and Moral Education*. Cambridge, Mass.: Laboratory of Human Development, Harvard University, 1973a.

Kohlberg, L. Continuities in childhood and adult moral development revisited. In P.B. Baltes & K.W. Schaie (Eds.), *Life-Span Developmental Psychology: Personality and Socialization*. New York: Academic Press, 1973b.

Kohlberg, L. Report to N.I.H. Review Committee on a grant proposal site visit. November 22, 1974, Harvard University.

Kohlberg, L. The cognitive-developmental approach: new developments and a response to criticisms. Paper presented at S.R.C.D. Convention, Denver, 1975.

Kohlberg, L. Moral stages and moralization: The cognitive-developmental approach. In T. Lickona (Ed.), *Moral Development and Behavior*. New York: Holt, Rinehart & Winston, 1976.

Kohlberg, L. The meaning and measurement of moral development. Invited address at the Convention of the American Psychological Association, Toronto, Canada, September 1, 1978.

Kohlberg, L. The meaning and measurement of moral development. Heinz Werner Lecture, Clark University, 1979.

Kohlberg, L., Colby, A., & Damon, W. Assessment of moral judgment in childhood and youth. Grant proposal to the National Institutes of Health, 1978.

Kohlberg, L., Colby, A., Gibbs, J., & Speicher-Dubin, B. *Moral stage scoring manual*. Cambridge: Center for Moral Education, Harvard University, 1976.

Kohlberg, L., Colby, A., Gibbs, J., & Speicher-Dubin, B. *Standard Form Scoring Manual*. Cambridge: Center for Moral Education, Harvard University, 1978.

Kohlberg, L. & Elfenbein, D. The development of moral judgments concerning capital punishments. *American Journal of Orthopsychiatry*, 1975, 45(4), 614-640.

Kohlberg, L., & Freundlich, D. The relationship between moral judgment and delinquency. Unpublished manuscript, Harvard University, 1973.

Kohlberg, L. & Hickey, J. Proposal to design and implement a correctional program based on moral development theory. Unpublished manuscript, 1972.

Kohlberg, L. & Kramer, R. Continuities and discontinuities in childhood moral development. *Human Development*, 1969, 12, 93-120.

Kohlberg, L. & Lockwood, A. Cognitive developmental psychology and political education. Paper presented at Social Science Consortium Convention, Boulder, Colorado, 1970.

Kohlberg, L. & Mayer, R. Development as the aim of education. *Harvard Educational Review*, 1972, 42(4), 449-496.

Kohlberg, L., Scharf, P., & Hickey, J. The justice structure of the prison: a theory and an intervention. *The Prison Journal*, 1972, 51(2), 3-14.

Kohlberg, L. & Selman, R. First things: a strategy for teaching values. Pleasantville, New York: Guidance Associates, 1973.

Kohlberg, L. & Turiel, E. Moral development and moral education. In G.S. Lesser (Ed.), *Psychology and Educational Practice*. Glenview, Illinois: Scott, Foresman and Co., 1971.

Kramer, R. Moral development in young adulthood. Unpublished doctoral dissertation, University of Chicago, 1968.

Krause, D. Personal communication, August 22, 1974.

Krebs, R.L. Some relations between moral judgment, attention, and resistance to temptation. Unpublished doctoral dissertation, University of Chicago, 1967.

Kuhn, D. Short term longitudinal evidence for the sequentiality of Kohlberg's early stages of moral judgment. *Developmental Psychology*, 1976, 12, 162-166.

Kuhn, D., Langer, J., Kohlberg, L., & Haan, N. The development of formal operations in logical and moral judgment. *Genetic Psychology Monographs*, 1977, 95, 97-188.

Kuhn, T.S. *The Structure of Scientific Revolutions*. Chicago: University of Chicago Press, 1962.

Kurtines, W. & Greif, E. The development of moral thought: Review and evaluation of Kohlberg's approach. *Psychological Bulletin*, 81(8), 1974, 453-470.

Latane, B. & Darley, J. Group inhibition of bystander intervention. *Journal of Personality and Social Psychology*, 1968, 10, 215-221.

Lawrence, J.A. Moral judgment intervention studies using the Defining Issues Test. Unpublished manuscript, University of Minnesota, 1977.

Lawrence, J.A. Review and rationale for moral judgment process research using the Defining Issues Test and the stimulated recall technique. Unpublished manuscript, University of Minnesota, 1977.

Lawrence, J.A. The component procedures of moral judgment-making. Unpublished doctoral dissertation, University of Minnesota, 1978.

Lee, L.C. The concomitant development of cognitive and moral modes of thought: a test of selected deductions from Piaget's theory. *Genetic Psychology Monographs*, 1971, 83, 93-146.

LeFurgy, W.G. & Woloshin, G.W. Immediate and long-term effects of experimentally induced social influence in the modification of adolescents's moral judgments. *Journal of Personality and Social Psychology, 1969, 12, 104-110.*

Leik, R.K. & Mathews, M. A scale for developmental processes. *American Sociological Review*, 1968, 33, 62-75.

Leming, J.S. An empirical examination of key assumptions underlying the Kohlberg rationale for moral education. *Foundational Studies 3*, 1975, 3-22.

Leming, J.S. Ego and conscience factors as determinants of resistance to cheating among college undergraduates. Unpublished manuscript, State University of New York at Stony Brook, 1976.

Leming, J.S. Cheating behavior, situational influence, and moral development. *Journal of Educational Research*, 1978, 71, 214-217.

Liebermann, M. Estimation of a moral judgment level using items whose alternatives form a graded scale. Unpublished doctoral dissertation, University of Chicago, 1971.

Lockley, O.E. Level of moral reasoning and student's choice of terminal and instrumental values. Unpublished doctoral dissertation, Rutgers, the State University, 1976.

Lockwood, A. Relations of political and moral thought. Unpublished doctoral dissertation, Harvard University, 1970.

Lockwood, A. *Moral Reasoning: The Value of Life*. Middletown, Conn.: American Education Publications, 1972.

Lockwood, A.L. Stages of Moral Development and Reasoning About Public Policy Issues. Unpublished manuscript, University of Wisconsin, 1973.

Lockwood, A.L. The effects of values clarification and moral development curriculum on school-age subjects: a critical view of recent research. Unpublished manuscript, University of Wisconsin, 1977.

Loevinger, J. Measuring personality patterns of women. *Genetic Psychology Monographs,* 1962, 65, 53-136.

Loevinger, J. The meaning and measurement of ego development. *American Psychologist,* 1966, 21, 195-206.

Loevinger, J. *Ego Development.* San Francisco: Josey-Bass, 1976.

Loevinger, J., & Sweet, B. Construction of a test of mothers' attitudes. In J.C. Glidewell (Ed.), *Parental Attitudes and Child Behavior.* Springfield, Illinois: Thomas, 1961.

Magowan S.A. & Lee, T. Some sources of error in the use of the projective method for the assessment of moral judgment. *British Journal of Psychology,* 1970, 61, 535-543.

Malinowski, C. Moral judgment and resistance to the temptation to cheat. Paper presented at the American Psychological Association Convention, Toronto, Canada, 1978.

Markus, H. Self schemata and processing information about the self. *Journal of Personality and Social Psychology,* 1977, 35, 63-78.

Marston, D. Social cognition and behavior problems in school: a three-year follow-up study of 38 adolescents. Unpublished manuscript, University of Minnesota, 1978.

Martin, R.M., Shafto, M., & VanDeinse, W. The reliability, validity and design of the Defining Issues Test. *Developmental Psychology, 1977, 13, 460-468.*

Masanz, J.A. Moral judgment development in adolescent girls. Unpublished master's dissertation, University of Minnesota, 1975.

McCall, R.B. Challenges to a science of developmental psychology. *Child Development,* 1977, 48(2), 333-344.

McColgan, E. Social cognition in delinquents, predelinquents and nondelinquents. Unpublished doctoral dissertation, University of Minnesota, 1975.

McColgan, E.B. Social cognition in delinquent, predelinquent and nondelinquent adolescents. Paper presented at the Convention of the Society for Research in Child Development, New Orleans, 1977.

McColgan, E.B. & Gott, S. Delinquency as a correlate of moral judgment: A review of the literature. Unpublished manuscript, University of Texas at Austin, 1977.

McDougall, W. *An Introduction to Social Psychology.* London: Metheun, 1908.

McGeorge, C.M. Situational variation in level of moral judgment. *British Journal of Educational Psychology,* 1974, 44, 116-122.

McGeorge, C. The susceptibility to faking of the Defining Issues Test of moral development. *Developmental Psychology,* 1975, 11, 108.

McGeorge, C. Some correlates of principled moral thinking in young adults. *Journal of Moral Education,* 1977.

McNamee, S. Relation of moral reasoning to experimental helping behavior. Unpublished manuscript, Harvard University, 1973.

Mead, G.H. *Mind, Self, and Society.* Chicago: University of Chicago Press, 1934.

Medairy, A.L. Moral judgment and Locus of Control in college freshmen and seniors. Unpublished manuscript, Whitman College, 1977.

Medinnus, G.R. Immanent justice in children: a review of the literature and additional data. *Journal of Genetic Psychology,* 1959, 94, 253-262.

Merelman, R.M. The development of political ideology: A framework for the analysis of political socialization. *The American Political Science Review,* 1969, 63(3), 750-767.

Merelman, R.M. The development of policy thinking in adolescence. *American Political Science Review,* LXV(4), 1971, 1033-1047.

Meyer, P.G. Intellectual development of college students as measured by analysis of religious content. Unpublished doctoral dissertation, University of Minnesota, 1975.

Milgram, S. Behavioral study of obedience. *Journal of Abnormal and Social Psychology*, 1963, 67, 371-378.

Miller, S.A. Nonverbal assessment of Piagetian concepts. *Psychological Bulletin*, 1976, 33(3), 405-430.

Mischel, W. Processes in delay of gratification. In L. Berkowitz (Ed.), *Advances in Social Psychology*, Vol. 7, New York: Academic, 1974.

Mischel, W. & Mischel, H.N. A cognitive social learning approach to morality and self-regulation. In T. Lickona (Ed.), *Moral Development Behavior*, New York: Holt, Rinehart & Winston, 1976, Chapter 4.

Moir, D.J. Egocentrism and the emergence of conventional morality in preadolescent girls. *Child Development*, 1974, 45, 299-304.

Moore, R. Personal communication, 1975.

Morrison, T., Toews, O., & Rest, J. An evaluation of a jurisprudential model for teaching social studies to junior high school students. Study in progress, University of Manitoba, 1973.

Mullen, P. Personal communication, November 5, 1975.

Nardi, P.M. & Tsujimoto, R.N. The relationship of moral maturity and ethical attitude. Unpublished manuscript, Pitzer College, 1977.

Nauman, C. The Defining Issues Test and MATC. Unpublished paper, Madison Area Technical College, 1976.

Neimark, E.D. Longitudinal development of formal operational thought. *Genetic Psychology Monographs*, 1975, 91, 171-225.

Nelson, K.H. *The Sierra Project: From Theory to Research*. Paper presented to the Moral Development and Psychological Education Conferences, 1976.

Newell, A. & Simon, H.A. *Human problem solving*. Englewood Cliffs, N.J.: Prentice-Hall, 1972.

Newmann, F.M. & Oliver, D. *Clarifying Public Controversy*. Boston: Little Brown, 1970.

Nicholls, J.G. Effects of moral maturity and perception of effort on achievement evaluation. Unpublished manuscript, Victoria University of Wellington, New Zealand, 1976.

Niebuhr, R. *Moral Man and Immoral Society: A Study in Ethics and Politics*, New York: Scribner, 1960.

Oliver, D.W. & Shaver, J.P. *Teaching Public Issues in the High School*. Boston: Houghton Mifflin, 1966.

Panowitsch, H.R. Change and stability in the Defining Issues Test. Unpublished doctoral dissertation, University of Minnesota, 1975.

Parke, R.D. & Walters, R.H. Some factors influencing the efficacy of punishment training for inducing response inhibition. *Monographs of the Society for Research in Child Development*, 1967, 32, 1 (Serial No. 109).

Perry, W.G. *Forms of intellectual and ethical development in the college years*. New York: Holt, Rinehart and Winston, 1970.

Piaget, J. *The Moral Judgment of the Child*, M. Gabain, trans. New York: The Free Press, 1965. (Originally published, 1932.)

Piaget, J. The general problem of the psycho-biological development of the child. In J.M. Tanner & B. Inhelder (Eds.), *Discussions on Child Development*. Vol. 4, New York: Internation Universities Press, 1960.

Pinard, A. & Laurendeau, M. "Stage" in Piaget's cognitive-developmental theory: exegesis of a concept. In D. Elkind & J.H. Flavell (Eds.), *Studies in Cognitive Development: Essays in Honor of Jean Piaget*. New York: Oxford University Press, 1969. Pp. 121-170.

Pittel, S.M. & Mendelsohn, G.A. Measurement of moral values: A review and critique, *Psychological Bulletin*, 1966, 66, 22-35.

Piwko, J. The effects of a moral development workshop. Unpublished manuscript, 1975.

Podd, M.H. Ego identity status and morality: The relationship between two developmental constructs. *Developmental Psychology*, 1972, 6, 497-507.

Popiel, M. The development of political thought and its relation to level of moral reasoning. Unpublished honors thesis, Bryn Mawr College, 1977.

Purpel, D. & Ryan, K. (Eds.), *Moral Education . . . . it comes with the Territory*. Berkeley, California: McCutchan, 1976.

Rapaport, A. and Chammah, A.M. *Prisoner's Dilemma: A Study in Conflict and Cooperation*. Ann Arbor: The University of Michigan Press, 1965.

Raths, L.E., Harmin, M., and Simon, S.B. *Values and Teaching*. Columbus, Ohio: Charles E. Merrill, 1966.

Rawls, J. *A Theory of Justice*. Cambridge, Mass.: Harvard University Press, 1971.

Rest, G.J. Voting preference in the 1976 Presidential Election and the influences of moral reasoning. Unpublished manuscript, University of Michigan, 1977.

Rest, J. Hierarchies of comprehension and preference in a developmental stage model of moral thinking. Unpublished doctoral dissertation, University of Chicago, 1969.

Rest, J. The hierarchical nature of moral judgment. *Journal of Personality*, 1973, 41, 86-109.

Rest, J.R. The cognitive-developmental approach to morality: the state of the art. *Counseling and Values*, 1974a, 18, 64-78.

Rest, J. Manual for the Defining Issues Test: an objective test of moral judgment development. Available from author (330 Burton Hall, University of Minnesota, Minneapolis, Minnesota 55455), 1974b.

Rest, J.R. Developmental psychology as a guide to value education: a review of "Kohlbergian" programs. *Review of Educational Research*, 1974c, 44(2), 241-259.

Rest, J. The validity of tests of moral judgment. In J. Meyer, B. Burnham, J. Cholvat (Eds.), *Value Education: Theory, Practice, Problems, Prospects*. Waterloo, Ontario, Canada: Wilfrid Laurier University Press, 1975a, 103-116.

Rest, J. Longitudinal study of the Defining Issues Test: a strategy for analyzing developmental change. *Developmental Psychology*, 1975b, 11, 738-748.

Rest, J. New approaches in the assessment of moral judgment. In T. Lickona (Ed.), *Moral Development and Behavior*. New York: Holt, Rinehart & Winston, 1976a, 198-220.

Rest, J.R. Moral judgment related to sample characteristics. Technical Report No. 2, University of Minnesota, 1976a.

Rest, J.R. A theoretical analysis of moral judgment development. Unpublished manuscript, University of Minnesota, 1976b (revised from 1971, 1974).

Rest, J.R. The stage concept in moral judgment research. Unpublished manuscript, University of Minnesota, 1977a.

Rest, J.R. Longitudinal study, in progress. University of Minnesota, 1977b.

Rest, J.R. *Revised Manual for the Defining Issues Test*. Minneapolis: Moral Research Projects, 1979. (Available from 330 Burton Hall, 178 Pillsbury Avenue, Minneapolis, Minnesota 55455.

Rest, J.R., Ahlgren, C., Mackey, J. Minneapolis Police Report. Unpublished manuscript, University of Minnesota, 1972.

Rest, J.R., Carroll, J., Lawrence, J., Jacobs, K., McColgan, E., Davison, M., & Robbins, S. Development in judging moral issues—a summary of research using the Defining Issues Test. Minnesota Moral Research Projects, *Technical Report #3*, 1977.

Rest, J.R., Cooper, D., Coder, R., Masanz, J., and Anderson, D. Judging the important issues in moral dilemmas—an objective test of development. *Developmental psychology*, 1974, 10(4), 491-501.

Rest, J.R., Davison, M.L., & Robbins, S. Age trends in judging moral issues: A review of cross-sectional, longitudinal and sequential studies of the Defining Issues Test. *Child Development*, 1978, 49(2), 263-279.

Rest, J.R. & Feldman, B. Correlations of the DIT with political attitudes. Study in progress, University of Minnesota, 1973.

Rest, J., Turiel, E. & Kohlberg, L. Level of moral development as a determinant of preference and comprehension of moral judgment made by others. *Journal of Personality*, 37, 1969, 225-252.

Rogers, C.R. *On Becoming a Person.* Boston: Houghton Mifflin, 1961.

Rokeach, M. *The Nature of Human Values.* New York: Free Press, 1973.

Ross, J. & Cliff, N. A generalization of the interpoint distance model. *Psychometrika*, 1964, 29, 167-176.

Rothman, G. The influence of moral reasoning on behavioral choices. *Child Development*, 1976, 47, 397-406.

Rubin, K.H. & Trotter, K.T. Kohlberg's moral judgment scale: some methodological considerations. Unpublished manuscript, University of Waterloo, 1977.

Rule, B.G., Nesdale, A.R., & McAra, M.J. Children's reactions to information about the intentions underlying an aggressive act. *Child Development*, 1974, 45, 794-798.

Ruma, E. & Mosher P. Relationships between moral judgment and guilt in delinquent boys. *Journal of Abnormal Psychology*, 1967, 72, 122-127.

Saltstein, H.D., Diamond, R.M. & Balenky, M. Moral judgment level and conformity behavior. *Developmental Psychology*, 1972, 7, 327-336.

Sanders, N. Pretesting in the pilot study schools of the skills for ethical action project. Unpublished manuscript, Research for Better Schools, Inc., 1976.

Satterstrom, L.S. Adolescents' choice of friends and leaders as a function of moral and ego development. Unpublished masters thesis, University of Minnesota, 1977.

Schaie, K.W. A general model for the study of developmental problems. *Psychological Bulletin*, 1965, 64, 92-107.

Schaie, K.W. A reinterpretation of age-related changes in cognitive structure and functioning. In L.R. Goulet and P.B. Baltes (Eds.), *Life-span Developmental Psychology: Research and Theory.* New York: Academic Press, 1970.

Schaie, K.W. & Labouvie-Vief, G. Generational versus ontogenetic components of change in adult cognitive behavior: a fourteen-year cross-sequential study. *Developmental Psychology*, 1974, 10, 305-320.

Schaie, K., Labouvie, G. & Buech, B. Generational and cohort-specific differences in adult cognitive functioning: a fourteen-year study of independent samples. *Developmental Psychology*, 1973, 9, 151-166.

Schneeweis, T.G. The relationship between the Allport-Vernon-Lindzey study of values and an objective measure of moral judgment. Unpublished master's dissertation, Moorhead State College, 1974.

Schomberg, S.F. Some personality correlates of moral maturity among community college students. Unpublished manuscript, University of Minnesota, 1975 (in progress).

Schomberg, S.F. Moral judgment development and its association with freshman year experiences. Unpublished doctoral dissertation, University of Minnesota, 1978.

Schomberg, S.F. and Balkcum, E. Evaluation of two instructional approaches in teaching ethics. Study in progress, University of Minnesota, 1976.

Schomberg, S.F. & Nelson, J. Evaluation of a Christian Ethics Course for Seminarians. Study in progress, University of Minnesota, 1976.

Schönemann, P.H. On metric multidimensional unfolding. *Psychometrika*, 1970, 35, 349-366.

Schwartz, S.H., Feldman, K.A., Brown, M.E. & Heingartner, A. Some personality correlates of conduct in two situations of moral conflict. *Journal of Personality*, 1969, 37, 41-57.

Selman, R. The relation of role-taking ability to the development of moral judgment in children. *Child Development*, 1971, 42, 79-91.

Selman, R. The relation of role-taking levels to stage of moral judgment: A theoretical analysis of empirical studies. Unpublished manuscript, Harvard University, 1973.

Selman, R. Toward a structural analysis of developing interpersonal relationship concepts:
Research with normal and disturbed preadolescent boys. In A. Pick (Ed.), *Tenth Annual
Minnesota Symposia on Child Psychology*, Minneapolis: University of Minnesota Press,
1976.

Selman, R., & Damon, W. The necessity (but insufficiency) of social perspective taking for
conceptions of justice at three early levels. In D.J. DePalma & J.M. Foley (Eds.), *Moral
Development: Current Theory and Research*. Hillsdale, N.J.: Lawrence Erlbaum, 1975,
57-74.

Selman, R.L. & Jaquette, D. Stability and oscillation in interpersonal awareness: a clinical
developmental analysis. In C. Keasey (Ed.), *The XXV Nebraska Symposium on Motivation*, University of Nebraska Press, 1977.

Selman, R.L. & Lieberman, M. An evaluation of a cognitive-developmental values curriculum for primary grade children. *Journal of Educational Psychology*, 1975.

Shaffer, P. Moral judgment: A cognitive-developmental project in psychological education.
Unpublished doctoral dissertation, University of Minnesota, 1973.

Shantz, C. The development of social cognition. In E.M. Hetherington (Ed.), *Review of
Child Development Research*, Vol. 5 Chicago: University of Chicago Press, 1975, Chapter 6.

Shantz, D.W. & Voydanoff, D.A. Situation effects on retaliatory aggression at three age levels.
Child Development, 1973, 44, 149-153.

Sheehan, J.T. Moral judgment as a predictor of clinical performance. Unpublished manuscript,
University of Connecticut Health Center, Farmington, 1979.

Siegal, M. An experiment in moral education: AVER in Surrey. Paper presented at Annual
Conference, Canadian Society for the Study of Education, Toronto, Ontario, 1974.

Smedslund, J. Concrete reasoning: A study of intellectual development. *Society for Research
in Child Development Monographs*, 1964, 29, No. 2 (Serial No. 93).

Smedslund, J. Psychological diagnostics. *Psychological Bulletin*, 1969, 71, 237-248.

Snow, R. Representative and quasi-representative designs for research on teaching. *Review
of Educational Research*, 1974, Vol. 44, No. 3, 265-292.

Spielburger, C.D., Goruch, R.L., & Lushene, R.E. *Manual for the State-Trait Anxiety Inventory*. Palo Alto, California: Consulting Psychologist Press, 1970.

Sprecher, P. Moral judgment in pre-adolescents: peer morality versus authority morality. Unpublished master's dissertation, University of Wisconsin, 1976.

Sprinthall, N.A. & Bernier, J.E. Moral and cognitive development for teachers: a neglected
area. Chapter for Fordham University Symposium: *Programs and Rational in Value—
Moral Education*, 1977.

Staub, E. To rear a prosocial child: reasoning, learning by doing, and learning by teaching
others. In D.J. DePalma & J.M. Foley (Eds.), *Moral development: Current theory and research*. Hillsdale, N.J.: Lawrence Erlbaum Associates, 1975, 113-136.

Standring, D.E. Values, Value change and attitudes to occupations as a function of moral
judgment level. Unpublished master's thesis, Victoria University of Wellington, New Zealand, 1976.

Sullivan, E.V. *Moral Learning*. New York: Paulist Press, 1975.

Sullivan, E.V., McCollough, G., & Stager, M. A developmental study of the relationship between conceptual, ego, and moral development. *Child Development*, 1970, 41, 399-411.

Tan-Willman, C. A look at the moral reasoning of prospective Canadian teachers. Unpublished
manuscript, University of Toronto, 1977.

Tapp, J.L. & Kohlberg, L. Developing sense of law and legal justice, *The Journal of Social
Issues*, 1971, 27, 65-91.

Tomkins, S. Left and right: a basic dimension of ideology and personality. In R. White (Ed.), *The Study of Lives*. New York: Atherton Press, 1963, 388-411.

Tomlinson-Keasey, C. & Keasey, C.B. The mediating role of cognitive development in moral judgment. *Child Development*, 1974, 45, 291-298.

Torgerson, W.S. *Theory and Methods of Scaling*. New York: Wiley, 1958.

Toussaint, N.A. An analysis of synchrony between concrete-operational tasks in terms of structural and performance demands. *Child Development*, 1974, 45, 992-1001.

Tracy, J.J. & Cross, H.J. Antecedents of shift in moral judgment. *Journal of Personality and Social Psychology*, 1973, 26, 238-244.

Troth, A.G. An assessment of impacts on students of the "Values" course. Unpublished manuscript, St. Olaf College, 1974.

Tsuijomoto, R.N. & Nardi, P.M. A comparison of Kohlberg's and Hogan's theories of moral development. Unpublished manuscript, Pitzer College, 1977.

Tsuijomoto, R.N. & Lucas, L.F. The relationship of moral judgment level to trust and self-actualization. Unpublished manuscript, Pitzer College, 1977.

Turiel, E. An experimental test of the sequentiality of developmental stages in the child's moral judgments. *Journal of Personality and Social Psychology*, 1966, Vol. 3, No. 6, 611-618.

Turiel, E. Developmental processes in the child's moral thinking. In P. Mussen, J. Langer & M. Covington (Eds.), *Trends and Issues in Developmental Psychology*. New York: Holt, Rinehart & Winston, 1969.

Turiel, E. Stage transition in moral development. In R.M. Travers (Ed.), *Second Handbook of Research on Teaching*. Chicago: Rand McNally, 1972.

Turiel, E. The effects of cognitive conflicts on moral judgment development. Unpublished manuscript, Harvard University, 1973.

Turiel, E. Conflict and transition in adolescent moral development. *Child Development*, 45, 1974, 14-29.

Turiel, E. Social Regulations and domains of social concepts. In W. Damon (Ed.), *New Directions for Child Development*, San Francisco: Jossey Bass, 1978, 45-74.

Turiel, E. and Rothman, G. The influence of reasoning on behavioral choices at different stages of moral development. *Child Development*, 1972, 43, 741-756.

Walker, L. The effect of a narrative model on stages of moral development. Unpublished manuscript, University of New Brunswick, Canada, 1974.

Weber, R.G. The nature of authoritarianism and its relationship to other personality variables and stages of moral judgment. Unpublished doctoral dissertation, University of Minnesota, 1974.

Weisbroth, S.P. Moral judgment, sex and parental identification of adults. *Developmental Psychology*, 1970, 2, 396-402.

White, C.B. Moral judgment in college students: the development of an objective measure and its relationship to life experience dimensions. Unpublished doctoral dissertation, University of Georgia, 1973.

White, C. Bushnell, N., & Regnemer, J. Moral development in Bahamian school children: a three year examination of Kohlberg's stages of moral development. *Developmental Psychology*, 1978, 14(1), 58-65.

White House Transcripts, New York Times, 1974.

Whiteley, J.M. The scope and purpose of the UCI residential education project. Unpublished manuscript, University of California, Irvine, 1976.

Whiteley, J.M. & Nelson, K.H. Personal communication, June 27, 1976.

Whiteman, J.L. An examination of the relationship between moral development and the perceptions of others. Unpublished manuscript, State of Indiana Department of Public Instruction, 1976.

Willging, T.E. Moral development in law school. Unpublished manuscript, The University of Toledo, College of Law, 1979.

Wilson, E. Personal communication, 1975.

Winocur, S. & Rogers, R.S. Individual differences, locus of issue and the resolution of moral dilemmas. Unpublished manuscript, University of Reading, 1975.

Wohlwill, J.F. Piaget's system as a source of empirical research. *Merrill Palmer Quarterly*, 1963, 9, 253-262(c).

Wohlwill, J.F. *The study of behavioral development*. New York: Academic Press, 1973.

Wohlwill, J.F., Devoe, S., & Fusaro, L. Research on the development of concepts in early childhood. Final Report NSF Grant G-5855, 1971.

Yussen, S.R. Moral reasoning from the perspective of others. *Child Development*, 1976, 47, 551-555.

APPENDIX

Defining Issues Test

For further information about test availability, administration, and scoring, write to Minnesota Moral Research Projects, 330 Burton Hall, 178 Pillsbury Drive S.E., Minneapolis, MN 55455.

Appendix

APPENDIX

OPINIONS ABOUT SOCIAL PROBLEMS

This questionnaire is aimed at understanding how people think about social problems. Different people often have different opinions about questions of right and wrong. There are no "right" answers in the way that there are right answers to math problems. We would like you to tell us what you think about several problem stories. The papers will be fed to a computer to find the average for the whole group, and no one will see your individual answers.

Please give us the following information:

Name _____ _____female

Age _____Class and period _____ _____male

School_____

* * * * * * * * *

In this questionnaire you will be asked to give your opinions about several stories. Here is a story as an example.

Frank Jones has been thinking about buying a car. He is married, has two small children and earns an average income. The car he buys will be his family's only car. It will be used mostly to get to work and drive around town, but sometimes for vacation trips also. In trying to decide what car to buy, Frank Jones realized that there were a lot of questions to consider. Below there is a list of some of these questions.

If you were Frank Jones, how important would each of these questions be in deciding what car to buy?

Instructions for Part A: (Sample Question)

On the left hand side check one of the spaces by each statement of a consideration. (For instance, if you think that statement #1 is not important in making a decision about buying a car, check the space on the right.)

IMPORTANCE:

Great	Much	Some	Little	No	
				✓	1. Whether the car dealer was in the same block as where Frank lives. (Note that in this sample, the person taking the questionnaire did not think this was important in making a decision.)
✓					2. Would a *used* car be more economical in the long run than a *new* car. (Note that a check was put in the far left space to indicate the opinion that this is an important issue in making a decision about buying a car.)
		✓			3. Whether the color was green, Frank's favorite color.
				✓	4. Whether the cubic inch displacement was at least 200. (Note that if you are unsure about what "cubic inch displacement" means, then mark it "no importance.")
✓					5. Would a large, roomy car be better than a compact car.
				✓	6. Whether the front connibilies were differential. (Note that if a statement sounds like gibberish or nonsense to you, mark it "no importance.")

Instructions for Part B: (Sample Question)

From the list of questions above, select the most important one of the whole group. Put the number of the most important question on the top line below. Do likewise for your 2nd, 3rd and 4th most important choices. (Note that the top choices in this case will come from the statements that were checked on the far left-hand side—statements #2 and #5 were thought to be very important. In deciding what is the *most* important, a person would re-read #2 and #5, and then pick one of them as the *most* important, then put the other one as "second most important," and so on.)

MOST	2ND MOST IMPORTANT	3RD MOST IMPORTANT	4TH MOST IMPORTANT
5	2	3	1

HEINZ AND THE DRUG

In Europe a woman was near death from a special kind of cancer. There was one drug that doctors thought might save her. It was a form of radium that a druggist in the same town had recently discovered. The drug was expensive to make, but the druggist was charging ten times what the drug cost to make. He paid $200 for the radium and charged $2,000 for a small dose of the drug. The sick woman's husband, Heinz, went to everyone he knew to borrow the money, but he could only get together about $1,000, which is half of what it cost. He told the druggist that his wife was dying, and asked him to sell it cheaper or let him pay later. But the druggist said, "No, I discovered the drug and I'm going to make money from it." So Heinz got desperate and began to think about breaking into the man's store to steal the drug for his wife.

Should Heinz steal the drug? (Check one)

_____Should steal it   _____Can't decide   _____Should not steal it

IMPORTANCE:

Great	Much	Some	Little	No	
					1. Whether a community's laws are going to be upheld.
					2. Isn't it only natural for a loving husband to care so much for his wife that he'd steal?
					3. Is Heinz willing to risk getting shot as a burglar or going to jail for the chance that stealing the drug might help?
					4. Whether Heinz is a professional wrestler, or has considerable influence with professional wrestlers.
					5. Whether Heinz is stealing for himself or doing this solely to help someone else.
					6. Whether the druggist's rights to his invention have to be respected.
					7. Whether the essence of living is more encompassing than the termination of dying, socially and individually.
					8. What values are going to be the basis for governing how people act towards each other.
					9. Whether the druggist is going to be allowed to hide behind a worthless law which only protects the rich anyhow.
					10. Whether the law in this case is getting in the way of the most basic claim of any member of society.
					11. Whether the druggist deserves to be robbed for being so greedy and cruel.
					12. Would stealing in such a case bring about more total good for the whole society or not.

From the list of questions above, select the four most important:

Most important_____   Second most important_____

Third most important_____   Fourth most important_____

STUDENT TAKE-OVER

At Harvard University a group of students, called the Students for a Democratic Society (SDS), believe that the University should not have an army ROTC program. SDS students are against the war in Viet Nam, and the army training program helps send men to fight in Viet Nam. The SDS students demanded that Harvard end the army ROTC training program as a university course. This would mean that Harvard students could not get army training as part of their regular course work and not get credit for it towards their degrees.

Agreeing with the SDS students, the Harvard professors voted to end the ROTC program as a university course. But the President of the University stated that he wanted to keep the army program on campus as a course. The SDS students felt that the President was not going to pay attention to the faculty vote or to their demands.

So, one day last April, two hundred SDS students walked into the university's administration building, and told everyone else to get out. They said they were doing this to force Harvard to get rid of the army training program as a course.

Should the students have taken over the administration building? (Check one)

____Yes, they should take it over ____Can't decide ____No, they shouldn't take it over

IMPORTANCE:

Great	Much	Some	Little	No	
					1. Are the students doing this to really help other people or are they doing it just for kicks?
					2. Do the students have any right to take over property that doesn't belong to them?
					3. Do the students realize that they might be arrested and fined, and even expelled from school?
					4. Would taking over the building in the long run benefit more people to a greater extent?
					5. Whether the president stayed withing the limits of his authority in ignoring the faculty vote.
					6. Will the takeover anger the public and give all students a bad name?
					7. Is taking over a building consistent with principles of justice?
					8. Would allowing one student take-over encourage many other student take-overs?
					9. Did the president bring this misunderstanding on himself by being so unreasonable and uncooperative.
					10. Whether running the university ought to be in the hands of a few administrators or in the hands of all the people.
					11. Are the students following principles which they believe are above the law?
					12. Whether or not university decisions ought to be respected by students.

From the list of questions above, select the four most important:

Most important_____   Second most important_____

Third most important_____   Fourth most important _____

ESCAPED PRISONER

A man had been sentenced to prison for 10 years. After one year, however, he escaped from prison, moved to a new area of the country, and took on the name of Thompson. For 8 years he worked hard, and gradually he saved enough money to buy his own business. He was fair to his customers, gave his employees top wages, and gave most of his own profits to charity. Then one day, Mrs. Jones, an old neighbor, recognized him as the man who had escaped from prison 8 years before, and whom the police had been looking for.

Should Mrs. Jones report Mr. Thompson to the police and have him sent back to prison? (Check one)

_____Should report him   _____Can't decide   _____Should not report him

IMPORTANCE:

Great	Much	Some	Little	No	
					1. Hasn't Mr. Thompson been good enough for such a long time to prove he isn't a bad person?
					2. Everytime someone escapes punishment for a crime, doesn't that just encourage more crime?
					3. Wouldn't we be better off without prisons and the oppression of our legal systems?
					4. Has Mr. Thompson really paid his debt to society?
					5. Would society be failing what Mr. Thompson should fairly expect?
					6. What benefits would prisons be apart from society, especially for a charitable man?
					7. How could anyone be so cruel and heartless as to send Mr. Thompson to prison?
					8. Would it be fair to all the prisoners who had to serve out their full sentences if Mr. Thompson was let off?
					9. Was Mrs. Jones a good friend of Mr. Thompson?
					10. Wouldn't it be a citizen's duty to report an escaped criminal, regardless of the circumstances?
					11. How would the will of the people and the public good best be served?
					12. Would going to prison do any good for Mr. Thompson or protect anybody?

From the list of questions above, select the four most important:

Most important_____   Second most important_____

Third most important_____   Fourth most important _____

THE DOCTOR'S DILEMMA

A lady was dying of cancer which could not be cured and she had only about six months to live. She was in terrible pain, but she was so weak that a good dose of pain-killer like morphine would make her die sooner. She was delirious and almost crazy with pain, and in her calm periods, she would ask the doctor to give her enough morphine to kill her. She said she couldn't stand the pain and that she was going to die in a few months anyway.

What should the doctor do? (Check one)

_____ He should give the lady an overdose   _____ Can't decide   _____ Should not give the
that will make her die   overdose

IMPORTANCE:

Great	Much	Some	Little	No	
					1. Whether the woman's family is in favor of giving her the overdose or not.
					2. Is the doctor obligated by the same laws as everybody else if giving her an overdose would be the same as killing her.
					3. Whether people would be much better off without society regimenting their lives and even their deaths.
					4. Whether the doctor could make it appear like an accident.
					5. Does the state have the right to force continued existence on those who don't want to live.
					6. What is the value of death prior to society's perspective on personal values.
					7. Whether the doctor has sympathy for the woman's suffering or cares more about what society might think.
					8. Is helping to end another's life ever a responsible act of cooperation.
					9. Whether only God should decide when a person's life should end.
					10. What values the doctor has set for himself in his own personal code of behavior.
					11. Can society afford to let everybody end their lives when they want to.
					12. Can society allow suicides or mercy killing and still protect the lives of individuals who want to live.

From the list of questions above, select the four most important:

Most important_____   Second most important_____

Third most important_____   Fourth most important_____

WEBSTER

Mr. Webster was the owner and manager of a gas station. He wanted to hire another mechanic to help him, but good mechanics were hard to find. The only person he found who seemed to be a good mechanic was Mr. Lee, but he was Chinese. While Mr. Webster himself didn't have anything against Orientals, he was afraid to hire Mr. Lee because many of his customers didn't like Orientals. His customers might take their business elsewhere if Mr. Lee was working in the gas station.

When Mr. Lee asked Mr. Webster if he could have the job, Mr. Webster said that he had already hired somebody else. But Mr. Webster really had not hired anybody, because he could not find anybody who was a good mechanic besides Mr. Lee.

What should Mr. Webster have done? (Check one)

_____ Should have hired Mr. Lee _____ Can't decide _____ Should not have hired him

IMPORTANCE:

Great	Much	Some	Little	No	
					1. Does the owner of a business have the right to make his own business decisions or not?
					2. Whether there is a law that forbids racial discrimination in hiring for jobs.
					3. Whether Mr. Webster is prejudiced against orientals himself or whether he means nothing personal in refusing the job.
					4. Whether hiring a good mechanic or paying attention to his customers' wishes would be best for his business.
					5. What individual differences ought to be relevant in deciding how society's roles are filled?
					6. Whether the greedy and competitive capitalistic system ought to be completely abandoned.
					7. Do a majority of people in Mr. Webster's society feel like his customers or are a majority against prejudice?
					8. Whether hiring capable men like Mr. Lee would use talents that would otherwise be lost to society.
					9. Would refusing the job to Mr. Lee be consistent with Mr. Webster's own moral beliefs?
					10. Could Mr. Webster be so hard-hearted as to refuse the job, knowing how much it means to Mr. Lee?
					11. Whether the Christian commandment to love your fellow man applies in this case.
					12. If someone's in need, shouldn't he be helped regardless of what you get back from him?

From the list of questions above, select the four most important:

Most important _____   Second most important _____

Third most important _____   Fourth most important _____

NEWSPAPER

Fred, a senior in high school, wanted to publish a mimeographed newspaper for students so that he could express many of his opinions. He wanted to speak out against the war in Viet Nam and to speak out against some of the school's rules, like the rule forbidding boys to wear long hair.

When Fred started his newspaper, he asked his principal for permission. The principal said it would be all right if before every publication Fred would turn in all his articles for the principal's approval. Fred agreed and turned in several articles for approval. The principal approved all of them and Fred published two issues of the paper in the next two weeks.

But the principal had not expected that Fred's newspaper would receive so much attention. Students were so excited by the paper that they began to organize protests against the hair regulation and other school rules. Angry parents objected to Fred's opinions. They phoned the principal telling him that the newspaper was unpatriotic and should not be published. As a result of the rising excitement, the principal ordered Fred to stop publishing. He gave as a reason that Fred's activities were disruptive to the operation of the school.

Should the principal stop the newspaper? (Check one)

_____ Should stop it   _____ Can't decide   _____ Should not stop it

IMPORTANCE:

Great	Much	Some	Little	No	
					1. Is the principal more responsible to students or to the parents?
					2. Did the principal give his word that the newspaper could be published for a long time, or did he just promise to approve the newspaper one issue at a time
					3. Would the students start protesting even more if the principal stopped the newspaper?
					4. When the welfare of the school is threatened, does the principal have the right to give orders to students?
					5. Does the principal have the freedom of speech to say "no" in this case?
					6. If the principal stopped the newspaper would he be preventing full discussion of important problems?
					7. Whether the principal's order would make Fred lose faith in the principal.
					8. Whether Fred was really loyal to his school and patriotic to his country.
					9. What effect would stopping the paper have on the student's education in critical thinking and judgments?
					10. Whether Fred was in any way violating the rights of others in publishing his own opinions.
					11. Whether the principal should be influenced by some angry parents when it is the principal that knows best what is going on in the school.
					12. Whether Fred was using the newspaper to stir up hatred and discontent.

From the list of questions above, select the four most important:

Most important_____   Second most important_____

Third most important_____   Fourth most important_____

INDEX

Index

See also Stage, Verbal expressiveness
—indexing: 275-58; Moral Maturity Index,
53, 72; highest stage of substantial use, 70;
predominant usage, 70; stage typing, 70,
73; curves of stage use, 71-72; Davison's
comparison of various DIT indices, 71,
223-45, 257-58; factor analyses 100;
experimentation with various indices,
100-5, 223-45, 257-58; calculation of
P index, 100-2; advantages of ranking
data, 103; exceptional usage, 104; correlations between various DIT and Kohlberg indices, 155-56; indexing summary,
257-58. *See also* Kohlberg; Stage
—validity and reliability: reliability, 54,
98, 223-45 *passim*, 239-41; test-retest
stability, 54, 239-41; Kohlberg's validation strategy, 96; predictive validity, 96-
97; validating strategy parallels to "knowledge of psychology," 97-100; face
validity, 98; criterion group validity, 98,
107-26 *passim*; longitudinal, 98, 126-45,
convergent-divergent, 98, 146-200
passim, 201-3, 249; experimental enhancement, 99, 204-14; test-taking sets,
fakability, 99, 152, 214-19; measurement
error, 130, 239; testing effects, 136,
141-42, discriminate validity, 201-3,
249; reliability of DIT, 239-41; validity
of the DIT—summary, 241-45, 247-51,
258-259. *See also* Comprehension—
validity; Kohlberg; Political attitudes,
Law and Order Test; Stage
Developmental character of moral judgment,
summary, 247-48
Dilemmas: Heinz and the Drug, 8, 291;
Captain's dilemma, 8; Similiarities between DIT and Kohlberg test, 156; complete set of DIT dilemmas, 289-96
Discriminant validity. *See* Developmental
assessment, validity
Disequilibrium, 219
Disjunctive scaling, 223-24
Distributive justice. *See* Behavior; Stage—
description of features of development
Doctors, clinical ratings of performance, 191
Dortzbach, J. R., 111-12

Education: Correlation with DIT, 111-13;
college, 133-35; interventions, 204-14;
mentioned, 219-22

Ego: factors related to moral judgment, 11;
ego strength, 177; ego identity, 199
Empathy, 18
Ennis, R., 209
Equilibrium: as balance of individual inter-
ests, 20, 22-23; at different stages,
35-36, 40
Erickson, V. L., 212
Erikson, E., 195
Ernsberger, D., 115-16, 226n
Estimate of standard error of measurement,
73, 239-41
Ethics philosophy class, 208-11. *See also*
Philosophers
Evil people, 178
Experimental method, 204-7
Eysenck, H. H., 40

Fairness. *See* Justice
Faking on the DIT, 152, 214-19
Fincham, F. D., 219
Five-B, Stage, 37
Flavell, J., 27, 48-64 *passim*, 171
Ford, G., President, 192-95
Form versus content. *See* Stage concept
Formal operations, 12, 73-74, 153
French, M. D., 212
Froming, W. J., 185-86, 266n

Galileo, G., 116-17
Geis, G., 142, 212
Generation effects, 137-41
Geographical area, 115
Gibbs, J., 154, 265n
Gilligan, C., 78
Goldiamond, I., 40
Graham, K., 219
Greif, E., 96, 106
Guilt, 11
Gunzberger, D. W., 186
Gutkin, D. C., 165, 167
Guttenberg, R., 219
Guttman, L., 233, 266n

Haan, N., 78, 176, 193
Harvey's Conceptual Systems, 153
Heinz and the Drug Dilemma, 8, 291
Helping behavior, 11. *See also* Behavior
Hickey, J., 78
Hierarchical reintegration, 219
Hits—Misses—Rejections, 24, 25-39 *passim*

Recognition versus production tasks, 60-63, 154-58. *See also* Developmental assessment—data sources
Reflective versus operational thought, 171-74
Regulation of society by moral rules, 18. *See also* Stage
Reliability. *See* Developmental assessment—validity and reliability; Kohlberg—research findings
Religion, 115-19
Rest, G., 192-95
Rest, J.: *1969* study, 21, 24-39 *passim, 62,* 88-90; *1973* study, 62; *1975* study, 221
Right wing-left wing. *See* political attitudes
Robbins, S., 223-45 *passim*, 265n
Rokeach Scale of Dogmatism, 165-66
Rokeach Value Survey, 196-98
Role taking: related to moral judgment, 12, 40, 73-74; reciprocal, 27; mind of rational person at Stages *5* and *6*, 32-33; at different moral judgment stages, 216-17. *See* Mutual expectations; Prerequisite components
Rosenberg's Scales, 199
Ross, J., 232
Rubin, R.A., 190

Sampling biases, 137, 142-43
Schaie, K., 112, 135-43 *passim*
Schomberg, S. F., 221
Schönemann, P. H., 225-29 *passim*, 266n
School behavior. *See* Behavior
Schostrum's Test, 201
Self-concept and self-esteem, 197, 199
Selman, R., 13, 27, 40
Sequential analyses, 137-41. *See also* Longitudinal studies
Sex, 120-24
Shafto, M. *See* Martin, R. M.
Sheehan, J. T., 191
Short form of DIT, 239-41
Short-term interventions, problems with, 205-6, 220
Siegal, M., 213
Simplex structure, 227, 233-34
Situational factors. *See* Performance and situational factors
Smedslund, J., 60
Social Learning theory, 144-45, 208. *See also* Bandura; Mischel

Socioeconomic status, 119
Sources of information, 255-57
Speicher-Dubin, B., 265n
Sprinthall, N., 213
Stage: correspondences, stage by stage, 74. *See also* Prerequisite components; stage typing. *See* Developmental assessment—indexing; exemplified in DIT items, 87; intercorrelations, 229; scale values, 230-33, 238
——descriptions of the features of development: 17-47, 254-55; alternative conceptions, 41, 47
——concept of, as model of development: 48-74, 251-54; as cognitive structures, 4-5, 42-46, 53; developmental sequence of, 5, 51, 64-67, 73; "simple stage" model, 49-74; "structured whole," 50, 56, 57; quantitative versus qualitative distinction, 50, 53, 61-63; mixture and pure types, 52, 57-60, 65; "all or nothing" view, 61-62, 63
Standring, D. E., 197-198
Stimulus characteristics, 55. *See also* Performance and situational factors
Story pull. *See* Developmental assessment
Strangelove, Dr., 207, 208
Suls, J., 165, 167
Superficial information about reflective thought, 174-75
Synchronous development. *See* Stage concept, stage mixture and pure types

Tapp, J., 76-77
Tennessee Self-Concept Scale, 199
Test characteristics in stories. *See* Performance and situational factors
Test retest stability, 54-55, 239-41. *See also* Developmental assessment—validity and reliability
Test taking sets, 99-100, 153, 214-19
Testing effects of DIT, 136, 141-42
Tests and testing. *See* Developmental assessment
Toews, O., 212
Torgerson, W. S., 225
Transition, periods of, 53, 66-67
Troth, A. G., 213
Trotter, K. T., 157
Tsujimoto, R. N., 165, 167
Turiel, E., 13, 173, 219